Single Again

THE UNCERTAIN JOURNEY

Single Again

THE UNCERTAIN JOURNEY

HOPE for the **DIVORCED** and **WIDOWED**

JIM SMOKE

VINE
BOOKS

SERVANT PUBLICATIONS
ANN ARBOR, MICHIGAN

Vine Books is an imprint of Servant Publications especially designed to
serve evangelical Christians.

Published in association with the literary agency of Alive Communications,
1465 Kelly Johnson Blvd., Suite 329, Colorado Springs, CO 80920.

Published by Servant Publications
P.O. Box 8617
Ann Arbor, Michigan 48107

Cover design: PAZ Design Group
Cover photograph: © Jill Sabella/FPG International LLC.

99 00 01 02 10 9 8 7 6 5 4 3 2 1

Printed in the United States of America
ISBN 1-56955-076-X

LIBRARY OF CONGRESS CATALOGING-IN-PUBLICATION DATA

Smoke, Jim.
    Single again : the uncertain journey / Jim Smoke.
        p.   cm.
    Includes bibliographical references (p.   ).
    ISBN 1-56955-125-1 (alk. paper).
    1.Divorced people—Religious life.   2. Widowers—Religious life.
3. Widows—Religious life.   4. Divorced people Life skills guides.
5. Widowers Life skills guides.   6. Widows Life skills guides.   I. Title.
BV4596.D58S58   1999
248.8'46—dc21   99-32957
                                                     CIP

Contents

Introduction

We live in a culture of instancy that has little time or patience for process. Pain, rejection, grief, and loss are often squeezed together in a four-line greeting card encouraging the reader to look beyond the dark clouds of struggle to the sunshine of tomorrow. If only our disappointments in life could be solved that easily!

As a counselor with single-again adults for the past twenty-five years, I have walked alongside thousands of men and women who have experienced loss of a spouse through divorce or death. I have watched many people go from a world of certainty to the scary uncertainties of being single again. My role has been to offer affirmation, practical guidance, and spiritual direction as they face one of life's toughest adjustments.

This is a book about walking through unfamiliar territory. It does not contain easy answers. There are none. But in order to dispel the many negatives you may hear upon entering this foreign wilderness, I offer a few thoughts I call "observations from the edge of my experience." I pray they will renew your hope for the days ahead.

- God is not prejudiced against single-again adults. He *loves* you.

- Most single-again adults hate the word "single" to describe their status in life, but you can be both happy and single again *at the same time.*

- Things you once thought certain quickly become uncertain, but God is with you on the journey.

- Loneliness goes with this new territory, but you will grow spiritually more than you ever dreamed you would.

- Singles meetings can be intimidating until you discover most of the people there are just like you: they would rather be someplace else.

- Dating as a single-again adult is scarier than it ever was as a teenager—the roller-coaster ride of your life.

- Being a single parent is a tough and totally exhausting job, but you can be a great and successful single parent.

- The majority of those who are single again do not want to remain that way for the rest of their lives.

- The thought of remarriage frightens most single-again adults, but the thought of never remarrying is even more frightening.

- When you become single again, the faces in your world change, but your needs, struggles, sorrows, and joys are the same as they were when you were married.

Throughout these pages, we will wrestle with the many uncertainties that cloud the horizon of the single-again experience. My prayer is that God's sunshine might brighten your new journey as you read.

Jim Smoke

Life Is a Journey Built on Hope

"For I know the plans I have for you," declares the Lord, "plans to prosper you and not to harm you, plans to give you hope and a future."

JEREMIAH 29:11

Sometime very early in life, you were taught that all your actions have consequences: bad actions result in bad consequences; good actions result in good consequences.

You came to adulthood with established patterns of behavior you hoped would bring rewards. You believed that if you loved someone with all your heart and soul—and he or she loved you—you would live happily for the rest of your life. Marriage vows publicly affirmed your lifelong intent. Family and friends celebrated your proclamation of vows.

No one informed you, however, that a marriage license does not come with a money-back guarantee. One party can jump ship at any time, deciding unilaterally to end the marriage. For more than 2.5 million Americans each year, the certainty of marriage turns into the uncertainty of becoming single again. Most of the men and women facing the task of picking up the pieces proclaim, "It's not fair!"

And no, it isn't. But don't give up hope.

HOPE IS A SEED

The seed of hope is planted in each human being at the moment of birth. But hope does not take form until you are old enough to recognize that it means wanting something just beyond your grasp.

You verbalize your hopes early in childhood. You tell your parents that you hope you will get this or that for a birthday or Christmas. Before long you realize parents and other people close to you play a major role in your hopes becoming reality. You move along through childhood and adolescence with some of your hopes realized and others delayed or abandoned.

Then in adulthood, a special person may enter your life. Many of your hopes plus a large piece of your future come together at a place called marriage. In marriage, two people, each with a unique set of hopes, attempt to adjust to a journey on the same pathway.

Through the years I have listened to couples articulate their hopes at the beginning of marriage. Most of them say, "We are meant for each other, and we'll be happily married forever." They promise they will share all their sorrows and joys and be faithful to their vows and to each other until death. They say goodbye to singleness forever, promising never to return to it.

You are probably thinking, *That's exactly how I felt when I got married—until my hopes were derailed.* You are among a large company of people who feel disappointed and disillusioned.

I received a call last week from one such derailed man, who between his anger and sorrow shared a familiar story. He had been married for more than twenty years and had just realized his career goals when his wife left him for another man. She had been having an affair for over a year. He said, "I was on top of my game, happy and successful until...!" His hope for the present and future collapsed.

DEALING WITH THE QUESTIONS

Certain words followed by actions, or actions followed by certain words, can often be the destroyers of hope. The words and phrases have changed little over the years. I have heard them from participants in divorce recovery workshops as well as in personal counseling with men and women. The most common are:

"I don't love you anymore."

"I don't think I ever really loved you."

"I love someone else."

"I don't have a problem; you have a problem."

"I don't need help."

The former spouses of over 70 percent of the men and women in my divorce recovery workshops left the marriage for another person. The remaining 30 percent of workshop participants chose to leave because they could no longer cope with the relationship. The most common reasons for leaving were physical, chemical, emotional, and sexual abuse, along with gambling and losing a spouse to homosexuality.

But whether a person is left by his or her spouse or decides to take that step personally due to painful circumstances, feelings of rejection will probably be overpowering. These feelings can shake self-worth and self-esteem to their roots. They wrap a person so tightly in a cloud of self-doubt that he or she lives in its nightmare twenty-four hours a day.

Hopes that were birthed at the altar of matrimony become hopes divided, then abandoned in divorce. You might view the loss of a spouse as receiving a cruel hand dealt by fate and as the termination of your happiness. Or you may view it as a mountain to climb, a new challenge to be conquered. But everyone has a long list of questions they want answered immediately if not sooner. Here is a short list of those most frequently asked—with an even shorter list of answers.

Will I make it through this mess?
Yes, but it will take time.

If I do, what kind of emotional shape will I be in?
It will be bad for a while, but it will get better.

Will I end up living on the street?

Only if you choose to do so.
Will my spouse and I get back together?
It's not likely. National statistics show few such reunions.

How will this change my life?
One of two ways, positively or negatively. The choice is yours.

Will I ever love anyone again?
Yes, you will if you want to because love is always a choice.

Will I remarry?
According to national statistics, it's very likely.

GIVE IT TIME

We have talked about divorce as the great divider and destroyer of hope. The affect that it has on a person is similar to that of the death of a spouse. In both cases people face uncertainties and the difficult task of discovering for themselves a new and different kind of hope. But however loss happens, the process of grief cannot be hurried. A person must process emotions and thoughts at the same time as he or she deals with practical matters. Bringing closure takes a while—usually two to three years. Give it time. Your hope will grow again.

I like what author Robert Veninga says in his powerful little book, *A Gift of Hope*:

Human pain does not let go of its grip at one point in time. There is a season of sadness, a season of anger, a season of tranquility, and a season of hope. But seasons do not follow one another in a lock step manner. The winters and springs of one's life are all jumbled together in a puzzling array. But when one affirms that the spring thaw will arrive, the winter winds seem to lose some of their punch.[1]

Most people would like to jump immediately from the cold suffering of winter to the growing season of spring and summer. But pain does not let go of you quickly. Even when you are moving forward, your mind can do a 360-degree turn, taking you back to the place where hope vanished.

Divorce and death of a spouse are not events; they are *processes*. It takes time to deal with shattering events because there is much to assimilate and there are many adjustments to make. Memories need to be sorted and filed. Grief needs to be absorbed. New plans must be drawn—both emotionally and practically. The longer one has been married, the longer this process may require. Emotional homework cannot be done in a hurry.

Of course, ours is a world of instant cures and quick fixes. Most of us do not ever want to feel pain, so we usually seek a cure that will work fast. One of my greatest fears is that a person in pain will find someone else just beyond the pain and form a relationship. When you are grieving loss, it seems like everyone has a "friend" they'd like you to meet, an antidote for your pain that may put you back on the road to hope. If that happens to you, beware! You are probably headed for a relationship collision. There are no instant pain relievers. Be patient. Lean into your emotions for a while. Sail right into those waves of discouragement.

LIVING WITH UNCERTAINTY

When your trust is betrayed, the most immediate challenge is survival. There are positive steps you can take to insure you'll not only make it but move ahead.

Develop total dependence on God. This should come first and foremost. He is the only one who promises, "Never will I leave you; never will I forsake you" (Heb 13:5b). He clearly proclaims through this promise that he will be by your side through every uncertainty you face. Not only does he promise his living presence, he promises he will meet your needs: "But my God shall supply all your need according to his riches in glory by Christ Jesus" (Phil 4:19, KJV).

But God's presence and promise do not supply a quick fix at the snap of your fingers. It unfolds into your life each day as you face your needs one by one. At the start of each morning, give that day to God and ask for his guidance. He will give it to you one moment at a time.

Develop a human support system that embraces you. People who have walked where you are now walking can give better directions and support than those who have never been there can. Those who are walking with God each day will be far more help to you than those who do not look to God for guidance will.

It may take some phone calls to track down a support group that fits your needs, but you will find one in your city or town if you look. Check newspapers, the Chamber of Commerce, and your phone book.

A support group will provide a safe place for you to belong as you undertake your new journey. You will meet fellow strugglers with whom you can talk over impending decisions.

Begin to embrace your faith, not your fears. We live in a world full of uncertainties, but that same world is full of opportunities. When uncertainties rain upon you, they can turn your boat upside down and drown your hope. Fears then get the upper hand.

Whether real or imagined, fears have a way of paralyzing you. This is why God gives us solid promises in the Bible upon which we can anchor our lives. One of my favorites is found in Jeremiah 29:11. It clearly defines the intentions of God for you and me: "'For I know the plans I have for you,' declares the Lord, 'Plans to prosper you and not to harm you, plans to give you hope and a future.'"

Also wrap your mind around this biblical promise from 2 Timothy 1:7 (KJV): "For God has not given us the spirit of fear; but of power, and of love, and of a sound mind." You are probably thinking this is a great verse except for the "sound mind" part! Certainly, experiencing any loss in life is somewhat crazy-making, but God's desire is to give you a clear, rational mental state capable of making good decisions during times of chaos.

When you find yourself facing any tough decision that seems beyond your coping abilities, stop and exclaim, "God is in charge here. I have nothing to fear!" As God's peace flows into your heart when you say that out loud, you will be amazed! (So will those standing around you!)

Divorce or Death of a Spouse— Is There a Difference?

I have found that widows and widowers typically do not want to be classified with divorced people, and many have told me they would not consider marrying a person who has been divorced. Somehow divorce carries the stigma of failure, even in this day and age.

Another significant difference is that the death of a spouse often leaves you with good memories of the marriage and your partner, while divorce can leave behind bitter memories and difficulty making sense of it all.

In addition, those who lose a spouse by death don't have to deal with the same kind of negative attachments as do divorced people, who may still be connected to former spouses and in-law networks through children. A divorced friend of mine often jokes, "There is a whole world of ex-spouses out there bent on causing havoc in our lives." Post-divorce wars rage through many blended families.

Many divorced men and women also face tough, ongoing financial battles, while the widowed may receive death benefits from life insurance. If there is no life insurance or other assets, the road of the widowed can be as tough as that of the divorced.

Acquaintances and even friends tend to leave

divorcing people alone, failing to offer support. One woman said, "I'm divorced *and* deserted." The widowed receive more frequent sympathetic gestures because death is usually a rallying cry for help.

Growing Strong at the Broken Places

It is when the rocks are rolling that
faith shows up best.

MALCOLM SMITH

When someone faces a crisis in life that cannot be immediately or neatly resolved, a kind of brokenness results. The pain of this brokenness is intense, and relief and healing seem to be a distant reality. Most people, single again or not, do not view broken places as life-enhancing opportunities to grow stronger. Broken places are usually seen as obstacles in the journey, to be avoided like potholes on the interstate. Yet those who have accepted their broken places will recount how the sharp edges became turning points, changing them and their lives in positive ways. Through the years I have heard countless people share how loss changed their lives for the better, even though they did not enjoy going through it.

People whose marriages and families are broken by divorce or death endure experiences that are intensely painful. How could these possibly be redeeming? Aren't they destructive to the human spirit? My dictionary defines *spirit* as "the animating principle of life, especially of humans: a vital essence."[1] In other words, when your essence—that fire within that keeps you moving forward each day—is quenched, you find it difficult to breathe, let alone do all the practical and emotional things life requires. You need to rebuild the fire. And to rebuild, you need to know what caused the problem.

WHAT CAUSES A BROKEN SPIRIT?

As I listened to thousands of single-again people, I identified a few major contributors to broken spirits. If your spirit is in a crunched mode right now, check off the ones that fit you.

Successive Major Disappointments

Most of us can handle a few of life's speed bumps, but when a series of major disappointments occur over time, it can put us on the sidelines. We have all heard of Murphy's Law: *If anything can go bad, it will.* Many people feel Murphy has moved into their house and taken over.

I work daily with people who carry enormous loads of personal issues that clearly reject immediate resolution due to a lack of cooperation from other parties involved. I often wonder how people who choose not to give God control keep going at all. On the other hand, I am constantly challenged by those who are recovering alcoholics because no matter what they face, they have learned to live one day at a time, one hour at a time, one minute at a time. They have learned that mountains in their journey are removed one stone at a time. I encourage you to follow their example.

I have come to realize that many of the disappointments in my life have turned out to be "his appointments." Always ask, *Is this disappointment or interruption sent by God to get my attention and make me ready to receive what he wants to do in my life?*

Disintegration of Self-Esteem

Enduring a barrage of words from another letting you know you are no good or you can never do anything right will destroy your sense of who you are and what you are worth. "I can't" begins to take the place of "I can," and a sense of helplessness takes up permanent residence.

So replace those negatives with positives. When the apostle Paul was warned not to go to Jerusalem, he chose to go anyway because he realized God was directing his way (see Acts 21). He knew he was walking toward suffering, but he replaced the human "I can't" with a divine "I can." You have that same choice in Christ.

Failure

We learn about failure early in our academic training. To pass a test is to announce that we are credible and smart. To fail is to move ourselves to the bottom of the list of "worthy" people. Most children are not taught that failure is just a rung on the ladder of success. We can use it to climb higher. Too many of us reach adulthood believing that if we fail at something, we automatically become failures.

The Bible is filled with stories of human failure. God doesn't leave you when you fail; he becomes more powerful because you need him more. Failure goes with the territory in life. Jesus said, "In this world you will have trouble. But take heart! I have overcome the world" (Jn 16:33).

Being Let Down by Others

It is easy to believe that if someone you trusted violated your trust, then everyone else will do the same. Broken trust is difficult to restore, and you must take great risk for that to happen. Fear of further hurt can keep a person running. The reality is that you cannot *trust* everyone and you cannot *distrust* everyone. You must find a balance between the two options.

Trust is active, not passive, and is restored only when you begin to take the first small steps. It grows as you take risks. There are no guarantees against broken trust, but when trust is reborn, there are great rewards.

Special to No One

Every one of us needs to be treasured by someone, and to treasure someone else. We all need someone in our life to whom we are special. That is what makes us feel significant.

Authors Les Carter and Jim Underwood talk about this in *The Significance Principle:*

> The basic, driving force of human behavior is the desire for acceptance, along with understanding, appreciation, and recognition. The need for significance is such a powerful aspect of our personality that it motivates us to identify with success and just as powerfully motivates us to avoid failure and conflict.[2]

When a man or woman becomes single again and the person they once thought special is no longer in their life, it leaves a hollow, lonely feeling. You can restore the lost feeling of being special by building new friendships with both men and women. You can choose to excel at your work or career. Everyone on Planet Earth goes through times of feeling insignificant and unimportant. Restoring self-worth comes from getting off the bench and back into the game of life.

Hopelessness

Many of you believe that nothing will change. You envision a future that will be no better than your present, bringing only more of the same. It is hard to pry open windows of hope.

A great danger in a period of hopelessness is searching for someone who you believe does have a future and will make you heir to it. I asked one woman about her plans to solve her financial problems. She said she planned to marry a man with money. I laughed at her response until I realized she was serious. She needed to regain her sense of personal control and destiny.

You can only do this if you learn to be responsible for your own present and future. People who wait to be rescued often end up becoming a prisoner of their rescuer. Your situation changes when you decide to become your own agent of change. Choose your future well because you have to live in it.

Illness and Physical Impairment

These lingering spirit-quenchers can become custom-made excuses for sitting on the sidelines in life and living in a constant state of self-pity. I have watched people in my church handle physical setbacks. Some use them as excuses to become non-participants in life, while others find ingenious ways to keep moving forward.

Steve was permanently confined to a wheelchair by a diving accident. I discovered he had gone from being a star athlete to being a two-wheeled wonder without missing a beat. If anything, Steve's pace of life accelerated to the point where his friends seldom noticed or thought of him as wheelchair-bound. He asked no favors and made no excuses. Today he is a psychologist in private practice.

We do not get to choose our afflictions, but we can choose how we will handle them.

QUESTIONS WE ASK
WHEN OUR SPIRIT IS BROKEN

Broken places are common life experiences. As a friend of mine frequently says, "Tough times never last, but tough people do!" Living in the broken places will teach you much as well as raise many questions. Here are a few of the most frequently asked questions, along with a few practical answers from the edge of my experience.

Is there a God? Does that sound like a funny question? At least it's honest. What you are really asking is, "If there is a God, why is he allowing this to happen to me?" You feel that a God who claims to love you would never let you go through a messy divorce or the death of a dearly beloved mate.

But Scripture says something positive about it: "No temptation has seized you except what is common to man. And God is faithful; he will not let you be tempted beyond what you can bear. But when you are tempted, he will also provide a way out so that you can stand up under it" (1 Cor 10:13). In this simple language, God is telling you he is still in charge. He will not let you go under.

If there is a God, where is he in my struggle? A more direct way to ask this would be, "Why is it taking God so long to get me out of this dehumanizing process?" One of the toughest issues to understand is why God is always in a different time zone. He is never in a hurry. You are tempted to jump in and give him a hand. But remember, you see only a small part of the picture, while God sees the whole panorama, beginning to end. You want answers while God is still evaluating your questions.

Throughout Scripture God kept people waiting while he worked his plan. Those who tried to run ahead of him ended up waiting even longer. An old priest once said, "He who hurries, delays the things of God." Don't hurry through this part of your journey.

How will I survive? You will not only survive, you will thrive if you invite God into your situation and turn it completely over to him. Do you know anyone else you would rather trust with your pain? You need only do four simple things: pray, trust, wait, and watch.

Where can I get help? Just ask. To ask is to drop the pride thing and exercise your humble spirit. First ask God for help. Then bring those around you into your struggle. People want to help those who ask for it. If necessary seek out a Christian therapist, who may suggest a structure for your process.

Does anybody care? Although there is no such thing as mass compassion, there are people who care about you. You only need a few who follow up with practical love in action. Meditate on the fact that an awesome God loves you and cares about you.

A SHORT VISIT TO THE ST. JAMES SCHOOL

I met a big, burly truck driver. He let me know quickly that life was tough and that he knew how to handle it. He summed up his earthy philosophy with these words: "Sometimes you get bad breaks. It's all a matter of luck and fate. Trust yourself, and get on with it." As he rolled his eighteen-wheeler out toward the interstate, I thought, *Many will agree.* But if the big man had only slowed down long enough, he might have realized there was a better way.

I'm sure he did not want to hear what James the apostle had to say about living in tough places and through tough times. James began his message by saying you should have an attitude of *joy* at broken places (see Jas 1:2). Now, if that were all James had said, you might question his sanity. But the reason he told you to have joy in the midst of struggles is that you are living the struggles for a reason. They are meant to teach you perseverance, maturity, and wisdom. God is taking you through a learning experience that will make you stronger, equipped to deal with anything. The end result is expressed in James 1:12:

"Blessed is the man who perseveres under trial, because when he has stood the test, he will receive the crown of life that God has promised to those who love him."

When you invite God into your broken places, no experience is wasted. God uses every one to make you strong, joyful, and transparent to others. I know it is difficult, if not nearly impossible, to understand right now that good can come from something as bad as what has happened to you, but look ahead.

You have a choice at your broken place: to get better or to get bitter. Which will you choose?

Practical Things You Can Do

- Realize that healing begins the moment you are broken, takes time, and works from the inside out.

- Relish time alone with God. Trust him.

- Lean on the promises in the Word of God starting with Psalm 34:18: "The Lord is close to the brokenhearted and saves those who are crushed in spirit."

- Begin a written prayer list of parts of your life that need rebuilding.

- Spend time with spiritual friends who lift your spirit.

- Ask for help. Strong people do, weaker people must.

- Don't allow yourself to focus on your struggles twenty-four hours a day. Find a way to reach out and empathize with others.

THREE

A Turning Point in an Uncertain Journey

Healthy things grow. Growing things change.
Changing things challenge us. Challenges cause us
to trust God. Trust leads to obedience. Obedience
makes us healthy. Healthy things grow.

JAMES RYLE

I got snagged on my own one-liner recently when I told someone his crisis would give him opportunity for "a fresh start and a new beginning." He smiled after I offered my words of hope and said, "I'm afraid at my age I'm not really starting over; I'm just continuing on!"

I thought about his comment after he walked away. I realized he's right. The truth is, none of us, no matter what our age, can go back to square one and start over. We only "continue on" and, hopefully, make wiser choices that change us for the better.

We are all riding the rapids of change every day, trying to accept the things we cannot change and change whatever we can. But if there is one word pasted on the forehead of every single-again adult, it is the word *change*. Every time you blink, it stares at you. In fact, it is a daily certainty. As disruptive as change can be, however, it is the one constant that pushes you toward turning points, and those turning points can become places for new growth to take root.

ACCEPT CHANGE AND MOVE WITH IT

Turning points are intersections in our life and are important to everyone, no matter what their station in life—married, divorced, widowed, or never-married. You will confront them in seven key areas. Accept them as gifts.

Crisis

A crisis is an unplanned or unexpected event, large or small, that upsets the status quo, often painfully. Divorce and death of a spouse are at the top of the list. While going through a crisis, most people would not call the experience positive. You won't spend much time thinking about the good side of it while you are stewing in the juices of your individual problem. In fact, when a crisis disrupts your life, your first thought is usually how to escape with minimal damage.

Still, as strange as it may seem now, your crisis is a turning point, an opportunity for growth, and can bear valuable fruit. It will clarify your focus, change your priorities, gently remind you of your humanity, and allow you access to the world of other hurting people. It will become a testing ground that can strengthen your personal faith in God and your entire Christian belief system. *You can embrace your crisis as God wraps his arms of love around you.*

Challenge

Challenges are stretching events that call forth your best resources and test your character. At the point of a challenge, you can opt out and stay in your comfort zone, or buy into it and be pushed onto a whole new playing field. The challenges associated with becoming single again will make your life a daily adventure. You may view the transition as a minefield to be avoided or as one through which you must carefully navigate.

Taken out of the comfortable cocoon of marriage, life naturally becomes unpredictable. The longer you were married, the tougher the challenges.

Some, feeling overwhelmed and without options, face their challenges with a sense of belligerence or hostility. That only makes people around them run for cover. Be brave, take on one challenge at a time, and keep going. I encourage you to take the risk of moving ahead even when you don't know exactly what is waiting. *Rise to the challenge, even though it scares you to death.*

And by the way, as you meet new people, go new places, and lean into new experiences, I'm aware that one of the toughest is attending your first-ever singles event. I've talked with hundreds of singles, even high profile managers and CEOs, who turn into Jell-O at such events. Don't let questions of acceptance or belonging send you running to the sanctuary of the restroom. Hang in there.

Boredom

One of my favorite authors, Henri Nouwen, said, "To be bored does not mean we have nothing to do, but that we question the value of the things we are so busy doing." Getting busy does not in itself remove boredom. Attributing value to you and others gives value to what you do. When you begin to feel your activities have significance, boredom is replaced with pleasure.

How many people do you know who complain about being bored but refuse to do anything about it? When I meet singles, I often ask, "How are things going?" only to have them reply, "Same ol', same ol'." I actually get excited when someone says, "Wow! You won't believe what's happening in my life."

Anyone can suffer boredom if they never welcome anything new and challenging into their lives. You will meet a turning point if you confront your own mediocrity and complacency. Your life is a ladder with rungs going both up and down. You alone choose which direction you want to go.

People

You are a human mosaic of the lives that have touched and influenced yours through the years. Your life story is not just about you. It is about the people who have been a part of your journey.

Some people are toxic to your growth, while others nourish and encourage. Some people block your progress, while others become door-openers to new opportunities. People can influence and motivate you or discourage and dismantle you. People can make you want to run away or run forward with enthusiasm.

The good news is that God uses people to help you through the hard places and affirm you in the good places. When you ask—and even sometimes when you don't—God has a unique way of putting people in your pathway just when you need them. They are God's primary resources in helping and loving you.

God did not create us to be Lone Rangers. It may be hard to reach out for help, but the alternative is dying inside from isolation. Can you name five people he has used in your life within the past ten years? How about the past year? How have they contributed to your growth? What gifts did they bring into your life? Who has God placed in your pathway recently to help you navigate the river of change? It is important to thank the people who have been there for you when things were tough. And when life threatens to bury you with problems, make this your prayer: *Lord, send some good people to help me out here.*

Call of God

In times of great change, your natural tendency is not to wait quietly for directions but to race off seeking them for yourself. If nothing appears to be happening, it is human nature to *make* something happen. Perhaps that's why the psalmist wrote, "Be still, and know that I am God" (Ps 46:10a). If you have ever lost patience with God and tried to make a way for yourself by your own strength, you most likely have suffered the disastrous consequences of running ahead. This always seems to lead to a dead end, not a turning point.

The call of God will often raise two questions: What is God doing at this place of change? And what is God saying at this place of change? These are good questions. Be willing to listen hard and maybe long. I seldom get answers when I am caught in a place of change, but when I do get them later, I understand why it took so long, or why I received a different answer than I expected. (I often expect God to use the world's standard of the instant. He doesn't.)

The call of God will never be heard unless you listen. Heart, mind, body, and spirit all need to be quiet to hear his voice. There is really no mystery in discovering how God wants to bring you through trouble: "Trust in the Lord with all your heart and lean not on your own understanding; in all your ways acknowledge him, and he will make your paths straight" (Prv 3:5, 6).

Feelings

Recently I asked a member of my recovery class how she was doing. She smiled, threw her hands in the air, and said, "Hey, it's crazy-making time. What do you expect?" Your cycles of change can definitely put you on the crazy-making highway of turning points. Trying to keep all the loose ends together can push your mind into overload. Then, as if that part of your life were not tangled enough, you soon realize your spirit also wants to be recognized and affirmed.

A vital part of making an uncertain journey more certain involves getting in touch with your feelings and learning to express them to people you feel safe with. Early in life you learn that expression and repression are the two basic ways of dealing with your feelings. You learn that expression can get you in trouble very quickly, so it's easier to repress them. The trouble is, repression keeps you out of trouble in the short term, but it slowly eats at your emotional and physical health.

People ask, "How are you doing?" but few appear willing to hang around for the answer. You learn to respond with "Fine," "OK," or "So-so" and hurry on your way. Not many of us will share deeper feelings with anyone unless we are certain they will really listen and care. If you grow up in a family system that is in any way dysfunctional, you are taught never to express your feelings and will probably not be in touch with them.

It is important to realize that feelings are neither right nor wrong. They are just feelings. We own them no matter what they are. Feelings only get us in trouble when we follow them with actions that are wrong. If I feel poverty-stricken, there is nothing wrong with that feeling. But if I feel poverty-stricken and then go rob a bank, I will be in trouble.

The great struggle for all of us is to stay in touch with our feelings and build supportive friendships so we can share them. When honest feelings are given and received, we feel significant, our authenticity is validated. We move ahead.

STAYING IN TOUCH WITH CHANGE

There is a powerful story of change in John 5:1-9. Jesus came to the pool of Bethesda and spotted a man who had been ill for thirty-eight years. Jesus asked him a strange question: "Do you want to get well?"

The man almost responded, saying, "You don't understand my problem." He told Jesus he had done everything required by the pool rules to achieve wellness, but alas, he was still sick.

Jesus responded by simply saying, "Get up! Pick up your mat and walk." The lame man followed Jesus' command and was instantly made whole.

What kind of changes do you think that man had to go through as a result of obeying Jesus? May I suggest a few that might sound familiar to you?

First, the lame man had to leave his daytime home of thirty-eight years. The pool of Bethesda was a place for sick people, not well people, so he no longer belonged there. He didn't belong anywhere else either. His healing dictated that he start an uncertain journey, wherever that would take him. This new situation was a challenge. Even a change from sickness to wellness has its stress and risks. Nevertheless, he gave up poolside residence and ventured out into a strange and about-to-be-hostile world.

Second, the lame man had to give up whatever security and

credibility his daily position by the pool afforded him. After thirty-eight years he probably had pool tenure along with pool perks. The length of his illness may have put him in the number-one poolside seat and made him well known as national record holder there. The man had an identity—as long as he stayed by the pool. With a few words from Jesus, all of that was removed, to be replaced by a world of healthy people who had their own struggles and problems. He must have soon discovered how unfriendly that world could be.

The lame man had to ask himself that burning question, *Who am I now?* The sick people, envious of his healing, did not want him hanging out at the pool any longer. The healthy people may have been suspicious, not accepting him in their community either. I imagine that man found himself stuck between two worlds. Does that sound familiar? He was probably caught in waves of rejection. Embarrassing questions may have been asked. I am sure he had moments wondering if wellness was worth the trauma. There will always be people who oppose your life changes, as well as those who accept them.

Finally, the man by the pool had to build a whole new life. He had to live life one day at a time, discovering for himself what options were available. He had to start again each and every morning. He may have asked himself, *Where will I live? How will I make a living? How will I make friends? What can I count on? Will I have enemies?* You can fill in more questions because these just may be your questions too.

When you entered single-again territory, you probably felt the same hesitancy. Losing a spouse by divorce or death forces unwanted, unplanned for, and unexpected change, scattering debris throughout your life and the lives of those you love. Change can come into your life by choice or by chance. But if you can pick up your bed and walk, then surely you can make other decisions as they are required.

You may be a few years into this journey and still feel like you are in a foreign land. The answers that worked before, in married life, do not work now. But God hasn't sentenced you to some singles' desert to live out your last days on Planet Earth.

Yes, your life will change. But you will change with it. You will grow with the responsibility. The good news is that you will not be alone. God has promised that he is with you and you will never be abandoned by him. So get serious about closing the gap between your changes and his realities. He still has a plan for your life. As you walk this new, uncertain journey, will you take a minute right now and place your hand in God's hand?

He is still up to something in your life!

FOUR

Getting on Track Spiritually and Staying There

And we know that in all things God works for the good of those who love him, who have been called according to his purpose.

ROMANS 8:28

God is in the renewal and reconstruction business. He is not the cause of the bad things that happen to us, but he can take a bad thing and bring good out of it. Sometimes we are hurt by the bad choices others make, as when someone runs a red light and hits our car. But God can use such events to give us the opportunity to witness or help others and to forgive those persons who have wronged us for the damage they caused.

Come to God prayerfully, talking to him about your situation and giving everything you know about it to him. Sound simple? That part usually isn't too tough. It gets tougher, though, when you realize what you give to God you have to leave with God—and not try to take it back. Unless you have previously developed a strong faith and walk securely in his love, this will not be easy.

When integrating spirituality with divorce or death of a spouse, the people I counsel usually have three different responses. If they have been on a spiritual path prior to their loss, they can reach deep into their well of faith and count on God to be their source and resource, guiding them safely through their crisis. This does not mean there will not be moments of doubt, confusion, anger, and frustration; those go with the territory of our humanity. What they will know is that God is in charge of everything and they can trust him as emotions rise and fall and tears flow. His grace will be clearly present.

A second response comes from people who have some spiritual background, but feel God has let them down. Praying their loss would be prevented, their prayer went unanswered, so they reason, "I counted on God, but since he did not give me the answer I desired, I can no longer trust him." These people may become angry or bitter. Some will drop out of church, abandon Christian friends, and disconnect from their walk with God.

A third response comes from those with little or no faith. Their crisis becomes a wake-up call. They turn their lives over to God for guidance and direction. Many divorced people have told me that God used their divorce experience to bring them to their knees and into a relationship with him. In the same breath they state they wish God could have used some far less destructive event to get their undivided attention.

For the past twenty-five years, I have had a sign on my desk that says, *God Is Up to Something.* Many single men and women pick it up and say, "I just wish I knew what God was up to right now!" Some days I wonder the same thing because God seldom gives me a road map for more than one day at a time. I have to replace any doubts I have about what God is up to with trust. If I really believe God is in charge and loves and cares for me, I can trust him with anything and everything. Notice that in Philippians 4:19 Paul writes, "And my God will meet all your needs according to his glorious riches in Christ Jesus." *Some* of your needs? No, not some, or the ones you really want, but *all* of them.

When you place everything in God's hands, you can move out of the starting gate. Then begin to address the following areas of your spiritual walk.

Church Life

Are you in a church family that loves, accepts, and cares for you as you rebuild your life? Sadly, many churches today are judgmental and critical of those going through divorce. They offer little compassion, help, or guidance, and often make those who are hurting feel isolated and demeaned. Those whose spouse has died will usually be treated better but will still feel some isolation because they are no longer part of a couple.

If you are in a church body that does not offer acceptance and nurturing, I believe you need to look prayerfully for a church that will offer you a loving home. If you are currently a part of any church family, I believe you need one that can encourage you and help you grow spiritually. You may have to do some searching, but I know that kind of church is out there because I have ministered in many of them. Warm, accepting, and healing churches do exist in cities large and small.

We all need and deserve support systems that can offer us love, care, affirmation, guidance, and healing.

Time With God

Every day spend private time with God in prayer, meditation, and Scripture reading. If you have no clue about how to do that effectively, visit your local Christian bookstore and purchase some of the many helpful tools available there. A good daily devotional guide can start you on the right track.

Every Christian I have ever met has confessed they struggle to be faithful and consistent in spending quiet time with God each day. A thousand good reasons for spending your time some other way will arise. Approach this assignment knowing you will have to establish a regular discipline of daily quiet time. It must become so much a regular part of your day that it cannot be put aside no matter what other claims are made on your time.

Thirty-four years ago I took up the daily routine of running a few miles. When I first started, I thought I was going to die in the first block. I used every excuse in the book not to run until a friend said, "Just keep running until it becomes as much of a daily habit as eating." It worked; I'm still running today. Meeting with God daily must become the number one priority in your life. Find the devotional practice that works best for you and just do it.

Small Group

We all need safe places where we can be our true selves and honestly share our hopes, fears, dreams, and hassles. Most churches have small study groups where men and women of all different ages and states in life commit to meet weekly. There are many workable formats for such groups and a huge quantity of available study materials. If you are in a large church, a small study group will give you a place to feel accepted and loved up close, and it will help you know fellow Christians on a deeper level.

Accountability

Every single one of us needs two or three people in our life who love us just as we are and with whom we can be brutally honest when necessary and allow them to be honest with us. We need people who accept spiritual authority in their own lives. They also should be free to ask us the hard questions that no one else is willing to ask.

Most people tell me they would welcome people to whom they could be accountable for actions, decisions, and overall spiritual progress. But when they find them, pride keeps them from accepting help. Willfulness or lack of humility can drive us away from those we need most as guides and mentors.

Finding a mentor takes time and prayer. God has to lead you to the person who will be best for you. Prayer is followed by keeping your eyes and ears open when you are with other people. If God impresses someone on your heart, have lunch with him or her and ask if they are interested. If their answer is no, move on in your search.

In the book *Connecting*, by Paul Stanley and Robert Clinton, mentoring is defined as:

> a relational process [in which a] mentor, who knows or has experienced something … transfers that something (resources of wisdom, information, experience, confidence, insight, relationships, status, etc.) to a mentoree, at an appropriate time and manner so that it facilitates development and empowerment.[1]

A great mentor will bring great accountability into your life.

Spiritual Disciplines

You will want to develop meditation, silence, solitude, contemplation, fasting, and Bible study skills. These are keys to ongoing spiritual growth. But I believe that all spiritual growth hinges on the discipline of prayer. Without that the others become hollow and mechanical. Spiritual disciplines do not form overnight. We live in a culture that resists these disciplines, emphasizing busyness, stress, competition, and worry. Spiritual disciplines counteract these and help us walk a different pathway, saturated with the peace of God.

If you are committed to building your walk with God, you may want to read these books: *The Divine Conspiracy,*[2] by Dallas Willard; *Embrace the Spirit,*[3] by Steven Harper; and *Celebration of Discipline,*[4] by Richard Foster.

THE COMBAT ZONE

The apostle Paul had great insight into the struggle of Christians. He wrote, "Don't let the world around you squeeze you into its mold, but let God remold your minds from within, so that you may prove in practice that the plan of God for you is good, meets all his demands, and moves toward the goal of true maturity" (Rom 12:2, PHILLIPS).

Paul's emphasis was on building our lives from the inside out, not the outside in. Nothing of great significance can happen in our outward lives that does not first happen inside us.

It is easy for most of us to operate by our own knowledge, intellect, and capabilities. Those are also gifts from God. But while we are quite able to do a spiritual song and dance for others to see, it will have no impact if we have no inner power. Our exterior walk with God will always reflect our interior walk.

When God works inside us through the spiritual disciplines, we develop spiritual muscles that will be available when we are called to carry heavy loads.

LISTEN TO GOD'S VOICE

"Listening to God" may sound oddly mystical to many people. After all, God doesn't talk out loud in English, does he? At least he hasn't yet used that approach with me. I believe there are four evident and practical ways that God *does* speak.

Scripture

God speaks through Scripture. Spend time reading God's Word each day. Give God the opportunity to speak to you through it. Your prayer should be that God would speak to you through its truth. Sometimes he gives clear directions and marching orders through what you are reading. At other times he gives guidelines for what to pray about. The Scripture says, "Do not merely listen to the word, and so deceive yourselves. Do what it says" (Jas 1:22).

God's Word is a book of instructions for living. It gives answers to life's toughest questions. In Matthew 7:7-8, we are told, "Ask and it will be given you; seek and you will find; knock and the door will be opened to you. For everyone who asks receives; he who seeks finds; and to him who knocks, the door will be opened."

I suggest you obtain several Bible translations. Modern translations read more like your daily newspaper and are easier to understand. Study Bibles contain notes and helps designed for more serious Bible study. *The Daily Walk Bible*[5] in the New Living Translation is extremely helpful if you want to read the

Bible through in one year. You might make this your year to do that. Get in God's Word every day and you will grow.

Life Circumstances
God speaks to us through our life circumstances as well. This is sometimes hard to understand because we often see negative circumstances as keeping us from serving God and living a fulfilling life. We seldom see them as opportunities for growth or new ways that God will reveal himself to us. But he really is in charge of our lives! God can use any experience to strengthen and build us up if we will give him the space and time to operate.

The next time you find yourself in a tough situation, stop and say, "Lord, I'm excited to see how you are going to work in this situation to help me grow." Then step back and get out of God's way.

Other Christians
God has a wonderful and unique way of putting the right people in your pathway at just the right time. I continue to be amazed by this. (Once in a while, God uses people that I wish he would put in someone else's life.) I am still learning to be more sensitive to the people I meet each day because God may be sending some of them into my path to help me grow.

The entire Bible contains stories of men and women God used to speak his message. We marvel at the stories of David and Jonathan, Ruth and Naomi. Jesus selected Peter, James, and John to be his inner circle of trusted friends and confidants. Even though he was the Messiah and came with the power of God, he still needed people. Equally amazing are the people in Scripture who were unimportant and unknown when God selected them to be part of his human drama.

God can use ordinary people to speak to your heart, mind, and spirit. The apostle Paul wrote, "Carry each other's burdens, and in this way you will fulfill the law of Christ" (Gal 6:2). There are times you do the carrying, and there are times when you will need to be carried. When you need to be carried, you aren't too concerned about who is doing the carrying. But it is wise to surround yourself with a few mature Christians.

An Inner Voice
Grasping the concept of inner voice is difficult for many people. It may sound mystical, maybe even dangerous. Aren't there too many people wandering around saying, "God told me this"? The implication is that they have a direct line to God and need nothing else for understanding. They employ a form of spiritual superiority that makes others feel inferior or spiritually immature.

I usually don't worry about what God told these people. I do worry when they say God told them to tell *me* something. The safety check on this kind of message is to compare it with the Word of God. Also look for other witnesses who can confirm it. When God seems to be impressing something on your heart and that impression just won't go away, always share it with a trusted Christian friend for evaluation. Pray God will give clarity and confirmation.

A few years ago, I was sitting in my office trying to figure out how to raise funds for our Divorce Recovery Center. (Yes, I am just like you, and I get unduly concerned over things like money.) As I was wrestling with this issue, a clear thought came into my mind: "I am going to give you a major gift from someone you do not know." My immediate mental response was, "Yeah, right. In my dreams!"

I went on with my day, and periodically that thought forced its way back into my mind. For the next several weeks, the thought kept recurring daily. I did not want to tell a soul because I thought they would think, *Nutcase!* About two months later I received a phone call from a friend, who said, "Someone you do not know has written a check for twenty-five thousand dollars for your center. When can I come by and drop it off?"

Wow! I thought. I knew in an instant that it was God who planted the original thought in my mind as an encouragement. Does that happen to me every day or every year? No. It rarely does. I do know it strengthened my faith and trust in God's ability to speak through an inner voice. It also helped me learn to let God be God, to do what may seem strange to me but is ordinary to him.

Once you turn your life over to God, there is a spiritual track running between you and him. You can get on it and stay on it, or you can lay your own track, run your own train, and remain uncertain of your destination. I hope you will be sure of where you are going and stay close to him.

FIVE

Staring Down Loneliness

God does not create us to live in isolation. He cre-
ated each of us incomplete, so we would need one
another, so we could help one another, so we could
reach out and touch one another's lives.

JOSEPH GIRZONE

Being alone is different from being lonely. Being alone comes from a choice or desire to be by oneself. After a long day of speaking and counseling, I usually want to be alone for about an hour to decompress. I relish other times when I can do something by myself. We all need to be able to rest and regroup in isolation. But being lonely is an entirely different thing.

My *Webster's New World Dictionary*[1] defines loneliness as "standing apart from others of its kind; isolated; unhappy at being alone, longing for friends, company, etc." My own, more succinct definition would be "suffering in social isolation."

Loneliness is reaching epidemic proportions in our culture, bringing with it perceived implications of failure, rejection, undesirability, and lack of value. No matter how you define it, loneliness can quickly burn a hole in the soul.

People who can admit to their struggle with loneliness are people who can work for resolution. Loneliness is not solved by denial of the problem. That only leads to depression and a total lack of motivation, even burnout and possibly a stay at a psychiatric hospital. Nor will you find the answer through chemical self-medication, overeating, emotional withdrawal, or frantically trying to fill your calendar so full you have no time to think or feel your pain.

FACING THE EMPTINESS

Loneliness is intertwined with loss. When a special person exits from your life, the many things they represented also disappear. You end up in a loneliness stare-down, wondering how to alleviate the emptiness. Let me encourage you to take the time to explore your feelings and talk them through with a trusted friend who may be able to offer insight.

Loss can be even more difficult because it may occur in several areas, such as the following:

Intimacy
When you share your life with someone for years, there are thousands of cords binding the two of you in varied levels of intimacy, some very deep. This intimacy is both physical and emotional. Now the person who understood you, accepted you as you were, and even read your mind occasionally is no longer there. When the cords are severed, a space is created

that cannot be filled by another person with whom you have no history.

Many people try to play the replacement game only to realize there is no such thing as instant intimacy—or that what feels like instant intimacy doesn't last. Some remarry quickly only to discover that a loneliness Band-Aid isn't enough. It is best to fully accept your loneliness and allow yourself to grieve your loss. Don't try to establish a new experience of intimacy too soon.

One of the key ingredients of physical intimacy is human touch. I hugged an older lady recently, and she started to cry. As I started to apologize, thinking I had squeezed too hard, she looked up and said, "Since George died, no one hugs me anymore." It's important to touch and hug people every day. It is one way we assure each other we are still alive. If people don't reach out to you, reach out to them and say, "I need a hug." They'll smile, hug you back, and you'll both feel better.

For many men and women, the loss of sexual intimacy is extremely difficult to deal with. The need for it is a powerful, pervasive drive. In a healthy marriage, sex enhances the emotional and spiritual relationship. When you lose a spouse, don't try to fill the void by having sexual relationships outside of marriage. I believe the Bible teaches this is wrong, discussed later in chapter 16. It is up to you to prepare your spirit and heart for the joy of sex within a possible remarriage. Many people testify to the fact that waiting is worth it!

Emotional intimacy is often most evident in conversation. But conversation is not about the words we speak to another; it's the emotional connection we make through what we have in common. You can speak to fifty people a day and receive from them only the standard, "Have a good day." Talking amounts only to a torrent of words if you are speaking with essentially nameless people with whom you have no life connection.

At the heart of any relationship, intimacy means there is someone listening and receiving what you are sharing. By sharing, I mean a soul and spirit kind of talk where two people share feelings, thoughts, dreams, and ideas together. Your innate need to be heard is perhaps far greater than your need to talk. Seek out a person who cares about you, and don't be afraid to say, "I need someone to talk to just for a few minutes. Don't feel you need to fix anything; will you please just listen?"

Support System
Within a year of becoming single again, you may lose 80 percent of your friends. It isn't that they have lost your telephone number. People just tend to group themselves with those in similar life situations. Married couples socialize with other couples. Single people gravitate to single people. Nothing strange and unusual about that! Though friendships do cross status and interest lines, we all tend to hang out with people like us.

Children, relatives, and friends form your closest circles of love. The death of a spouse usually draws those support systems even closer. In divorce, however, support systems sometimes fall apart. Friends may continue support depending on their interpretation of what happened. You may lose people you thought would stand by you. Children may go to live with the other parent. You may end up wondering where everyone went, feeling like a walking want ad. Hang in there. Keep active. Work on becoming stable. When you lose a connection with one group of people, you enter the process of choosing to build a new friendship circle or remaining alone. With time you can make new friends who are loyal and caring.

Understanding

You thought marriage was forever. You believed the person you married would love, respect, and care for you until death. No one told you that living relationships die but there is no burial when divorce is the victor.

Now you feel like you've lost your ability to understand your life. You know only that things have gone berserk and the damage left in the wake is scattered about your life. "Why" comes up in almost every discussion you have—even in the ones you don't have. You seldom know the answer to the "whys" but think if you did, somehow everything would make sense and you could move on to the next space on your Monopoly board of life.

The bad news is you may not understand things for a long time to come. The good news is you can trust the One who holds the past and future. God will eventually help you make sense of what happened. In the meantime move ahead. You don't need to understand everything to take your first steps forward into a brand new life.

Community Respect

In a healthy marriage, husbands and wives are a team and present a united front to the community. They are an intimate community relating to a larger community beyond themselves. In that larger community, there is usually respect for that team and the imprint it leaves. Loss of that community respect constitutes a form of social isolation. When the team no longer exists, unfair as this is, both members can be locked out of the larger community, even a church fellowship. A friend of mine bemoans the fact that often, "The Christian army shoots its wounded." Some churches do it in the name of theology and denominational standards. Others simply show a lack of compassion and caring.

Even when lovingly accepted, former spouses rarely stay in the same church. Some church communities will embrace the person left behind and help them adjust to the single-again experience. A church that welcomes newly single-again men and women will usually have a large crowd. Look for that, and be willing to start over.

Vocation

In today's world, the loss of a person's vocational community rarely happens—except for members of the clergy, and even that is changing dramatically. Still, many men and woman use divorce's corridor of change to launch a new career. Many women find they must work outside the home now due to reduced economic status. Others have long wanted a career of their own. Women in both situations find they can make it just fine. Many pursue brand new dreams; others pull an old one out of mothballs.

If you have lost your vocational community, it may be time to visit your local community college and talk with a career counselor. Most schools have programs that can sift your interests and target your giftedness and undeveloped capabilities. Career counselors are up to date on which careers are obsolete and which are emerging. There are incredible new options today for anyone wanting a new career challenge.

Identity

Personal identity is a powerful thing. You cannot get on a plane or write a check in a store without being asked for ID. We all reach for our driver's license so that the airline employee or store clerk can look at us, then at our picture, and decide if we are who we claim to be.

But identity is far more than a picture. Men and women

sometimes define themselves through the person to whom they are married. In unhealthy marriages a person can lose their personal identity by allowing their spouse to control them, dictate to them, or demean them. I meet people coming out of long-term marriages who have no clue as to who they are because along the way another person either squashed their identity or stole it.

I will never forget a lady who sat in my office with tears running down her cheeks as she begged me to help her find herself. A marriage of over thirty-five years had ended, and the person who dictated to her was no longer present. Her identity, such as it was, went with him. I knew it would take a long time and hard work for her to establish her identity as a single-again woman.

No one should ever be allowed to rob you of who you are. Independent, dependent, and codependent relationships may have become thieves that stole your personhood. If you have had your identity stolen in a marriage that has ended, it would be wise for you to spend time examining how that happened. If you later choose remarriage, you had better do a lot of talking first and go into it with a solid game plan. Many remarriages take on the same baggage as first ones. People tell me constantly that they married the same kind of person as they did the first time and are now rerunning the same problems. There are many things to be learned from a failed marriage. Take the time you need to learn them.

WRESTLING WITH LONELINESS

I meet some people who use loneliness as a badge of martyrdom to hide behind. They blame everyone for their problem.

When I invited a professed lonely man to a singles meeting recently, he said he did not want to be in a room with a hundred other people like himself. So he stayed away and perpetuated his lonely journey.

Self-pity and blaming everyone else for your life situation are not the answer. Admission that you need other people is the first step to finding a workable solution. There are a few simple, positive things you can do that really work.

Talk to the Lord about your feelings and struggles with loneliness. God understands what loneliness is all about because he faced it in his humanity. For a time he was cut off from human relationships. He gave us assurance that when we are cut off, he will always be with us and we will never be alone.

Commit to becoming part of a supportive and sustaining community. You have to search for it. When you find it, you have to take ownership in it. To belong to any support system, you must give as well as take. Community doesn't happen overnight. Not every group will fulfill your expectations and dissolve your loneliness in two short weeks. Relationship-building is slow, hard, grinding work. Always remember that you have to dig for the diamonds.

Find a few other people who are also struggling with loneliness so you can help each other. I have never seen a newspaper ad for a loneliness recovery group, but any kind of group works with that problem as part of building human wholeness. People need to belong to other people who understand their problems and share the goal of finding constructive answers. Ask single people you meet to go out for coffee with you, see a movie, or join you for skiing. Look for new interests to cultivate together with others.

Work at building your own self-worth and self-esteem. This is more of a private project than a public one, but it is vital to your growth. Personal counseling can help here, along with taking a few career classes at a community college and doing some instructive reading. Remember, when changes invade your life, it's time to hang out a sign that says, *Please Be Patient With Me—I'm Under Construction.* Don't be afraid of a long-term project. Only mushrooms grow overnight.

Take responsibility for your physical health and fitness. The physical is always connected to the emotional and mental. Join a health club and go regularly. Take up a new sport or hobby. The Bible says your body is a temple (see 1 Cor 6:19). You are responsible for keeping it in good condition. I meet too many lonely people who are drastically overweight, walk no further than from their house to their car, spend all their free time in front of the TV, and wonder why they feel frustrated. Growth means getting outside and assuming responsibility for yourself.

Be good to yourself. Do something you have always wanted to do. Do something without having to ask permission from any-one. Try something daring and different. One lady in a seminar I was teaching decided to take up flying as a hobby. That hobby eventually led her into racing airplanes on the national circuit. When I asked her how she got into this, she told me her husband never permitted her to take flying lessons. The minute he left her for another woman, she headed for the airport and signed up. She could have sat down on her couch and been swallowed up by loneliness. Instead she flew right through it!

Set goals for yourself and start working on a life plan that is uniquely yours, not someone else's. Stop waiting for someone to come along with a custom-made set of plans for your future. If they do come along, the plans will probably be theirs. Remember that growing people build their own plans—with God's help.

UNTIE THE RIBBON ON GOD'S GIFT

There is no escape from times of loneliness as long as we are alive. But we do not need to become imprisoned by them. Loneliness is a gift that reminds us of our humanity. It drives us to a relationship with God and each other. It can draw us into community, giving us the warmth to fuel our spirit and keep windows of hope wide open. The first step is always talking to God. The second is taking the risk to reach out and build a new community of friends. You will feel uncertain at first, but your confidence will grow. Loneliness is always painful, but it is full of treasure if you dig deep.

In Search of a New Community

*The moving finger of God in human history
points ever in the same direction. There must be
community.*

HOWARD THURMAN

I grew up in the country, in an era when everyone knew their neighbors, everyone helped their neighbors, and everyone cared about their neighbors. In my early twenties I ended up in a college in the suburbs of New York City where no one knew anyone else and everyone suspected everyone else. During the forty years since college, I have lived in cities, small and large, and have seldom known my neighbors beyond a nod and a passing greeting. Somewhere along the road of progress, we Americans have severed our relationship with neighbors, choosing to go our solitary way.

Community is a basic human need. Yet sometimes it seems the only thing that calls us back to community is some form of disaster—hurricane, flood, tornado, or fire. Out of every disaster come incredible stories about people helping each other, often performing acts of great courage and selflessness. Human barriers quickly disappear in the face of the need to survive. But once life gets back to normal, the close bonds formed in crisis are usually left behind.

A new housing development not far from my home is advertising houses built after a post–World War II model. They boast of large front porches, lots of green grass, and lampposts along the street. Their object is to create a community that invites people to form relationships, not live cut off from each other behind tall fences and prominent garages. The developers have created playgrounds, ball fields, park benches, and wide greenbelts with inviting places to sit. But building the structure of a community won't automatically make these relationships happen.

Many people admit to living too much in isolation but feel no great motivation to change. They bemoan a lack of deeper friendships and neighborliness but continue their frantic pace of life, promising to make the needed changes "when things slow down."

I conducted a funeral recently. The crowd was pretty sparse. When I said something about it to someone, she remarked, "I guess people just don't have the time anymore to go to funeral services." Where I grew up, a funeral was often an all-day affair. People came before the service, stayed through it, ate lunch together afterwards, and seldom went home before dark. My grandfather once remarked that you always knew how many friends a person had by counting the cars following their funeral coach to the cemetery. People in those days supported the grieving by being physically present. They formed community by attending and helping at funerals, barn raisings, harvest, and family celebrations.

A community is a place where we meet people to whom we belong. In our lifetimes, we have the option to form and be a part of numerous communities, some short-lived, others permanent. When you marry, you start a new community called a family. You connect to other primary units to become a family system. In a healthy family, you feel loved, accepted, and cared for. When your family experiences a loss through divorce or death, the entire family community is weakened by fragmentation. Many single-again men and women tell me they felt they had been dropped into a giant black hole. They wondered if they would ever belong anywhere again. There is a keen sense of loss, and a desire to rebuild.

BUILDING AGAIN

Where *do* you belong when you become single again? How do you build a support system that won't fall apart every time you go through a crisis? I asked those two questions in a group of newly single-again men and women. Responses ranged from elation to frustration. Some were discouraged. Others felt they were building a better support system than they had when married. All of them did agree on one thing: Building a new community where you truly feel a sense of belonging is difficult. It takes a major investment of time and energy.

There are several realities you need to accept as you build new friendship circles. First, you will lose many of the friends you had when you were married. Your life is now very different from theirs. Some fade away, even when they previously had assured you they would be there for you. Others seem to back off from the beginning. There will be days when you wonder if you are carrying the Ebola virus around with you.

Work hard to keep the friends you don't want to lose. Ask for continued friendship. And look for ways you can be a good friend to others.

Second, understand that it is possible to spend too much time with other divorced people. You risk developing a dislike for anyone who is not divorced or divorcing, an "us-versus-them" mentality. Don't start living on the defensive. Being with fellow strugglers is important to your healing process, but you don't want to turn them into your personal army.

Going to singles groups every night of the week is not a satisfying experience. Yes, you do need to connect, but you can burn out by making singles the centerpiece of your new life. As I speak at singles groups in my city, I often see the same people at different groups. You cannot belong anywhere if you are busy visiting everywhere. I believe most single-again people need a singles group for about two to three years. After that you need to move on and get interested in other kinds of people with a variety of interests. Be enthusiastic and excited about life as a whole. A healthy singles group is a recovery room to help you heal, but you can't stay there.

Third, if you are a single parent, you won't have much time left over for building a new community. And when you do have time, it will most likely include your children. Time for you is at a premium. Those with whom you work and fellowship should respect that. You can join other single parents and their children for activities you enjoy together. For a start, take the initiative and invite others for potluck dinners or picnics.

WHAT DOES A SUPPORTIVE
COMMUNITY PROVIDE?

Each of us is busy practicing to become the person God designed us to be. None of us has arrived. A healthy, supportive community is a safe place where you can practice your *becoming*. When you are part of one, you will be around people who love you as you are and help you struggle to get where you want to be. A healthy community will have particular characteristics for which you should look.

It will provide a place where you share the deep truths of your life with others—and allow others to share their deep truths with you. The ultimate goal of any community is to allow its members to be real there, to feel a genuine sense of acceptance. Then you will open up and allow your life to be transparent.

It will provide a forum made up of people who will challenge you to move forward into tomorrow, and not remain stuck in yesterday. On a radio talk show about forgiveness, a lady called in, then rattled on and on about a husband who had left her, how he had hurt her, and how she would never consider forgiving him. I could barely get a word in. Finally, when she took a breath, I asked how long ago her marriage ended. Everyone in the studio was stunned when she said "twenty-two years ago." Later the announcer looked at me and said, "That woman needs to get a life."

In fact she desperately needed a group of people who would not allow her to remain angry after twenty-two years or to live without forgiving. A healthy community will hold you to some degree of accountability for moving forward. If your community doesn't challenge you once in a while, it may mean their level of compassion isn't very high.

It will help you set goals and become responsible for some part of your future. You will be better equipped to live your future if you have a few productive goals equipping you once you get there. Weight Watchers, for example, is a community that is incredibly effective in helping people lose weight. When you attend weekly sessions, you have to step on a scale and read the results. With thirty people staring over your shoulder at the numbers on the scale, your weight loss increases dramatically. Why? Because people keep us accountable, and people cheer us on. You can count your own calories, but if your cheerleading squad is lost, weight loss is a hollow victory. You want to succeed. Your community wants you to succeed. You want them to succeed.

It will provide a networking system that builds bridges to help you reach important goals. Finding a job, a good dentist, a reliable mechanic, or the right doctor is best accomplished by asking around for tips and recommendations. Networking fills 80 percent of all job openings, not placing ads in the newspaper. In a supportive community you have a myriad of ties to different people, places, and things.

The struggle for most of us is that we do not want to ask for help because we do not want to bother anyone or experience their rejection if they don't help us. Pride often preempts our need and keeps us from using help available to us. You will be amazed how quickly you can move ahead when you network in your community. The larger your community, the greater your resources.

One of the positive things I have done for years is ask people in a singles meeting if they have any needs the group can assist them in. I ask for those who can talk with individuals after the meeting. People are always challenged and excited by the opportunity to help. There is no better feeling than to know you are part of helping someone move ahead.

It will provide people with whom you can do things socially. There is little satisfaction in doing alone things you enjoy. Most singles groups have extensive social calendars. Their events offer safe opportunities to meet and get to know other people, building friendships. Take the risk of reaching out to others.

You are a stranger only the first time you enter a new group. Those first steps are very difficult to take because you are entering the unknown. You don't have to be single again to be fearful of new things. Everyone faces that feeling several times a week.

It will help form three kinds of relationships, all of which serve our needs. The first kind of relationship can best be described as casual. Casual relationships usually involve people who have names and faces we recognize but who for the most part populate the fringes of our life. I describe them as the "Hi, how are you? Fine. How are you?" people. Our contact with casual acquaintances is limited and usually for a brief, specific purpose.

The second kind of relationship is friendship. At this level you relate with people socially—in bowling, ball games, church committee work, task forces, or choir. You don't spend great amounts of time with these friends, but you keep them within reach. You usually remain comfortable at the housekeeping levels of life but rarely share at a deep level.

Intimate relationships are the third and closest kind. These people are allowed to see your vulnerability and the deepest concerns of your soul. They know you inside out. You know them the same way. It takes years to build that kind of relationship because it requires a shared history to build trust. That history will take you through the joys, heartaches, losses, and wins of each other's lives.

Intimate friendships involve total acceptance on both sides. You seldom build more than three or four relationships like this in a lifetime, but women typically have more than men do. Women are by nature more relational and nurturing, while men tend to be more private, hiding caring feelings to avoid seeming unmanly. Women participate more readily in small group discussions. Men tend to sit silently for several weeks before they take the risk of open sharing. Once they open up, though, look out; often the dam breaks and the tears flow. Intimate relationships can be risky when they are with members of the opposite sex. A safe standard to hold to is men need men, women need women.

CONCENTRIC CIRCLES

Everyone needs concentric circles of relationships, including all levels of life, if we are to be healthy members of a community. Too many of one kind of relationship and too few of another will keep us relationally unbalanced.

If I were to relive my life, I would put more time and energy into building healthy relationships. Though I have an abundance of them today, I have let good ones fall by the wayside. At midlife I realize so much that occupies our time is simply just *stuff*.

Any relationship is a risk. From the moment you say hello,

you can never be sure where this new friendship will go. You can never be sure if the other person is a giver or a taker and what that might mean in the long run. But communities are meant to be strong enough to foster healthy friendships like bridges connecting us in life.

Ask yourself the following questions in order to see if you are growing in your community.

Am I safely becoming what God wants me to be? Are my hurts being healed? People who are beginning the rebuilding process need a warm, loving, and safe place to fellowship. I have spoken to singles who were not in the healthiest place possible for growth and healing. Some groups were filled with judgment, argument, and a preoccupation with negative things while they gave out spiritual Band-Aids. Look around you. If the people in your community are not getting well, your chances may be rather slim too. You should have room to stretch, struggle, and grow, with no one forcing you to fit a certain mold.

Are my emotional, spiritual, psychological, and physical needs being met? Am I becoming whole? The joy of a healthy community is that other people share their personal giftedness with you, becoming participants in your growth. A newly divorced man in our church shared how the leaders and other participants in our divorce recovery seminar had affected him. He said he owed his life to God and the men and women who stood by him and helped meet his needs as he journeyed through his broken places. He felt his highs and lows were becoming balanced again. He was choosing to act on situations rather than react to them. He was experiencing God's love and forgiveness through God's people, and as a result, his depression was beginning to lift and his ability to concentrate was restored. I listened to the threads of hope that ran through this man's conversations. Like many before him, he came through the doorway of despair but chose not to take up permanent residence there.

Am I receiving help and guidance that is helping me resolve my fears because the promises of God's Word are believed and taken seriously? For years I have told teachers of singles that my goal is to present relational and practical guidance that is biblical. Your community should be about changing lives. If it's not, ask yourself what it *is* about. Should you remain in it? If you are not growing, you are dying.

This past summer, I was given three rose bushes to add to the one I already had, one called the *Billy Graham* rose. I placed the new plants in pots on the patio. They looked pretty small and scared when we got them settled down in their new homes. I wondered if they would survive and bloom or take one look at us and give up the ghost.

For months the bushes have produced crop after crop. It's now December, and we just picked the last two roses of the season. Did the little bushes just take off and grow by themselves all summer and fall? No, I had to give them more attention that most other flowers, with fertilizer and water heading the list. Pruning followed, along with a few other touches here and there. Nurture and care made the difference. Nothing does well without it—roses or people.

Many people enter the single-again community dragging with them a long list of promises broken by other people. The newcomers' defenses are high and their hopes are low. They look like my frightened rose bushes. Skepticism and defiance may be evident as some people wonder, *Will this group make a positive difference in my life?* Some challenge the group almost the minute they open the door. But in a loving community, no one laughs at your fears. They stand with you, pray with you, and assist as you search for answers in God's Word.

Is my life taking a new direction? Am I working on God-sized goals for the future? Too many formerly married men and women seem content to park in a singles group with little vision for their future. The tide of growth and change in a healthy community should keep you moving ahead. People can and will affirm your goals as they see them becoming reality.

A healthy community should have a number of mentors, guides, and examples with whom you can talk and pray and from whom you take guidance. Some of them should be a little further down the road than you are, willing to reach back, grab your hand, and pull you along.

A year from now you should be at a different place than you are today. But that will not happen by chance. It will happen when you become responsible for your life, and share it with people in your community.

Am I experiencing "anyhow" love? There are three kinds of love:

If Love

Because Love

Anyhow Love

The first two are conditional and performance-oriented. Children know they will receive certain things they want if they do certain things adults ask. Good actions are rewarded and the bad are punished. We learn early in life how to play the game, and we move into adulthood hauling the game board with us. But when God comes into our lives bringing unconditional love, we learn that this love is based upon acceptance, not performance. It begins creeping into human relationships, changing you and those around you. For some who have grown up learning and practicing conditional love, it's tough to make the switch. If your community claims the name "Christian" for itself, Anyhow Love had better be growing there.

I am fortunate to work in a church that allows me to be a shepherd and a healer to those who are hurting. Some days I feel we have a huge magnetic sign out on the street that says, *Hurting People Welcome Here—We Dispense Anyhow Love Without Limits.* Does that mean we have a perfect church? No. We work hard at accepting, and we attract many people who need that in their lives. We have discovered that where love flows, a person grows.

JESUS HAD A COMMUNITY

If the headlines of the local newspaper in Jesus' time had read, "Lone Messiah Does Miracles," the message of the Gospel might have been confined to the hillsides around Bethlehem and Nazareth. Knowing his message was for an entire world, Jesus brought together a community that would carry his message once he was gone. In the beginning it consisted of his immediate family. Later he called his disciples. Inside that band Jesus called Peter, James, and John to be closer to him than the others. They formed what we would call an intimate circle. He also gathered around himself other friends like Mary, Martha, and Lazarus, and later he called seventy people to do missionary work throughout the land. After the resurrection, he called one hundred twenty into an upper-room encounter. And so his circles of community grew. Today we have that community known as the Christian church.

Jesus the man needed those who could receive and give to him, listening to his teaching and observing the miracles he performed. In many different ways he told his friends, "You are loved. You are forgiven. You belong to my family." No wonder the church spread throughout the world.

You and I need community if we are to be healthy spiritually and be effective in changing our world. It is a place to practice our *becoming!*

SEVEN

Reaffirming My Identity: Who Am I Anyway?

I am not afraid of my life.

SUSAN MUTO

On a recent flight I found myself seated next to a talkative woman. We had no sooner taken to the skies than she finally asked me the big question, "What do you do?" I knew that the instant I replied truthfully, I would find myself immersed in a two-hour conversation that would rob me of the time in which I had planned to read. Now, like you, when I am asked the great identity-revealing question, I have a variety of answers. I can say I am a harmonica player, roller-blader, grandfather, author, minister, husband, ex-hockey player, and about sixty-two other things. Any one of my responses can lead the ensuing conversation down its own individual path. When I say I am an author, everyone tells me they are going to write a book someday, or that they've already written the first page.

I have found the answer that shuts people down quickly is, "I am a minister." "That's nice," most people comment as they go back to whatever they were doing, leaving me to my solitude.

My response when asked what I do is usually the first step in telling people who I am. I begin to unwrap my identity in a public way. Of course, I can limit how far I want to go with that revelation and just how much I want someone else to know. We all form conclusions about people based on what they tell us about what they do. We file people in categories *important* or *unimportant* based on their vocation.

Perhaps a better question to someone we have never met would be, "Are you someone important or famous?" One segment of contemporary culture is known as the *groupies*. Groupies are people with little or no identity of their own who hang around movie and music stars. They want everyone to know whom they are following. By being with the famous (or infamous), they hope to form an identity. They serve the purpose of making famous people more famous, while the famous use them to make themselves *feel* famous. As one singer said, "I must be famous; everyone comes to hear me sing."

We are name-droppers when it comes to knowing someone a little higher on the ladder in life. We feel if we can identify with them, we will somehow be more important. Why else would four hundred Little Leaguers hang around the players' exit at major league ballparks? If they can come home and show their friends Roger Clemens' autograph, their status rises to new levels. For many people, identity is not who you are but whom you know.

The world of merchandising says we are what we can afford to buy and flaunt. Economic status defines our identity according to lifestyle. The bigger and more expensive the car, the more superior the identity of the driver. Expensive clothing conveys the same message.

It is little wonder Scripture asks, "What good will it be for a man if he gains the whole world, yet forfeits his soul?" (Mt 16:26a). In God's economy other things contribute to the forming of your identity. Who you are goes way beyond what you do, whom you know, what kind of car you drive or house you live in, or what clothes you wear.

WHO AND WHAT DETERMINES MY IDENTITY?

The first and foremost influence on your identity is the family into which you were born. You had no choice in selecting that family. You were placed within it at birth and will be forever tied to it whether it is a blessing or a burden. Whether you like it or not, in your formative years that family made an imprint larger than any DNA. Whatever they contributed to your development will remain with you for the whole journey through life. When people study their genealogies, they ask, "Where did I come from? What were my ancestors like? How has my heritage influenced me?"

I frequently meet people who tell me they come from a dysfunctional family. They assume they have little chance to be anything other than dysfunctional. I always challenge that because each person is an individual who reaches an age where he or she is capable of making personal choices. You cannot deny your origins, but you do not have to duplicate bad choices made in your family of origin.

A second contributor to your identity is educational background. Many parents want their children to go to big-name colleges so they can use that college name as part of their own identity as well as the child's. The competition to get into the right college is strong for families who feel academics, career, and identity are tied together. Parents may feel if their child is a doctor, lawyer, or corporate chief it will mean a better identity than those who become carpet cleaners or truck drivers.

A good and expansive education is a confidence-builder as well as a vocation-builder. Education opens a person's mind to a broader view. When education is limited, vocational options are few. Someone once said, "Big people talk about ideas, average people talk about things, and little people talk about other people." Strive to live in the world of ideas! Also, educated people tend to gravitate to and socialize with other educated people. Education truly does open doors.

Third, identity is formed through friends and support systems. Much of the battle for identity is wrapped up in our desperate need to belong somewhere—and to someone. When we have a place to belong, we can shake our fist at the world and yell, "See, I'm not alone. I know who I am. I belong to, or with, _____."

Remember when you were a teenager, and your parents warned you about some of your companions? The warning seemed to be, "Hang out with those in trouble, and you will get in trouble." There is a lot of truth in that.

The flip side of that truth is the positive value of friendships within a strong peer group with members who have high standards, high morals, dedicated motivation, and a desire to be responsible citizens of society. In my early years working with the juvenile court system and Youth for Christ, I saw what peer groups did to teenagers. Negative groups buried teenagers in a sea of bad influence, while positive groups built productive lives. This is equally true of adult lives. Look for strong peer groups!

A fourth identity-builder is what I call "life stuff." It is composed of all the life experiences that build character or contribute to its destruction, helping form the good and bad qualities of our characters.

Any experience can be a builder of good, however, if you can learn something from it. Periodically I meet people who are ten years beyond the loss of a spouse and still buried by the event. You have a choice to live under the pile of negative experience or on top of it. Bad things happen to good people, but the good people will look at them as "life stuff" that can make their character stronger.

The other day I asked a divorced man how he was doing. His answer was, "Stronger." Maybe five years down the road, people meeting him for the first time will marvel at how strong he is. Only he will know that his strength is born out of bad "life stuff." The apostle Paul said, "When I am weak, then I am strong" (2 Cor 12:10b). He could say that because he knew where his strength came from. It came from God in the middle of "life stuff"!

A final identity-builder is your belief system. What do you believe? It takes a lifetime to form a belief system. After you lose a spouse, some things you once believed, you no longer believe. Some things you did not believe, you now believe.

I grew up in a zealous and rigid church of strong convictions. I believed our church was better, bigger, stronger, and more biblical than any other was. I also believed we were right and other churches were wrong. My church defined my identity in a big way when I was growing up. It wasn't until well beyond college, when I was in full-time ministry, that I realized other churches with different signs out front also preached the gospel. After seventeen years of traveling across America and speaking in all kinds of churches, I have come to believe you can't tell what is going on inside a church by the sign out front. God's people just happen to be everywhere and in the most unexpected places. My belief system has changed.

The Christian's spiritual belief system is anchored in the cement of the Word of God. Spiritual beliefs that change from day to day and situation to situation have no home in the heart of a follower of God. If all a Christian had in his possession was a copy of the Beatitudes, the Ten Commandments, and the discourse from the Mount of Olives, he would have a rock-solid belief system upon which to anchor his life.

Most of the identity-builders I have described deal with external things. They do influence our identity, but they are neither the sum total nor the final word. Our external situation can change quickly, and we are often forced to change with it. In some of those changes, vital parts of who we were may disappear and we may wonder, *Who am I anyway?*

AM I WHO I WAS?

One of the biggest identity changes in life comes with marriage. A woman's actual name usually changes. In the ensuing months, many other changes take place. Two individuals are now a couple and begin to build an identity as a couple. A new family structure is created. Personal dreams are often sacrificed as corporate dreams are born. Childhood dreams are replaced by adopting the dreams of a spouse. Geographical and job changes become a way of life. Children are born, careers are advanced, and houses are purchased.

In some marriages the identities of husband and wife as individuals grow and are strengthened by the union. In others one individual identity is strengthened while the other is weakened or even lost. Some people lose their identity by becoming what a spouse wants them to be. I meet many men and women who marry, only to wake up years later with no clue as to who they really are.

A person who assumes the identity of a spouse, giving up his or her own identity, forms a *dependent* relationship. Dependent relationships become *codependent* when identity boundary lines are lost and one spouse is trapped in the behavior and lifestyle of the other. A healthy marriage identity can grow when an *interdependence* is formed: both build personal identities along with an identity as a couple.

Either divorce or death of a spouse can send your identity spinning out of control, taking away what you did have—and what you did not have. The more your identity was drawn from your spouse, the greater the loss. It can leave you standing alone wondering where in the world you should be going. With economics changed, faith shaken, family life disrupted, and friends beating a hasty retreat, one might truthfully ask, *Who am I now?*

A BRIEF IDENTITY CHECK

When your identity has been lost or badly beaten, it is hard to look up and rebuild hope. Many years ago I thought it would be a good idea to have participants in a divorce recovery seminar stand each night and say out loud, "I am God's unique, unrepeatable miracle." I could barely get anyone to talk above a mumble. I realized that as much as I believed this for them, and wanted them to believe it, they did not even feel close to any miracle. Nevertheless it is true.

Do you believe God really loves you?

Do you believe you are a gifted and talented human being?

Do you believe God is bigger than any problem you have right now?

Do you believe God can use your situation to make you stronger?

Do you believe you are loved?

Do you believe God has a life for you beyond where you now are?

Do you believe God is in the forgiveness business?

If you can answer yes to a few of these questions, you have good building blocks with which to start rebuilding your identity. It is no overnight project. It will take time.

I tried to tell that to a woman who came into my office today. Her divorce was final, her family roots were two thousand miles away, and, except for elderly parents, she was very much alone. I wish I could have let her see a year ahead into her future so she could know this wasn't the end of her story, just an intersection.

Jeremiah 29:11 helps raise the banner of hope: "'For I know the plans I have for you,' declares the Lord, 'plans to prosper you and not to harm you, plans to give you hope and a future.'"

THE VALUE OF LOVE

I had just finished a seminar and was hurriedly packing my briefcase for the mad dash to the airport. As I was going out the door, a lady came up and asked if she could pin a button on my lapel. I answered yes, thanked her, and ran for my ride. After I checked in at the airport, I remembered the button, looked down, and read, *You Are Loved.* All my tiredness disappeared as I reflected on those three words. It was one giant affirmation helping me understand that a big part of who I am involves giving and receiving love.

Love really isn't love until you give it away. If you are free to give it, you will receive it. If you don't have it, you desperately need it. The key to understanding who you are is found in the truth of knowing *you are loved.* It starts with God's love. If God loves you, you can love yourself; you are a created work of his love. If God loves you and you love you, you can love others and they can love you back.

THREE GOALS TO
BUILDING YOUR IDENTITY

Identity asks three questions:

Who was I?

Who am I?

Where am I headed?

These involve your past, present, and future. How would you answer? You are formed from the bits and pieces of yesterday. You are adding what you are discovering today. Your goal is to take it all with you into tomorrow. There are three words that will help you on your today and tomorrow part of the journey.

Becoming. You are in the process of finding out what God wants you to be and what God wants you to do. If your identity comes from knowing and following God in your life, no one can steal that from you. As you grow in your ability to follow him, along with becoming what he wants you to be, you will have a strong sense of belonging to him before anything else.

Relating. Relating involves the way you function with the significant others in your life. To a large extent, what you become is related to the people with whom you spend time. Choose Christian friends who know and love God and follow him. Right relationships can have a deep and profound influence on your life.

Achieving. Most of us spend the larger part of every day trying to achieve the myriad things we set out to do. Achievements validate our existence. Achieving is asking questions about God's goals for our lives and asking what direction he would want our paths to take. God always gives directions when we ask for them—and are willing to wait for the answers.

Achieving also involves affirmation. When I write the last page of this book, I will feel a sense of accomplishment. That feeling of satisfaction will remain limited until someone someday says, "Thank you for that book you wrote. It helped me immensely." From childhood to adulthood, we wait each day for affirmation of achievement.

A CHANGE OF DIRECTION
AND A NEW IDENTITY

Does God have the power to change your direction and give you a new identity? There is a model in the book of Acts. We are introduced to Saul of Tarsus in the seventh chapter. When we first meet him, Stephen is being stoned to death for his beliefs. Saul looks on and passes out the stones. Later (chapter nine), Saul picks up the pace somewhat. He is described as "breathing out murderous threats" to the followers of Jesus and trying to imprison as many as possible. His identity is wrapped up in hating the followers of Jesus (see Acts 9:1-2).

God dramatically interrupts Saul's life as Saul travels to Damascus in order to persecute more Christians. Confronted on a dusty road by God, Saul is blinded and falls to the ground. In this dramatic encounter he is forever changed. So is his name. We learn, "So Saul stayed with them and moved about freely in Jerusalem, speaking boldly in the name of the Lord" (Acts 9:28). Saul had a one-on-one with God and came away with a new identity and a new mission. He wrote a vast amount of the New Testament and planted churches everywhere he traveled. Read the story in the book of Acts, then ask yourself, *Can God still do what he did in Saul's life? Might he do that in my life?*

If God said, "Stand up right now and identify yourself," what would you say?

EIGHT

Goals: The Stepping Stones to Tomorrow

Trust in the Lord with all your heart and lean not on your own understanding; in all your ways acknowledge him, and he will make your paths straight.

PROVERBS 3:5-6

A wise person once said, "Shoot at nothing, and that's exactly what you will hit." I meet men and women in the single-again world who appear to be shooting at nothing. And they are hitting it dead center. When I question them about goals for their future, they often respond by telling me their life is far too uncertain to think about that. They usually add that once their life returns to normal, they will try to set a few.

When you live like that, you can become a victim of cir-cumstances. Depression may set in, and you may begin to self-destruct emotionally. You need to set goals *now* in order to get your life back on track.

There are those who commit personally to very little, always keep their options open, and hope their circumstances will somehow change. Too many single adults feel the only goal they really need is to start a relationship with someone, attach their life to that person, adopt that person's goals, and begin to march toward the future. The grave danger here is that you have no personal ownership and investment in someone else's goals. You can never attain personal fulfillment by living out another person's dream.

Waiting until you find a new mate, new job, new career, or new house will only put control of your life into someone else's hands. What if those things never happen because you were hoping someone else would take care of them? When setting goals, never surrender leadership to anyone else. Keep yourself in the driver's seat.

A holding-pattern mentality drives leaders and pastors in single-again ministry over the edge. Single adults usually wait until the last minute to register for or attend anything. As one woman stated, "Hey, you have to keep all your options open. You might get a better offer." I understand her reasoning, but she might waste the rest of her life *waiting* for something better when she could be setting goals to *move* toward something better.

Some people delay goal setting out of fear that locking goals into place will limit their present and future freedom. If they set any goals at all, they may place them so far in the future they will never have to face the challenge of reaching them. Goals are dreams with an anchor attached. When we accept them as attainable, they can change our lives.

We all face personal crossroads from time to time. We need

to take one growth step after another and become responsible for our own destinies. Fear of moving forward leaves a person sitting on the curb in life while everyone else heads on down the street. Nothing changes unless you take personal responsibility for making it happen.

I was once involved in a serious auto accident but escaped without injury. The moment I climbed out of that totally demolished car, I knew the accident was a wake-up call from God. I knew I would have to return to my educational pursuit and get my life back on the track from which it had been derailed. My goal was to do it on down the road until a friend said, "You need to do it now, not later." The accident happened in August. I was back in school in September.

I have learned over the years that *someday goals* can easily become *no-day goals*. Workable time frames have to be nailed down or your goals will merely become good intentions lost in the sea of daily living.

Most effective goals fall into three categories: short-term, intermediate, and long-term. You need a sprinkling of all three when you move into serious goal setting. If all your goals are long-term, the danger is you will never start on any of them. If all of them are short-term, you will accomplish them too easily and your perseverance will remain unchallenged.

Goals also need to be shared with others so there will be both accountability and encouragement. When a goal is achieved, there should always be a celebration of some kind. Attainment of all goals, big or small, should be recognized in some way. Accomplishment is always a builder of self-esteem, and we will seldom have an overabundance.

SEVEN WAYS TO MAKE GOALS HAPPEN

Write down your goals. List goals in their order of importance. Indicate the time frame within which you want to accomplish them. Then post the list in several places to remind yourself of what you are working on. Keep the list in your daily organizer and refer to it several times a week. When you achieve a goal, cross it off your list and move on to the next. Trying to remember goals without writing them down seldom works because other needs start claiming your attention every day and you get sidetracked.

I had always lived with a Month-at-a-Glance yearly calendar and a legal pad. Every day I would make my *to do* list and check my appointments, and between these two tools, try to keep my life organized. Then one day while visiting with a friend, I pulled out my dynamic duo to write something down. My friend asked if that was how I organized my life. I told him it had worked for me for many years. He smiled and told me he worked for a large national time-organizer company, and he invited me to attend one of their seminars and begin using their organizer. I resisted at first, feeling that my rather archaic system worked fine. I did not feel I needed his two-hundred-fifty-dollar wizardry. He told me he would give me the whole thing free if I would attend. What a deal!

A month later I found myself in his seminar with a mound of new material sitting on the desk in front of me. Six hours later I went home, stacked it all on a shelf, and continued on my merry old way. He called within a month and asked me how it was going. I told him it wasn't. He encouraged me to do it for thirty days. Since it was free, I felt I owed him at least that much. I have been using his system now for over ten years, and it has revolutionized my life. I would be lost without it.

The reason I share this is to show you I am no different than you. New goals scare me. I am hesitant to give up what works for me, even if there is something close by that works better. We are all creatures of habit, developing comfort zones we are hesitant to leave. Setting and pursuing new goals kicks us out of our comfort zones and moves us forward.

Make a number of your goals personal. Some adults I have counseled are still trying to reach the goals their parents set for them—even when their parents are no longer alive. A personal goal is a goal born in your own heart, not someone else's heart.

In athletic competition there is a concept called "personal best." It says that any athlete must compete against his own best record before competing against anyone else. What everyone else does is second in importance to the best you can do. You will climb over impossible obstacles to achieve goals by competing against your personal best.

Avoid contingency goals. The control and input of too many other people—or your own fantasy world—limit your contingency goals. Many people say, "When I get a lot of money ..." or "When I get the job I want ..." they will do such and such. If you think or plan that way, you need a reality check. Goals prefaced by the word "if" or "when" tend to be about as solid as melting ice cubes.

It is fine to have dreams, and some dreams can become goals, but you need to be clear about the difference between your own dreams and goals. For example, I often dream about winning a new car in a contest, but I have no control over that dream. However, if it is my *goal* to have a new car, there are numerous ways I can go about making that happen.

Share your goals with people who will not laugh at you but encourage and affirm you. Everyone needs a few cheerleaders when they are shaping their dreams into realistic goals. One of your best cheerleaders should always be screaming into your right ear, "Yes, you can!" When goals are shared with people you trust, people help you open doors, offering guidance and suggestions.

The road to goal fulfillment is often long and lonely. Encouragement is one of the most powerful motivators. Friends are vital to the survival of goals.

Set some goals from which you can receive payback more quickly than from the rest. You need to build a ladder of goal accomplishment so you will be able to see how far you have come even though you still have a long way to go. Your journey always needs to include joy that can fire you up for what is ahead.

People in sales know the pendulum swings every month from goal setting to goal meeting. Managers keep raising the bar on their sales people so they will not rest on their laurels after achieving a particular goal. The motivation may be added income, awards, or company perks. But beyond exterior motivation, there always needs to be inner satisfaction that says, "I knew I could do it." Your personal confidence will always grow when goals are reached.

I got a glimpse of the satisfaction of reaching a quick-payback goal a few years ago. I was leaving a seminar when a lady asked if I had a few minutes to look at the new car she had just purchased. As we walked across a large church parking lot, my mind began to picture the kind of car this little, gray-haired, demure, and rather quiet lady had selected. I pictured a big, old Buick or Oldsmobile in a muted shade of blue or black, with living-room-sized seats. Suddenly she pointed to a corner of the lot and said, "Well, there it is! What do you think?"

I saw a bright white Mustang convertible with red racing stripes and "mag" wheels. The crowning adornment was a long whip antenna with a flag attached to it. The lady jumped into the car and started it up to the tune of custom racing exhausts. With a big smile, she told me she always wanted a car like that, but her conservative husband would not allow it. After her divorce she had one quick-payback goal: get the car she always wanted. And she did!

I can still see her racing up and down the streets of Whittier, California, revving up the engine at every stoplight. Quickly attainable goals can change your image and your life!

Incorporate stretch goals into your planning. Stretch goals take you beyond the place you are now. They move you from your feel-good comfort zone into the challenging stretched-out zone. Stretch goals put you beyond your known capabilities. Some people are afraid to go there because they fear failure. Applause is not guaranteed. You may fail, but at least you will have tried.

Every time I write a book, I am forced out of my comfort zone. I would rather look at the ones I have written sitting on my bookshelves and feel good about them. A new writing assignment means I have to go to the well of creativity and hope it hasn't dried up. I have to set aside time to write when I would rather be running or walking the beach. I always wonder if what I write will help anyone. Writing pushes me out of my comfort zone for a time and stretches me.

Stretch goals also help me develop new areas of my life. They push me to the edge of embarrassment. Will my weaknesses be exposed and people laugh at me? It is less threatening to continue to live in the safety zone of what I know than to reach out and stretch my capabilities. But it is also boring, limits my growth, and reduces the challenge of life. That is not where I want to live.

GOALS ON WHICH TO BUILD YOUR LIFE

Goals are often born of two things: need and desire. Deciding which goal is most important is always difficult. What seems important today may appear irrelevant tomorrow. If you are living in pain of any kind, the goal is usually to get out of it. But when healing begins the goal changes.

Goals to acquire *things* are not enduring or important. Goals to build intangible *qualities* into your life are far more durable and life-sustaining. A solid set of goals can be identified from meditating on Galatians 5:22, which lists the fruits of the Spirit: love, joy, peace, patience, kindness, goodness, faithfulness, gentleness, and self-control. You won't find *these* on sale at your local Wal-Mart. They are interior life goals for every person who decides to follow God.

I want to break down the challenge of setting goals into some practical, everyday categories. The questions that appear under each category comprise a homework assignment for you.

Relational Goals

- *Who do I need in my life as part of a new and growing support system?*
- *Do I need to build new friendships?*
- *Do I need to let go of some old friendships?*

- *Are there any toxic people in my life I need to get away from?*
- *Do I need to find a new church home?*
- *Do I need to spend more prime time building relationships?*

Vocational Goals

- *Does my current job cause me more happiness than unhappiness?*
- *Where will I be if I am still in this job five years from now?*
- *If I were now in my ideal job, what would that job be?*
- *Is that ideal job attainable for me?*
- *Am I doing the job I really want to do?*
- *What parts do education and finances play in my future job or career goals?*
- *Is it time to shift vocational gears?*

Geographic Goals

- *Am I happy living where I now live?*
- *If I am not happy living where I do now, where would I rather live?*
- *What would keep me from living where I really want to live?*
- *If I am a parent, is this the best place for my children to live?*
- *What are the benefits of living where I now live?*
- *What are the liabilities in living here?*

Financial Goals

- *What kind of financial shape am I in?*
- *What kind of financial shape would I like to be in?*
- *What do I need to do to get into my desired financial shape?*

- *What needs to change about the way I handle money in order to improve my financial condition?*
- *Where do I want to be financially five years from now?*
- *Am I a giver or a taker?*
- *Do I tithe to my church?*
- *Am I willing to get some guidance in financial matters?*

Health Goals

- *What kind of physical shape am I in?*
- *Is it time for a full medical examination by my doctor?*
- *What kind of physical shape do I want to be in?*
- *Who can help me the most in achieving my desired physical condition?*
- *Is my current health affecting my job?*

Family Goals

- *What are the greatest assets of my family?*
- *What are the weaknesses of my family?*
- *What are my family's areas of greatest need?*
- *How has my family changed in the past three years?*
- *Is God at the center of my family?*
- *What do I want my family to be in the years ahead?*

Spiritual Goals

- *How would I explain my spiritual journey?*
- *What areas do I need to pursue and grow in spiritually?*
- *Where in my spiritual life am I strong?*
- *Where in my spiritual life am I weak?*

- *Do I have friends who keep me accountable on my spiritual journey?*
- *Is God really in charge of my life?*
- *Does my church meet my spiritual needs?*
- *Do I read the Bible daily?*
- *Do I pray daily?*
- *Am I farther ahead today in my spiritual life than I was two years ago?*
- *Am I working on the inner goals from Galatians 5:22?*

If you think of some other goals, add them to your list. The important thing is to start forming goals. They keep you focused and on target. We all suffer from times of scattered attention. Staying in focus is a form of discipline that gives direction and a sense of destination.

As you think and plan your goals, always put God at the center of them. As you follow him in every area of your life and ask him to give you the right goals, you also need to allow him to shift your goals and send you in a new direction. If or when God puts new plans and goals into operation in your life, you probably won't understand why at first. Your trust will be called into play, and you will have to allow God to unfold his reasons.

The apostle Paul had a strong goal orientation and kept his goals directly in his vision. Shipwreck, stoning, imprisonment, and other human threats had little impact on his determination. Like a giant bulldozer, he kept moving ahead toward the goal God had set before him. He said, "Brothers, I do not consider myself yet to have taken hold of it. But one thing I do: Forgetting what is behind and straining toward what is ahead, I press on toward the goal to win the prize for which God has called me heavenward in Christ Jesus" (Phil 3:13-14).

NINE

Navigating the Dating Rapids

Love is a mutual self-giving which ends
in self-recovery.

FULTON J. SHEEN

Leaders say any time you want a large turnout at a singles event, just advertise the topic of sex and dating. Many men and women wrestle with a string of questions associated with their need to risk a new relationship. It is probably the number-one issue and the number-one fear. As I travel and speak at divorce recovery seminars, I find the questions are pretty much the same; only the faces of the questioners change. About halfway through one singles seminar, a tall, handsome man in his mid-forties stood up and asked a rather risky question. In a quiet voice he said, "How do you ask a woman for a date, what do you say and do on a date, and what do you say and do at the end of one?"

I expected the room to fill with nervous laughter, as it would

have if he were eighteen. Instead it became deathly quiet as a
few heads nodded affirmatively to the question. As the man sat
down, I was afraid to break the stillness. It's a serious question
when you realize you are no longer brash and carefree, but
older and cautious. Dating raises the issue of rejection, and if
that was a central issue in your divorce, you are not eager to
revisit it.

Observing the singles world from the sidelines, and talking
to thousands of you on the front lines, I have formed some
conclusions about dating that I want to share.

SOME THINGS TO THINK ABOUT ALONG THE DATING ROAD

*Don't get involved in any man-woman relationship until the
wounds from your divorce or the death of your spouse have ade-
quately healed.* My rule of thumb is that you need two to three
years to put your own life back together before you even consider dating again. The majority of professional counselors and
therapists agree, and some even argue for a longer time. To
become a whole person with well-healed wounds takes time
and work. You cannot hurry the process any more than you
can hurry the healing of a cut finger.

One stop sign you may encounter on the dating road says,
Help! Please Rescue Me! Some people start dating the day their
divorce is final. Many are remarried within six months or a year,
divorced and single again within another year. Of course, each
feels he is the exception to the rule. Many single-again men and
women are so overwhelmed by their burden in life they just
want to find someone—anyone—who will rescue them from
their problems.

One worn-out-looking single mother told me she would

marry the next man who asked because she just needed help to survive. Over the years many single mothers have expressed the same thought. That's a desperate and dangerous place to be. I have great admiration and respect for every single parent. They are all doing a sometimes-impossible job. Marrying a housekeeper or wage earner is not the answer, however. You don't need someone to rescue you, and you don't need to rescue anyone else.

So please, don't panic! Many singles speed up relationships so they can get to the altar before it closes. But desperate people attract equally desperate people. This kind of match is mutually destructive.

It may actually take longer for you to find God's person for your life if you hurry. Remember that God is never in a hurry, and your haste could delay the things of God. Besides, the person God has for you may not be ready for you yet—or *you* may not be ready for that person. To watch, wait, and pray is the order of the day.

Once you are in a serious relationship, wait at least a year before you marry. You need to watch the other person through all the things one might face in a given year and see how they handle the good and the bad. You seldom find that out in four months.

Just about everyone I know wants to keep their life moving at warp speed, but relationships are like roses: they need time to bloom. You can get too close too soon and ruin a good relationship that just needed more time to grow. Emotional collisions produce human wreckage that can send you back into the recovery room for a long time.

You can learn a lot about a person by getting to know the people in his or her world. One year is also a great time frame in which to do that. Don't forget that in a first marriage you marry a person with a short history on Planet Earth, but the second time around you marry a person with a much longer and more complex history. You need to know as many people as possible from your friend's history book or family tree. If you are ever in a relationship with a person who hides their family from you, you have a right to become concerned.

When you begin dating a person, look long and hard at his or her family of origin. It may be able to tell you things you need to know without saying a word. When you are around the family, do you witness dysfunctional relationships? Do you see any of that in the person you are dating? We take the good things from a primary family with us and also the not-so-good things. Become an observer not blinded by romance. Also remember that some people from difficult backgrounds can be set free, grow, and become healthy people.

Another of my top reasons for a long recovery before remarriage is that you need to know you can survive and grow without anyone in your life. There is something to prove to yourself! You cannot build a healthy and growing relationship with another person until you really know yourself. Crisis changes a person. The crisis of divorce and death puts every survivor into a class called Identity 101. You will be a different person after divorce or the death of your spouse than you were before. If you aren't well acquainted with that new and changing person, it will be difficult to build and sustain a relationship.

A Christian walks on dangerous ground if he or she dates non-Christians. When you marry someone who is from a different faith background—or from no faith background—you deliberately place roadblocks in your path to a successful remarriage. The spiritual intimacy that is at the heart of a Christian marriage cannot develop in an interfaith marriage because God is not at the center of it. For this reason, the Christian partner often experiences a growing sense of aloneness, and feels that he or she must choose between God and the new spouse. Some non-Christian partners will attend church early on in the relationship in order to please their partner. However, in many cases their attendance sharply declines after the marriage takes place—forcing the Christian partner either to go alone or to stop going as well.

If and when the marriage is blessed with children, the pressure and discord intensify as the parents try to decide in "which faith," if any, the children should be raised. The disagreements that stem from this issue can overlap into extended family systems, causing further division and unrest.

Perhaps you are not thinking of marriage right now. I have done verbal battle with those who insist, "I'm just going out on a date. I'm not going to marry the person!" Every marriage starts with a first date. You have no idea before that first date if you will eventually marry a person or not. I did not plan to marry my wife when I dated her. I just wanted to have a fun evening with an attractive young woman who caught my eye.

If you doubt it would be risky for you to date a non-Christian, just ask the many who have done it, thinking they would win someone over to a personal faith in Christ. I am not suggesting you interrogate a person about his or her religious life before you date them, but you usually can get a hint of where they are spiritually. You can find out more on the first date, then close the door to future dates if you find out this person does not share your spiritual journey.

Before you start dating, you should have a personal set of criteria for the kind of person with whom you want to share your life. I know that sounds uncomfortably like using some kind of shopping list, but using clear guidelines will prevent wasting time and money on people who do not fit your standards. You need to establish which points are non-negotiable and remain strong on those. Others can be less important. All of us get in trouble when we betray the standards we have set for our lives. I meet some people who daily shift their standards according to whom they are dating. Shifting standards make shifty people.

I have listened for years to what single-again people desire in a potential mate. For a long time the highest ideals were "honest, hardworking, responsible, and kind—and he or she should also be a Christian." In recent years I have watched that change. Most of the single-again people with whom I work would say their number-one requirement for a mate is that he or she must be deeply committed to Christ and mature in their walk with him.

People are looking for life partners who take their faith seriously. I challenge you to take your time and think this question through: If you choose remarriage, what criteria for a spouse would you put on your list? Write down the eight or ten things most important to you and tuck that list away in your wallet or purse. Read it often and pray that God will honor it.

You can receive good directions on the dating road if you ask your friends what they think and how they feel about the person you are dating. When you are a teenager, you take your date home to meet Mom and Dad. When the date is over, your first question is, "Well, what do you think?" You desperately want your choice to be approved by the ones you love most. It is a little harder to do that when you are forty or fifty years old, but you do need to ask the question of a few people you trust so that you can get an honest answer.

There is a wide assortment of people in the dating jungle. Some are caretakers. Others are rescuers. Some are unhealthy. Others are healthy. Single-again men and women are like everyone else. They have lost a marriage partner, but that does not make them all losers. Faithful friends will tell you the truth. They are outside the situation and not romantically tied to it. They will be more objective. You need to know what they see and feel. Don't defend. Just listen and weigh carefully what they have observed.

The other side of running your relationship through your friendship screen is to screen the friends of your new relationship. People are known by the company they keep. You can learn a great deal about someone by meeting his or her closest friends. Listen, observe, question, and keep your radar on. When someone in my group is dating someone I do not know, I jokingly say, "Hey, bring them around. I would like to see if they pass my litmus test." If I care about the people I work with, I will care about the people they are getting serious about. This may not always be possible, of course. In our mobile culture, your new friend may be "starting over" in a new area, and may not have any "long-term friends" for you to get to know. In this case you will need to be more observant as you watch how your friend relates to your other friends, and what your friends think and feel.

Spend time sharing dreams with the person you are dating. Everyone needs to have a few old and new dreams of his or her own to pursue. They also need to dream new dreams together with their spouse, ones that will give them a unity together. The very ability to dream again can be reborn in a healthy second marriage.

At some point in time, dreams need to match. When dreams go in opposite directions, a relationship goes downhill fast. One woman married a man who had a good job. She had an even better job. They were dreaming of working hard, saving money, and some day retiring together. Two months after they married, he quit his job and said he was retiring, but she could keep working. She worked, he loafed, and the marriage dissolved into a second divorce.

How can you guarantee this kind of thing will not happen to you? You can't! There are no guarantees. But you need to do your homework before you remarry. Some have sat in my office with a second marriage breaking up and told me they swept certain warning signs under the rug and went blindly ahead. The sages say, "Love is blind." I say, "People in love are blind." You can have all the premarital counseling and personality testing in the world (and you should have), but if you are operating without your radar on, in mid-marriage you could collide with an unknown object called your spouse. Go slowly. Keep your radar on and your eyes open. Meet reality head on before you get married.

Spiritual compatibility is a vitally important part of sharing dreams and goals. One's personal spiritual journey, church denomination, and theological perspective are but a few ingredients to mix into a new relationship. This doesn't mean you will both agree on everything, but it does mean that if the relationship locks in, you need to be kindred spirits spiritually.

Some people are far ahead of others in their spiritual journey. Others are just starting out. It is often hard to grow spiritually when there are disparities in the spiritual dimension. One single father I know ended a relationship that appeared altarbound because his fiancée announced that if they had a child, the child would be raised in the church of her childhood. He said, "No way." She left. As difficult as that was on him, life might have been much worse if either of them had had to compromise deeply held convictions in the hope the problem would go away. Never assume anything when it comes to spiritual convictions and compatibility. Do your homework when you are in a dating relationship, not five years after you have remarried.

THE DATING PROGRESSION

It is difficult to list a dating progression for single-again people. A relationship starts with the first date but doesn't move inevitably or instantly to "going steady." Usually, if a relationship is going to continue, a single date leads into a bunch of dates and eventually to the investment of an increasing amount of time building the relationship. After some time the M-word is brought up and the couple bump it back and forth for a while.

When any relationship becomes serious and appears headed for M-word country, I recommend premarital counseling and testing with a competent therapist or psychologist. The many people I encourage to do this always come back and thank me profusely because it has helped them so much.

You can never do too much homework. When you are on the dating road and thinking idle thoughts of possible remarriage, you will want to answer these questions.

Would you marry someone with children still at home?

Would you want to have more children when you remarry?

Would you want to be a part-time stepparent?

Would you marry a divorced person?

Would you marry a widowed person?

Do you really like his or her children?

Would you marry someone who has never been married before?

Would you marry someone younger or older than yourself?

Are you willing to be a part of a blended family?

Single adults are somewhat naive when it comes to second marriage issues. They want to let their heart run away with their head. It is easy to say, "If you really love someone, those things won't matter." But they do. Only you can decide where you fit. You may be able to handle certain situations but not others. Just *think through* the questions.

WHAT ABOUT NOT DATING?

When you feel ready to enter the dating world again, what happens if no dates come your way? You can walk around with a T-shirt announcing your availability, but that doesn't mean anyone will necessarily line up with a date book. You can register with a dating service only to discover that it can be a bizarre and frustrating experience. You look around at the field of potential candidates and utter a sigh of despair.

Then you realize something. When you gave your life to God and trusted Jesus as your Savior, you accepted his promise that he would never leave you and that he would always take care of your needs. So you prayerfully say, "Lord, this dating thing has to be *your* thing, so I place it all in your hands and ask you to lead and guide me every step of the way. Help me to go only where you want me to go, and keep me away from the spirit of desperation. And Lord, while I'm waiting, give me great patience to know you are in charge."

The prophet wrote, "But they that wait upon the Lord shall renew their strength; they shall mount up with wings as eagles; they shall run, and not be weary; and they shall walk, and not faint" (Is 40:31, KJV). I believe the key to not wearing out in waiting for someone special in your life is to trust God with your need.

A WORD ABOUT REJECTION

She was angry when she came into my office. After a few minutes of ranting and raving, she quieted down long enough for me discover the reason for her anger. The story she told me sounded familiar. She was dating a man in our singles group, and the relationship was moving toward marriage. Suddenly he ended the relationship by saying he just wasn't ready for marriage and hoped she understood. Two days later, he was dating another woman. Her comment to me was, "I can't go through this rejection stuff anymore. No more men, no more dating."

That has happened at least once to most of us. The only difference is that it probably happened when we were teenagers, when resilience is far greater than in midlife. In the area of relationships, the world of the single-again adult is a lot like the world of the teenager, but the thought of starting new relationships in midlife can be emotionally draining. The fear that relationships will wear out after you have put so much into them is discouraging.

Rejection in any form is always painful, especially when your hopes are high. If you live to be one hundred years old, you will still encounter some form of rejection from time to time. Of course you can avoid it simply by not risking anything, hiding in a cave and avoiding all human contact. Few of us want to live that way.

To risk reaching out to another person is to know you are still alive and part of the human family. To withdraw is to cut yourself off from the sustaining strength of real community and friendships. Many people choose the road of the loner. Everyone makes the choice to isolate or relate. The latter always comes with risk. There is no way to avoid it.

When a long-term or even short-term marriage ends with any form of rejection, it is easiest to pack up your hurts and run. There are no guarantees when you reenter the dating world. You may fall madly in love with the first person you date, marry, and live happily ever after. But if I could give that kind of guarantee, there would be a very long line outside my door.

The suggestions in this chapter may take some of the thorns out of the dating bushes, but you still must take the risk. Every one of us experiences rejection of some kind every day. Much of it is not major. We accept it as a part of living and move on. But we will never outlive its possibility. To be alive is to risk rejection. To take a job is to risk rejection. To build friendships is to risk rejection.

To laugh is to risk appearing the fool.
To weep is to risk appearing sentimental.
To reach out for another is to risk involvement.
To expose feelings is to risk exposing your true self.
To place your ideas and your dreams before the crowd is
    to risk their loss.
To love is to risk not being loved in return.
To live is to risk dying.
To try is to risk failure.

But risks must be taken, because the greatest hazard in life
    is to risk nothing.

The person who risks nothing, does nothing, has nothing,
    and is nothing.

He may avoid suffering and sorrow.

But he simply cannot learn, feel, change, grow, love, and
    live.

Chained by his certitudes, he is a slave.

He has forfeited freedom.

Only the person who risks is free.

ANONYMOUS

Is Dating Worth the Hassle?

I've been asked this question more times than I can remember. The answer comes when I stand at the altar of marriage and look in the eyes of two people who have suffered great loss and pain and now stand ready to make life commitments to each other. I share in their happiness and excitement. I watch their tears of joy and frequently add mine to the mix. Many of those couples came into my life in a divorce recovery seminar or at a memorial service. I became a part of their journey through the valley of pain. I now watch that journey continue on the mountaintop.

If you ever considered for a moment *not* taking a risk in a relationship that could lead to marriage, stop by and catch the joy of the union of two people who took the risk. When remarriage is right for both people, I will lead the celebration!

Although a vast majority of single-again people choose remarriage, some are not interested in remarriage or even dating. Lest you get the idea that I am trying to propel everyone in the direction of marriage, let me say that it is perfectly normal and genuinely sane not to head down that trail. I have many single-again friends who have elected to stay single and thoroughly enjoy their lifestyle. It is a matter of choice. That choice is yours to make with God's guidance.

TEN

Facing the Fears That Paralyze

When I am afraid, I will trust in you. In God, whose word I praise, in God I trust; I will not be afraid. What can mortal man do to me?

PSALM 56:3-4

She huddled down in my office chair and wrapped her arms tightly around her body. Her voice was barely above a whisper as she spoke. "I am so afraid," she said.

When I asked the woman what she was fearful of, she responded, "Everything." I thought about asking her to be specific, but I already knew what she would say. Her husband, the anchor of her life, had left her for another woman. Now she faced the battle of leading their three children into the future. She had no job, little income, and even less direction. Everything in her world had become an occasion for fear. The only words of hope she spoke in our hour of discussion were, "I really don't want to be afraid."

Well, nobody wants to be afraid, but at some point in life, everybody is.

The battle for a new beginning after what seems like a final ending is often hard to frame. There is no instant prescription for the transition from sharing responsibilities with a spouse to assuming sole responsibility for yourself and your children. It is painfully hard to believe there is life beyond loss. But you will reach a place where your fears are fewer than your hopes!

TURN ON THE LIGHT

Winning the war over fear starts by identifying those particular fears that traumatize and immobilize you. Pretending that those troubling you most will just go away is a form of denial. It will do nothing to help you win your battle.

When you were a child, you were probably afraid of the dark just like other children. But it wasn't the dark that made you fearful; it was the things you thought lurked in the dark. It was little consolation that those things were imaginary. Only when the lights were turned on once more were your fears quelled. If the lights were turned off again, your fears returned with a vengeance. Parents discovered night-lights, closet lights, and hall lights and put them to use to make nighttime bearable. The only thing that removes the fear of darkness, and the monsters hiding within it, is light. The Bible talks about this in numerous places: 2 Samuel 22:29, Psalm 27:1, Isaiah 2:5, John 3:19 and 8:12, and 1 John 1:5-7.

During my work with single adults, I have compiled a long list of fears people shared with me. Some are of major importance, while others are just distractions. Here are my top twenty. Check yours as you read the list.

- The fear of living alone.
- The fear of growing old alone with no one to care for me.
- The fear of never marrying again.
- The fear of marrying again.
- The fear of losing my job or career.
- The fear of economic disaster (running out of money).
- The fear of losing old friendships from my married years.
- The fear of relocating geographically.
- The fear of relationship abuse.
- The fear of no support system.
- The fear of reentering the workforce.
- The fear of changes in my lifestyle.
- The fear of the impact of death or divorce on my family.
- The fear that my reason to live is gone.
- The fear of inadequacy.
- The fear of failure.
- The fear of rejection.
- The fear of what the future holds.
- The fear of failing health.
- The fear of what God may do with my life if I give it totally to him.

After thinking through this list, you may fear that you have too many fears! I want to give you hope so you can begin to move from fear-based living to faith-based living.

THE FEAR OF LIVING ALONE

It may sound strange, but this fear can be resolved by simply learning how to live alone with confidence. You may be thinking your resolution would be to find a spouse. That may be one answer, but we will put it at the bottom of the list here. Begin to conquer your fear of living alone by attacking your specific worries related to it.

You're afraid someone will break into your home, rob you, beat you, and leave you for dead. Working to resolve this, you might move to a safer area or install your own home security system.

You feel very uncomfortable when the house is silent. Try filling your home with music and sound as soon as you come in the door. Keep an inexpensive phone handy in every room, and ask someone to check on you every day.

On the other hand, silence and solitude can also be gifts that help the healing process. In the Scriptures, Jesus used times alone to pray, rest, and be in touch with his Father. You can experience times of great spiritual growth as you use times of silence and solitude to deepen your walk with God. *Celebration of Discipline* by Richard Foster is a good guide to exploring the use of silence and solitude as well as other spiritual disciplines.

You dread that empty feeling. Get a pet that will be glad to see you at the end of the day, even if it is just a goldfish.

You worry about not knowing how to maintain your house or car. Take a class at the community college.

You have trouble coping with the lack of companionship. Find a roommate or two and build an extended family. Get to know your neighbors so they can be a secure network around you. Use your residence as a place to entertain others.

THE FEAR OF GROWING OLD ALONE

The fears of abandonment, loneliness, loss of relationship, and that your life is no longer worth living fuse together as you age. Aging may also increase your concern about rejection. Quality of life is an issue too.

It is your personal responsibility to decide what kind of life you want and then live it. One of the best ways to resolve fears related to rejection is to build strong friendships every day, not waiting until you desperately need them. Good friendships will age with you. Make friends of younger people too. You need all ages in your community circle to thrive.

If your health is strong, signs of aging are not as prevalent and the fear is reduced. Once health begins to decline, the fear rises. There are three basic ways to deal with declining health. You cannot prevent the aging process, but you can build some guardrails so you aren't ravaged by it. Gather friends and family members around you. Have good medical care close by. (Go to a physician who emphasizes wellness and exercise.) And most important, keep moving even if you are going at turtle speed. Age may be inevitable, but rusting out is not.

The strength of your faith usually comes into play as you age. Everything you face can now be met with the words of Jesus, "Lo, I am with you always" (Mt 28:20b, KJV). God will not abandon you or leave you without hope. He is with you in every struggle and every fear. This does not mean your struggles will be over or your fears will disappear. It means you can call upon God to quiet your fears and soothe raw emotions. You prove his faithfulness when you trust him with difficult issues. As you grow, you make deposits in a reservoir of faith. You can go to that reservoir when your faith is lacking and draw from it.

Spiritual depth and spiritual friends are the two strongest antidotes to any fear. But the bottom line is that only God can fill the empty and fearful spaces. Even Moses felt he could not face Pharaoh or lead the Israelites out of Egypt. It was not until he grabbed hold of God's promise, "I will be with you" (Ex 3:12a), that Moses was able to get his sandals pointed in the right direction. When any fear invades your life, it is the size of your God, not the size of your fear, which counts. If you have chosen to follow God, you will not grow old alone. You will grow on with God.

THE FEAR OF NEVER MARRYING AGAIN

When you move out of your forties into your fifties and sixties, you may fear the opportunities for remarriage grow slimmer. Don't panic. Age is never a barrier to remarriage. I do more and more weddings with older couples. If your heart's desire is to remarry, you can find someone who desires the same thing, even if you are ninety-five years old.

I have also noticed as men and women age, their desire for remarriage lessens. There will always be those whose desire is to welcome and appreciate the single-again lifestyle. When I jokingly asked one man in his sixties if he thought much of remarriage, he responded, "Not anymore. I am happy where I am, have great friends to do things with, and only have to clean up after one." Does that mean he would turn down a good opportunity? I doubt it.

Many single-again men and women with grown children and grandchildren say they like the idea of being responsible for themselves and having full freedom to choose what they want to do. The longer one remains single-again, the more comfortable that feeling becomes and the less one wants an intruder on the life that already satisfies. I have heard many describe where they are as being "comfortably single," and barring any divine interruption, they plan to stay that way.

With younger men and women, the fear of never remarrying is strongest for those who have children. As one single mother of five puts it, "I get plenty of dates until the guys start counting the number of bicycles in my driveway. Most men do a quick U-turn and keep right on going past my house." It may take a man with courage, financial security, patience, and love to move into that kind of situation, but they are out there. Remember that men lose families, too, and some crave the family feeling that comes with a warm house full of life and love.

Bart was one of those men who felt no woman would ever marry him because he had five children to raise after his wife died. He seldom dated. Then he met Jean, a divorcée with three children. When they began dating, group members smiled and said, "No way. Too much baggage."

After sixteen months Bart and Jean took the plunge and landed in one home with their eight children. They were dubbed the "Brady Bunch" by some folks, but the struggles they faced would be a little too raw for prime-time TV. They learned that blended families take time to blend, but when love is strong and God is at the center, it is doable.

During the past twenty-five years, I have performed more second marriages than first marriages. Some did not make it.

The vast majority did. All of them learned it was far more work than any first marriage. They also learned that you don't quit and run at the first sign of struggles or differences. Many churches today offer ministry groups for remarrieds where they can share problems, laugh and cry together, and find answers that work.

When couples entering a second marriage go through strong premarital programs, they discover that they are better equipped to remain strong and grow in that new relationship. A vast majority of first marriage failures had no premarital classes, psychological tests, or instruction that would help them survive struggles and differences. If you are contemplating a second trip to the altar, be good to yourselves—and your future marriage. Sign up for premarital counseling. It works!

THE FEAR OF CHANGE

Many people find it is easy to own the problem of fear but far more difficult to implement recovery. In order to move ahead and reduce fear, there must be change. But many people fear all change—even change for the good. I have watched women cling to physically and emotionally abusive husbands because their fear of being alone was greater than their fear of being beaten. They readily admitted the danger of their situation to everyone, but fear of change kept them from moving into a shelter and working to change their lives. It saddens me when I hear people admit their fears but refuse to deal with them.

Someone asked me the other day, "How do you know what is on the other side of change?" I could only answer, "You don't!" But when the situation you are dealing with becomes worse than the risk of change, you will probably take the risk and change.

THE FEAR OF LOSING A JOB OR CAREER

One of the biggest needs for single-again people is money. Since jobs supply money, concern usually shifts in that direction when a person is divorced or his or her spouse dies.

Personal loss can hurt productivity. Attention wanders to crises outside of work. Stress, lack of sleep, lateness, and inability to focus all decrease one's effectiveness. One divorcing woman told me she was fired from her job because of a lack of concentration.

Pressure-created job loss is a growing problem in the workplace. If you cannot function, you cannot work. If you cannot work, you will have financial troubles. It is extremely difficult to be productive and attentive at work when every day you are struggling to clean up emotional debris outside of work. It is hard to switch gears in your head and focus your energies where they need to be.

When problems at home cloud your mind at work, stop long enough to ask yourself this question: "Will allowing my mind to dwell on the outside stuff change any of it while I am at work?" I think the universal answer would be "No!"

So stop focusing on outside stuff. Get a copy of the serenity prayer and repeat it out loud before you leave for work and before you go to bed. Fear always says, "I might lose something." Faith always says, "I can find something."

Job security doesn't exist in our culture anymore anyway. When downsizing hits your workplace, or your company is sold, you may stand in danger of losing your job—and with it, your lifestyle and economic security. Fear of poverty can settle in. Scripture says, "We live by faith, not by sight" (2 Cor 5:7).

Trust is about the only thing that can replace fear. "Trust in the

Lord with all your heart and lean not on your own understanding; in all your ways acknowledge him, and he will make your paths straight," wrote King Solomon (Prv 3:5, 6). Remember: your job, your career, and your future are in God's hands.

Standing right next to faith and trust in God for your career is the practical side of what you can do to prepare for downsizing, buyouts, early retirements, and obsolescence. Too many men and women just go to work every day and come home every night without a thought about where their company or career might be heading—or not heading. Survival of the employee means getting ahead of the company just as companies work to get ahead of the competition. Ask yourself the hard questions: Where are we going as a company? What is going on in this industry? What are my options if I lose my job? What will I do if I lose it? What can I do now?

Get the idea? Look down the road, thinking ahead, and you won't be blindsided. The average man or woman will hold nine different jobs by the time they are thirty. Read, get more education, take career testing. God trusts you to use the intelligence he gave you.

THE FEAR OF A LIFESTYLE CHANGE

Housing arrangements change overnight when you lose a spouse. Things once taken for granted, like groceries, house payments, utilities, insurance, and car payments, come up for grabs. Children often lose music lessons, sports, extra school activities, and even allowances. One father recently told me his financial condition was turned upside down during his divorce. He ended up filing for bankruptcy and losing all his toys and status symbols. On the other hand, he added, his entire value system changed. He now appreciates the simple things of life more than ever.

We live in a culture where our values are largely derived from the media and merchandising, both of which say, *More is better*. A good example of this is lined up inside my garage: athletic shoes. I will not tell you how many pairs I have; I just know I don't need them all. I run, play tennis and racquetball, walk, and loaf. My favorite sports store tells me I need different shoes for each activity. I also need a couple pairs of worn shoes to walk the beach. The most recent athletic shoe ads invite me to dump all those I have and buy the newest high-tech shoes now filtering into the market. Maybe I'll just go barefoot!

It sometimes takes losing *more* for us to get back to the basics like those referred to in Philippians 4:19: "And my God will meet all your needs according to his glorious riches in Christ Jesus." I watched God bring this promise home to a single mother this past Christmas season. She was struggling along, trying to make ends meet as she went through a job transition. Her faith was strong, and she said little about her needs to anyone, even as things became more desperate. Then I received a phone call from someone who wanted to give money to a single mother with urgent needs. This and other outpourings of support, meeting each of her needs, overwhelmed the praying and trusting single mother. Though lifestyle, career, and family structure changes, God is ever the same.

THE FEAR OF RELATIONAL ABUSE

I wish more single-again adults had the fear of relational abuse. It could help them avoid some of the pain and hurt they are prone to incur.

Both divorce and death leave painful scars on the heart, and it's natural to want to make that hurt go away. In an attempt to bring about healing, singles often turn to others to help ease the pain. On a simple caring level, there is nothing wrong with this, but you can get into trouble when you dump your entire load of hurt on someone else, expecting him or her to make your pain disappear.

You are most vulnerable to abusive relationships when your pain level is high and your self-esteem is low. Hurting people have an extremely high degree of vulnerability. Until healing begins and self-confidence starts to grow, you will be a prime candidate for emotional marauders who only dole out further hurt. During my years in singles ministry, I have witnessed self-appointed rescuers take far more than they give and become abusers in the process.

If any form of relational abuse has victimized you in your past, your trust level will be low. The surest way to find freedom from past injuries is to visit a highly qualified counselor or therapist. Support groups may also be effective. It takes time to heal wounds in this extremely delicate area. But if you don't work toward healing, the emotional fallout will follow you into future relationships.

FEAR OF THE FALLOUT

Divorce divides, disrupts, and destroys family systems and structures. Relatives often choose up sides. Verbal and emotional battles are commonplace. Relationships that were once close and caring may no longer exist. Family warmth can be replaced with cold indifference. Holidays and celebrations become trials to be slogged through with a glued-on smile. Once secure family units can disappear overnight and ultimately be replaced by a confusing web of blended families.

Beyond the realm of family loss, there can be a great loss of Christian friends. Divorced people are often forced to leave a church that was home for many years, leaving behind many years of history and friendship. It is sad when this happens to a person who already has to deal with the rejection of a spouse. When the rejection is compounded, the person may choose to walk away from all churches and never return.

The best way I know to deal with fallout is to not waste time trying to win battles that are not winnable. Don't spend more than a few seconds wondering what other people are thinking or saying. You will never change the mindset or attitude of your church or the friends you once had. Don't waste energy trying. I have told many people caught in fallout, "Look to Jesus, and keep moving down the road." You can work hard at keeping the friendships you desire, but if they don't choose you, it's time to move on. There is always fallout to deal with, but you cannot waste time on situations beyond your control.

FEAR OF FAILURE

Fear of failure was planted in you when the schoolteacher said, "Take out a pencil and a sheet of paper. We are going to have a pop quiz." If you were up to date in your classroom studies, you smiled and awaited the challenge. If you were behind in your homework, a cold, clammy sweat began to cascade down your face. Your greatest fear was failing the test, followed by the fear of looking bad, followed by the fear of your parents punishing you for flunking the quiz. From those early days on, fear of failure was accompanied by the dread of ending up a failure in life.

It is bad to own a failed experience, but worse is not learning anything from it. I have asked many divorced people what they learned from their failed marriages. Some give good answers, like, "I will never let anyone devalue me again," and "I want a home and life where God is first." Others simply say, "Don't get married." Failure is always an occasion of learning if we are open to the teaching. We never stop learning and we never stop failing. To fail is to come back strong and try again.

There is a great lesson we can learn from baseball. Batters do not get a hit every time they come to bat. About two-thirds of the time they strike out, ground out, fly out, or are called out by the umpire. Batters hit the ball and get on base only one-third of the time. No matter how hard they work on batting skills, their failure rate remains about the same. We pay ballplayers millions of dollars every season to fail two out of every three times they come to bat!

Baseball and life are much alike—except for the salaries. When you fail at something, don't give up and quit. Learn what you can, and take another shot at it. Life is not batting a thousand. Life is batting every day and not giving up.

THE BIBLE SPEAKS ON FEAR

Fear is the great destroyer of faith. Fear is also basic distrust of God. Fear sends us into hiding, but faith sends us marching into life. David, the writer of the Psalms, told us, "The Lord is my light and my salvation—whom shall I fear? The Lord is the stronghold of my life—of whom shall I be afraid?" (Ps 27:1). In other words, when you have the Lord in your life, there is nothing to fear.

Proverbs 29:25 is another fear-fighter. It says, "Fear of man will prove to be a snare, but whoever trusts in the Lord is kept safe." Fear can drag you down, but faith in the Lord will lift you up. A third fear evaporator is found in 2 Timothy 1:7: "For God did not give us a spirit of timidity, but a spirit of power, of love and of self-discipline." If you are living fearfully, the origin of that fear is not God because God gives strength.

Fear is a part of life. There are healthy fears, like that of stepping in front of a moving bus. There are unhealthy fears, such as the feeling that something bad will always happen to you. The fear that everyone is out to get you is common but very unhealthy. The constant fear that you will become ill and die haunts many people. But any negative, consuming fear can put your life off track and haunt the corridors of your mind on a daily basis.

You always have a choice in how you respond to your fears. First, admit and face them. Denial only leads to defeat. Admission leads to freedom. Second, pray and give them over to God. Scripture says, "Cast your cares on the Lord and he will sustain you; he will never let the righteous fall" (Ps 55:22).

Third, don't be afraid to seek counseling if you are obsessed with your fears. God can use a gifted Christian therapist to bring healing. Fourth, memorize Bible promises about fear removal. Get an arsenal of God's good words stored in your mind. When fear attacks, pull them out and say them out loud. Fifth, build enduring friendships with people who are not fearful, but faithful. They can become your cheerleading squad when fear tries to immobilize you.

Letting go of anything, even if it is destructive, is not easy. Letting go of your fears is a daring attempt at *real* living.

Always remember that as you let go of your fears with one hand, God is holding onto your other one.

ELEVEN

Remarriage: "I Do, I Do!" Again

Insanity is doing the wrong things over and over,
and yet expecting different results.

ANONYMOUS

You cannot be around a group of single-again adults long before someone brings up the topic of remarriage. At some point in the discussion, the group usually divides into three highly opinionated subgroups: the majority who definitely want and plan to remarry sometime, those who proclaim loudly that remarriage is nowhere on their agenda, and those who have no opinion one way or the other. Of course, there is a period of time in the beginning of loss when the thought of being with another person doesn't cross your mind or is only a fleeting thought. This is a long and tender journey you must undertake before thoughts of remarriage can be validated.

But there is always a small segment of single-again men or women who instantly seek remarriage. A prime motive may be to prove to a former spouse they can find someone who will love them and who chooses life with them. Most of us had a similar response when we were teenagers. For sixty seconds we vowed never to date again while on Planet Earth. Then we raced to the phone to find a replacement. Our most immediate thought was, *I'll show you! You can't do this to me.* It may seem rather strange to find yourself somewhere in midlife acting like you did at seventeen.

Many newly divorced men and women overreact to their divorce by remarrying with little thought given to what kind of match this would be. This kind of impulsiveness can have devastating consequences. Certain combinations of personalities and life experiences are less workable than others. Please read the next few pages carefully so you may avoid emotional collisions.

TOUGH COMBINATIONS

At the end of a recent counseling session, I was asked a rare question: "What are some of the toughest matchups in remarriage?" Most men and women still assume you can fall in love with anyone and the human dynamics won't matter at all. I have worked with singles long enough to believe this assumption is not true. You can love someone desperately and be destroyed by the differences in the combination.

One of the most difficult combinations in remarriage happens when a never-married man or woman, or a formerly married man or woman without children, marries a divorced or widowed person with children. If the children are very young and have little or no contact with the other parent, this combination is a little more workable. If the children are teenagers, the chances of success are reduced dramatically. There are few men and women who can inherit an instant family and make it work.

It is supremely difficult for a never-married man or woman to go from a self-oriented lifestyle to living in the midst of a family hurricane. I have watched the battle for survival in this area, and I have witnessed the crash and burn of remarriages within a year. It takes a unique and caring person to walk successfully into this arena. A blended family comes with carrying charges, and a new person walking into it is often thought of as an invader to be dealt with and dismissed as quickly as possible.

A second tough combination involves a single-again person marrying someone far younger or far older, say, with a fifteen-year age gap between the two. It appears that some people who do this are happy and the marriage is good. The real struggles take place, however, as the couple ages and the differences naturally increase. A sixty-eight-year-old man will face issues a fifty-two-year-old woman cannot comprehend.

Some people look for a father or mother figure to afford them security in life only to realize they have little in common with each other after a few months of marriage. We hear now of many people jumping into this kind of marriage, but the disastrous end results are seldom reported. When an older man marries a younger woman, she is often called his "trophy wife." Too often a man falls into the midlife crisis pothole, dumping his family and sometimes his career to marry a youthful and attractive woman who will make him feel young and others envious. We look at couplings like this and wonder what the real motivations are. The answer is often prestige, power, and money. For some younger women, the motivation is making the quantum leap from anonymity to popularity.

I watched one of those marriages in a singles ministry many years ago. It lasted only a year. When I asked the woman what happened, she replied that her ex-husband had already done the many things she wanted to do, and they had little in common for the future. Remember, what looks good in attractive wrapping paper may not look so good unwrapped. If you want a trophy, go buy one at the trophy shop.

A third difficult matchup happens when a committed Christian marries someone who does not share that commitment. Many of today's divorces happen because a person's first marriage was that kind of combination. The hope of making someone else believe what you believe apparently dies hard. When someone tells me they are in a serious relationship, I always ask if that person is a committed Christian. I get really nervous when the answer is, "Well, sort of. He [or she] does attend church with me, and he [she] did go to Sunday school for a few years in their childhood."

The prophet asks, "Do two walk together unless they have agreed to do so?" (Am 3:3). This did not refer to unity in marriage, but it is certainly a good guideline for people proposing to share life's journey. You cannot compartmentalize your faith. If it is real, it will penetrate every area of your relationship. If your wish is to create and share a Christian home, your mate has to share that same desire. Many who are married to someone who does not share their faith in Christ attend church alone week after week, except for Easter and Christmas. It is a lonely journey when you cannot share with the one you love your faith, your spiritual growth, answered prayer, biblical standards for living, and the hope and joy of one day meeting God face to face.

A fourth difficult pairing involves a divorced person marrying a widowed person. Although both have suffered acute loss, the person whose spouse died usually has plenty of good memories from the marriage and will often hold up a former spouse as an icon and measuring stick. The divorced person may have feelings that run the gamut from deep affection and love to total unconcern and indifference. And yet, if children were born into that relationship, there will always be ties to the former spouse. With those ties come varying degrees of conflict that rarely disappear with time. Some widowed persons have told me they would never marry a divorced person because there are too many strings to other people that might cause them pain and problems. If you move into that territory, you will need to understand where the land mines are planted.

A final combination, often a struggle, happens when one person wants one or more children to be created in the new union while the other person proclaims, "No way!" The issue of *none* versus *more* needs to be resolved way back down the dating road. Too many men and women think that once they get a foothold in another person's life, they can convince him or her of anything. Wrong! It only postpones the battle to a later date. The result is a stalemate.

I had a friend, single for many years, who became involved in a relationship with a never-married woman who wanted to have children. He had a child grown and out of the home and did not want to go back to square one and start again. I watched the issue batted back and forth until the relationship finally ended. It was good they did not marry, hoping to resolve the issue at some future time. While the issue is not as great between ages twenty and forty, beyond forty the strong feelings build and declarations are nailed down. This is not a case of right and wrong. It is a matter of personal choice, and people have a right to live out their choices.

If you are thinking about remarriage, you again need to

establish your own criteria. As you eliminate potential marriage candidates, you also remove potential conflicts. Remember, do your homework before the test comes, not after.

SOME RULES ON THE REMARRIAGE ROAD

I have presided over the weddings of many couples entering a second marriage. I have also watched many second marriages crumble, coming to an untimely end. I meet people in workshops who have been married four and five times. When they share that with me, there is a strong sense of shame attached. My concern for them is to help them stop and learn, and not continue their marriage-losing streak. Those who have had a string of divorces usually jump from the ending of one marriage to a new marriage in six months or less. The two-to-three-year rule would probably have prevented that from happening because their focus would have been on recovery, not remarriage.

Here are a few points to remember. They can serve you well as guidelines when you do decide to remarry.

Strive for spiritual compatibility. One partner should not be way ahead of the other spiritually. Share your spiritual journeys with one another. Note the areas where you are together and those where you are at a distance. What do both of you need to do to close the gap? What keeps the other person growing spiritually? What keeps you growing spiritually? Can you read, study, and pray together comfortably? What are your personal spiritual priorities, and what spiritual priorities will you form together as a couple?

Don't push someone who is not as ready for remarriage as you are. A newly divorced or widowed person may meet someone four years out of the experience who is ready to find a new mate, settle down, and remarry. If that situation pops up on your relationship radar, let the other person know you understand there is a lot of healing to do before he or she is ready for remarriage. You cannot do recovery work for someone else. It may be tempting to think you can because the person you love may appear together and whole, but you can't.

Resist any rescue attempts from those who have already recovered. Always be willing to accept a helping hand; just make sure the hand isn't connected to a person who is after you as a marriage partner. Commonplace emotional collisions look like great shortcuts to wholeness. But they don't catapult you forward. They send you backwards. You will need to set up boundaries so other people are kept where they need to be while you are rebuilding. Remember that grief and loss are life experiences that cannot be resolved by anyone other than the one who owns the experience.

Take time to houseclean your life prior to thoughts of remarriage. Unresolved childhood issues and unclaimed emotional baggage often come to the surface during a time of bereavement or divorce. You may need some professional counseling during this time to resolve previously hidden issues. You need someone to ask you the hard questions and not let you off with easy answers. This is a time to sweep things clean.

In the past few years, I have noticed that men and women come to recovery groups with divorce issues but then discover the stuff hidden away in the closets of their life. These unexpected issues seem to fall out in our small group discussion times. For many, divorce recovery is the beginning of healing old hurts that predate marriage.

Take all the time you need to get to know the other family system. Allow the person you are dating to get to know yours. Beware of the person who says, "Hey, you have me. You don't need to worry about my family." I don't care if you remarry at eighty; you still marry into the family of another person.

If the family you are marrying into has children, take time to build a personal friendship with each of them. To many children, a potential stepparent looms as the enemy. Most children want their real mother and father back together again. The appearance of a potential stepparent is a guarantee that what they want will not happen. It is little wonder they are often full of resentment and anger. It will take time, energy, and love to break through that kind of wall. It will not be easy. Love wins over time, but we never know how long it will take.

Dreams for a new marriage need to be shared. Each person brings his or her own dreams into a relationship. Those dreams need to be nurtured and shared. New dreams created by the couple need to be owned. Dreams form bedding soil in which goals may be planted. Always remember that you never sacrifice your personal dreams when you enter a remarriage. You bring them into that new relationship, fuse them with the other person's dreams, and work hard to see them grow. Some people are specialists at killing other people's dreams and inserting their own. If anyone tries to do that to you, run for your life. Better to pursue your own dream alone than have another person stamp it out as the price tag for relationship.

Remember that you are becoming a part of another person's history. He or she has formed a life and previously lived it without you in it. The person you love has family albums full of celebrations and vacations, houses and apartments, and a whole world of memories that did not include you. In a remarriage of two people in their forties or fifties, a combination of eighty to one hundred years of history goes into that union. The good times and bad times of your life are now merged with another person's. Now a new history will be born. Making new memories and creating a new history have priority in a second marriage. The focus needs to be on what you are *building*, with an eye to what you have *learned* from prior experiences.

Children in a second marriage need plenty of time getting used to the idea before the marriage takes place. The only children that seem to welcome stepparents are those who lived in highly dysfunctional families, were abused in one way or another, or were shown little attention and love. But even abused children dream of mother and father together again in a normal home. The vast majority of healthy children usually stand in strong opposition to their parent getting remarried. I remember doing a wedding where the son of the groom was his best man. Throughout the entire ceremony the boy glared at me with a look of disgust on his face. I am sure he thought I was to blame for what he was witnessing.

It takes time and energy to build relational bridges with another person's children. Too many want it to happen overnight, and it does not. If you don't spend time with them before the new marriage, they won't spend time with you after it. They can become your worst nightmare and wipe out everything you try to do.

Children face three basic struggles in a remarriage. Jealousy is usually the first dragon to raise its ugly head in a blended family. It takes a while to establish fair and even treatment for all children involved. Until that is established, jealousy in just about every area will be a daily struggle. When children from both families have to live together seven days a week, the tension of jealousy will be on public display for all to see and all to resolve.

The second dragon is resentment. Resentment is worse than the flu, because the flu goes away eventually but resentment settles in for a lifetime. Children, like adults, need a forum to express their feelings. If their feelings are walled off from their reality, resentment grows. After all, they have a lot to resent: a new stepparent, new housing, new schools, new friends, loss of old friends, new disciplines, new schedules, loss of status. (And those are only a few of the possibilities.) Resentments need to be talked through so that feelings are validated. If that is denied, it won't be long before you will know you are living on top of a rumbling volcano.

The third dragon is sibling rivalry. Bad enough in a family of origin, it tends to be worse in a blended family. When children lose their status in family ranking and are forced to share it in a new system, rivalry enters the picture. I have watched children fall right through the cracks in a second marriage because they lost their status and importance. One teen told me that he just wasn't a "player" in his family any longer. He said he would work and hang on until graduation, then he would be out the door.

When you are aware that children have feelings, you face these and assorted other issues. You can take the time to work through them before they become combustible.

You know about another person only what they want you to know, and what they tell you. This is a final warning sign on the road to remarriage that may sound strange and be difficult for many. It is based on my twenty-five years of working in the single adult community. Some of the tragic experiences I've witnessed could have been avoided with a little homework. Once you fall in love with someone, logic, reasoning, and clear thinking will take a backseat. So here are a few things to consider doing before your heart runs away with your head.

Before you say, "I do," make sure both of you are tested for HIV. In most states that is part of the blood test required for a marriage license. I know someone who died of AIDS in a second marriage because he did not do a test.

If there are any question marks regarding finances in the life of your about-to-be spouse, take the time to run a credit check. I know, you are thinking that is a sign of distrust. But I know many people who trusted and were taken to the financial cleaners in a second marriage. You have a right to know what kind of financial background and credit rating your special person has. A single mother told me recently she had worked for five years to get her credit reestablished after a bad marriage. She stated she would not marry anyone without his permission for a credit check. Smart lady!

One of the wisest things any couple contemplating a second marriage can do is spend some time prior to the marriage with a wise and caring financial consultant. He or she can go over each person's financial history, including any financial investments, and give good direction in setting up a future plan that will work for both parties.

If one or both parties are bringing financial obligations into a new marriage (such as children from previous marriages), talk about how you will meet these obligations as a couple. It may be wise to talk with a lawyer about establishing living trusts or provisions in your wills. Working through these financial issues before you are married, with the help of qualified consultants, can save you hours of haggling and allow both partners to go into the second marriage on the same "financial page."

If there are time periods in a person's life that are blank, and he or she can give no explanation, this may be considered a red flag. You might well consider a police check. I am not suggesting doing this when there is no good reason, but when doubts are there, wisdom should take over. I could tell you sad stories you would find hard to believe when some people did not read the signs well and suffered immense pain as a result. Yes, you can be *too* trusting.

Premarital counseling is a must before second marriages. Find a skilled therapist and ask him or her to work the both of you over. There are some great tests that will reveal a lot and help you pinpoint potential struggles. I recommend this to everyone I work with in remarriage. They all agree it is tremendously helpful and a good start on a new future.

Finally, get a copy of my book *Growing in Remarriage,*[1] read it together from cover to cover, and talk about it. It covers a lot of ground, such as how to prepare for remarriage, how to blend children into a new relationship, how to get help when you feel the marriage is in trouble, and how to sort out expectations. It addresses the issues everyone faces in remarriage, along with offering the Remarriage Test.

I believe in remarriage, but I believe there is plenty of homework to do prior to that time. Many of the marriages I have performed over the last twenty-five years are still going strong. People have worked hard to build them and create something good. You can, too! Keep your eyes open, your prayers directed, your mind questioning, and your homework ready to be turned in.

TWELVE

Learning to Accept Where You Are

*We shall find that the spheres God brings us into
are not meant to teach us something but to make us
something.*

OSWALD CHAMBERS

The blizzard hit town overnight, and I found myself stuck in the Pittsburgh Airport with grounded planes and hundreds of unhappy travelers. We were told it would be hours before any flights would be called to Los Angeles, where it never snows and the planes fly every day. Being from L.A., I did not want to be stuck where I was.

Grounded passengers are generally an unhappy lot. They fret, fuss, stomp, stew, and mumble as they walk back and forth, waiting for melting snow and plowed runways. I was one of these unhappy campers until I realized there was nothing I could do to change the situation. I settled down in a quiet corner, opened my briefcase, and went to work in my portable office. My plans for the day were in the hands of other people and God.

Many hours later my flight was called, and we finally headed west. But I learned a valuable life lesson that long day. You may not always like where you are. You may desperately want to be somewhere else. But until you can get there, you will be happier if you accept the situation and make good use of the experience.

Many express deep resentment at becoming single again when what they wanted was to stay married. Venting feelings of anger, sadness, and betrayal may be therapeutic at times, but that will not change your situation. Growth always begins when you learn to accept where you are and turn a negative experience into a positive one. I know that sounds like hype, but you always have a choice in how you handle an experience. There were many people in the Pittsburgh airport that wintry day who spent their time complaining and stomping from one airline to the next. The longer they complained, the angrier they became. Emotions changed nothing that day. They will change very little about your single-again status and impede your journey toward new experience.

Positive growth starts by affirming your present situation verbally, mentally, and spiritually. It's difficult to explain, "I'm divorced" or "I'm widowed." There are no awards given for your declaration. If you receive anything, it usually comes in the form of, "Oh, I didn't know. I'm so sorry." I have known men and women who continue to wear their wedding rings long after their spouse is gone. They tell me it keeps the body snatchers away and lessens the number of questions they have to answer. But it also becomes an anchor to yesterday that denies you opportunity to begin a new journey. Admitting where you are unlocks the door to acceptance. Accepting where you are is the key to recovery and growth. Any recovery program in the country knows this and practices it.

The opposite of accepting where you are is denial. I have met some single-again people who practice their own form of denial. One man told me he wasn't single; he was just between marriages. Other singles have told me they refuse to attend singles meetings because they are not like the other people who attend them. We all want to feel unique, but there is a time when a "Me too" will move you further down the road than a "Not me."

GOOD-FOR-YOU AFFIRMATIONS

One of the good steps in accepting your current residency in the single-again world is to practice saying the following six affirmations every day.

> *I am divorced [widowed].*
> *I am single today.*
> *I am OK.*
> *I am a good and gifted person.*
> *God loves me.*
> *I have a future that is in God's hands.*

You might be thinking my suggestion is silly and a waste of time. If you do, just go to any sales meeting anywhere in the country and listen to what is being said. Or stop by the locker room before any sports event and listen to the coach talk to the players. All you will hear is positive affirmations and a timeworn theme, "You can do this!" Does it work? Ask a salesman or football player. Or visit your friendly local bookstore and purchase a copy of *The Little Engine That Could*. You probably read it to your children to encourage them to believe they could do anything. It may be time for you to read it again. Another great book is *OH! The Places You'll Go* by Dr. Seuss.

THE ROAD TO ACCEPTANCE

For most of us, reaching a place of acceptance is a journey. Each day on that road feels a little more comfortable. You will experience some sidetracks along the way, though, if you are normal (and most of us would like to believe we are normal).

Some time is always spent in denial. We somehow feel that if we don't talk about the problem, don't think about it, and pretend it doesn't exist, it does not exist. When someone is diagnosed with cancer or another life-threatening disease, there is always a time of denial when heart and brain battle each other. I watch people sidetracked in denial all the time. They choose fantasy over reality. A man who recently filed for bankruptcy told me he spent weeks denying his reality, even when his accountant showed him convincingly that he was beyond bankruptcy.

Another sidetrack on the acceptance pathway is resistance. For many single-again adults, resistance says, "I won't join in or become a part of this new world because I am not going to be here long enough to need it." There is resistance to getting to know others on the same pathway. Secular stereotypes of single-again men and women can cause some resistance because the picture often painted is not positive and may even be degrading. Any time the single-again world is represented in the media, some reporter and a cameraman visit a singles bar or after-work hangout, shoot some footage, and ask dumb questions. Film at eleven!

Real single-again men and women have little time to hang out in a bar after work. They are usually picking up children from daycare, cooking dinner, helping with homework, doing laundry, and falling into bed, dead by eleven o'clock. Weekends are filled with sports, grocery shopping, housecleaning, and church and school activities. No one gets excited about putting that on the late news.

A big part of growth on the road to acceptance is learning to live through transitions. Living in the midst of ever-changing uncertainty is like living out of a suitcase for a month or a year. You are limited in your choices and confined to restrictions that may be uncomfortable. Stability will keep you focused on your daily journey. It provides certainties needed for a healthy balance in life. When your stability is shaky, you become indecisive, uncertain, and insecure. Good decisions do not take root where instability reigns.

Keeping life simple helps a person live with transitions. There is a growing interest in living more simply in a society that is becoming more complex. A number of best-selling books in the past months have emphasized how to achieve that. Read them and form a plan to implement some of the ideas.

The danger in living with transitions is that you can develop a *tentative* lifestyle. Being tentative is being uncertain, and that can cause a person to make no decisions on anything. I meet people who have moved from one place to another but never completely unpacked because they don't know how long they will be at their new location. Many years ago a friend gave me some good advice on moving from one city to another in ministry. He told me to always unpack totally and to settle in permanently, as if I were planning to spend the rest of my life in that place. Good advice! I have tried to practice that. It removes the temptation of the tentative, giving me a sense of belonging and ownership. Everyone is faced with uncertainties that cannot be resolved quickly. You need to learn to live with them but not give in to them.

You can become a visitor in the single-again world, or you can take up residency. You can unpack and enjoy, or you can stay packed and avoid reality. Acceptance of this part of your journey through life will help you grow free in new areas. I hear this oft-repeated comment from many of the people I work with: "I just cannot believe how much I have grown in every area of my life since being single." They are learning what I learned in the Pittsburgh Airport!

AFTER ACCEPTANCE ... GROWTH!

I am a strong believer in growth. There are five areas that are helpful to target. You will not grow automatically by reading about them here. You have to do them.

Honest Communication

One of the most important keys in communication is learning to express your feelings. Feelings are neither right nor wrong; they are just feelings. We need to express them so that others will know what is going on inside of us. We need friends we can trust with our feelings when we share them. We don't share them so someone else will have to act on them; *we* don't even have to act on them. We just need to know someone will hear them, and in hearing them, authenticate that we are alive, experiencing emotions.

People often leave my office saying, "Thanks for all your help." Sometimes I have to smile to myself at that comment because all I have done for one hour is listen attentively while saying nothing. I have discovered that my help was just listening to what others were feeling about what was happening in their lives. One therapist recently described his profession as being a "paid listener." As the importance of technology increases in our world, the need for human listening and interaction is climbing dramatically.

When you communicate honestly, you speak truthfully. Scripture tells us to speak "the truth in love" (Eph 4:15). Learning to do that is difficult because we may not be sure what the truth is. Or we are afraid that the one we are speaking to may not receive truth the way we intended. A worthy goal would be to communicate what you feel honestly. This may be a new challenge, but it will help you in your struggle to express your thoughts and feelings more authentically.

Flexibility

A vital part of living with a new role is to resist the stereotypes and boxes in which other people want to place you. You may feel as though you are viewed by those outside the single-again world as inferior to a married person. You may even feel discriminated against. A case in point: It took many years for churches to get serious in establishing singles ministries. If a church had a singles ministry, it was often a no-budget group that met in a broom closet once a month. Thankfully, this is changing. Though it was a while before singles gained recognition as a legitimate community with important needs and concerns, there are singles ministries all over the country today.

Meanwhile you may find your new role is in fact a composite of several roles, each bringing its own kind of challenges. One of the toughest roles to live out is that of a single parent. It is not easy when the children are still at home and need everything two parents should be giving, yet have only one to depend on. The role of the single parent has many faces and many demands.

Another role is that of the dating person. This role is seldom comfortable because it is accompanied by the risk of being rejected or hurt. It is also the grid through which potential candidates for remarriage enter your life. It magnifies uncertainties. It often leads to making a scary decision.

The reverse of the dating role is the role of the nondating person. In a singles group, those who are healing their loss, wholesome and normal, and yet not dating anyone are often looked upon as suspect. One nondating man told me that he wanted to wear a shirt printed with the words, *Don't Shoot Me, I'm Normal!* A lady told me that you are treated with suspicion if you date all the time or if you never date at all. She felt like she could not win in the role game.

Being flexible within these roles is not easy. Choosing flexibility means not nailing yourself in a corner. People attempt to superimpose roles and definitions on you all the time. You can choose to resist their attempts. At other times, you place those roles upon yourself and limit your capabilities when you do. Flexibility is being able to ebb and flow with the daily currents of life much as the tides in the oceans do. The roles may change frequently, making you feel uncertain. But growing is learning who you are and feeling secure in who you are. Then you will exude a confidence that others will read and respect.

New Experiences

The longer one is married, the more predictable life experiences become. This provides security and a safety net for life. The exchanging of marriage vows is believed to be a guarantee that our mate will always be there for us and we will always be there until death intervenes. Divorce is unexpected. Death is expected, though only in the twilight years of life. When something pulls that security away, your life changes in an instant. Loss cancels all the certainties.

I have told you the response of one lady when I asked, "What are you doing that's new and challenging?" She told me she was racing airplanes. I smiled knowingly, thinking she meant model airplanes on Saturday morning at the local park, until she explained she was in national competition with the Women's Powder Puff National Air Races. After divorce she added her own dramatic new experience to the one she did not invite, being single again.

After a marriage ends, the only boundaries are self-imposed. For some the challenge is a new career. For others it's living in another city, state, or country. Some go back to school and complete work on their long-delayed academic goals. Some single-again people have gone to a mission field for a few years to fulfill a longtime dream.

The good news when you are single again is that you don't have to ask anyone's permission to accept invitations to new experiences.

Trust

Anyone who is trying to follow God learns that means to trust where God leads. Proverbs 3:5-6 gives good advice in this area. The more uncertain life's pathway looks, the more you will need the Lord to guide you through tough times and tough places. The more you trust God to lead, the deeper your reservoir of trust becomes. Trust is renewable daily. It never wears out. If you have never been on a journey of faith, now is the time to reach for God's hand and begin an adventure.

Do you believe you can trust God with every detail, every

day of your life? Do you believe you can place every impossible situation in his hands? Do you believe he will supply all your needs? Most of us have a surface kind of trust where we say we trust God, but attempt to keep control of certain situations ourselves. Trust is giving something to God and then getting out of the way so he can take control. Miracles can happen when we give God room to do what he wants to do.

A second part of trust involves learning to trust yourself again. Many singles say they made such a bad marriage choice the first time, they would never trust themselves again. It takes a big chunk of time to rebuild. You begin that process by risking again, once healing has taken place in your life. You can trust yourself when you are learning and growing through your mistakes.

We live in a world suffering under a gigantic collapse of trust. People and institutions, from the halls of government to the halls of industry to the halls of your own church, have violated public trust. We wake up each morning wondering who will not disappoint. Perhaps our coins sum up the answer: "In God we trust." That is all you need.

Acceptance, Not Performance

You work hard to define who you are by what you do, your vocation or career. The question is, *who are you when you are not doing what you do*? Like everyone else, you struggle long and hard to perform in life in order to gain affirmation and acceptance. Death or divorce can blindside you by quickly taking away the world in which you performed well. And so you are foced to answer this question again, as someone newly single: "Who are you now? How will you gain acceptance?"

It is a challenge for others simply to accept you for who you are. I remember asking a question in a singles group about identity. A woman stood and loudly proclaimed, "I'm tired of the label 'single.' I want to be known as a human being. A person. Nothing more or less." Everyone in the group applauded her in agreement. Labels are for cans and jars. But God always accepts us as we are. Make it your goal to do that for each other, basing identity on acceptance, not performance.

Writing to early Christians in the fourth chapter of Philippians, the apostle Paul talked about three things that I believe are important for single-again adults. He said he had learned to accept where he was, grow where he was, and keep on building. Circumstances were unimportant, he said. The goal was to keep moving ahead undeterred. Even skeptics and doubters did not sidetrack Paul. He accepted those roadblocks as a part of his journey. He refused to focus on them in place of his calling. Paul kept moving ahead with Christ as his model and leader.

Accepting where you are is hard when you would rather be somewhere else. But your roots grow best in the soil of acceptance. God accepts you exactly as you are. You do not need to perform for him.

THIRTEEN

Guidelines for Single Parents

I can do everything through him who gives me strength.

PHILIPPIANS 4:13

Lines showed on her face as she slumped in a chair. Her voice was weary and barely audible. A single working mother with two children, she told me she didn't have enough money to meet expenses or enough time to nurture her children. After about twenty minutes she finally said, "I'm just too tired and worn down in every area of my life. I can't do this anymore." Her eyes filled with tears as she looked away from me.

Does this sound familiar? I have listened to that scenario more times than I can remember. There are many burned-out single moms and dads struggling to make sense of circumstances forced upon them. If this were the whole story, we would have a national burnout epidemic on our hands.

All single parents face the reality of too little time, too little sleep, too little money, and too little help. Are you living this script? If raising children in a two-parent home is a tough job, it can seem overwhelming in a single-parent family. The good news is that I have watched thousands of single parents around the country accept the challenge and, over the long haul, do an incredible job. I have watched children growing up in those homes turn out to be competent and capable adults who refuse to let the loss of a parent damage their lives. The woman in my office would find a way to be among these families.

I need to say that I have also watched some single parents do an incompetent job and have witnessed the results in the lives of the children. Some adults forget that you do not divorce your children, or abandon them while you mourn the death of a spouse.

Since joint or shared custody of children is now a legal option in most states, many parents are working harder to be physically present and available to their children. Tragically, some never get past the divorce war zone. For those that do, the goal of being the best parent possible to each child can be achieved.

WHAT DO SINGLE PARENTS NEED?

Any struggle can seem overwhelming unless one carefully and prayerfully has a plan of attack. There are specific needs on which you must focus as you seek to be an effective single parent.

Trust in God
God will always be bigger than the biggest problem you face. A strong spiritual center, with a complete faith and trust in

God, is at the heart of success as a single parent. One single father recently summed up how he felt about trusting God for the ability to be an effective parent. He said, "I get up every morning and pray, 'Lord, help!' And he does!"

That is where it all starts. The Bible says, "You do not have, because you do not ask God" (Jas 4:2b). Jesus gave another strong directive about asking for things: "Ask and it will be given to you; seek and you will find; knock and the door will be opened to you. For everyone who asks receives; he who seeks finds; and to him who knocks, the door will be opened" (Mt 7:7-8).

God understands your needs and waits patiently for you to ask for his help. He is the power source and best resource for every mom and dad. Without God at the center of your single-parent home, daily survival will be an exhausting and overpowering experience.

Time and Love

The most important gifts you can give your children are time and love. I have listened too often over the years to sad, angry, and lonely children tell me they wished their mom and dad would spend more time doing things with them. Physical presence is a powerful gift to give your child and one of the strongest ways to build an album of happy memories with him or her. Your presence tells a child he or she is important, and valuable enough that you want to be with him or her. Many children listen to the parental promise, "When I have more time, I will spend some of it with you." Seldom is that promise fulfilled.

Children grow up in the blink of an eye. They are born one day, go to college the next, and get married the next. Time not invested can never be reclaimed. Relationships demand time.

You can buy a child everything under the sun, but that will never be an adequate substitute for the investment of your personal time and attention.

The gift of love from parent to child can be expressed in countless ways. One of the best is to tell your child daily, "I love you." It doesn't matter if they are six, sixteen, or thirty-six. Along with the verbal expression of love, children of all ages need to be hugged. The power of touch is vital to healthy humanity. Most of us never get enough of it.

Knowing you are loved is knowing you have worth and value. Not knowing you are loved robs you of your worth as a person and devalues your humanity.

In counseling many people tell me their parents rarely said, "I love you" while they were growing up, or even later when they lived on their own. Those same people seldom received a hug. I find that hard to believe, but I know it's true. When affection is absent, self-worth and self-esteem suffer. Reassured daily, a child will have the inner strength to go through difficult times. You can never express too much love.

Many single parents have experienced rejection by a divorcing spouse and may feel love-starved. As a consequence they may have a difficult time keeping the river of love flowing toward and through their children. The good news is that your children can return love to you if you can just manage to prime the pump. They will help fill the empty reservoir in your own life.

While younger children often respond to you with affection, older children may be nonaffectionate, angry and resentful, or just not home very much. I have talked with hundreds of high school students who remain fueled by their hostilities toward a parent. While you hope they will become more understanding and mellow as they grow older, keep reaching out with whatever affection or pats of approval you can spare. They need it more than ever, though they don't show it.

Someone has said that love isn't love until you give it away. I would add that love given away will also be given back to you.

A Whole Family

I heard a single mom describe her home recently as "half a family." That instantly pushed one of my buttons. I told her I understood why she felt that way, but if her children believed her comment, they would feel demeaned. It is important to help your children understand that a single-parent home is still a family.

Your family is your family regardless of the shortage of another resident parent. Sometimes I hesitate to use the term "single-parent family" because it may portray a negative tone to children. Always refer to your children and yourself as a whole family.

A Support System

Parents need to be with others who face the same difficulties in raising children as they do as well as the same joys, needs, and desires. Children need the opportunity to build friendships with other children. Both need to belong to something bigger than themselves and their families that will expand their world and help them build strong relationships.

Children need to be included in as many social events as possible. The fastest-growing groups in many churches are those formed around meeting the needs of single parents and their children. Most single parent fellowship groups across the country hold events each year that include children, activities like camping, sports, picnics, parties, and bike rides.

Knowing How

There are several ways to learn how to fulfill your role as a single parent most effectively. One is to visit your local Christian bookstore, which will have current titles from the most important books on this subject. Do some browsing. Then buy and read a few of your finds.

A group approach could include organizing workshops on the subject, led by professionals who can teach and inspire. Or use relevant materials in your small group discussions, where people can share their experiences and insights. You could start a single-parent class on Sunday morning so fellowship and teaching could be combined.

You don't need to find an expert before you begin helpful programs. You don't need to have a staff pastor create what you need. You are on the road. Band together, form a team, dream, and share the work. Some of the best programs I have been in around the country have been run totally by laypeople in the church who are single parents. If you have this need, take the challenge to build a support system that can help you and others.

Becoming a single parent will definitely put a new face on parenting. It is far more than a full-time job, but it is being done every day by people in my church and countless others around the country. The single parents I know deserve gold medals for their efforts and commitment to their children.

MEETING THE NEEDS OF THE CHILDREN

Children, like adults, have specific needs fundamental to their survival. From my experience of working with children in divorce, I want to share some of the most important ones.

Love

Children need to be told they are loved and to feel loved. We can *say*, "I love you," but love is always something you *do*. Loving actions must follow loving words if that love is to be felt. One of the struggles for a child in divorce country is to know that the noncustodial parent still loves him or her even though he may not be as physically available. I know noncustodial parents who love their children effectively and have a great relationship with them. I also know some who appear to care little about their children. The children feel the pain, and they may carry those feelings into adulthood.

Freedom From Fear of Abandonment

There are two forms of abandonment, physical and emotional. From my perspective they are equally devastating. Physical abandonment is just not being physically present in the child's life. Emotional abandonment is being bodily present but mentally and emotionally absent. Emotional starvation results in emotional isolation. When a child is older, he will often go in search of someone to fill that emptiness. Too often it is filled with the wrong kind of people and the wrong kind of experience. Many teens who join gangs are trying to fill a void left by the lack of acceptance, love, and support that should have come from their parents.

Another detrimental form of abandonment involves lack of financial support. Financial abandonment is the curse of child-support collectors across America. When a parent reneges in this area, not only do the child and the custodial parent suffer material problems, but the child also receives a message that says, "I don't love you."

Hundreds of millions of back child-support payments are owed across our country. New laws have been enacted to try to solve this problem. Another of my personal hot buttons is a parent who does not pay child support at all. If you are in my singles group, you had better run for cover if that describes you. No child should be forced to pay for his or her parents' divorce by being financially abandoned.

Information

Too often children are kept in the dark and told not to worry, with a quick promise that everything will be OK. It doesn't take long for them to figure out that things are *not* OK and may not be OK for a very long time. When information is scarce, fear invades the life of a child.

It is a good practice to hold frequent family forums where everyone is informed and asked to be part of the solution. A family is a team. Team members need to be part of decisions that will affect them. Children have a right to respond to the things that will affect them or the family. A child also needs a place to express his or her feelings where they will be heard. It is a big mistake to leave your children on the outside while you or other adults make all the decisions.

In addition, a child needs to know about the family financial picture. Many parents lock the children out of this knowledge and thus do not gain their support when finances are tight. Older children especially need to know the reasons why things are tight at any given moment. They can improve finances by working part time for things they need or to contribute to the budget. This is an opportunity for them to do something positive.

Though children may resent the financial stress a divorce places on life and family, this is a reality they need to deal with. Financial struggles will impact their lives as well as yours. Be honest with them and ask for their help and suggestions as team members.

A Role in Planning

A dream is what keeps hope alive, and children need to be part of the decision making for your family's future. Those decisions may involve geographical relocation, career and school changes, changing friends, and blending family. As an adult's relationships change due to death or divorce, so do those of the child. Being forced to change neighborhoods and schools means new friendships have to be made, and if that is scary for an adult, it is even worse for a child. He needs to have a say in the plotting and planning.

I am not suggesting that children be given the power to approve or negate decisions. They just need to feel part of the process. This is even more important when you have teenagers. Too many parents call their family together and bluntly announce a twenty-five-hundred-mile move from the sun of San Diego to the cold of Boston because grandparents said, "Bring the kids and come on home. We will help you." Those offers may sound like the deal of the week, but you need to process it with the children, giving attention to how it will impact their lives.

Talk with your children, listen to them, and make them part of the solution, not the problem.

Understanding of Parents' Dating

The majority of children go through their parents' divorce dreaming privately that Mom and Dad will get back to together and home will be like it once was. The finalization of divorce papers means little. But when a parent begins to date, the message becomes clear: their dream is not to be. The permanence of the divorce begins to sink in, and the child's emotions can run the gamut from hate to excitement to total indifference. Fear of the entrance of an unkind stepparent may push a child's response to an even more extreme level.

Too many parents just start dating with no explanation, and expect their children to understand. That seldom works out for the children, and it will work against you. There should be a family forum where a parent explains the human need to have someone special in his or her life. This forum should happen before a parent starts dating again. The children also need time to accept, know, understand, and trust someone new in their mom or dad's life. Everyone you date is a potential candidate for marriage, and I believe kids need to meet the people you date from day one.

Make dating an adventure you can share with your children. Even if they are not of dating age now, the day will come, and you can teach them a lot about dating by opening your heart and feelings to them. They can cry, laugh, and commiserate with you, go through your matchups and breakups, and understand you are very human. Don't make the mistake of thinking it is none of their business. When you bring someone into their lives, it may be for a lifetime.

Divorce and Adult Children

An increasing number of divorces occur between people who have been married thirty or forty years. Half of the men and women in my divorce recovery workshops had been married for more than twenty-five years. This new dynamic means that Grandpa and Grandma are now going through divorce. This is a shock to the family system. Grandparents are expected to spoil grandchildren and live to a ripe old age. No one ever expects them to divorce before they die.

Adult children often have an extremely hard time dealing with the divorce of their parents. Even though they are married and have established their own homes, this traumatic event can shake them to the core. One lady remarked, "I feel like someone dropped a nuclear bomb on my family and totally wiped it out." A man told me he wanted to kill his grandfather for divorcing his grandmother. I have seen grandchildren and children rage at the older adults in their lives who have betrayed them by divorcing.

This bomb blast only worsens when Grandpa or Grandma decides to remarry, connecting to a whole new family system. Allegiances and commitments change dramatically. Everyone gets confused, angry, sad, and revengeful. The splintered family has little chance for any healing. Some say, "Let bygones be bygones. Forgive and forget. Hold a big family reunion with all the new add-ons." Biting that kind of bullet gives most people lead poisoning. Life always seems to go on, but there are usually more losses than wins in this kind of family fracture. One man said, "I lost both my mom and dad somewhere when they divorced."

But whether you are the adult child of divorce or the divorcing grandparents, you must choose to live through the experience, set your boundaries, and ask God for daily wisdom. You are responsible for yourself before God. You are responsible for the children God has placed in your care. You live that responsibility one day at a time and call upon God for the strength you need each day.

FOURTEEN

What Would Jesus Do?

God has the right to interrupt your life.

HENRY BLACKABY

It was a phenomenon that swept across the country. Hundreds of thousands of children and adults had a bracelet on their wrist with a message containing four letters and a question mark: *WWJD?* The slogan was derived from the classic best-selling story *In His Steps,*[1] by Charles M. Sheldon, about a church that decided to follow Jesus instead of merely finding expedient solutions to everyday problems. In both the original edition written by Sheldon and the revised edition written by his grandson, a Christian community wrestles with hard issues about honoring God. In every situation they stop long enough to ask the question, "What would Jesus do?"

Like every other trend, this Christian fad spawned an entire industry of jewelry, clothing, cards, caps, bumper stickers, and devotional books. I am uncertain as to whether this attempt to ask the right question at the right time had any lasting impact on society. I do know many businesspeople made a great deal of money.

Most of us have been on the Christian pathway long enough to know that asking this question is seldom easy and usually demands hard answers. I often fall into the category of the disciples who fell asleep in the garden: "The spirit is willing, but the body is weak" (Mt 26:41b). I always start out with an honorable intention of trying to do things God's way. I know the end result will be better if I follow the leading of the Lord in my decisions. I just have a big problem with the waiting, watching, listening, and doing parts. If I were to rephrase the WWJD question in the culture of Southern California, where I live, it would probably sound like this: "What would Jesus do if he were in a hurry like me?" I am afflicted with the disease of today's culture; I want an instant answer.

Doing things God's way is more of a process than an instant response. Since I am more acclimated to the instant, I tend to rush that process, rather than wait for God's timing. I have a hard time asking the WWJD question because I have learned that God is never in a hurry. I will do much better if I allow God to move on his timetable rather than try to squeeze him into mine, but I struggle with wanting to see *my* results to my questions rather than waiting for the results that God will bring. I often impatiently tell God, "Don't worry, Lord. I'll take care of it," to which God probably responds, "I'm sure you will."

In the spiritual dimension it doesn't matter if you are single *still*, single *again*, or married. In each case, whenever you follow God and seek to do his will, you follow the same road map, the Bible. I believe the questions single-again people ask God are no easier or more difficult than the questions anyone else would ask. We all want to know what God wants us to do at moments of decision. Even if we decide to follow him at a one particular point in time, we constantly have to ask for his leading and direction.

LEARNING TO WAIT

Doing things God's way always starts with the process of waiting. The most outstanding example of waiting in Scripture is found in the book of Exodus and in the life of the nation of Israel. The Hebrew people spent forty years waiting to enter the Promised Land. I am sure that after the first three days of waiting in the wilderness, they were ready to roll into Canaan and set up camp. But there were lessons to be learned and it was going to take a long time to learn them.

The humbling process is often long and slow. Waiting includes *waiting* before the Lord, that is, spending time with him while *listening* for his direction. I come before him, *presenting myself.* It also means waiting for the Lord to do things in *his way* and on *his time schedule.* I wait for him to *direct* me. These principles are simple to understand but hard to act upon.

In Psalm 37:7 the psalmist tells us to, "Rest in the Lord and wait patiently for Him. Do not fret because of him who prospers in his way, because of the man who carries out wicked schemes" (NASB). Some of our reason for not being willing to wait on the Lord lies in the second part of this verse. We are afraid that while we are waiting, someone else will get ahead of us on the road to prosperity, success, or popularity. We fear that while we are waiting for God, others may be out there doing, and we will end up looking spiritually incompetent.

Many people hastily do something and ask God's blessing on it later, or they take God's blessing for granted. Worse still, they do something, then tell everyone God told them to do it, when in fact God did no such thing. There is a big difference between God getting the credit and God getting the blame.

As I speak and travel around the single-again world, a constant theme seems to be *growth, action, progress,* and *motion.* That's not bad unless its origin is more human than divine. We not only need to ask, "Is God in my own life?" but to ask the same question about activities within the family of God.

Sometimes spiritual discernment is replaced by the thrill of religious progress. In a fast-paced, high-tech world, waiting for God's leading and direction can appear outmoded, even archaic. I can only wonder how much further ahead we would be if we would only heed the psalmist's direction.

In a recent conversation with a newly single man, I asked how he felt about this new pathway. He commented, "It's like one big waiting room. Everyone is waiting for something different, but everyone is still waiting." The thought that crossed my mind was, *What do you do while waiting? Attend singles meetings, singles seminars, singles potlucks, singles retreats, and buy singles food portions at the local supermarket?* Wisdom told me not to express my question. There is more to becoming single again than just attending events.

LEARN TO LISTEN

What do you do while waiting for God to give directions on important decisions in your life? The psalmist tells us to rest (see Ps 91:1), an admonition few of us know how to follow. Let me expand that. We need to rest *and listen!* Did you ever meet someone who asked questions constantly but never waited for the answers? Many of us do that with God. Our questions pour out from troubled hearts and broken spirits, but we are unwilling to wait for answers. It is true that some questions will not be answered in this life. Those we must trust to God's wisdom. But the questions that can be answered in God's timing need a receptive person listening.

Listening is a lost art in today's world of information-giving and information-gathering. Everyone wants to talk, but few appear to listen. Listening to God means listening to his heart. It is allowing God to place his thoughts and directions within you, much like he did to a young man named Samuel. Samuel's sleep was interrupted by a voice he thought came from a man named Eli. Eli discerned that Samuel had heard the call of God and said to him, "It is the Lord; let Him do what seems good to Him" (1 Sm 3:18b, NASB). God will place his thoughts and directions within you if you will just listen.

Listening to God is most often a private process. It is fine-tuning your spiritual ear to the inner prompting and urging of God's spirit. Sometimes that means getting away from your daily routine to a place of quiet where you can concentrate on hearing God's voice. This is why Scripture says, "Be still, and know that I am God" (Ps 46:10a). *Knowing* thrives in stillness. Stillness precedes listening. Listening takes a receptive and quiet spirit.

To insure good results, you are to evaluate the inner voice by comparing it to what Scripture teaches. God's inner voice will never betray the Bible. It is also helpful to listen to fellow believers. God works as he has always worked, in and through his people. That's you and me! God used Eli to verify Samuel's call. If you and I are receptive to what God wants to say and do in our lives, we need to listen to Christian friends and teachers that God puts in our pathways. Those who walk closest to us are usually the ones who pray for us and care about us.

When you feel God is speaking in a definitive way to you, bounce what you are hearing off those friends for verification and confirmation. If they express concern and caution, you do the same. Remember that God is *never* in a hurry.

FOLLOW THROUGH

If doing things God's way starts with asking the right question, followed by waiting, then listening for the answer, it continues by following the directions God gives just as we follow the doctor's orders after an illness has been diagnosed. The struggle in following God lies in the will to obey. As we view the panorama of Bible characters stumbling through its pages, one truth becomes clear: they all received directions intact but failed to follow them.

Obedience is seldom easy for any of us because it means giving up our own will and accepting God's will. Getting in harness with him means following his directions and allowing him to do things his way. His way sometimes flies in the face of convention. It does not take much study in the Bible to discover that God often throws the predictable out the window. Jesus repeatedly got in trouble because he refused to follow the established ways and methods of worship. He respected tradition, yet refused to allow it to rule. I believe he desires to work in us today the same way.

There are those who think God's way of doing things has changed since Jesus' earthly ministry and the birth of the early church. I believe that kind of thinking limits God in much the same way the religious leaders limited Jesus in his day. God defies stereotypes. He is a specialist in breaking molds. When you give him the freedom he desires in your life, he will set you free beyond your wildest dreams. God's freedom allows you to be creative in serving him. It allows your faith to be stretched as you learn to trust God for things you once thought impossible. His freedom says all things are possible when his strength is flowing through you. When someone tells you, "No way," God's freedom says, "Yes, when it's God's way."

LIVE ON THE EDGE WITH GOD

Anticipating the unexpected brings the joy of watching how God will bring things together for his glory and purpose. Once I heard a person say, "Most things in life are pretty predictable, except for God." That stopped me in my mental tracks. God is totally unpredictable. When you ask him what to do in any situation, you had better be prepared to live on the edge. Rarely does he give out in advance the game plan for how he will resolve our problems. If he did, we surely would not need faith and trust for the journey. If our Christian life is to be the adventure God intended it to be, we will have to become permanent residents amidst the messiness of life's fray.

Once I overheard a person say, "I wish God would do in my life what he is doing in Larry's life." I have listened to powerful testimonies of how God worked in another person's life only to hear the last line, "And don't forget, what God did in my life he can do in yours." Essentially that is true—if God so chooses. But it is easy to look at good things happening in another person's life and want God to photocopy that for you. I have learned God doesn't seem impressed by that idea. He operates differently in each of our lives because he is unique. God is God; he can break all the molds if he so chooses. He works his plan according to who we are and what we need, not according to what has happened in someone else's life. Look at Jesus' healing ministry in the Bible. Each event stood alone and different from any preceding event. What never changed was Jesus' feeling of compassion for the afflicted and his desire and power to heal them.

I cringe when I hear someone tell an about-to-be-divorced person, "God put our marriage back together, and if he could do that for us, he can do that for you." I never doubt the "what God can do" part. I just know it always takes two people desiring restoration to make it happen. Since God gives each of us the freedom to make our own choices, some will make the wrong choice and some marriages will dissolve as a result. If we could order God to heal all broken relationships caused by divorce, we could also order God to heal the world from hunger, wars, crime, violence, and human injustice.

God does not force his will on us. Instead he allows us the freedom to make good and bad decisions. When we desire God's direction and will in our lives, we allow him to implement his unique plan for us. His question to you and me is, "What will you do?"

NO NEED TO EXPLAIN GOD

Have you ever spent time trying to explain to someone what you think God is doing in your life, why he is doing it, and what you feel the end results will be? Perhaps you are unable to accept what he is doing, or you want others to cheer what you feel he is doing. God must have a good laugh with all the angels when you try to do that. If you truly are willing to allow God to be God in your life, you must quit trying to explain him. Simply stand in awe and reverence seeing the results.

When the walls of Jericho came tumbling down, it was impossible on a human level to explain. The less we try to explain the *how* and *why* of God, the freer we will be to enjoy the result. To stand in awe of what God has done and is doing is to have a strong sense of reverence for his power made real in your daily journey.

Sometimes we worry too much about what others will think about what God is doing or not doing. We can critique everything, from theological viewpoints to the songs we sing in worship. Analyzing judgments appear to abound. Evaluating what God is doing in the lives of others can easily fall into such judgment. It is not easy to follow God's directions when somebody questions or criticizes us. Worrying what others think, we sometimes get off track.

Apart from verifying God's direction with trusted Christian friends, we must follow the directions that God gives us regardless of the criticism that comes our way. Our lives are to be reflections of him, not the opinions of others. You can weigh every comment and criticism carefully, but follow through with what you know to be God's will.

JUST DO IT

Loss of a spouse by death or divorce will bring a change of direction into your life. You will be faced with many decisions once the loss is processed and healing and hope have been restored. You will face the discrepancy between, *What would Jesus do?* and, *What would I do?*

Holding out for God's answer will not always be easy when the answer doesn't appear in the time you have allotted for God. But God's way is always the way of adventure and challenge. There is nothing boring about following him. There is always the thrill of wondering how God will accomplish his purpose in your life. To see God at work will encourage you to be totally open to letting him do things his way.

God asks you this question right now: "Are you willing to let me take control over the things you have no control over anyway?" The best answer you can give is "Yes!"

FIFTEEN

Healing the Hurts

For I am the Lord who heals you.

EXODUS 15:26b

There are not enough words, Hallmark cards, grief seminars, or sage wisdom to bring overnight healing of hurt caused by losing someone you loved. You cannot fill your life with enough distractions to free your mind from dealing with pain. Tangible problems can be managed, directed, resolved, and filed far more easily than the things of the heart, mind, memory, and spirit.

I frequently talk with men and women three and four years removed from the loss of a spouse only to find they still have gaping wounds. Some people have not worked hard enough at the healing process. Others have played the games of denial and self-pity, failing to face responsible healing.

The gaping wounds need care. To live is to risk hurt, and to be hurt is to be human, but God is in the healing business. We are both the hurting and the healing as we make our journey through life.

HEALING PRIDE

Wounded pride may be one of the things you first confront. Divorce is basically the failure of a relationship. When you fail at something, your capabilities are questioned and you feel you look bad. You get angry with yourself first, then at the person who wounded you. Divorce wars become the fallout because a divorce generally leaves a live and moving target to shoot at. Blame is tossed back and forth like a Ping-Pong ball. You say, "You hurt me, and I am going to find a way to hurt you back." Those who lose a spouse by death may also feel angry, but about the only thing they can do is kick dirt on the tombstone. (I have met some who have done that and a little bit more.)

The desire for revenge is usually stirred up when you have been wronged. The family law and courts are designed for an adversarial process. The system seems to welcome and cheer on the pursuit of vengeance. No matter how small or large the wrong has been, getting even is looked upon as proper repayment.

And yet, Scripture is clear on this issue. "Do not take revenge, my friends, but leave room for God's wrath, for it is written: 'It is mine to avenge; I will repay,' says the Lord" (Rom 12:19). The problem is that most want to know when God will do the repaying so they can be present to cheer him on. But when vengeance is turned over to the Lord, a healing release begins to take place. You will be set free to experience God's touch.

HEALING HOPELESSNESS

The wound of hopelessness is opened when the past is always in instant replay. I meet too many single-again men and women who say things like, "It isn't fair," and, "I wasted too many years," or, "I'll be single until I die." They act, think, look, and live the word *hopeless.*

Healing a hopeless spirit involves appropriating the words of the apostle Paul in Romans 8:28: "And we know that in all things God works for the good of those who love him, who have been called according to his purpose." All you and I have to do is love God, and God will bring hope. We become daily participants in the healing process. From time to time, it is wise to seek professional help in healing things that appear impossible to resolve. But even in the hands of a therapist, healing will take time and hard work on your part.

HEALING OF MEMORIES

Each day we live is a page in the book of memories. Some are good and others bad. Most of us tend to maximize the bad ones and minimize the good ones. The news media lead the parade in this regard, with bad news getting the featured role and good news being consigned to the last five minutes on TV or placed on the back pages of the newspaper. Other people seem to deal with bad *and* good memories by denying they ever existed. They dismiss them and block them from consciousness. Other people learn from the bad memories and celebrate the good ones, accepting both as part of the landscape of life.

What do you do with the memories that are painful to you?

Do you try to file them away but find the drawer keeps falling open and dumping their remains back into your lap? Hurtful memories must be prayerfully given over to God for ultimate resolution, healing, and filing. Prayer lifted to God should express both how you feel at the moment and how you would like to feel down the road. It should ask God to take your feelings, unscramble them, resolve them, and give you his peace. You also ask God to take care not only of past pain but also of present and future hurts. God is waiting for you to ask so he can begin the process.

I often meet people who want to keep the bad memories alive so the pain will keep fueling them to live on the defensive. In some strange way they feel this will protect them from future hurt. Underneath this is unresolved anger that can infect a life for years. I recently talked with a bitter man whose anger spilled out in his conversation with me. When I questioned him about the well of resentment in his life, he informed me he had a perfect right to be angry. He then gave me a long list of injustices that legitimized it. His list sounded familiar. A vast majority of single-again people have walked through the same debris. The difference between this man and many others is that he is choosing to stay embittered and is spewing it out on everyone else. Many who have had similar experiences have chosen to work through the bad memories, move beyond them, and not let them impact the present and future.

Healing bad memories starts with a willingness to let go of them. The longer you hold on, the less chance you have to be healed, and unhealed memories can make for a heavy load. They become roadblocks to growth and wholeness. Although many memories are hard to deal with because they lie deep within and are difficult to verbalize, it is helpful to write them out as collections of thoughts, words, and feelings.

Other helpful suggestions appear in Dennis and Matthew Linn's book *Healing Life's Hurts.*[1] The authors suggest five progressive stages toward healing:

> *I don't admit I was ever hurt.* That's denial.
> *I blame others for hurting and destroying me.* That's anger.
> *I set up conditions to be fulfilled before I'm ready to forgive.*
>   That's bargaining.
> *I blame myself for letting hurt destroy me.* That's depression.
> *I look forward to growth from hurt.* That's acceptance.

Where are you today in experiencing healing of your memories? Are they on the front burner, stealing your energy and souring your spirit, or are they filed away in a box labeled *Resolved?* Yesterday's experiences can teach us many things. They cannot be erased, but they can be healed by the grace of God and put to rest.

HEALING THROUGH FORGIVENESS

One of the greatest gifts God has given to us is the gift of forgiveness. It is the most difficult gift to employ and process because it must come from a heart of humility and be coupled with a spirit of human kindness. It is a detergent that God provides to clean up relational differences and roadblocks. It is the glue that holds us together in community. It mends broken places and helps heal hurt.

Forgiveness is something that needs to operate on a daily basis. You cannot live if you do not forgive. Jesus taught it to the disciples more than once. He put it right in the middle of the Lord's Prayer. He set no limits on it and wanted everyone to practice it. There are four principles of forgiveness:

God forgives me.
I forgive myself.
I ask my former spouse to forgive me.
I grant forgiveness to my former spouse.

This fourth point is the toughest for many people. If one spouse sets the stage for forgiveness but the other refuses all opportunities for forgiveness, you have to allow that person to be, and focus on moving your life ahead. You are only responsible for your part. The other person is responsible for what he or she chooses to give or withhold. Don't tie into someone else's negative attitude. Be forgiving and move on. You are not accountable for anybody's attitude but your own.

Forgiveness is a mountain to climb and it will take thought, prayer, and often a change of attitude for it to happen. God has to do some long-term work in your heart before you are ready to use this process post-divorce. But I have listened to hundreds of forgiveness stories over the years, and I know it can happen when you work at it.

One of the most powerful examples of forgiveness comes from the life of Joseph, in Genesis 37-45. Joseph's brothers sold him into Egyptian slavery. Separated from his family, he went through harrowing experiences during his ascent to the second-highest position of leadership in Egypt. Years later a famine brought his brothers to Egypt to buy grain. When Joseph saw his brothers for the first time, he wept but did not reveal who he was. As the interactions between Joseph and his family increased, Joseph's heart began to melt with the spirit of forgiveness. When he finally disclosed who he was, the forgiveness became a river and washed his entire family clean.

God used Joseph's journey to fulfill a divine purpose. Next

to Christ dying on the cross to forgive your sins and mine, Joseph is perhaps the next-best model of thorough forgiveness in the Bible. If forgiveness were not a healing stream running through his life, Joseph might have died at the bottom of the well where his brothers dumped him or in an Egyptian prison.

Forgiveness doesn't always have a "Joseph ending." You can forgive others, but you cannot make them forgive you. And you may have to live your forgiveness challenges open-ended. But you are only responsible for your part in the process. You cannot extract it from someone who does not want to give it. Peace will come when you do your part. You will be freed and healed and will begin to grow.

THE HEALING ROLE OF SOLITUDE

Vital parts of your healing process can only take place in solitude. This means being alone and not caught up in the whirl of activity and the constant demands of your regular world. For most hyperkinetic beings, this kind of stepping out of regular life will not come easily. It will take discipline and setting some time apart, but it is in just such a space that you can best allow God's quietness, assurance, and peace to wash over you. Monasteries are good places to do this. A cabin or retreat center can also be used. Many are vacant during the week, making it possible for you to rent a room.

In a noisy and busy world there is an increasing need for times of solitude in our lives. So many strings are pulled by other people that sometimes only the frayed ends are left for us to grasp at the end of our workweek. We have to establish a center for ourselves where we can rediscover who we are and focus on what we really want. It takes discipline to pull yourself apart from the world to think, observe, reflect, and pray. Two good things happen when we plan for these times. First, we get in touch with ourselves. Reflecting, thinking, journaling, meditating, and sorting out feelings is best done in places of quiet.

A second advantage of solitude is to get in touch with God. The Bible tells us, "Be still, and know that I am God" (Ps 46:10a). Leaders in the Bible often refused to move a muscle until God talked to them. We are too used to moving on our own without seeking God first, hoping that he will sanction our move later.

Time alone with God is vital in the healing process. Even Jesus set the model for this by periodically getting away by himself and leaving the world and his ministry behind. Being alone with God is vital not only to healing our hurts, but also to our spiritual survival.

HEALING THROUGH COMMUNITY

Solitude and community may appear to be direct opposites, but they are actually companions, both vital to wholeness. When you think about healing in community, you might think about a hospital, where you find people healing from diseases or physical problems. When that kind of healing has progressed sufficiently, you are free to leave the hospital and go home. Your church or support system of Christian friends should be a healing community for you. But unlike the hospital, you don't leave when healing is accomplished. You stay to celebrate your healing and become instrumental in the healing of others.

Henri Nouwen describes what a healing community should look like:

Each of us matters to God.

① Dear B. Laring!
I know your
heart is making
progress! God can
see all the little
details. He wants to
be your first love
before any others!
Hoping this book
will give you some
direction! Trust in

He cares for you.
1 Peter 5:7

God and He will
direct you! He wants
what is best for
you!
Keeping you in
my good thoughts
and prayers.
I love you!
He loves you
even more!
love, Carrie
xox

70725

U.S. 40
Canada 75

0 42516 70725 7

A Christian community is therefore a healing community, not because wounds are cured and pains are alleviated, but because wounds and pains become openings or occasions for a new vision. Mutual confession then becomes a mutual deepening of hope, and sharing weakness becomes a reminder to one and all of the coming strength.[2]

What Nouwen says here is that in a sense we are all wounded healers. As our wounds are healed, we become equipped to be healers to others.

A good, healthy singles group should offer two things to those who come through the door: healing and wholeness. I am not intimidated by single men and women who come through that door sick and falling apart. I am always amazed at the kind of help people in divorce recovery workshops can give each other. They all come the first night focused on their own pain. By the third night, some of their focus has shifted to what others are feeling and going through. By the end of the seminar, recovery and healing become a community thing, not a solitary experience.

The gifts a group can give to hurting people are encouragement, affirmation, guidance, and the knowledge that none are alone. Medical science has discovered that those who best help the ill are those with the same illnesses.

HEALING FAMILY RELATIONSHIPS

Living through loss and uncertainty means living with families that are affected by both. There will be gains and losses, misunderstanding and isolation for all the people involved. Questions will be asked to which there are no immediate answers. Strong relationships will vanish. Families will take sides, and people will be hurt. Healing will be desperately needed but will often appear far away. It may take years to repair and heal severed family relationships. Losing in-laws that you were close to can leave giant sinkholes. Inheriting a new family by a new marriage somehow doesn't always remove the sting of losing treasured people.

Isolation in divorce is a cruel and lonely experience. How do you bring a healing touch to your fragmented family? The first step is always to commit your concerns to prayer and ask God to bring healing. This can be a slow process because things have to happen to other people to make them open to healing. Those do not happen overnight. Fearlessly go to family members you want in your life and ask for their friendship. Silence can only deepen the chasm of separation. You may discover they want the same thing but were afraid to ask. Building a bridge starts with one person reaching out. Ask friends to help in the restoration and healing process with family. God can use them when there is little you can do. Leave the matter in God's hands, then do what you can do to move your life ahead.

There is a powerful healing promise in Exodus 15:26 with which I want to close this chapter. God makes a promise to the nation of Israel saying, "If you listen carefully to the voice of the Lord your God and do what is right in his eyes, if you pay attention to his commands and keep all his decrees, I will not bring on you any of the diseases I brought on the Egyptians, for I am the Lord who heals you." The dynamic of this promise is simply that God is always the healer. He will bring healing to your life when you seek and follow him.

SIXTEEN

Coming to Grips With the S-Word

God wants you to live a pure life.

Keep yourselves from sexual promiscuity.

Learn to appreciate and give dignity to your body,

not abusing it, as is common among those who

know nothing of God.

1 THESSALONIANS 4:3-5, THE MESSAGE

No, the S-word I am talking about is not "sin." It is "sex." Speaking about this issue to any single-again audience will usually triple the average attendance. The question most men and women want answered is this: *Is it right to have a sexual relationship outside of marriage?* All single-again adults came from having a sexual relationship with their spouse and often make the assumption that once sex is a part of your life, it is all right after a marriage ends as long as the other person desires it too.

We are constantly pounded with highly sexual media images and see a variety of sexual expression widely accepted in our culture. You do not have to watch too many movies or television programs to get the apparent message that it is acceptable to have sexual relationships with anyone, anytime, and almost anywhere. When you are bombarded by that message, it will affect your thoughts and actions even if you are a committed Christian trying to live by God's standards.

THE THREE ATTITUDES

Every person has a choice among three attitudes regarding sexual involvement. The first attitude proposes that if it feels good and the other person agrees, a sexual relationship is OK—no barriers, no limits, no rules. The second attitude is somewhat more restrictive; it accepts sex only if you are in a serious relationship with intentions of marriage. The third attitude rejects any sexual relationship except that between marriage partners. We might describe these three attitudes as wanton sex, selective sex, and no sex. I often ask newly single-again adults which of the three attitudes would best describe them, only to receive an answer like, "Well, I'm not sure. It all depends."

It is not my job to be a moral cop to anyone, but it is my responsibility to present the standards set forth in Scripture regarding the issue of sexuality. When a person decides to turn his life over to God and commits to following him, that person is under a new set of standards, which are clearly stated in the Bible. If a person is not attempting to follow God and his Word, he can do anything he wants as long as it is within the laws of our country.

Only the Christian is bound by the teachings of Scripture. When I talk about sexual standards, my first question is always, "Have you given your life to God, and is it your desire to follow and obey him?" If the answer is yes, my next question is, "What does the Bible teach about sexual issues?" After a blank look or two, I point to the instructions found in the Bible.

WHAT THE BIBLE SAYS

Paul gives a general principle for all behavior, saying, "So whether you eat or drink or whatever you do, do it all for the glory of God" (1 Cor 10:31). If that "whatever" had been left out, it would narrow our obedience level. But it is there, and it is comprehensive. You might feel the "whatever" means things like going to church, doing good deeds, relating to others, or being honest. But it also means how you relate to others sexually. The big question here is, *Can a sexual relationship outside of marriage bring glory to God?* If you are struggling with the issue of sex, you had better give a lot of thought and prayer to answering this question.

In all decisions we face, we should ask,

What would Jesus do?
Will what I am about to do bring glory to God?
Is this what God intends as his best for my life?

In most decision-making, those questions can be answered rather quickly and honestly, even though we may not want to follow the answer.

We add to this a second guideline found in 1 Corinthians 6:13-20, where the issue was whether early Christians could eat certain foods and still honor God. Paul stated his instructions clearly:

"Food for the stomach and the stomach for food"—but God will destroy them both. The body is not meant for sexual immorality, but for the Lord, and the Lord for the body. By his power God raised the Lord from the dead, and he will raise us also. Do you not know that your bodies are members of Christ himself? Shall I then take the members of Christ and unite them with a prostitute? Never! Do you not know that he who unites himself with a prostitute is one with her in body? For it is said, "The two will become one flesh." But he who unites himself with the Lord is one with him in spirit.

Flee sexual immorality. All other sins a man commits are outside his body, but he who sins sexually sins against his own body. Do you not know that your body is a temple of the Holy Spirit, who is in you, whom you have received from God? You are not your own; you were bought at a price. Therefore honor God with your body.

That's one solid piece of biblical advice. These are some of the toughest instructions regarding the body that Paul wrote. His warning is that you cannot just do whatever you want when you belong to God. You are compelled to do what God wants because you belong to him. The question is not, *What can I get away with?*, but *What pleases God?* When God lays down rules for living, they are not temporary and flexible. They are not easy. They require dedication, discipline, and commitment.

The sexual ethics of a Christian are determined by what God intended when he gave mankind the gift of sex. I believe God stamped that package with the words *Fragile! Handle With Care*, and, *Before Using, Read Instructions!* Sex was intended for pleasure and procreation only within the context of a marriage relationship. You can search for all the loopholes you want, but you will not find them in the Word of God. God does not specialize in situation ethics, standards that change daily depending on the situation.

God sets tough, lasting standards to live by. When they are followed, life is filled with joy and blessing. When they are not, well, just take a look around. Characters in Scripture who had sexual relationships outside of marriage fell under God's judgment. I appreciate people who can admit this area is a struggle for them but who want to work on it. They will find God's answer.

WHAT WILL YOU DO?

Read what the Bible teaches. If you don't like it, argue with God. Read a few books on sexuality from the Christian perspective. Spend time talking to God about it. He won't be shocked. Talk with other Christians about your feelings and struggles. God gives us a community to help at the hard places. Work to arrive at what you believe about sexual issues, and communicate them honestly. When you have a Christian standard and someone tries to get you to bend or discard that standard, you need to be strong enough not to allow it.

The temptation to engage in a sexual relationship can come from the nicest people you ever met at your friendly local Christian singles group. They may carry a ten-pound Bible everywhere, sing great praise and worship songs, and witness to everyone they meet. That can throw you the biggest curve ball in your life because you will say, "This person is a devout Christian, so engaging in sex with them can't be wrong." It is wrong and always will be if you believe what God's Word teaches. Temptation often comes from those you want to trust the most. Be careful out there!

GUIDELINES THAT WILL SERVE YOU WELL

Dealing with sexuality will always be present in the land beyond marriage. Questions, emotions, and feelings need to be sifted and sorted. The following guidelines come from years of listening to and empathizing with the single-again men and women that God has put in my pathway.

State your convictions about your sexual standards early on in a dating relationship. When you bring your standards for a sexual relationship into a discussion, you needn't share with an "I'm better than you" spiritual attitude. Be kind and matter-of-fact. Convictions shared are convictions strengthened. You may be helping your date clarify his or her standards also. Whatever you do, don't wait until the guessing games start: *Does he [she] have sex with any and all consenting adults? Is he [she] a prude? Is he [she] willing to compromise standards?*

The media promote sexual relationships outside the bonds of marriage as perfectly normal, and you can easily fall into that trap. The only thing that will keep you from absorbing secular standards is to adopt biblical ones, concluding with a "no compromise" clause. If you wait until someone is trying to wrestle you emotionally into a sexual relationship, it is too late to state your convictions and expect the other person to honor them.

Avoid the sexual traps. Too much time alone with someone in whom you are interested is dangerous ground. I've noticed many people vanish from singles groups once they start dating.

There is nothing wrong with spending time with somebody you like. You need to invest in a relationship for it to grow. But you also need accountability and community. Avoid being alone in a house or apartment when "The kids are with [a former spouse] for the weekend." Keep doing group activities. Let your circle of friends know how you are doing and that you are still around. Hang out with other people besides the person you are dating.

Feelings of rejection will also lead you into a trap if you give into them instead of trusting God to heal you. Many formerly married men and women who suffer from lack of love and attention go looking for it among fellow sufferers to prove they are still desirable and acceptable. Quite a few have told me privately they have been sleeping around because they were desperate to fill the emotional vacuum in their lives. They further admit that after a while it just doesn't work, isn't satisfying, and is downright dumb. Learn from that and don't start having sex just because you are hurt or lonely. Wait to date until you are well on the healing road.

Set up sexual boundaries. Boundaries are convictions with fences around them. A lack of boundaries shows up in comments like, "Let's live together and see if we're compatible," or, "Sex between us is OK because we're committed to marry eventually." Many Christians have told me God will understand because their end goal is marriage. Others say a signed certificate does not make a marriage happen anyway. But living together or having sex outside marriage is a nonverbal way of saying, "Rules are made for others; I am different." Vows, promises, and commitments are what make a marriage happen. The signed marriage certificate is a clear-cut boundary around them. After all, we sign documents when we buy a car, a home, or sign on for a credit card because a signature is the legal cultural way to agree on something. Is signing for *things* more important than signing for spiritual realities?

Should you make up your own rules in one of life's longest and most meaningful commitments? The nation of Israel felt they could bend the rules many times to fit their own game plan, only to have God bring judgment on them. Ultimate happiness comes from playing by his rules.

Don't lose control of your emotions. Keep yourself under control.
When we are in control of our emotions, life moves along fairly well. But when we are not, life gets pretty bumpy and can get distorted. In a relationship emotions often dictate what will happen next. Emotions are wrapped up in our sexuality, and our sexuality is often expressed through our emotions.

Years ago while I was in youth ministry, I spent a great deal of time trying to help teens understand the huge part emotions play in the sex drive and relationships. I told them it is hopeless to try to control your emotions after you have been "making out" in the car for a couple of hours on a perfect date. That is the wrong time to make a decision about sexual standards. The sexual act is a result of a chain reaction built into our human frame. Once set in motion, it is hard to throw the emotional switch into the off position.

These things are just as true for adults. But it is more difficult to dispense the rules to grown-ups who have been married and enjoyed the freedom of a sexual relationship. Without patronizing single-again men and women by setting down specific advice, let me simply say, get in touch with your emotions and know them. Begin to distinguish for yourself between affection and temptation. It may keep you from someday saying, "I don't know what came over me," or, "It just happened." Keep in touch with healthy emotions, and keep in touch with God.

Consider the consequences of sex before marriage. We are all familiar with the axiom, "For every action there is an equal and opposite reaction." Biblically we say, "Be sure your sin will find you out" (Nm 32:23b, KJV). Breaking a standard that God set is sin. Sin has consequences attached. I realize many people don't think in those terms today, but the rules haven't changed. If we keep God's rules, we experience the benefits: maintaining our integrity, building character, the absence of guilt and fear, enhanced self-esteem, the permanent joy of knowing you did the right thing by giving up a temporary high.

It is easy to join the bandwagon and say, "Everyone is doing it, so it must be OK." Some even say, "My feelings about this person are so strong, it can't be wrong." Remember Joseph? He had an opportunity to relax his sexual standards and sleep with Potiphar's wife. Scripture tells us he did a very simple thing. He ran away so fast he left his coat in her hands. No logic, no reason. He just ran. Think about that as you walk the dating road.

Avoid pseudo-intimacy. In their classic book *The Intimate Marriage,* authors Howard and Charlotte Clinebell say,

> Pseudo-intimacy is physical familiarity without interpersonal relatedness. Adolescents and older persons who are still adolescents emotionally often confuse a kind of mechanical sexual gratification with genuine human sexuality, which must include relatedness. Impersonal sex is dehumanized sex; it lacks that which makes human sex more than animal sex, an ongoing multileveled interpersonal relationship.[1]

There is a whole lot more to intimacy than sex. The Clinebells say, "[Sex] is being together both physically and emotionally, sharing in each others' worlds of feelings, hopes, anxieties and dreams, that keeps in good repair the bridge that joins two persons."[2] Most men and women desire that kind of complete human intimacy. When you realize that a sexual relationship outside of marriage cannot contain the other elements needed for fulfillment, you realize it is wise to raise the banner of sexual abstinence.

There are no easy answers about how to embrace your God-given sexuality without engaging in sex. The solution is not in rushing to the altar or in being standoffish and judgmental. But being a sexual person carries with it the responsibility to take care of yourself. It implies that you honor your body, protect it, supervise its activities, and realize its many functions are interwoven and dependent on each other. There is joy in being responsible to yourself, and loving yourself enough to say no when it's called for.

God's standards and directives bind a Christian. The Bible will not tell you if you should hold hands and kiss good night on your first date. It will not tell you how to handle raging hormones and the loss of human intimacy. It *will* tell you that God loves you very much and will not abandon you if you seek him. You have a choice: Do I want to live and walk in God's ways? Do I want to establish my own rules and live life my way? God gives you the right to decide. Choose well.

SEVENTEEN

Single Again and Stressed Out

He who is in a hurry delays the things of God.

St. Vincent de Paul

If all the issues and struggles talked about in this book were lumped into one person's existence, you would have someone suffering a mega-stress syndrome. Individual issues can be tough enough, but they are nearly impossible when compounded by fifteen others.

Twenty-five years ago, the word *stress* wasn't associated with the everyday struggle to survive. Today, it is the most-used response when someone says, "How are you doing?" Like we said in chapter one, when everything that can go wrong does go wrong, Murphy and his law become permanent tenants in your life. Stress becomes a mountain range that grows higher and higher with each passing day. We are stressed at the gym, where we go to relieve stress, at church, where we go to give our stress to God, and even when we sleep (even after taking our melatonin)—and whenever we think about how stressed we are! It would appear Planet Earth should be renamed Planet Stress.

How do you learn to live with focus and not have your goals constantly diverted by the forces of stress? Let's look at six kinds of stress. Identify the ones that are eating away at your spirit. Then I will offer practical and spiritual steps you can take to lower your stress level.

Emotional stress. The most common stress results from the continuous submerging of your own feelings in order to meet the emotional needs of everyone around you. Single parents know this firsthand because they usually try to take care of all their children's needs, desires, and concerns while ignoring their own. One mother said, "By the time I get around to meeting some of my emotional needs, I've been asleep for an hour!" Most single parents I know are tapped dry by the end of each day. They go to bed wondering if they can muster enough strength to meet the emotional challenges of tomorrow.

When you allow your life to be lived on that kind of treadmill, you will not only be stressed out but burned out as well. And when you are burned out, you become emotionally dead. You probably spend too little time checking the water level in your emotional well. When it suddenly runs dry, you are in trouble.

A good way to monitor your emotional needs is to take time to ask yourself, *Where am I emotionally right now? What emotional needs are not being met in my life?*

A good second step is to ask what it would take to meet some of those needs. Then make plans to do some of those things. If you are a single parent of small children, you need to have a few adult conversations during the week. If you are running a household and an office, once in a while you need freedom just to be yourself and not have to fulfill any obligations. If you are the problem-solver in everything, you need periods of time when there are no demands placed upon you. If your days are jammed with things to do every waking hour, you need to have a day to do anything you want—or absolutely nothing.

The two biggest emotional stresses are worry and fear. They gnaw away at the edges of your life and cause you to doubt your own strength and capabilities. I have learned that most of the things I worry about never happen. I have wasted good energies that could have been invested in better things. The fears I have had were best handled by building a strong faith and trust that God is always in charge. Scripture talks about mountain-moving faith. It takes that kind of faith to deal with emotional stress and the uncertainties of life.

Physical stress. The body breaks down when the emotions wage war. Any worthwhile physician will tell you quickly that emotions have a significant effect on the physical body, and when you are under emotional stress your body will start going downhill. If you believe your body is a gift from God and a temple for him, begin to monitor how your emotions affect your health.

The business community knows that good health means productivity, while declining health due to emotional and physical stress means loss of productivity and job dissatisfaction. There is a huge wellness movement in business supporting and encouraging physical care. Many corporations now have gyms, exercise programs, and recreational opportunities designed to keep their employees fit and healthy. The companies near the church where I work have their employees out walking every lunch hour. I have to be careful not to be mowed down by this moving mob at noontime.

My own medical clinic doesn't just treat illness, but emphasizes the need to be in better shape than you are at any given time. My personal doctor is constantly after me to run, work out, eat right, and get stronger.

Think about how you could become healthier. The more vital you are physically, the more vital you will feel and the more spiritual energy you will have, and vice versa.

Occupational stress. There was a time in our history when a person could accept employment with a giant corporation and expect to retire someday from that same corporation. Sometime in the 1980s that promise turned to myth, and the corporate world has been turned upside down. A friend of mine just accepted a position in another city. He will commute for four months, then move his family. I asked him the other day if his new job was secure enough to make this move. He laughed and said, "No job is secure anymore." We live in an era of vocational uncertainty. Occupational stress occurs in a world of downsizing, mergers, layoffs, buyouts, transfers, replacements, obsolescence, promotions, lack of promotions, and the bottom line, profits.

I oversee the men's ministry in my church and daily touch the lives of men and women who experience occupational stress, many the victims of downsizing or layoffs. Once I was asked to speak to forty corporate executives and their wives on the topic "How to keep your family together when your vocation is falling apart." Everyone is looking for vocational security. No one is finding it.

Single-again men and women are vulnerable to occupational stress because there is no backup by the salary of a spouse contributing to the family income. The stress level in a family where employment is uncertain is gigantic. That kind of stress affects daily life, future planning, economic survival, and emotional stability. Whatever stresses were in the family prior to the loss only get larger.

Relational stress. When emotional, physical, and occupational stress start shredding your life, it comes home and ends up becoming family stress. What happens *out there* ends up *in here* at the dining room table.

We live in the era of the changing face of family and the pain that accompanies the change. Even families that don't suffer loss of a spouse are struggling to keep up socially, spiritually, economically, physically, and emotionally. I have watched once stable and strong families come apart for many reasons. I doubt there has ever been a time in human history when more pressure has been placed upon the family. Children are divided, homes sold, possessions split, and everyone prays that all the members will survive on their own. Yes, a lot of prayer is needed along with maintaining personal disciplines and belonging to community.

We all struggle to keep relationships healthy and in balance. We try to build and maintain healthy relationships with God, ourselves, and each of the significant people in our lives. One man told me he could best be described as "a relational juggler." It takes a lot of time and energy to keep relationships in balance and growing.

Relational stress can also come when we spend too little time with the right people and too much time with the wrong people. Or it can be caused by the demands that relationships place upon us. The biggest demand in any relationship is simply the time you spend being physically present with the other and in doing things with him or her. Are you doing what they prefer to do or are they doing what you prefer? People become irritable when always actualizing the other person's agenda. You need to spend time doing some of each, and make sure some of your needs are also being met.

In the world of single-again men and women, relational stress can also be caused by losing relationships you value and struggling to build new ones. I overheard a group of single adults laughing, joking, and kidding each other about finding the right person. Then one of them asked the others, "How long do you guys think it will take all of us to find the right person?" Good question. I just pray the answer won't cause them more relational stress!

I cannot overemphasize how important a support system is to your well-being and personal growth. Good relational balance means building right relationships that are part of your life during good and bad times.

Spiritual stress. This may sound strange because the spiritual area should bring joy, not stress, right? Spiritual stress often centers on what we think God demands of us, what our church demands of us, and what we demand of ourselves. We measure ourselves by comparing our spirituality to that of people around us, even though this is not how God measures any of us. His measuring stick for us is our personal relationship to Jesus Christ and God's Word, the Bible. Remember that he saved you and me because he loved us all. Love and grace is his motivation toward and plan for us.

We get that mixed up with works and then contend with spiritual burnout. This happens to people who get too involved in their church or too involved in themselves. I am not saying that being spiritual will cause burnout. But if you try to do more spiritually than you are capable of doing, you will grow.

A good sermon or two on dedication and commitment can raise your guilt barometer enough to keep you solidly on the burnout track. Most churches will keep you going seven days a week attending their functions, serving on their committees and filling ministry vacancies, and working hard to get the Outstanding Christian Volunteer of the Year Award. I believe everyone in church should have one job and do it well. If that were so, guilt and burnout would vanish overnight.

Too many Christians cling to the *performance* model of spiritual growth, rather than the *faith* model. God is not impressed with how much we do. He is concerned with who we are and how faithful we are in following him. Some days we need to step back and ask, "Where is God in all this I am so busy doing?"

The accountability thing. We all need a few people who can circle their wagons around us once in a while and give us a stress test. We need kindred spirits who can ask us the right questions and challenge us to give truthful answers. Of course, everyone tells me they want that until they are faced with accountability. Then they want to make their own decisions, regardless of how poor those decisions might be.

I have a few guidelines that help me keep from becoming stressed out. You might find them helpful in getting and keeping your life in balance.

- Learn to say, "No." "Yes" people burn out faster than "no" people do.
- Realize you are not the Messiah. Jesus still is.
- Run away for a while when you really need to. Jesus did that.
- Get your priorities straight. Nonpriorities will bury you.
- Be good to yourself. Occasionally do something just for you.

- Plan times of inner renewal. Find a monastery!
- Don't take yourself too seriously. Others don't.
- Set some boundaries in your life. No one else will.
- Find some accountability people. Become accountable.
- Listen when God speaks. He likes that.

These ten guidelines are not meant just to be read and then passed by. They are meant to be done. They will take some time to accomplish, but I guarantee the stress levels in your life will descend rapidly if you do them. You can apply this verse to the assignment: "Commit to the Lord whatever you do, and your plans will succeed" (Prv 16:3). Live it out in your daily journey.

You cannot avoid sources of stress, but you can make a choice about how to deal with them. You can allow them to run you down, or you can run them down. You can act upon them, or you can react to them. God is bigger than any stress that will come into your life. He is a specialist in stress resolution. He waits for you to give him the opportunity.

Afterword

Any life crisis can turn you in a direction you had not planned to go. It can present you with foreboding challenges. It can shake your faith to its foundations, or build your faith to new heights. It can knock you off your track and set you on another, headed for a new destination.

Becoming single again will do all of the above and a whole lot more. The despair and new hope of this uncertain journey was made real to me this morning when one of our divorce recovery leaders grabbed me after church and proudly showed me her new engagement ring. She and her soon-to-be husband wore rainbows of smiling happiness. I congratulated them, and we talked about setting the wedding date. I walked away thinking of the night three years before when that same woman had attended the first night of a divorce recovery seminar. She had been broken, crushed, and emotionally shattered by the ominous thought of facing the world as a single parent. Between our first meeting that night and our happy encounter today, she has lived through many of the struggles addressed in these pages.

It is this lady and others like her who keep me working in a challenging ministry to single-again men and women. These people have shown me the healing and happiness that happens when the issues and principles described in this book are lived out one day at a time. With the help of God and a strong supportive community, you can move beyond the loss of a spouse and open a window of hope to a new tomorrow.

I want to ask one final question before you close this book. It comes from the life of the prophet Elijah (1 Kgs 18-19). Elijah had just celebrated his most triumphant victory as a prophet of the living God. The power of God had ignited his altar fire, while the prophets who had prayed to the false god Baal continued to stare at their wet and unlit altar. The people rejoiced and declared their desire to follow the one true God. It was a moment of great celebration and victory for Elijah. But the celebration was cut short when Queen Jezebel declared that Elijah would pay with his life.

Elijah took off running into the wilderness to hide from Jezebel and her troops. 1 Kings 19:9 tells us, "He went into a cave, and spent the night in that place; and behold, the word of the Lord came to him, and He said to him, "What are you doing here, Elijah?"(NKJV).

Elijah's answer was simple: "I am running away to save my life."

God instructed him to go and stand on the mountain, and when he did, God displayed a set of heavenly fireworks like Elijah had never seen. At the conclusion of the violent windstorm, the crashing earthquake, and the incendiary fire, God spoke to him in a still, small voice, again asking the question, "What are you doing here, Elijah?"

That is my question to you today. *What are you doing here, wherever you are today?*

God had performed a great miracle for Elijah. The enemy issued a death warrant. The prophet hit the road, ran into the wilderness, and found a cave, in which he hid from both the good and bad that had happened. God gave Elijah a little lesson about himself by performing awesome deeds with awesome power. He was literally shouting, "Hey, Elijah! Remember that altar fire? Well, I am still the same God, and these three things I have just shown you should remind you of that! Now Elijah, if you know that, what in the world are you doing hiding out in this cave?"

What are you doing, wherever you are today? Good and bad are, and always will be, part of your uncertain journey. You will always have a choice to make: hide out or face God and trust him. Get the picture? You may have forgotten just how powerful God is as you walk along this new road. You do not need to run away from God or your fears. You do not need to go hide in a cave somewhere. You can boldly place your hand in God's hand and with his help and guidance, take steps confidently and courageously forward every day.

If God's question to Elijah is the one he is asking you today, what is your answer? If it is, "I don't know what I'm doing here," then it is time to ask God for his directions. Remember Proverbs 3:5-6? "Trust in the Lord with all your heart and lean not on your own understanding; in all your ways acknowledge him, and *he will make your paths straight*" (emphasis added).

The journey ahead may look uncertain, but God is certain to guide you if you let him.

LIFE EVALUATION QUESTIONS

Change comes about in our lives when we are asked the right questions and are given freedom to wrestle with the answers. The following questions will be helpful for you to think about. Write your responses on a separate sheet of paper. Don't hurry. This can't be done quickly. Be thoughtful and prayerful as you answer.

THE PEOPLE IN MY LIFE

Who are the most valuable people in my support system?

What does each of them add to my life?

Are there some people in my life that shouldn't be there?

Do I have friends that allow me to be who I am?

What type of friends do I value the most?

Who are my mentors?

Do I need a mentor in my life right now?

Among my friendships, who are my heroes or role models?

Which of my friends are willing to ask me the hard questions?

To whom in my life do I need to say, "Thank you"?

If I had to lose all my friends but one, whom would I keep?

Who in my life holds me accountable for who I am and what I do?

Who helps me see my relationships and mission in life clearly?

Who encourages and affirms me the most?

How do I define myself in terms of my relationships?

Do I make any unreasonable demands on people?

Do people make any unreasonable demands on me?

How does it seem other people view me?

MY PERSONAL LIFE

Who am I, and what do I value?

In what ways am I talented?

What would I be willing to die for?

Where in my life do I feel trapped?

Do I like who I am?

Am I too self-critical?

Do I relate to others well?

Do I share my feelings honestly?

Whom do I blame when I fail?

What have I learned from the defeats in my life?

How do I cope with stress and pressure?

What kind of shape am I in physically?

What are my inner needs?

Do I accept challenges readily?

What would I change if I could change anything about the yesterdays in my life?

What dreams do I have that I fear sharing with others?

Do I wish I were someone else? Who?

Do I feel good about who I am?

Do I feel I am a person of great worth to others?

Do I know that I am God's unique, unrepeatable miracle?

Has life has been unfair to me?

What is my most valuable possession?

How can I be more effective in helping others?

How do I handle my fears?

MY SPIRITUAL LIFE

Who are my spiritual friends?

Who makes God more real to me?

When in my life have I most powerfully felt God's presence?

If I could be any biblical character, who would I be and why?

What are my spiritual gifts?

Do I have strong convictions of my own?

Where have I adopted the convictions of others?

How would I describe myself spiritually?

How would I describe my daily walk with God?

What is the biggest prayer request God answered in my life?

What would I tell God if I had five minutes with him?

What five spiritual convictions are strongest in my life?

With which known spiritual leader would I like to spend time?

What would I ask that person?

If God gave me only one prayer, what would it be?

How would I measure my spiritual growth the past two years?

What was the spiritual high point in my life to date?

What was the spiritual low point to date?

How well do I know the Lord?

Have I committed my life to the Lord?

Am I willing to follow wherever he leads me?

What spiritual gifts do I possess that I am not using?

MY JOB (CAREER)

Does my job cause me more happiness than unhappiness?

Career-wise, where do I want to be five years from now?

If I could have any job, what would it be?

If I could quit working, what would I do with my time?

Am I trapped in my career?

MY GOALS

What is the most significant change I have made during the past year?

What do I want to be doing in ten years? In five years?

What changes would I like to make in my life this year?

Am I missing anything in my life that is important to me?

What am I passionate about?

What would I do if I knew I could not fail?

If I could live anywhere on earth, where would it be?

What unexpressed dreams do I have?

If I could roll back time, where would I stop and why?

Is the window of hope wide open in my life?

AND FINALLY ...

What other questions may become measuring sticks as I grow?

Endnotes

CHAPTER 1

1. Robert Veninga, *A Gift of Hope* (New York: Ballantine, 1996).

CHAPTER 2

1. *Webster's College Dictionary* (New York: Random House, 1996).

2. Les Carter and Jim Underwood, *The Significance Principle* (Nashville, Tenn.: Broadman and Holman, 1998).

CHAPTER 4

1. Paul Stanley and Robert Clinton, *Connecting* (Colorado Springs, Colo.: NavPress, 1992).
2. Dallas Willard, *The Divine Conspiracy* (San Francisco: Harper, 1998).
3. Steven Harper, *Embrace the Spirit* (Wheaton, Ill.: Victor Books, 1987).
4. Richard Foster, *Celebration of Discipline* (San Francisco: Harper and Row, 1978).

5. *The Daily Walk Bible* (Wheaton, Ill.: Tyndale, 1997).

CHAPTER 5

1. *Webster's New World Dictionary of the American Language* (New York: Simon and Schuster, 1964).

CHAPTER 11

1. Jim Smoke, *Growing in Remarriage* (Grand Rapids, Mich.: Fleming Revell, 1990).

CHAPTER 14

1. Charles Monroe Sheldon, *In His Steps* (New York: Grosset and Dunlap, 1935).

CHAPTER 15

1. Dennis and Matthew Linn, *Healing Life's Hurts* (New York: Paulist Press, 1978).
2. Henri Nouwen, *The Wounded Healer* (Garden City, N.Y.: Image Books, 1979), 94.

CHAPTER 16

1. Howard and Charlotte Clinebell, *The Intimate Marriage* (San Francisco: Harper and Row, 1970), 48.
2. Clinebell, 9.

Virgin River

Robyn Carr

MILLS & BOON

Mills & Boon
An imprint of HarperCollins*Publishers* Ltd
1 London Bridge Street
London SE1 9GF

This paperback edition 2020

First published in Great Britain by MIRA,
an imprint of HarperCollins*Publishers* Ltd 2008

ISBN: 978-1-84845-820-8

MIX
Paper from
responsible sources
FSC   **FSC™ C007454**
www.fsc.org

This book is produced from independently certified FSC™ paper
to ensure responsible forest management.

For more information visit: www.harpercollins.co.uk/green

Printed and bound in Great Britain by
CPI Group (UK) Ltd, Croydon, CR0 4YY

This novel is dedicated to Pam Glenn,
Goddess of Midwifery,
my friend and sister of my heart.

Also available from Robyn Carr

Sullivan's Crossing
WHAT WE FIND
THE FAMILY GATHERING
THE BEST OF US

Virgin River
VIRGIN RIVER
SHELTER MOUNTAIN
WHISPERING ROCK
A VIRGIN RIVER CHRISTMAS
SECOND CHANCE PASS
TEMPTATION RIDGE
PARADISE VALLEY
FORBIDDEN FALLS
ANGEL'S PEAK
MOONLIGHT ROAD
PROMISE CANYON
WILD MAN CREEK
HARVEST MOON
BRING ME HOME FOR CHRISTMAS
HIDDEN SUMMIT
REDWOOD BEND
SUNRISE POINT
MY KIND OF CHRISTMAS

Virgin River

One

Mel squinted into the rain and darkness, creeping along the narrow, twisting, muddy, tree-enshrouded road, and for the hundredth time thought, *Am I out of my mind?* And then she heard and felt a thump as the right rear wheel of her BMW slipped off the road onto the shoulder and sank into the mud. The car rocked to a stop. She accelerated and heard the wheel spin but she was going nowhere fast.

I am so screwed, was her next thought.

She turned on the dome light and looked at her cell phone. She'd lost the signal an hour ago when she left the freeway and headed up into the mountains. In fact, she'd been having a pretty lively discussion with her sister Joey when the steep hills and unbelievably tall trees blocked the signal and cut them off.

"I cannot believe you're really doing this," Joey was saying. "I thought you'd come to your senses. This isn't *you,* Mel! You're not a small-town girl!"

"Yeah? Well, it looks like I'm gonna be—I took the job and sold everything, so I wouldn't be tempted to go back."

"You couldn't just take a leave of absence? Maybe go to a small, private hospital? Try to think this through?"

"I need everything to be different," Mel said. "No more hospital war zone. I'm just guessing, but I imagine I won't be called on to deliver a lot of crack babies out here in the woods. The woman said this place, this Virgin River, is calm and quiet and safe."

"And stuck back in the forest, a million miles from a Starbucks, where you'll get paid in eggs and pig's feet and—"

"And none of my patients will be brought in hand-cuffed, guarded by a corrections officer." Then Mel took a breath and, unexpectedly, laughed and said, "Pig's feet? Oh-oh, Joey—I'm going up into the trees again, I might lose you…"

"You wait. You'll be sorry. You'll regret this. This is crazy and impetuous and—"

That's when the signal, blessedly, was lost. And Joey was right—with every additional mile, Mel was doubting herself and her decision to escape into the country.

At every curve the roads had become narrower and the rain a little harder. It was only 6:00 p.m., but it was already dark as pitch; the trees were so dense and tall that even that last bit of afternoon sun had been blocked. Of course there were no lights of any kind along this winding stretch. According to the directions, she should be getting close to the house where she was to meet her new employer, but she didn't dare get out of her swamped car and walk. She could get lost in these woods and never be seen again.

Instead, she fished the pictures from her briefcase in an attempt to remind herself of a few of the reasons why she had taken this job. She had pictures of a quaint little hamlet of clapboard houses with front porches and dormer windows, an old-fashioned schoolhouse, a stee-pled church, hollyhocks, rhododendrons and blossom-ing apple trees in full glory, not to mention the green pastures upon which livestock grazed. There was the pie and coffee shop, the corner store, a tiny one-room, freestanding library, and the adorable little cabin in the woods that would be hers, rent-free, for the year of her contract.

The town backed up to the amazing sequoia red-woods and national forests that spanned hundreds of miles of wilderness over the Trinity and Shasta moun-tain ranges. The Virgin River, after which the town was named, was deep, wide, long, and home to huge salmon, sturgeon, steel fish and trout. She'd looked on the internet at pictures of that part of the world and was easily convinced no more beautiful land existed. Of course, she could see nothing now except rain, mud and darkness.

Ready to get out of Los Angeles, she had put her résumé with the Nurses' Registry and one of the recruit-ers brought Virgin River to her attention. The town doc-tor, she said, was getting old and needed help. A woman from the town, Hope McCrea, was donating the cabin and the first year's salary. The county was picking up the tab for liability insurance for at least a year to get a practitioner and midwife in this remote, rural part of the world. "I faxed Mrs. McCrea your résumé and let-ters of recommendation," the recruiter had said, "and she wants you. Maybe you should go up there and look the place over."

Mel took Mrs. McCrea's phone number and called her that evening. Virgin River was far smaller than what she'd had in mind, but after no more than an hour-long conversation with Mrs. McCrea, Mel began effecting her move out of L.A. the very next morning. That was barely two weeks ago.

What they didn't know at the Registry, nor in Virgin River for that matter, was that Mel had become desperate to get away. Far away. She'd been dreaming of a fresh start, and peace and quiet, for months. She couldn't remember the last time she'd had a restful night's sleep. The dangers of the big city, where crime seemed to be overrunning the neighborhoods, had begun to consume her. Just going to the bank and the store filled her with anxiety; danger seemed to be lurking everywhere. Her work in the three-thousand-bed county hospital and trauma center brought to her care the victims of too many crimes, not to mention the perpetrators of crimes hurt in pursuit or arrest—strapped to hospital beds in wards and in Emergency, guarded by cops. What was left of her spirit was hurting and wounded. And that was nothing to the loneliness of her empty bed.

Her friends begged her to stave off this impulse to run for some unknown small town, but she'd been in grief group, individual counseling and had seen more of the inside of a church in the last nine months than she had in the last ten years, and none of that was helping. The only thing that gave her any peace of mind was fantasizing about running away to some tiny place in the country where people didn't have to lock their doors, and the only thing you had to fear were the deer getting in the vegetable garden. It seemed like sheer heaven.

But now, sitting in her car looking at the pictures by the dome light, she realized how ridiculous she'd been. Mrs. McCrea told her to pack only durable clothes—jeans and boots—for country medicine. So what had she packed? Her boots were Stuart Weitzmans, Cole

Haans and Fryes—and she hadn't minded paying over a tidy four-fifty for each pair. The jeans she had packed for traipsing out to the ranches and farms were Rock & Republics, Joe's, Luckys, 7 For All Mankind—they rang up between one-fifty and two-fifty a copy. She'd been paying three hundred bucks a pop to have her hair trimmed and highlighted. After scrimping for years through college and post-grad nursing, once she was a nurse practitioner with a very good salary she discovered she loved nice things. She might have spent most of her workday in scrubs, but when she was out of them, she liked looking good.

She was sure the fish and deer would be very impressed.

In the past half hour she'd only seen one old truck on the road. Mrs. McCrea hadn't prepared her for how perilous and steep these roads were, filled with hairpin turns and sharp drop-offs, so narrow in some places that it would be a challenge for two cars to pass each other. She was almost relieved when the dark consumed her, for she could at least see approaching headlights around each tight turn. Her car had sunk into the shoulder on the side of the road that was up against the hill and not the ledge where there were no guardrails. Here she sat, lost in the woods and doomed. With a sigh, she turned around and pulled her heavy coat from the top of one of the boxes on the backseat. She hoped Mrs. McCrea would be traversing this road either en route to or from the house where they were to meet. Otherwise, she would probably be spending the night in the car. She still had a couple of apples, some crackers and two cheese rounds in wax. But the damn Diet Coke was gone—she'd have the shakes and a headache by morning from caffeine withdrawal.

No Starbucks. She should have done a better job of stocking up.

She turned off the engine, but left the lights on in case a car came along the narrow road. If she wasn't rescued, the battery would be dead by morning. She settled back and closed her eyes. A very familiar face drifted into her mind: Mark. Sometimes the longing to see him one more time, to talk to him for just a little while was overwhelming. Forget the grief—she just missed him—missed having a partner to depend on, to wait up for, to wake up beside. An argument over his long hours even seemed appealing. He told her once, "This—you and me—this is forever."

Forever lasted four years. She was only thirty-two and from now on she would be alone. He was dead. And she was dead inside.

A sharp tapping on the car window got her attention and she had no idea if she'd actually been asleep or just musing. It was the butt of a flashlight that had made the noise and holding it was an old man. The scowl on his face was so jarring that she thought the end she feared might be upon her.

"Missy," he was saying. "Missy, you're stuck in the mud."

She lowered her window and the mist wet her face. "I... I know. I hit a soft shoulder."

"That piece of crap won't do you much good around here," he said.

Piece of crap indeed! It was a new BMW convertible, one of her many attempts to ease the ache of loneliness. "Well, no one told me that! But thank you very much for the insight."

His thin white hair was plastered to his head and his bushy white eyebrows shot upwards in spikes; the rain glistened on his jacket and dripped off his big nose. "Sit tight, I'll hook the chain around your bumper and pull you out. You going to the McCrea house?"

Well, that's what she'd been after—a place where everyone knows everyone else. She wanted to warn him not to scratch the bumper but all she could do was stammer, "Y-yes."

"It ain't far. You can follow me after I pull you out."

"Thanks," she said.

So, she would have a bed after all. And if Mrs. Mc-Crea had a heart, there would be something to eat and drink. She began to envision the glowing fire in the cottage with the sound of spattering rain on the roof as she hunkered down into a deep, soft bed with lovely linens and quilts wrapped around her. Safe. Secure. At last.

Her car groaned and strained and finally lurched out of the ditch and onto the road. The old man pulled her several feet until she was on solid ground, then he stopped to remove the chain. He tossed it into the back of the truck and motioned for her to follow him. No argument there—if she got stuck again, he'd be right there to pull her out. Along she went, right behind him, using lots of window cleaner with her wipers to keep the mud he splattered from completely obscuring her vision.

In less than five minutes, the blinker on the truck was flashing and she followed him as he made a right turn at a mailbox. The drive was short and bumpy, the road full of potholes, but it quickly opened up into a clearing. The truck made a wide circle in the clearing so he could leave again, which left Mel to pull right up to…a *hovel!*

This was no adorable little cottage. It was an A-frame with a porch all right, but it looked as though the porch was only attached on one side while the other end had broken away and listed downward. The shingles were black with rain and age and there was a board nailed over one of the windows. It was not lit within or without; there was no friendly curl of smoke coming from the chimney.

The pictures were lying on the seat beside her. She blasted on her horn and jumped immediately out of the car, clutching the pictures and pulling the hood of her wool jacket over her head. She ran to the truck. He rolled down his window and looked at her as if she had a screw loose. "Are you sure this is the McCrea cottage?"

"Yup."

She showed him the picture of the cute little A-frame cottage with Adirondack chairs on the porch and hanging pots filled with colorful flowers decorating the front of the house. It was bathed in sunlight in the picture.

"Hmm," he said. "Been a while since she looked like that."

"I wasn't told that. She said I could have the house rent free for a year, plus salary. I'm supposed to help out the doctor in this town. But this—?"

"Didn't know the doc needed help. He didn't hire you, did he?" he asked.

"No. I was told he was getting too old to keep up with the demands of the town and they needed another doctor, but that I'd do for a year or so."

"Do what?"

She raised her voice to be heard above the rain. "I'm a nurse practitioner. And certified nurse midwife."

That seemed to amuse him. "That a fact?"

"You know the doctor?" she asked.

"Everybody knows everybody. Seems like you shoulda come up here and look the place over and meet the doc before making up your mind."

"Yeah, seems like," she said in some self-recrimination. "Let me get my purse—give you some money for pulling me out of the—" But he was already waving her off.

"Don't want your money. People up here don't have money to be throwing around for neighborly help. So," he said with humor, lifting one of those wild white eyebrows, "looks like she got one over on you. That place's been empty for years now." He chuckled. "Rent free! Hah!"

Headlights bounced into the clearing as an old Suburban came up the drive. Once it arrived the old man said, "There she is. Good luck." And then he laughed. Actually, he *cackled* as he drove out of the clearing.

Mel stuffed the picture under her jacket and stood in the rain near her car as the Suburban parked. She could've gone to the porch to get out of the elements, but it didn't look quite safe.

The Suburban's frame was jacked up and the tires were huge—no way that thing was getting stuck in the mud. It was pretty well splashed up, but it was still obvious it was an older model. The driver trained the lights on the cottage and left them on as the door opened. Out of the SUV climbed this itty-bitty elderly woman with thick, springy white hair and black framed glasses too big for her face. She was wearing rubber boots and was swallowed up by a rain slicker, but she couldn't have been five feet tall. She pitched a cigarette into the mud and, wearing a huge toothy smile, she approached Mel. "Welcome!" she said gleefully in the same deep, throaty voice Mel recognized from their phone conversation.

"Welcome?" Mel mimicked. "Welcome?" She pulled the picture from the inside of her jacket and flashed it at the woman. "This is not that!"

Completely unruffled, Mrs. McCrea said, "Yeah, the place could use a little sprucing up. I meant to get over here yesterday, but the day got away from me."

"Sprucing up? Mrs. McCrea, it's falling down! You said it was *adorable! Precious* is what you said!"

"My word," Mrs. McCrea said. "They didn't tell me at the Registry that you were so melodramatic."

"And they didn't tell me you were delusional!"

"Now, now, that kind of talk isn't going to get us anywhere. Do you want to stand in the rain or go inside and see what we have?"

"I'd frankly like to turn around and drive right out of this place, but I don't think I'd get very far without four-wheel drive. Another little thing you might've mentioned."

Without comment, the little white-haired sprite stomped up the three steps and onto the porch of the cabin. She didn't use a key to unlock the door but had to apply a firm shoulder to get it to open. "Swollen from the rain," she said in her gravelly voice, then disappeared inside.

Mel followed, but didn't stomp on the porch as Mrs. McCrea had. Rather, she tested it gingerly. It had a dangerous slant, but appeared to be solid in front of the door. A light went on inside just as Mel reached the door. Immediately following the dim light came a cloud of choking dust as Mrs. McCrea shook out the tablecloth. It sent Mel back out onto the porch, coughing. Once she recovered, she took a deep breath of the cold, moist air and ventured back inside.

Mrs. McCrea seemed to be busy trying to put things right, despite the filth in the place. She was pushing chairs up to the table, blowing dust off lampshades, propping books on the shelf with bookends. Mel had a look around, but only to satisfy her curiosity as to how horrid it was, because there was no way she was staying. There was a faded floral couch, a matching chair and ottoman, an old chest that served as a coffee table and a brick and board bookcase, the boards unfinished. Only a few steps away, divided from the living room by a counter, was the small kitchen. It hadn't seen a cleaning since the last person made dinner—presumably years ago. The refrigerator and oven doors stood open, as did most of the cupboard doors. The sink was full of pots and dishes; there were stacks of dusty dishes and plenty of cups and glasses in the cupboards, all too dirty to use.

"I'm sorry, this is just unacceptable," Mel said loudly.

"It's a little dirt is all."

"There's a bird's nest in the oven!" Mel exclaimed, completely beside herself.

Mrs. McCrea clomped into the kitchen in her muddy rubber boots, reached into the open oven door and plucked out the bird's nest. She went to the front door and pitched it out into the yard. She shoved her glasses up on her nose as she regarded Mel. "No more bird's nest," she said in a voice that suggested Mel was trying her patience.

"Look, I'm not sure I'd make it. That old man in the pickup had to pull me out of the mud just down the road. I can't stay here, Mrs. McCrea—it's out of the question. Plus, I'm starving and I don't have any food with me." She laughed hollowly. "You said there would be adequate housing ready for me, and I took you to mean clean and stocked with enough food to get me through a couple of days till I could shop for myself. But this—"

"You have a contract," Mrs. McCrea pointed out.

"So do *you*," Mel said. "I don't think you could get anyone to agree this is adequate or ready."

Hope looked up. "It's not leaking, that's a good sign."

"Not quite good enough, I'm afraid."

"That damned Cheryl Creighton was supposed to be down here to give it a good cleaning, but she had excuses three days in a row. Been drinking again is my guess. I got some bedding in the truck and I'll take you to get dinner. It'll look better in the morning."

"Isn't there some place else I can stay tonight? A bed-and-breakfast? A motel on the highway?"

"Bed-and-breakfast?" she asked with a laugh. "This look like a tourist spot to you? The highway's an hour off and this is no ordinary rain. I have a big house with no room in it—filled to the top with junk. They're gonna light a match to it when I die. It would take all night to clear off the couch."

"There must be something…"

"Nearest thing is Jo Ellen's place—she's got a nice spare room over the garage she lets out sometimes. But you wouldn't want to stay there. That husband of hers can be a handful. He's been slapped down by more than one woman in Virgin River—and it'd be a bad thing, you in your nightie, Jo Ellen sound asleep and him getting ideas. He's a groper, that one."

Oh, God, Mel thought. Every second this place sounded worse and worse.

"Tell you what we'll do, girl. I'll light the hot water heater, turn on the refrigerator and heater, then we'll go get a hot meal."

"At the pie and coffee shop?"

"That place closed down three years back," she said.

"But you sent me a picture of it—like it was where I'd be getting lunch or dinner for the next year!"

"Details. Lord, you do get yourself worked up."

"Worked up!?"

"Go jump in the truck and I'll be right along," she commanded. Then ignoring Mel completely, she went to the refrigerator and stooped to plug it in. The light went on immediately and Mrs. McCrea reached inside to adjust the temperature and close the door. The refrigerator's motor made an unhealthy grinding sound as it fired up.

Mel went to the Suburban as she'd been told, but it was so high off the ground she found herself grabbing the inside of the open door and nearly crawling inside. She felt a lot safer here than in the house where her hostess would be lighting a gas water heater. She had a passing thought that if it blew up and destroyed the cabin, they could cut their losses here and now.

Once in the passenger seat, she looked over her shoulder to see the back of the Suburban was full of pillows, blankets and boxes. Supplies for the falling-down house, she assumed. Well, if she couldn't get out of here tonight, she could sleep in her car if she had to. She wouldn't freeze to death with all those blankets. But then, at first light...

A few minutes passed and then Mrs. McCrea came out of the cottage and pulled the door closed. No locking up. Mel was impressed by the agility with which the old woman got herself into the Suburban. She put a foot on the step, grabbed the handle above the door with one hand, the armrest with the other and bounced herself right into the seat. She had a rather large pillow to sit on and her seat was pushed way up so she could reach the pedals. Without a word, she put the vehicle in gear and expertly backed down the narrow drive out onto the road.

"When we talked a couple weeks ago, you said you were pretty tough," Mrs. McCrea reminded her.

"I am. I've been in charge of a women's wing at a three-thousand-bed county hospital for the past two years. We got all the most challenging cases and hopeless patients, and did a damn fine job if I do say so myself. Before that, I spent years in the emergency room in downtown L.A., a very tough place by anyone's standards. By tough, I thought you meant medically. I didn't know you meant I should be an experienced frontier woman."

"Lord, you do go on. You'll feel better after some food."

"I hope so," Mel replied. But, inside she was saying, *I can't stay here. This was crazy, I'm admitting it and getting the hell out of here.* The only thing she really dreaded was owning up to Joey.

They didn't talk during the drive. In Mel's mind there wasn't much to say. Plus, she was fascinated by the ease, speed and finesse with which Ms. McCrea handled the big Suburban, bouncing down the tree-lined road and around the tight curves in the pouring rain.

She had thought this might be a respite from pain and loneliness and fear. A relief from the stress of patients who were either the perpetrators or victims of crimes, or devastatingly poor and without resources or hope. When she saw the pictures of the cute little town, it was easy to imagine a homey place where people needed her. She saw herself blooming under the grateful thanks of rosy-cheeked country patients. Meaningful work was the one thing that had always cut through any troubling personal issues. Not to mention the lift of escaping the smog and traffic and getting back to nature in the pristine beauty of the forest. She just never thought she'd be getting this far back to nature.

The prospect of delivering babies for mostly uninsured women in rural Virgin River had closed the deal. Working as a nurse practitioner was satisfying, but midwifery was her true calling.

Joey was her only family now; she wanted Mel to come to Colorado Springs and stay with her, her husband, Bill, and their three children. But Mel hadn't wanted to trade one city for another, even though Colorado Springs was considerably smaller. Now, in the absence of any better ideas, she would be forced to look for work there.

As they passed through what seemed to be a town, she grimaced again. "Is this the town? Because this wasn't in the pictures you sent me, either."

"Virgin River," she said. "Such as it is. Looks a lot better in daylight, that's for sure. Damn, this is a big rain. March always brings us this nasty weather. That's the doc's house there, where he sees patients when they come to him. He makes a lot of house calls, too. The library," she pointed. "Open Tuesdays."

They passed a pleasant-looking steepled church, which appeared to be boarded up, but at least she recognized it. There was the store, much older and more worn, the proprietor just locking the front door for the night. A dozen houses lined the street—small and old. "Where's the schoolhouse?" Mel asked.

"What schoolhouse?" Mrs. McCrea countered.

"The one in the picture you sent to the recruiter."

"Hmm. Can't imagine where I got that. We don't have a school. Yet."

"God," Mel groaned.

The street was wide, but dark and vacant—there

were no streetlights. The old woman must have gone through one of her ancient photo albums to come up with the pictures. Or maybe she snapped a few of another town.

Across the street from the doctor's house Mrs. McCrea pulled up to the front of what looked like a large cabin with a wide porch and big yard, but the neon sign in the window that said Open clued her in to the fact that it was a tavern or café. "Come on," Mrs. McCrea said. "Let's warm up your belly and your mood."

"Thank you," Mel said, trying to be polite. She was starving and didn't want an attitude to cost her her dinner, though she wasn't optimistic that anything but her stomach would be warm. She looked at her watch. Seven o'clock.

Mrs. McCrea shook out her slicker on the porch before going in, but Mel wasn't wearing a raincoat. Nor did she have an umbrella. Her jacket was now drenched and she smelled like wet sheep.

Once inside, she was rather pleasantly surprised. It was dark and woody with a fire ablaze in a big stone hearth. The polished wood floors were shiny clean and something smelled good, edible. Over a long bar, above rows of shelved liquor bottles, was a huge mounted fish; on another wall, a bearskin so big it covered half the wall. Over the door, a stag's head. Whew. A hunting lodge? There were about a dozen tables sans tablecloths and only one customer at the bar; the old man who had pulled her out of the mud sat slumped over a drink.

Behind the bar stood a tall man in a plaid shirt with sleeves rolled up, polishing a glass with a towel. He looked to be in his late thirties and wore his brown hair cropped close. He lifted expressive brows and his chin in greeting as they entered. Then his lips curved in a smile.

"Sit here," Hope McCrea said, indicating a table near the fire. "I'll get you something."

Mel took off her coat and hung it over the chair back near the fire to dry. She warmed herself, vigorously rubbing her icy hands together in front of the flames. This was more what she had expected—a cozy, clean cabin, a blazing fire, a meal ready on the stove. She could do without the dead animals, but this was what you got in hunting country.

"Here," the old woman said, pressing a small glass of amber liquid into her hand. "This'll warm you up. Jack's got some stew on the stove and bread in the warmer. We'll fix you up."

"What is it?" she asked.

"Brandy. You gonna be able to get that down?"

"Damn right," she said, taking a grateful sip and feeling it burn its way down to her empty belly. She let her eyes drift closed for a moment, appreciating the unexpected fine quality. She looked back at the bar, but the bartender had disappeared. "That guy," she finally said, indicating the only customer. "He pulled me out of the ditch."

"Doc Mullins," she explained. "You might as well meet him right now, if you're okay to leave the fire."

"Why bother?" Mel said. "I told you—I'm not staying."

"Fine," the old woman said tiredly. "Then you can say hello and goodbye all at once. Come on." She turned and walked toward the old doctor and with a weary sigh, Mel followed. "Doc, this is Melinda Monroe, in case you didn't catch the name before. Miss Monroe, meet Doc Mullins."

He looked up from his drink with rheumy eyes and regarded her, but his arthritic hands never left his glass. He gave another single nod.

"Thanks again," Mel said. "For pulling me out."

The old doctor gave a nod, looking back to his drink.

So much for the friendly small-town atmosphere, she thought. Mrs. McCrea was walking back to the fireplace. She plunked herself down at the table.

"Excuse me," Mel said to the doctor. He turned his gaze toward her, but his bushy white brows were drawn together in a definite scowl, peering over the top of his glasses. His white hair was so thin over his freckled scalp that it almost appeared he had more hair on his brows than his head. "Pleasure to meet you. So, you wanted help up here?" He just seemed to glare at her. "You didn't want help? Which is it?"

"I don't much need any help," he told her gruffly. "But that old woman's been trying to get a doc to replace me for years. She's driven."

"And why is that?" Mel bravely asked.

"Couldn't imagine." He looked back into his glass. "Maybe she just doesn't like me. Since I don't like her that much, makes no difference."

The bartender, and presumably proprietor, was carrying a steaming bowl out of the back, but he paused at the end of the bar and watched as Mel conversed with the old doctor.

"Well, no worries, mate," Mel responded, "I'm not staying. It was grossly misrepresented. I'll be leaving in the morning, as soon as the rain lets up."

"Wasted your time, did you?" he asked, not looking at her.

"Apparently. It's bad enough the place isn't what I

was told it would be, but how about the complication that you have no use for a practitioner or midwife?"

"There you go," he said.

Mel sighed. She hoped she could find a decent job in Colorado.

A young man, a teenager, brought a rack of glasses from the kitchen into the bar. He sported much the same look as the bartender with his short cropped, thick brown hair, flannel shirt and jeans. Handsome kid, she thought, taking in his strong jaw, straight nose, heavy brows. As he was about to put the rack under the bar, he stopped short, staring at Mel in surprise. His eyes grew wide; his mouth dropped open for a second. She tilted her head slightly and treated him to a smile. He closed his mouth slowly, but stood frozen, holding the glasses.

Mel turned away from the boy and the doctor. She headed for Mrs. McCrea's table. The bartender set down a bowl along with a napkin and utensils, then stood there awaiting her. He held the chair for her. Close up, she saw how big a guy he was—over six feet and broad-shouldered. "Miserable weather for your first night in Virgin River," he said pleasantly.

"Miss Melinda Monroe, this is Jack Sheridan. Jack, Miss Monroe."

Mel felt the urge to correct them—tell them it was Mrs. But she didn't because she didn't want to explain that there was no longer a Mr. Monroe, a Dr. Monroe in fact. So she said, "Pleased to meet you. Thank you," she added, accepting the stew.

"This is a beautiful place, when the weather cooperates," he said.

"I'm sure it is," she muttered, not looking at him.

"You should give it a day or two," he suggested.

She dipped her spoon into the stew and gave it a

taste. He hovered near the table for a moment. Then she looked up at him and said in some surprise, "This is delicious."

"Squirrel," he said.

She choked.

"Just kidding," he said, grinning at her. "Beef. Corn fed."

"Forgive me if my sense of humor is a bit off," she replied irritably. "It's been a long and rather arduous day."

"Has it now?" he said. "Good thing I got the cork out of the Remy, then." He went back behind the bar and she looked over her shoulder at him. He seemed to confer briefly and quietly with the young man, who continued to stare at her. His son, Mel decided.

"I don't know that you have to be quite so pissy," Mrs. McCrea said. "I didn't sense any of this attitude when we talked on the phone." She dug into her purse and pulled out a pack of cigarettes. She shook one out and lit it—this explained the gravelly voice.

"Do you have to smoke?" Mel asked her.

"Unfortunately, I do," Mrs. McCrea said, taking a long drag.

Mel just shook her head in frustration. She held her tongue. It was settled, she was leaving in the morning and would have to sleep in the car, so why exacerbate things by continuing to complain? Hope McCrea had certainly gotten the message by now. Mel ate the delicious stew, sipped the brandy, and felt a bit more secure once her belly was full and her head a tad light. *There,* she thought. *That is better. I can make it through the night in this dump. God knows, I've been through worse.*

It had been nine months since her husband, Mark, had stopped off at a convenience store after working a long night shift in the emergency room. He had wanted milk for his cereal. But what he got was three bullets, point-blank to the chest, killing him instantly. There had been a robbery in progress, right in a store he and Mel dropped into at least three times a week. It had ended the life she loved.

Spending the night in her car, in the rain, would be nothing by comparison.

Jack delivered a second Remy Martin to Miss Monroe, but she had declined a second serving of stew. He stayed behind the bar while she ate, drank and seemed to glower at Hope as she smoked. It caused him to chuckle to himself. The girl had a little spirit. What she also had was looks. Petite, blonde, flashing blue eyes, a small heart-shaped mouth, and a backside in a pair of jeans that was just awesome. When the women left, he said to Doc Mullins, "Thanks a lot. You could have cut the girl some slack. We haven't had anything pretty to look at around here since Bradley's old golden retriever died last fall."

"Humph," the doctor said.

Ricky came behind the bar and stood next to Jack. "Yeah," he heartily agreed. "Holy God, Doc. What's the matter with you? Can't you think of the rest of us sometimes?"

"Down, boy." Jack laughed, draping an arm over his shoulders. "She's outta your league."

"Yeah? She's outta yours, too," Rick said, grinning.

"You can shove off anytime. There isn't going to be anyone out tonight," Jack told Rick. "Take a little of that stew home to your grandma."

"Yeah, thanks," he said. "See you tomorrow."

When Rick had gone, Jack hovered over Doc and said, "If you had a little help, you could do more fishing."

"Don't need help, thanks," he said.

"Oh, there's that again," Jack said with a smile. Any suggestion Hope had made of getting Doc some help was stubbornly rebuffed. Doc might be the most obstinate and pigheaded man in town. He was also old, arthritic and seemed to be slowing down more each year.

"Hit me again," the doctor said.

"I thought we had a deal," Jack said.

"Half, then. This goddamn rain is killing me. My bones are cold." He looked up at Jack. "I did pull that little strumpet out of the ditch in the freezing rain."

"She's probably not a strumpet," Jack said. "I could never be that lucky." Jack tipped the bottle of bourbon over the old man's glass and gave him a shot. But then he put the bottle on the shelf. It was his habit to look out for Doc and, left unchecked, he might have a bit too much. He didn't feel like going out in the rain to be sure Doc got across the street all right. Doc didn't keep a supply at home, doing his drinking only at Jack's, which kept it under control.

Couldn't blame the old boy—he was overworked and lonely. Not to mention prickly.

"You could've offered the girl a warm place to sleep," Jack said. "It's pretty clear Hope didn't get that old cabin straight for her."

"Don't feel up to company," he said. Then Doc lifted his gaze to Jack's face. "Seems you're more interested than me, anyway."

"Didn't really look like she'd trust anyone around here at the moment," Jack said. "Cute little thing, though, huh?"

"Can't say I noticed," he said. He took a sip and then said, "Didn't look like she had the muscle for the job, anyway."

Jack laughed. "Thought you didn't notice?" But he had noticed. She was maybe five-three. Hundred and ten pounds. Soft, curling blond hair that, when damp, curled even more. Eyes that could go from kind of sad to feisty in an instant. He enjoyed that little spark when she had snapped at him that she didn't feel particularly humorous. And when she took on Doc, there was a light that suggested she could handle all kinds of things just fine. But the best part was that mouth—that little pink heart-shaped mouth. Or maybe it was the bottom.

"Yeah," Jack said. "You could've cut a guy a break and been a little friendlier. Improve the scenery around here."

Two

When Mel and Mrs. McCrea returned to the cabin, it had warmed up inside. Of course, it hadn't gotten any cleaner. Mel shuddered at the filth and Mrs. McCrea said, "I had no idea, when I talked to you, that you were so prissy."

"Well, I'm not. A labor and delivery unit in a big hospital like the one I came from is pretty unglamorous." And it struck Mel as curious that she had felt more in control in that chaotic, sometimes horrific environment than in this far simpler one. She decided it was the apparent deception that was throwing her for a loop. That and the fact that however gritty things got in L&D, she always had a comfortable and clean house to go home to.

Hope left her in possession of pillows, blankets, quilts and towels, and Mel decided it made more sense to brave the dirt than the cold. Retrieving only one suitcase from her car, she put on a sweatsuit, heavy socks, and made herself a bed on the dusty old couch. The mattress, stained and sagging, looked too frightening.

She rolled herself up in the quilts like a burrito and huddled down into the soft, musty cushions. The bathroom light was left on with the door pulled slightly closed, in case she had to get up in the night. And thanks to two brandies, the long drive and the stress of spoiled expectations, she fell into a deep sleep, for once not disturbed by anxiety or nightmares. The softly drumming rain on the roof was like a lullaby, rocking her to sleep. With the dim light of morning on her face, she woke to find she hadn't moved a muscle all night, but lay swaddled and still. Rested. Her head empty.

It was a rare thing.

Disbelieving, she lay there for a while. *Yes,* she thought. *Though it doesn't seem possible under the circumstances, I feel good.* Then Mark's face swam before her eyes and she thought, *what do you expect? You summoned it!*

She further thought, *There's nowhere you can go to escape grief. Why try?*

There was a time she had been so content, especially waking up in the morning. She had this weird and funny gift—music in her head. Every morning, the first thing she noticed was a song, clear as if the radio was on. Always a different one. Although in the bright light of day Mel couldn't play an instrument or carry a tune in a bucket, she awoke each morning humming along with a melody. Awakened by her off-key humming, Mark would rise up on an elbow, lean over her, grinning, and wait for her eyes to pop open. He would say, "What is it today?"

"'Begin the Beguine,'" she'd answer. Or, "'Deep Purple.'" And he'd laugh and laugh.

The music in her head went away with his death.

She sat up, quilts wrapped around her, and the morning light emphasized the dirty cabin that surrounded her. The sound of chirping birds brought her to her feet and to the cabin's front door. She opened it and greeted a morning that was bright and clear. She stepped out onto the porch, still wrapped in her quilts, and looked up—the pines, firs and ponderosa were so tall in daylight—rising fifty to sixty feet above the cabin, some considerably taller. They were still dripping from a rain that had washed them clean. Green pinecones were hanging from branches—pinecones so large that if a green one fell on your head, it might cause a concussion. Beneath them, thick, lush green fern—she counted four different types from wide-branched floppy fans to those as delicate as lace. Everything looked fresh and healthy. Birds sang and danced from limb to limb, and she looked into a sky that was an azure blue the likes of which she hadn't seen in Los Angeles in ten years. A puffy white cloud floated aimlessly above and an eagle, wings spread wide, soared overhead and disappeared behind the trees.

She inhaled a deep breath of the crisp spring morning. *Ah,* she thought. Too bad the cabin, town and old doctor didn't work out, because the land was lovely. Unspoiled. Invigorating.

She heard a crack and furrowed her brow. Without warning the end of the porch that had been sagging gave out completely, collapsing at the weak end which created a big slide, knocking her off her feet and splat! Right into a deep, wet, muddy hole. There she lay, a filthy, wet, ice-cold burrito in her quilt. "Crap," she said, rolling out of the quilt to crawl back up the porch, still attached at the starboard end. And into the house.

She packed up her suitcase. It was over.

At least the roads were now passable, and in the light of day she was safe from hitting a soft shoulder and sinking out of sight. Reasoning she wouldn't get far without at least coffee, she headed back toward the town, even though her instincts told her to run for her life, get coffee somewhere down the road. She didn't expect that bar to be open early in the morning, but her options seemed few. She might be desperate enough to bang on the old doctor's door and beg a cup of coffee from him, though facing his grimace again wasn't an inviting thought. But the doc's house looked closed up tighter than a tick. There didn't seem to be any action around Jack's or the store across the street, but a complete caffeine junkie, she tried the door at the bar and it swung open.

The fire was lit. The room, though brighter than the night before, was just as welcoming. It was large and comfortable—even with the animal trophies on the walls. Then she was startled to see a huge bald man with an earring glittering in one ear come from the back to stand behind the bar. He wore a black T-shirt stretched tight over his massive chest, the bottom of a big blue tattoo peeking out beneath one of the snug sleeves. If she hadn't gasped from the sheer size of him, she might've from the unpleasant expression on his face. His dark bushy brows were drawn together and he braced two hands on the bar. "Help you?" he asked.

"Um… Coffee?" she asked.

He turned around to grab a mug. He put it on the bar and poured from a handy pot. She thought about grabbing it and fleeing to a table, but she frankly didn't like the look of him, didn't want to insult him, so she went to the bar and sat up on the stool where her coffee waited. "Thanks," she said meekly.

He just gave a nod and backed away from the bar a bit, leaning against the counter behind him with his huge arms crossed over his chest. He reminded her of a nightclub bouncer or bodyguard. Jesse Ventura with attitude.

She took a sip of the rich, hot brew. Her appreciation for a dynamite cup of coffee surpassed any other comfort in her life and she said, "Ah. Delicious." No comment from the big man. Just as well, she thought. She didn't feel like talking anyway.

A few minutes passed in what seemed like oddly companionable silence when the side door to the bar opened and in came Jack, his arms laden with firewood. When he saw her, he grinned, showing a nice batch of even, white teeth. Under the weight of the wood his biceps strained against his blue denim shirt, the width of his shoulders accentuated a narrow waist. A little light brown chest hair peeked out of the opened collar and his clean-shaven face made her realize that the night before his cheeks and chin had been slightly shadowed by the day's growth of beard.

"Well, now," he said. "Good morning." He took the firewood to the hearth and when he stooped to stack it there, she couldn't help but notice a broad, muscular back and a perfect male butt. Men around here must get a pretty good workout just getting through the rugged days of rural living.

The big bald man lifted the pot to refill her cup when Jack said, "I got that, Preacher."

Jack came behind the bar and "Preacher" went through the door to the kitchen. Jack filled her cup.

"Preacher?" she asked in a near whisper.

"His name is actually John Middleton, but he got that nickname way back. If you called out to John, he wouldn't even turn around."

"Why do you call him that?" she asked.

"Ah, he's pretty straight-laced. Hardly ever swears, never see him drunk, doesn't bother women."

"He's a little frightening looking," she said, still keeping her voice low.

"Nah. He's a pussycat," Jack said. "How was your night?"

"Passable," she said with a shrug. "I didn't think I could make it out of town without a cup of coffee."

"You must be ready to kill Hope. She didn't even have coffee for you?"

"'Fraid not."

"I'm sorry about this, Miss Monroe. You should've had a better welcome than this. I don't blame you for thinking the worst of this place. How about some eggs?" He gestured over his shoulder. "He's a fine cook."

"I won't say no," she said. She felt that odd sensation of a smile on her lips. "And call me Mel."

"Short for Melinda," he said.

Jack hollered through the door to the kitchen. "Preacher. How about some breakfast for the lady?" Back at the bar, he said, "Well, the least we can do is send you off with a good meal—if you can't be convinced to stay a couple of days."

"Sorry," she said. "That cabin. It's uninhabitable. Mrs. McCrea said something about someone who was supposed to clean it—but she's drinking? I think I got that right."

"That would be Cheryl. Has a bit of a problem that way, I'm afraid. She should've called someone else. Plenty of women around here who'd take a little work."

"Well, it's irrelevant now," Mel said, sipping again. "Jack, this is the best coffee I've ever had. Either that, or I had a bad couple of days and am easily impressed by some creature comforts."

"No, it's really that good." He frowned and reached out, lifting a lock of her hair off her shoulder. "Do you have mud in your hair?"

"Probably," she said. "I was standing on the porch, appreciating the beauty of this nice spring morning when one end gave way and spilled me right into a big, nasty mud puddle. And I wasn't brave enough to try out the shower—it's beyond filthy. But I thought I got it all off."

"Oh, man," he said, surprising her with a big laugh. "Could you have had a worse day? If you'd like, I have a shower in my quarters—clean as a whistle." He grinned again. "Towels even smell like Downy."

"Thanks, but I think I'll just move on. When I get closer to the coast, I'm going to get a hotel room and have a quiet, warm, clean evening. Maybe rent a movie."

"Sounds nice," he said. "Then back to Los Angeles?"

She shrugged. "No," she said. She couldn't do that. Everything from the hospital to the house would conjure sweet memories and bring her grief to the surface. She just couldn't move on as long as she stayed in L.A. Besides, now there was nothing there for her anymore. "It's time for a change. But it turns out this was too big a change. Have you lived here all your life?"

"Me? No. Only a little while. I grew up in Sacramento. I was looking for a good place to fish and stayed on. I converted this cabin into a bar and grill and built on an addition to live in. Small, but comfortable. Preacher has a room upstairs, over the kitchen."

"What in the world made you stay on? I'm not trying to be flip—there doesn't seem to be that much of a town here."

"If you had the time, I'd show you. This is incredible country. Over six hundred people live in and around town. Lots of people from the cities have cabins up and down the Virgin River—it's peaceful and the fishing is excellent. We don't have much tourist traffic through town, but fishermen come in here pretty regularly and some hunters pass through during the season. Preacher is known for his cooking, and it's the only place in town to get a beer. We're right up against some redwoods— awesome. Majestic. Lots of campers and hikers around the national forests all through the summer. And the sky and air out here—you just can't find anything like it in a city."

"And your son works here with you?"

"Son? Oh," he laughed. "Ricky? He's a kid from town. He works around the bar after school most days. Good kid."

"You have family?" she asked.

"Sisters and nieces in Sacramento. My dad is still there, but I lost my mother a few years back."

Preacher came out of the kitchen holding a steaming plate with a napkin. As he sat it before Mel, Jack reached beneath the bar and produced silverware and a napkin. On the plate was a luscious-looking cheese omelet with peppers, sausage patties, fruit, home fries, wheat toast. Ice water appeared; her coffee was refilled.

Mel dipped into the omelet and brought it to her mouth. It melted there, rich and delicious. "Mmm," she said, letting her eyes close. After she swallowed she said, "I've eaten here twice, and I have to say the food is some of the best I've ever had."

"Me and Preacher—we can whip up some good food, sometimes. Preacher has a real gift. And he wasn't a cook until he got up here."

She took another bite. Apparently Jack was going to stand there through her meal and watch her devour every bite. "So," she said, "what's the story on the doctor and Mrs. McCrea?"

"Well, let's see," he said, leaning his back on the counter behind the bar, his arms wide, big hands braced on either side of him. "They tend to bicker. Two opinionated, stubborn old farts who can't agree on anything. The fact of the matter is, I think Doc could use help—but I imagine you gathered he's a bit on the obstinate side."

She made an affirmative noise, her mouth full of the most wonderful eggs she'd ever eaten.

"The thing about this little town is—sometimes days go by without anyone needing medical attention. Then there will be weeks when everyone needs to see Doc—a flu going around while three women are about to give birth, and right then someone will fall off a horse or roof. So it goes. And although he doesn't like to admit it, he is seventy." Jack gave a shrug. "Next town doctor is at least a half hour away and for rural people out on farms and ranches, over an hour. The hospital is farther yet. Then, we have to think about what will happen when Doc dies, which hopefully won't be too soon."

She swallowed and took a drink of water. "Why has Mrs. McCrea taken on this project?" she asked. "Is she really trying to replace him, as he says?"

"Nah. But because of his age, it's about time for some kind of protégé, I would think. Hope's husband left her enough so she'll be comfortable—she's been widowed a long time now, I gather. And she seems to do whatever she can to keep the town together. She's also looking for a preacher, a town cop and a schoolteacher, grades one through eight, so the little ones don't have to bus two towns over. She hasn't had much success."

"Doctor Mullins doesn't seem to appreciate her efforts," Mel said, blotting her lips with the napkin.

"He's territorial. He's in no way ready for retirement. Maybe he's worried that someone will show up and take over, leaving him with nothing to do. Man like Doc, never married and in service to a town all his life, would balk at that. But...see... There was an incident a few years ago, just before I got here. Two emergencies at the same time. A truck went off the road and the driver was critically injured, and a kid with a bad case of flu that turned to pneumonia stopped breathing. Doc stopped the bleeding on the truck driver, but by the time he got across the river to the kid, he was too late."

"God," she said. "Bet that leaves some hard feelings."

"I don't think anyone really blames him. He's saved some lives in his time here. But the feeling he could use some help gets more support." He smiled. "You're the first one to show up."

"Hmm," she said, taking a last sip of coffee. She heard the door open behind her and a couple of men walked in.

"Harv. Ron," Jack said. The men said hello and sat at a table by the window. Jack looked back at Mel. "What made you come up here?" he asked.

"Burnout," she said. "I got sick of being on a first-name basis with cops and homicide detectives."

"Jesus, just what kind of work did you do?"

"Ever been to war?" she asked.

"As a matter of fact," he replied with a nod.

"Well, big-city hospitals and trauma centers get like that. I spent years in the emergency room in downtown L.A. while I was doing my post-grad work to become a family nurse practitioner, and there were days it felt like a battle zone. Felons transported to E.R. after incurring injuries during arrest—people who were still so out of control and impossible to subdue that three or four cops had to hold them down while one of the nurses tried to start an IV. Addicts with so much junk in them, three hits with an officer's Taser wouldn't even slow 'em down, much less a dose of Narcan. O.D.s, victims of violent crimes and, given it was the biggest trauma center in L.A., some of the ugliest MVAs and GSWs... Sorry. Motor vehicle accidents and gunshot wounds. And crazy people with no supervision, nowhere to go, off their meds and... Don't get me wrong, we did some good work. Excellent work. I'm real proud of what we got done. Best staff in, maybe, America."

She gazed off for a second, thinking. The environment was wild and chaotic, yet while she was working with and falling in love with her husband, it was exciting and fulfilling. She gave her head a little shake and went on.

"I transferred out of E.R. to women's health, which I found was what I'd been looking for. Labor and delivery. I went to work on my certification in midwifery. That turned out to be my true calling, but it wasn't always a sweeter experience." She laughed sadly and shook her head. "My first patient was brought in by the police and I had to fight them like a bulldog to get the cuffs off. They wanted me to deliver her while she was handcuffed to the bed."

He smiled. "Well, you're in luck. I don't think there's a pair of handcuffs in town."

"It wasn't like that every day, but it was like that often. I supervised the nurses on the L&D ward for a couple of years. The excitement and unpredictability zooped me up for a long time, but I finally hit a wall. I love women's health, but I can't do city medicine like that anymore. God, I need a slower pace. I'm wiped out."

"That's an awful lot of adrenaline to leave behind," he said.

"Yeah, I've been accused of being an adrenaline junkie. Emergency nurses often are." She smiled at him. "I'm trying to quit."

"Ever live in a small town?" he asked, refilling her coffee.

She shook her head. "Smallest town I've ever lived in had at least a million people in it. I grew up in Seattle and went to Southern California for college."

"Small towns can be nice. And they can have their own brand of drama. And danger."

"Like?" she asked, sipping.

"Flood. Fire. Wildlife. Hunters who don't follow the rules. The occasional criminal. Lotta pot growers out here, but not in Virgin River that I know of. Humboldt Homegrown, it's called around here. They're a tight-knit group and usually keep to themselves—don't want to draw attention. Once in a while, though, there'll be crime associated with drugs." He grinned. "But you never had any of that in the city, right?"

"When I was looking for change, I shouldn't have made such a drastic one. This is kind of like going cold turkey. I might have to downsize a little more gradually. Maybe try out a town with a couple hundred thousand people and a Starbucks."

"You aren't going to tell me Starbucks can beat that coffee you're drinking," he said, nodding at her cup.

She gave a short laugh. "Coffee's great." She favored him with a pleasant smile, deciding that this guy was okay. "I should've considered the roads. To think I left the terror of Los Angeles freeways for the heart-stopping curves and cliffs in these hills… Whew." A tremor ran through her. "If I did stay in a place like this, it would be for your food."

He leaned toward her, bracing hands on the bar. Rich brown eyes glowed warm under serious hooded brows. "I can get that cabin put right for you in no time," he said.

"Yeah, I've heard that before." She put out a hand and he took it. She felt his calluses as he gently squeezed her hand; he was a man who did hard, physical work. "Thanks, Jack. Your bar was the only part of this experiment I enjoyed." She stood and began fishing for her wallet in her purse. "What do I owe you?"

"On the house. The least I could do."

"Come on, Jack—none of this was your doing."

"Fine. I'll send Hope a bill."

At that moment Preacher came out of the kitchen with a covered dish wrapped in a towel. He handed it to Jack.

"Doc's breakfast. I'll walk out with you."

"All right," she said.

At her car, he said, "No kidding. I wish you'd think about it."

"Sorry, Jack. This isn't for me."

"Well, damn. There's a real dearth of beautiful young women around here. Have a safe drive." He gave her elbow a little squeeze, balancing the covered dish in his other hand. And all she could think was, what a peach of a guy. Lots of sex appeal in his dark eyes, strong jaw, small cleft in his chin and the gracious, laid-back manner that suggested he didn't know he was good-looking. Someone should snap him up before he figured it out. Probably someone had.

Mel watched him walk across the street to the doctor's

house, then got into her car. She made a wide U-turn on the deserted street and headed back the way she had come. As she drove by Doc's house, she slowed. Jack was crouched on the porch, looking at something. The covered dish was still balanced on one hand and he lifted the other, signaling her to stop. As he looked toward her car, his expression was one of shock. Disbelief.

Mel stopped the car and got out. "You okay?" she asked.

He stood up. "No," he said. "Can you come here a sec?"

She left the car running, the door open, and went up on the porch. It was a box, sitting there in front of the doctor's door, and the look on Jack's face remained stunned. She crouched down and looked within and there, swaddled and squirming around, was a baby. "Jesus," she said.

"Nah," Jack said. "I don't think it's Jesus."

"This baby was not here when I passed his house earlier."

Mel lifted the box and asked Jack to park and turn off her car. She rang the doctor's bell and after a few tense moments, he opened it wearing a plaid flannel bathrobe, loosely tied over his big belly and barely covering a nightshirt, his skinny legs sticking out of the bottom.

"Ah, it's you. Never know when to quit, do you? You bring my breakfast?"

"More than breakfast," she said. "This was left on your doorstep. Have any idea who would do that?"

He pulled at the receiving blanket and revealed the baby. "It's a newborn," he said. "Probably only hours old. Bring it in. Ain't yours, is it?"

"Come on," she said in aggravation, as though the doctor hadn't even noticed that she was not only too thin to have been pregnant, but also too lively to have just given birth. "Believe me, if it were mine, I wouldn't have left it here."

She walked past him into his house. She found herself not in a home, but a clinic—waiting room on her right, reception area complete with computer and filing cabinets behind a counter on her left. She went straight back on instinct and when she found an exam room, turned into it. Her only concern at the moment was making sure the infant wasn't ill or in need of emergency medical assistance. She put the box on the exam table, shed her coat and washed her hands. There was a stethoscope on the counter, so she found cotton and rubbing alcohol. She cleaned the earpieces with the alcohol—her own stethoscope was packed in the car. She listened to the baby's heart. Further inspection revealed it was a little girl, her umbilicus tied off with string. Gently, tenderly, she lifted the baby from the box and cooing, laid her on the baby scale.

By this time the doctor was in the room. "Six pounds, nine ounces," she reported. "Full term. Heartbeat and respirations normal. Color is good." The baby started to wail. "Strong lungs. Somebody threw away a perfectly good baby. You need to get Social Services right out here."

Doc gave a short laugh just as Jack came up behind him, looking into the room. "Yup, I'm sure they'll be right out."

"Well, what are you going to do?" she asked.

"I guess I'm going to rustle up some formula," he said. "Sounds hungry." He turned around and left the exam room.

"For the love of God," Mel said, rewrapping and jiggling the baby in her arms.

"Don't be too hard on him," Jack said. "This isn't L.A. We don't put in a call to Social Services and get an immediate house call. We're kind of on our own out here."

"What about the police?" she asked.

"There's no local police. County sheriff's department is pretty good," he said. "Not exactly what you're looking for, either, I bet."

"Why is that?"

"If there's not a serious crime, they would probably take their time," he said. "They have an awful lot of ground to cover. The deputy might just come out and write a report and put their own call in to Social Services, which will get a response when they're not overworked, underpaid, and can rustle up a social worker or foster family to take over this little…" He cleared his throat. "Problem."

"God," she said. "Don't call her a problem," she admonished. She started opening cupboard doors, unsatisfied. "Where's the kitchen?" she asked him.

"That way," he said, pointing left.

"Find me towels," she instructed. "Preferably soft towels."

"What are you going to do?"

"I'm going to wash her." She left the exam room with the baby in her arms.

Mel found the kitchen, which was large and clean. If Jack was delivering the doctor's meals, it probably wasn't used that much. She tossed the dish rack onto the floor in the corner and gently laid the baby on the drain board. Under the sink she found cleanser and gave the sink a quick scrub and rinse. Then she tested the temperature and filled the sink with water while the baby, most annoyed at the moment, filled the kitchen with the noise of her unhappiness. Fortuitously, there was a bar of Ivory soap on the sink, which Mel rinsed off as thoroughly as possible.

Rolling up her sleeves, she lifted the naked little creature into her arms and lowered her into the warm water. The cries stopped. "Aw," she said. "You like the bath? Does it feel like home?"

Doc Mullins came into the kitchen, dressed now, with a canister of powdered formula. Behind him trailed Jack, bearing the towels he was asked to fetch.

Mel gently rubbed the soap over the baby, rinsing off the muck of birth, the warmth of the water hopefully bringing the baby's temperature up. "This umbilicus is going to need some attention," she said. "Any idea who gave birth?"

"None whatsoever," Doc said, pouring bottled water into a measuring bowl.

"Who's pregnant? That would be a logical place to start."

"The pregnant women in Virgin River who have been coming here for prenatal visits wouldn't give birth alone. Maybe someone came from another town. Maybe I've got a patient out there who gave birth without the benefit of medical assistance, and that could be the second crisis of the day. As I'm sure you know," he added, somewhat smugly.

"As I'm sure I do," she returned, with equal smugness. "So, what's your plan?"

"I imagine I will diaper and feed and become irritable."

"I think you mean *more* irritable."

"I don't see many options," he said.

"Aren't there any women in town who could help out?"

"Perhaps on a limited basis." He filled a bottle and popped it in the microwave. "I'll manage, don't you worry." Then he added, somewhat absently, "Might not hear her in the night, but she'll live through it."

"You have to find a home for this baby," she said.

"You came here looking for work. Why don't you offer to help?"

She took a deep breath and, lifting the baby from the sink, laid her in the towel being held by Jack. She cocked her head in appreciation as Jack took the infant confidently, wrapping her snugly and cuddling her close. "You're pretty good at that," she said.

"The nieces," he said, jiggling the baby against his broad chest. "I've held a baby or two. You going to stay on a bit?" he asked.

"Well, there are problems with that idea. I have nowhere to stay. That cabin is not only unacceptable for me, it's more unacceptable for this infant. The porch collapsed, remember? And there are no steps to the back door. The only way in is to literally crawl."

"There's a room upstairs," Doc said. "If you stay and help out, you'll be paid." Then he looked at her over the rims of his reading glasses and sternly added, "Don't get attached to her. Her mother will turn up and want her back."

Jack went back to the bar and placed a call from the kitchen. A groggy, thick voice answered. "Hello?"

"Cheryl? You up?"

"Jack," the woman said. "That you?"

"It's me. I need a favor. Right away."

"What is it, Jack?"

"Weren't you asked to clean that McCrea cabin for the nurse coming to town?"

"Uh… Yeah. Didn't get to it though. I had… I think it was the flu."

It was the Smirnoff flu, he thought. Or even more likely, the Everclear flu—that really evil 190-proof pure grain alcohol. "Can you do it today? I'm going out there to repair the porch and I need that place cleaned. I mean, really cleaned. She's here and is staying with Doc for now—but that place has to be whipped into shape. So?"

"You're going to be there?"

"Most of the day. I can call someone else. I thought I'd give you a crack at it first, but you have to be sober."

"I'm sober," she insisted. "Totally."

He doubted it. He expected she would have a flask with her as she cleaned. But the risk he was taking, and it was not a pleasant risk, was that she would do it for him, and do it very well if it was for him. Cheryl had had a crush on him since he hit town and found excuses to be around him. He tried very hard never to give her any encouragement. But despite her struggle with alcohol, she was a strong woman and good at cleaning when she put her mind to it.

"The door's open. Get started and I'll be out later."

He hung up the phone and Preacher said, "Need a hand, man?"

"I do," he said. "Let's close up and get the cabin fixed up. She might be persuaded to stay."

"If that's what you want."

"It's what the town needs," he said.

"Yeah," Preacher said. "Sure."

If Mel practiced any other kind of medicine, she might've put the baby in the old doctor's arthritic hands and gotten in her car to leave. But a midwife would never do that—couldn't turn her back on an abandoned newborn. For that matter, she couldn't shake a profound concern for the baby's mother. It was settled within seconds; she couldn't leave the baby to an old doctor who might not hear her cry in the night. And she had to be close by if the mother sought medical attention because women in childbirth and postpartum were her specialty.

During the rest of the day, Mel had ample opportunity to check out the rest of Doc's house. The spare room he provided turned out to be more than something for overnight guests—it was furnished with two hospital beds, an IV stand, tray table, bedside bureau and oxygen canister. The only chair in the room happened to be a rocking chair, and Mel was sure that was by design, for the use of a new mother and baby. The baby was provided with a Plexiglas incubator from the downstairs exam room.

The doctor's house was completely functional as a clinic and hospital. The downstairs living room was a waiting room, the dining room was fronted by a counter for check-in. There was an exam room, treatment room, both small, and the doctor's office. In the kitchen there was a small table where he no doubt ate his meals when he wasn't at Jack's. No ordinary kitchen, this one had an autoclave for sterilizing and a locked medicine chest for narcotic drugs kept on hand. In the refrigerator, a few units of blood and plasma, as well as food. More blood than food.

The upstairs had two bedrooms only—the one with the hospital beds and Doc Mullins's. Her accommodations were not the most comfortable, though better than the filthy cabin. But the room was cold and stark; hardwood floors, small rug, rough sheets with a plastic mattress protector that crinkled noisily. She already missed her down comforter, four-hundred-count sheets, soft Egyptian towels and thick, plush carpet. It had occurred to her that she would be leaving behind creature comforts, but she thought it might be good for her, thought she was ready for a big change.

Mel's friends and sister had tried to talk her out of this, but unfortunately they had failed. She had barely gotten over the traumatic experience of giving away all of Mark's clothes and personal items. She'd kept his picture, his watch, the cuff links she had given him on his last birthday—platinum—and his wedding ring. When the job in Virgin River came available, she'd sold all the furniture in their house then put it on the market. There was an offer in three days, even at those ridiculous L.A. prices. She'd packed three boxes of little treasures—favorite books, CDs, pictures, bric-a-brac. The desktop computer was given away to a friend, but she'd brought the laptop and her digital camera. As far as clothes, she'd filled three suitcases and an overnight and gave the rest away. No more strapless dresses for fancy charity events; no more sexy nighties for those nights that Mark didn't have to work late.

Mel was going to be starting over no matter what. She had nothing to go back to; she hadn't wanted anything to tie her to L.A. Now that things in Virgin River were not going as planned, Mel decided to stay and help out for a couple of days and then head out to Colorado. *Well,* she thought, *it'll be good to be near Joey, Bill and the kids. I can start over there as well as anywhere.*

It had been just Mel and Joey for a long time now. Joey was four years her senior and had been married to Bill for fifteen years. Their mother had died when Mel was only four—she could barely remember her. And their father, considerably older than their mother had been, had passed peacefully in his La-Z-Boy at the age of seventy, ten years ago.

Mark's parents were still alive and well in L.A., but she had never warmed to them. They had always been stuffy and cool toward her. Mark's death had brought them briefly closer, but it took only a few months for her to realize that they never called her. She checked on them, asked after their grief, but it seemed they'd let her drift out of sight. She was not surprised to note that she didn't miss them. She hadn't even told them she was leaving town.

She had wonderful friends, true. Girlfriends from nursing school and from the hospital. They called with regularity. Got her out of the house. Let her talk about him and cry about him. But after a while, though she loved them, she began to associate them with Mark's death. Every time she saw them, the pitying looks in their eyes were enough to bring out her pain. It was as if everything had been rolled up into one big miserable ball. She just wanted to start over so badly. Someplace where no one knew how empty her life had become.

Late in the day, Mel handed off the baby to Doc while she took a badly needed shower, scrubbing from head to toe. After she had bathed and dried her hair and donned her long flannel nightgown and big furry slippers, she went downstairs to Doc's office to collect the infant and a bottle. He gave her such a look, seeing her like that. It startled his eyes open. "I'll feed her, rock her and put her down," she said. "Unless you have something else in mind for her."

"By all means," he said, handing the baby over.

Up in her room, Mel rocked and fed the baby. And of course, the tears began to well in her eyes.

The other thing no one in this town knew was that

she couldn't have children. She and Mark had been seeking help for their infertility. Because she was twenty-eight and he thirty-four when they married, and they'd already been together for two years, they didn't want to wait. She had never used birth control and after one year of no results they went to see the specialists.

Nothing appeared to be wrong with Mark, but she'd had to have her tubes blown out and her endometriosis scraped off the outside of her uterus. But still, nothing. She'd taken hormones and stood on her head after intercourse. She took her temperature every day to see when she was ovulating. She went through so many home pregnancy tests, she should have bought stock in the company. Nothing. They had just completed their first fifteen-thousand-dollar attempt at in vitro fertilization when Mark was killed. Somewhere in a freezer in L.A. were more fertilized ovum—if she ever became desperate enough to try to go it alone.

Alone. That was the operative word. She had wanted a baby so badly. And now she held in her arms an abandoned little girl. A beautiful baby girl with pink skin and a sheer cap of brown hair. It made her literally weep with longing.

The baby was healthy and strong, eating with gusto, belching with strength. She slept soundly despite the crying that went on in the bed right beside her.

That night Doc Mullins sat up in bed, book in his lap, listening. So—she was in pain. Desperate pain. And she covered it with that flip wit and sarcasm.

Nothing is ever what it seems, he thought, flicking off his light.

Three

Mel woke to the ringing of the phone. She checked the baby; she had only awoken twice in the night and still slept soundly. She found her slippers and went downstairs to see if she could rustle up some coffee. Doc Mullins was already in the kitchen, dressed.

"Going out to the Driscolls'—sounds like Jeananne might be having an asthma attack. There's the key to the drug box. I wrote down the number for my pager—cell phones aren't worth a damn out here. If any patients wander in while I'm gone, you can take care of them."

"I thought you just wanted me to babysit," she said.

"You came here to work, didn't you?"

"You said you didn't want me," she pointed out to him.

"You said you didn't want us, either, but here we are. Let's see what you got." He shrugged on his jacket and picked up his bag. Then jutted his chin toward her, lifted his eyebrows as if to say, *Well?*

"Do you have appointments today?"

"I only make appointments on Wednesdays—the rest are walk-ins. Or call-outs, like this one."

"I wouldn't even know what to charge," she argued.

"Neither do I," he said. "Hardly matters—these people aren't made of money and damn few have insurance. Just make sure you keep good records and I'll work it out. It's probably beyond you, anyway. You don't look all that bright."

"You know," she said, "I've worked with some legendary assholes, but you're competing for first place here."

"I'll take that as a compliment," he said gruffly.

"That figures," she answered tiredly. "Incidentally, the night was fine."

No comment from the old goat. He started for the door and on his way out, grabbed a cane. "Are you limping?" Mel asked him.

"Arthritis," he said. He dug an antacid out of his pocket and popped it in his mouth. "And heartburn. Got any more questions?"

"God, no!"

"Good."

Mel got a bottle ready and while it was in the microwave, she went upstairs to dress. By the time that was accomplished, the baby started to stir. She changed her and picked her up and found herself saying, "Sweet Chloe, sweet baby…" If she and Mark had had a girl, she was to be Chloe. A boy would be Adam. What was she doing?

"But you have to be someone, don't you?" she told the baby.

When she was coming down the stairs, the baby swaddled and held against her shoulder, Jack was opening the front door. He was balancing a covered dish on his hand, a thermos tucked under his arm. "Sorry, Jack—you just missed him."

"This is for you. Doc stopped by the bar and said

I'd better get you some breakfast, that you were pretty cranky."

She laughed in spite of herself. "I'm cranky, huh? He's a giant pain in the ass! How do you put up with him?"

"He reminds me of my grandfather. How'd it go last night? She sleep?"

"She did very well. Only woke up a couple of times. I'm just about to feed her."

"Why don't I give her a bottle while you eat. I brought coffee."

"Really, I didn't know they made men like you," she said, letting him follow her into the kitchen. When he put down the plate and thermos, she handed over the baby and tested the bottle. "You seem very comfortable with a newborn. For a man. A man with some nieces in Sacramento." He just smiled at her. She passed him the bottle and got out two coffee mugs. "Ever married?" she asked him, then instantly regretted it. It was going to lead to him asking her.

"I was married to the Marine Corps," he said. "And she was a real bitch."

"How many years?" she asked, pouring coffee.

"Just over twenty years. I went in as a kid. How about you?"

"I was never in the marines," she said with a smile.

He grinned at her. "Married?"

She couldn't meet his eyes and lie, so she concentrated on the coffee mug. "I was married to a hospital, and my bitch was as mean as your bitch." That wasn't a total lie. Mark used to complain about the schedules they kept—grueling. He was in emergency medicine. He'd just finished a thirty-six-hour shift when he stopped at the convenience store, interrupting the robbery. She shuddered involuntarily. She pushed a mug toward him. "Did you see a lot of combat?" she asked.

"A lot of combat," he answered, directing the bottle into the baby's mouth expertly. "Somalia, Bosnia, Afghanistan, Iraq. Twice."

"No wonder you just want to fish."

"Twenty years in the marines will make a fisherman out of just about anyone."

"You seem too young to have retired."

"I'm forty. I decided it was time to get out when I got shot in the butt."

"Ouch. Complete recovery?" she asked, then surprised herself by feeling her cheeks grow warm.

He lifted a corner of his mouth. "Except for the dimple. Wanna see?"

"Thanks, no. So, Doc left me in charge and I have no idea what to expect. Maybe you should tell me where the nearest hospital is—and do they provide ambulance service to the town?"

"That would be Valley Hospital—and they have ambulance service, but it takes so long to get here, Doc usually fires up his old truck and makes the run himself. If you're desperate and have about an hour to spare, the Grace Valley doctors have an ambulance, but I don't think I've seen an ambulance in this town since I've been here. I heard the helicopter came for the guy who almost died in the truck accident. I think the helicopter got as much notice as the accident."

"God, I hope these people are healthy until he gets back," she said. Mel dug into the eggs. This seemed to be a Spanish omelet, and it was just as delicious as the one she'd eaten the day before. "Mmm," she said appreciatively. "Here's another thing—I can't get any cell phone reception here. I should let my family know I'm here safely. More or less."

"The pines are too tall, the mountains too steep. Use the land line—and don't worry about the long distance cost. You have to be in touch with your family. Who is your family?"

"Just an older married sister in Colorado Springs. She and her husband put up a collective and huge fuss about this—as if I was going into the Peace Corps or something. I should've listened."

"There will be a lot of people around here glad you didn't," he said.

"I'm stubborn that way."

He smiled appreciatively.

It made her instantly think, *Don't get any ideas, buster. I'm married to someone. Just because he isn't here, doesn't mean it's over.*

However, there was something about a guy—at least six foot two and two hundred pounds of rock-hard muscle—holding a newborn with gentle deftness and skill. Then she saw him lower his lips to the baby's head and inhale her scent, and some of the ice around Mel's broken heart started to melt.

"I'm going into Eureka today for supplies," he said. "Need anything?"

"Disposable diapers. Newborn. And since you know everyone, could you ask around if anyone can help out with the baby? Either full-time, part-time, whatever. It would be better for her to be in a family home than here at Doc's with me."

"Besides," he said, "you want to get out of here."

"I'll help out with the baby for a couple of days, but I don't want to stretch it out. I can't stay here, Jack."

"I'll ask around," he said. And decided he might just forget to do that. Because, yes, she could.

Little baby Chloe had only been asleep thirty minutes after her morning bottle when the first patient of the day arrived. A healthy and scrubbed looking young farm girl wearing overalls in the middle of which protruded a very large pregnant tummy, carrying two large jars of what appeared to be preserved blackberries. She put the berries on the floor just inside the door. "I heard there was a new lady doctor in town," she said.

"Not exactly," Mel said. "I'm a nurse practitioner."

Her face fell in disappointment. "Oh," she said. "I thought it would be so nice to have a woman doctor around when it's time."

"Time?" Mel asked. "To deliver?"

"Uh-huh. I like Doc, don't get me wrong. But—"

"When are you due?" Mel asked.

She rubbed her swollen belly. "I think about a month, but I'm not really sure," she said. She wore laced-up work boots, a yellow sweater underneath the overalls and her brown hair was pulled back in a ponytail. She looked twenty years old, at most. "It's my first."

"I'm a midwife, as well," Mel said, and the young woman's face lit up in a beautiful smile. "But I have to warn you—I'm only here temporarily. I'm planning to leave as soon as—" She thought about what she should say. Then, instead of explaining about the baby, she said, "Have you had a checkup recently? Blood pressure, weight, et cetera?"

"It's been a few weeks," she said. "I guess I'm about due."

"Why don't we do that since you're here, if I can find what I need," Mel said. "What's your name?"

"Polly Fishburn."

"I bet you have a chart around here somewhere," Mel said. She went behind the counter and started opening file drawers. A brief search turned up a chart. She went in search of litmus, and other obstetric supplies in the exam room. "Come on back, Polly," she called. "When was the last time you had an internal exam?"

"Not since the very first," she said. She made a face. "I was dreading the next one."

Mel smiled, thinking about Doc's bent and arthritic fingers. That couldn't be pleasant. "Want me to have a look? See if you're doing anything, like dilating or effacing? It might save you having Doc do it later. Just get undressed, put on this little gown and I'll be right back."

Mel checked on the baby, who was napping in the kitchen, then went back to her patient. Polly appeared to be in excellent health with normal weight gain, good blood pressure, and... "Oh, boy, Polly. Baby's head is down." Mel stood and pressed down on her tummy while her fingers stretched toward the young woman's cervix. "And... You're just barely dilated and effaced about fifty percent. You're having a small contraction right now. Can you feel that tightening? Braxton Hicks contractions." She smiled at her patient. "Where are you having the baby?"

"Here—I think."

Mel laughed. "If you do that anytime soon, we're going to be roommates. I'm staying upstairs."

"When do you think it'll come?" Polly asked.

"One to four weeks, and that's just a guess," she said. She stepped back and snapped off her gloves.

"Will you deliver the baby?" Polly asked.

"I'll be honest with you, Polly—I'm planning to

leave as soon as it's reasonable. But if I'm still here when you go into labor, and if Doc says it's okay, I'd be more than happy to." She put out a hand to help Polly sit up. "Get dressed. I'll see you out front."

When she walked out of the exam room and back toward the front of the house, she found the waiting room was full of people.

By the end of the day Mel had seen over thirty patients, at least twenty-eight of whom just wanted a look at "the new lady doctor." They wanted to visit, ask her questions about herself, bring her welcome gifts.

It was at once a huge surprise to her, and also what she had secretly expected when she took the job.

By six o'clock, Mel was exhausted, but the day had flown. She held the baby on her shoulder, gently jiggling her. "Have you had anything to eat?" she asked Doc Mullins.

"When, during our open house, would I have eaten?" he shot back. But it was not nearly as sarcastic as Mel imagined he wished it to be.

"Would you like to walk across the street while I feed the baby?" she asked. "Because after you and little Chloe have eaten, I really need some fresh air. No, make that—I'm desperate for a change of scenery. And I haven't eaten since breakfast."

He put out his old, gnarled hands. "Chloe?" he asked.

She shrugged. "She has to be called something."

"Go," he said. "I'll see that she's fed. Then I'll poke around here for something."

She handed over the baby with a smile. "I know you're trying to act miserable and just can't pull it off," she said. "But thank you—I'd really like to get out of here for an hour."

She grabbed her jacket off the peg by the front door and stepped out into the spring night. Out here, away from the smog and industry of city life, there were at least a million more stars. She took a deep breath. She wondered if a person actually got used to air like this—so much cleaner than the smog of L.A., it shocked the lungs.

There were quite a few people at Jack's—unlike that stormy night when she'd arrived. Two women she'd met earlier in the day were there with their husbands—Connie and Ron of the corner store, and Connie's best friend Joy and husband, Bruce. Bruce, she learned, delivered the mail and was also the person who would take any specimens to the lab at Valley Hospital, if needed. They introduced her to Carrie and Fish Bristol and Doug and Sue Carpenter. There were a couple of guys at the bar and another two at a table playing cribbage—by their canvas vests she took them for fishermen.

Mel hung up her jacket, gave her sweater a little tug to bring it over the waist of her jeans and popped up on a bar stool. She did not realize she was wearing a smile. That her eyes shone. They had all come out to see her, welcome her, tell her about themselves, ask her for advice. When the day was full of people who needed her—even those who weren't necessarily sick—it filled her up inside. Passed for happiness, if she dared go that far.

"Lot of action across the street today, I hear," Jack said, giving the bar a wipe at her place.

"You were closed," she said.

"I had things to do—and so did Preacher. We stay open most of the time, but if something comes up, we put up a sign and try to get back by dinner."

"If something comes up?" she asked.

"Like fishing," Preacher said, putting a rack of glasses under the bar, then he went back to the kitchen. Out of the back came the kid, Ricky, bussing tables. When he spied Mel he grinned hugely and came over to the bar with his tray of dishes. "Miss Monroe—you still here? Awesome." Then he went to the kitchen.

"He is too cute."

"Don't let him hear you say that," Jack advised. "He's at the crush age. A very dangerous sixteen. What do you feel like?"

"You know—I wouldn't mind a cold beer," she said. And it instantly appeared before her. "What's for dinner?" she asked.

"Meat loaf," he said. "And the best mashed potatoes you'll ever experience."

"You don't have anything like a menu, do you?"

"Nope. We get whatever Preacher's in the mood to fix. You wanna enjoy that beer for a minute? Or, you want your supper fast?"

She took a pull. "Give me a minute." She took another sip and said, "Ahhh." It made Jack smile. "I think I met half the town today."

"Not even close. But the ones who came out today will spread the word about you. Have any real patients, or were they all just checking you out?"

"I had a couple. You know, I really didn't have to come over here—the house is full of food. When they come, they bring food, whether they're really sick or not. Pies, cakes, sliced meat, fresh bread. It's very… country."

He laughed. "Careful," he said. "We'll grow on you."

"You have any use for a couple of jars of canned berries? I think it was a patient fee."

"You bet. Preacher makes the best pies in the county. Any news about the baby's mother?"

"I call the baby Chloe," she said, expecting a sting of tears that, remarkably, didn't come. "No. Nothing. I hope the woman who gave birth isn't sick somewhere."

"With the way everyone around here knows everyone's business, if there were a sick woman out there, word would get out."

"Maybe she did come from another town."

"You look almost happy," he said.

"I almost am," she returned. "The young woman who brought the berries asked me to deliver her baby. That was nice. The only problem seems to be that she's going to be having her baby in my bedroom. And she could be doing that pretty soon, too."

"Ah," he said. "Polly. She looks like that baby's ready to fall out of her."

"How did you know? Oh, never mind—everyone knows everything."

"There aren't that many pregnant women around," he laughed.

She turned on her stool and looked around. Two old women were eating meat loaf at a table by the fire and the couples she had met, all in their forties or fifties, seemed to be socializing; laughing and gossiping. There were perhaps a dozen patrons. "Business is pretty good tonight, huh?"

"They don't come out in the rain so much. Busy putting buckets under the leaks, I suppose. So—still feel like getting the hell out of here?"

She drank a little of her beer, noting that on an empty stomach the effects were instantaneous. And, actually, delightful. "I'm going to have to leave, if for no other reason than there's nowhere around here to get high-lights put in my hair."

"There are beauty shops around here. In Virgin River, Dot Schuman does hair in her garage."

"That sounds intriguing." She lifted her eyes to his face and said, "I'm getting a buzz. Maybe I better do that meat loaf." She hiccupped and they both laughed.

By seven, Hope McCrea had wandered in and took the stool next to her. "Heard you had a lot of company today," she said. She pulled her cigarettes out of her purse and as she was going to shake one out, Mel grabbed her wrist.

"You have to wait until I'm done with dinner, at least."

"Oh, foo—you're a killjoy." She put the pack down. "The usual," she ordered. And to Mel, "So—how was it? Your first real day? Doc scare you off yet?"

"He was absolutely manageable. He even let me put in a couple of stitches. Of course, he didn't compliment my work, but he didn't tell me it was bad, either." She leaned closer to Hope and said, "I think he's taking credit for me. You might want to stand up for yourself."

"You're staying now?"

"I'm staying a few days, at least. Until we get a couple of things that need attention ironed out."

"I heard. Newborn, they say."

Jack put a drink down in front of Hope. "Jack Daniel's, neat," he said.

"Have any ideas on the mother?" Mel asked Hope.

"No. But everyone is looking at everyone else strangely. If she's around here, she'll turn up. You done pushing food around that plate yet? Because I'm ready for a smoke."

"You shouldn't, you know."

Hope McCrea looked at Mel in impatience, grimacing. She pushed her too-big glasses up on her nose. "What the hell do I care now? I've already lived longer than I expected to."

"That's nonsense. You have many good years left."

"Oh, God. I hope not!"

Jack laughed and in spite of herself, so did Mel.

Hope, acting like a woman with a million things to do, had her drink and cigarette, put money on the bar, hopped off the stool and said, "I'll be in touch. I can help out with the little one, if you need me."

"You can't smoke around the baby," Mel informed her.

"I didn't say I could help out for hours and hours," she answered. "Keep that in mind." And off she went, stopping at a couple of tables to pass the time on her way out.

"How late do you stay open?" Mel asked Jack.

"Why? You thinking about a nightcap?"

"Not tonight. I'm bushed. For future reference."

"I usually close around nine—but if someone asks me to stay open, I will."

"This is the most accommodating restaurant I've ever frequented," she laughed. She looked at her watch. "I better spell Doc. I don't know how patient he is with an infant. I'll see you at breakfast, unless Doc's out on a house call."

"We'll be here," he offered.

Mel said goodbye and on her way to her coat, stopped at a couple of the tables to say good night to people she had just met. "Think she'll stay on awhile?" Preacher quietly asked Jack.

Jack was frowning. "I think what she does to a pair of jeans ought to be against the law." He looked at

Preacher. "You okay here? I'm thinking of having a beer in Clear River."

It was code. There was a woman in Clear River. "I'm okay here," Preacher said.

As Jack drove the half hour to Clear River, he wasn't thinking about Charmaine, which gave him a twinge of guilt. Tonight he was thinking about another woman. A very beautiful young blonde woman who could just about bring a man to his knees with what she looked like in boots and jeans.

Jack had gone to a tavern in Clear River for a beer a couple of years ago and struck up a conversation with the waitress there—Charmaine. She was the divorced mother of a couple of grown kids. A good woman; hard-working. Fun-loving and flirtatious. After several visits and as many beers, she took him home with her and he fell into her as if she were a feather bed. Then he told her what he always made sure women understood about him—that he was not the kind of man who could ever be tied down to a woman, and if she began to have those designs, he'd be gone.

"What makes you think all women want to be run by some man?" she had asked. "I just got rid of one. Not about to get myself hooked up to another one." Then she smiled and said, "Just the same, everyone gets a little lonely sometimes."

They started an affair that had sustained Jack for a couple of years now. Jack didn't see her that often—every week, maybe couple of weeks. Sometimes a month would go by. He wasn't sure what she did when he wasn't around—maybe there were other men—though he'd never seen any evidence of that. He never caught her making time in the bar with anyone else;

never saw any men's things around her house. He kept a box of condoms in her bedside drawer that didn't disappear on him, and he'd let it slip that he liked being the only man she entertained.

As for Jack—he had a personal ethic about one woman at a time. Sometimes that woman could last a year, sometimes a night—but he didn't have a collection he roved between. Although he wasn't exactly breaking that rule tonight, he wasn't quite sticking to it, either.

He never spent the night in Clear River and Charmaine was not invited to Virgin River. She had only called him and asked him to come to her twice—and it seemed a small thing to ask. After all, he wasn't the only one who needed to be with someone once in a while.

He liked that when he walked in the tavern and she saw him, it showed all over her that she was happy he'd come. He suspected she had stronger feelings for him than she let show. He owed her—she'd been a real sport about it—but he knew he'd have to leave the relationship before it got any more entangled. So sometimes, to demonstrate he had a few gentlemanly skills, he'd drop in for just a beer. Sometimes he'd bring her something, like a scarf or earrings.

He sat down at the bar and she brought him a beer. She fluffed her hair; she was a big blonde. Bleached blonde. At about five foot eight, she'd kept her figure, mostly. He didn't know her exact age, but he suspected late forties, early fifties. She always wore very tight-fitting clothes and tops that accentuated her full breasts. At first sight you'd think—cheap. Not so much tawdry or low-class as simple. Unrefined. But once you got to know Charmaine and how kind and deep down earnest she was, those thoughts fled. Jack imagined that in younger years she was quite the looker with her ample chest and full lips. She hadn't really lost those good looks, but she had a little extra weight around the hips and there were wrinkles at the corners of her eyes.

"Hiya, bub," she said. "Haven't seen you in a while."

"It's only been a couple of weeks, I think."

"More like four."

"How've you been?" he asked.

"Busy. Working. Went over to Eureka to see my daughter last week. She's having herself a lousy marriage—but what should we expect? I raised her in one."

"She getting divorced?" he asked politely, though in truth he didn't care that much. He didn't know her kids.

"No. But she should. Let me get this table. I'll be back."

She left him to make sure the other customers were served. There were only a few and once Jack showed up the owner, Butch, knew that Charmaine would want to leave a little early. He saw her take a tray of glasses back behind the bar and talk quietly with her boss, who nodded. Then Charmaine was back.

"I just wanted to have a beer and say hello," Jack said. "Then I have to get back. I have a big project going on."

"Oh, yeah? What's that?"

"I'm fixing up a cabin for one of the women in town. I put on a new porch today and tomorrow I'm going to paint it and build back steps."

"That so? Pretty woman?"

"I guess you could say she's pretty. For seventy-six years old."

She laughed loudly. Charmaine had a big laugh. It was a good laugh that came from deep inside her. "Well, then, I guess I won't bother being jealous. But do you think you can spare the time to walk me home?"

"I can," he said, draining his beer. "But I'm not coming in tonight."

"That's fine," she said. "I'll get my coat."

When they were outside, she looped her arm through his and began to talk about her last couple of weeks, as she always did. He liked the sound of her voice, deep and a little raspy, what they called a whiskey voice though she wasn't much of a drinker. She could go on and on about next to nothing but in a pleasant way, not an irritating way. She would talk about the bar, the people in the town, her kids, what she'd bought lately, what she'd read. News items fascinated her—she would spend the mornings before work watching CNN, and she liked to tell him her opinion of breaking stories. She always had some project going on in her little house— wallpaper or paint or new appliances. The house was paid for; an inheritance of some kind. So the money she made, she spent on herself and her kids.

When they got to the door he said, "I'll shove off, Charmaine. But I'll see you before long."

"Okay, Jack," she said. She tilted her head up for a kiss and he obliged. "That wasn't much of a kiss," she said.

"I don't want to come in tonight," he said.

"You must be awful tired," she said. "Think you have enough energy to give me a kiss that I'll remember for an hour or two?"

He tried again. This time he covered her mouth with his, allowed his tongue to do a little exploring, held her close against him. And she grabbed his butt. Damn! he thought. She ground against him a little bit, sucked on his tongue. Then she hooked her hand into the front of his jeans and pulled him forward, letting her fingers drift lower against his belly.

"Okay," he said weakly, a little vulnerable, stirred up. "I'll come in for a few minutes."

"That's my boy," she said, smiling at him. She pushed open the door and he followed her inside. "Just think of it as a little sleeping pill."

He dropped his jacket on the chair. Charmaine wasn't even out of hers when he grabbed her around the waist, pulled her against him and devoured her with a kiss that was sudden, hot and needy. He pushed her jacket off her shoulders and walked her backwards toward the bedroom and dropped with her onto the bed. He pulled at her top and freed her breasts, filling his mouth with one and then the other. Then off came her pants, and down came his. He ran his hands over her lush body, down over her shoulders, hips, thighs. He reached over to the bedside table, retrieved one of the condoms kept there for him, and ripped the package open. He put it on and was inside her so quickly, it startled even him. He thrust and plunged and drove and she said, "Oh! Oh! Oh, my God!"

He was ready to explode, but held himself back while her legs came around his waist and she bucked. Something happened to him—he went a little out of his mind. Didn't know where he was or with whom. When she finally tightened around him, he let himself go with a loud groan. She panted beneath him, the sound that told him she was completely satisfied.

"My God," she said when she finally caught her breath. "What's got you so hot?"

"Huh?"

"Jack, you don't even have your boots off!"

He was shocked for a moment, then rolled off her. *Jesus,* he thought. *You can't treat a woman like that.* He might not have been thinking, but at least he wasn't thinking about anyone else, he consoled himself. He had no brain power involved in that at all—it was all visceral. His body, reaching out.

"I'm sorry, Charmaine. You okay?"

"I'm way more than okay. But please, take your boots off and hold me."

It was on his mind to say he had to go, he wanted to go, but he couldn't do that to her after this. He sat up and got rid of the boots and pants and shirt, everything hitting the floor. After a quick visit to the bathroom he was back, scooped her up in his arms and held her. Her heavy, soft body was cushiony against his.

He stroked her, kissed her and eventually made love to her again, as opposed to what he'd done before. This time sanely, but no less satisfactorily. At one in the morning he was searching around the floor for his pants.

"I thought you might be staying the night this time," she said from the bed.

He pulled on his pants and sat on the bed to put on his boots. He twisted around and gave her a kiss on the cheek. "I can't," he said. "But you'll be fine now." He smiled at her. "Think of it as a little sleeping pill."

As he drove back to Virgin River he thought, *It's over now. I have to end it. I can't do that anymore, not with a clear conscience. Not when something else has my attention.*

Four

Jack drove out to the cabin, the truck bed loaded with supplies. It was his third day in a row. When he pulled up, Cheryl came out of the house, onto the new porch. "Hey, Cheryl," he called. "How's it going? Almost done in there?"

She had a rag in her hands. "I need the rest of the day. It was a real pigsty. Will you be here tomorrow, too?"

He would. But he said, "Nah. I'm about done. I want to paint the porch this morning—can you get out the back door? I haven't built steps yet."

"I can jump down. Whatcha got?" She came down the porch steps.

"Just stuff for the cabin," he said, unloading a big Adirondack chair for the porch, its twin in the truck bed.

"Wow. You really went all out," she said.

"It has to be done."

"She must be some nurse."

"She says she's not staying, but the place has to be fixed up anyway. I told Hope I'd make sure it was taken care of."

"Not everyone would go to so much trouble. You're really a good guy, Jack," she said. She peeked into the truck. He had a new double-size mattress inside a large plastic bag lying flat in the bed. On top of that, a large rolled-up rug for the living room, bags from Target full of linens and towels that were new as opposed to the graying, used ones borrowed from Hope's linen closet, potted geraniums for the front porch, lumber for the back step, paint, a box full of new kitchen things. "This is a lot more than repair stuff," she said. She tucked a strand of hair that had escaped her clip around her ear. When he chanced a glance at her, he saw those sad eyes filled with longing. He looked away quickly.

"Why go halfway?" he said. "It ought to be nice. When she leaves, maybe Hope can rent it out to summer people."

"Yeah," she said.

Jack continued unloading while Cheryl just stood around. He tried to ignore her; he didn't even make small talk.

Cheryl was a tall, big-boned woman of just thirty, but she didn't look so good—she'd been drinking pretty hard since she was a teenager. Her complexion was ruddy, her hair thin and listless, her eyes red-rimmed and droopy. She had a lot of extra weight around the middle from the booze. Every now and then she'd sober up for a couple of weeks or months, but invariably she'd fall back into the bottle. She still lived with her parents, who were at their wits' end with her drinking. But what to do? She'd get her hands on booze regardless. Jack never served her, but every time he happened upon her, like now, there was usually a telltale odor and half-mast eyes. She was holding it together pretty good today. She must not have had much.

There had been a bad incident a couple of years ago that Cheryl and Jack had had to get beyond. She had a little too much one night and went to his living quarters behind the bar, banging on his door in the middle of the night. When he opened the door, she flung herself on him, groping him and declaring her tragic love for him. Sadly for her, she remembered every bit of it. He caught her sober a few days later and said, "Never. It is never going to happen. Get over it and don't do that again." And it made her cry.

He moved on as best he could and was grateful that she did her drinking at home, not in his bar and grill. She liked straight vodka, probably right out of the bottle and, if she could get her hands on it, Everclear—that really mean, potent stuff. It was illegal in most states, but liquor store owners usually had a little under the counter.

"I wish I could be a nurse," Cheryl said.

"Have you ever thought about going back to school?" he asked as he worked. He was careful not to give her the impression he was too interested. He hauled the rug out of the back of the truck, hefted it over his shoulder and carried it to the house.

To his back she said, "I couldn't afford it."

"You could if you got a job. You need a bigger town. Throw your net a little wider. Stop relying on odd jobs."

"Yeah, I know," she said, following him. "But I like it here."

"Do you? You don't seem that happy."

"Oh, I'm happy sometimes."

"That's good," he said. He threw the rolled rug down in the living room. He'd spread it out later. "If you have the time, could you wash up those new linens I bought and put them away? Fix up the bed when I get the new mattress on it?"

"Sure. Let me help you with the mattress."

"Thanks," he said, and together they hauled it into the house. He leaned it against the wall and grabbed the old one off the bed. "I'll go by the dump on the way home."

"I heard there was a baby at Doc's. Like a baby that was just left there."

Jack froze. Oh, man, he thought. Cheryl? Could it be Cheryl's? Without meaning to, he looked her up and down. She was big, but not obese. Yet fat around the middle and her shirt loose and baggy. But she'd been out here cleaning that very day—she couldn't do that, could she? Maybe it wasn't the Smirnoff flu. Wouldn't she be bleeding and leaking milk? Weak and tired?

"Yeah," he finally said. "You hear of anyone who could have done that?"

"No, but when I'm done here, I could help out with the baby."

"Uh, I think that's covered, Cheryl. But thanks. I'll tell Doc." He carried the old mattress out and leaned it against the truck bed. God, that was an awful-looking thing. Mel was completely right—that cabin was horrific. What had Hope been thinking? She'd been thinking it would be cleaned up—but had she expected the new nurse to sleep on that thing? Sometimes Hope could be oblivious to details like these. She was pretty much just a crusty old broad.

He reached into the truck and hauled out the bags of linens. "Here you go," he said to Cheryl. "Now get inside—I have to start painting. I want to get back to the bar by dinner."

"Okay," she said, accepting the bags. "Let me know if Doc needs me. Okay?"

"Sure, Cheryl." *Never,* he thought. Too risky.

* * *

Jack was back at the bar by midafternoon with time enough to do an inventory of bar stock before people started turning out for dinner. The bar was empty, as it often was at this time of day. Preacher was in the back getting started on his evening meal and Ricky wasn't due for another hour at least.

A man came into the bar alone. He wasn't dressed as a fisherman; he wore jeans, a tan T-shirt under a denim vest, his hair was on the long side and he had a ball cap on his head. He was a big guy with a stubble of beard about a week old. He sat several stools down from where Jack stood with his clipboard and inventory paperwork, a good indication he didn't want to talk.

Jack walked down to him. "Hi. Passing through?" he asked, slapping a napkin down in front of him.

"Hmm," the man answered. "How about a beer and a shot. Heineken and Beam."

"You got it," Jack said, setting him up.

The man threw back the shot right away, then lifted the beer, all without making any eye contact with Jack. *Fine, we won't talk,* Jack thought. *I have things to do anyway.* So Jack went back to counting bottles.

About ten minutes had passed when he heard, "Hey, buddy. Once more, huh?"

"You bet," Jack said, serving him another round. Again silence prevailed. The man took a little longer on his beer, time enough for Jack to get a good bit of his inventory done. While he was crouched behind the bar, a shadow fell over him and he looked up to see the man standing right on the other side of the bar, ready to settle up.

Jack stood just as the man was reaching into his pocket. He noticed a bit of tattoo sneaking out from the

sleeve of his shirt—the recognizable feet of a bulldog—
the Devil Dog. Jack was close to remarking on it—the
man wore an unmistakable United States Marine Corps
tattoo. But then the man pulled a thick wad of bills out,
peeled off a hundred and said, "Can you change this?"

Jack didn't even have to touch the bill; the skunk-
like odor of green cannabis wafted toward him. The
man had just done some cutting—pruning or harvesting and, from the stinky cash, had made a sale. Jack
could change the bill, but he didn't want to advertise
how much cash he kept on hand and he didn't want that
money on the premises. There were plenty of growers
out there—some with prescriptions for legal use, conscious of the medical benefits. There were those who
thought of marijuana as just any old plant, like corn. Ag-
riculture. A way to make money. And some who dealt
drugs because the drugs would offer a big profit. This
part of the country was often referred to as the Emer-
ald Triangle for the three counties most known for the
cannabis trade. Lots of nice, new, half-ton trucks being
driven by people on a busboy's salary.

Some of the towns around these parts catered to
them, selling supplies illegal growers needed—irriga-
tion tubing, grow lights, camouflage tarps, plastic sheet-
ing, shears in various sizes for harvesting and pruning.
Scales, generators, ATVs for getting off-road and back
into secretive hideaways buried in the forest. There were
merchants around who displayed signs in their windows that said, CAMP Not Served Here. CAMP being
the Campaign Against Marijuana Planting that was a
joint operation between the county sheriff's department
and the state of California. Clear River was a town that
didn't like CAMP and didn't mind taking the growers'
money, of which there was a lot. Charmaine didn't ap-

prove of the illegal growing, but Butch wouldn't turn down a stinky bill.

Virgin River was not that kind of town.

Growers usually maintained low profiles and didn't cause problems, not wanting to be raided. But sometimes there were territorial conflicts between them or booby-trapped grows, either one of which could hurt an innocent citizen. There were drug-related crimes ranging from burglary or robbery to murder. Not so long ago they found the body of a grower's partner buried in the woods near Garberville; he'd been missing for over two years and the grower himself had always been a suspect.

You couldn't find anything in Virgin River that would encourage an illegal crop, one means of keeping them away. If there were any growers in town, they were real, real secret. Virgin River tended to push this sort away. But this wasn't the first one to pass by.

"Tell you what," Jack said to the man, making long and serious eye contact. "On the house this time."

"Thanks," he said, folding his bill back onto the wad and stuffing it in his pocket. He turned to go.

"And buddy?" Jack called as the man reached the door to leave. He turned and Jack said, "Sheriff's deputy and California Highway Patrol eat and drink on the house in my place."

The man's shoulders rose once with a silent huff of laughter. He was on notice. He touched the brim of his hat and left.

Jack walked around the bar and looked out the window to see the man get into a black late model Range Rover, supercharged, big wheels jacked up real high, windows tinted, lights on the roof. That model would go for nearly a hundred grand. This guy was no hobbyist. He memorized the license plate.

Preacher was rolling out pie dough when Jack went into the kitchen. "I just served a guy who tried to pay for his drinks with a wad of stinky Bens as big as my fist," Jack told him.

"Crap."

"He's driving a new Range Rover, loaded, jacked up and lit up. Big guy."

"You think he's growing around town here?"

"Have no idea," Jack said. "We better pay attention. Next time the deputy's in town, I'll mention it. But it's not against the law to have stinky money or drive a big truck."

"If he's rich, it's probably not a small operation," Preacher said.

"He's got a bulldog tattoo on his upper right arm."

Preacher frowned. "You kind of hate to see a brother go that way."

"Yeah, tell me about it. Maybe he's not in business around here. He could have been just scoping out the town to see if this is a good place to set up. I think I sent the message that it's not. I told him law enforcement eats and drinks on the house."

Preacher smiled. "We should start doing that, then," he said.

"How about a discount, to start? We don't want to get crazy."

Mel got her sister, Joey, on the phone.

"Oh, Jesus, Mel! You scared me to death! Where have you been? Why didn't you call sooner?"

"I've been in Virgin River where I have no phone and my cell doesn't work. And I've been pretty busy."

"I was about to call out the National Guard!"

"Yeah? Well, don't bother. They'd never be able to find the place."

"You're all right?"

"Well… This will probably make you perversely happy," Mel told her. "You were right. I shouldn't have done this. I was nuts. As usual."

"Is it terrible?"

"Well, it definitely started out terrible—the free housing turned out to be a falling-down hovel and the doctor is a mean old coot who doesn't want any help in his practice. I was on my way out of town when—you'll never believe this—someone left an abandoned newborn on the doctor's porch. But things have improved, if slightly. I'm staying for at least a few more days to help with the baby. The old doc wouldn't wake up to those middle-of-the-night hunger cries. Oh, Joey, my first impression of him is that he was the poorest excuse for a town doctor I'd ever met. Mean as a snake, rude as sour milk. Fortunately, working with those L.A. medical residents, especially those dicky surgeons, prepared me nicely."

"Okay, that was your first impression. How has it changed?"

"He proves tractable. Since my housing was uninhabitable, I'm staying in the guest room in his house. It's actually set up to be the only hospital room in town. This house is fine—clean and functional. There could be a slight inconvenience at any moment—a young woman who asked me to deliver her first baby will be having it here—in my bedroom, which I share with the abandoned baby. Picture this—a post-partum patient and a full nursery."

"And you will sleep where?"

"I'll probably hang myself up in a corner and sleep

standing up. But that's only if she delivers within the next week, while I'm still here. Surely a family will turn up to foster this baby soon. Although, I wouldn't mind a birth. A sweet, happy birth to loving, excited, healthy parents…"

"You don't have to stay for that," Joey said firmly. "It's not as though they don't have a doctor."

"I know—but she's so young. And she was so happy, thinking there was a woman doctor here who could deliver her rather than this ornery old man."

"Mel, I want you to get in your car and drive. Come to us. Where we can look after you for a while."

"I don't need looking after," she said with a laugh. "Work helps. I need to work. Whole hours go by without thinking about Mark."

"How are you doing with that?"

She sighed deeply. "That's another thing. No one here knows, so no one looks at me with those sad, pitying eyes. And since they don't look at me that way, I don't crumble so often. At least, not where anyone can see."

"Oh, Mel, I wish I could comfort you somehow…"

"But Joey, I have to grieve this, it's the only way. And I have to live with the fact that I might never be over it."

"I hope that's not true, Mel. I know widows. I know widows who have remarried and are happy."

"We're not going there," she said. Then Mel told Joey about what she knew of the town, about all the people who'd been drifting into Doc's house just to get a look at her, about Jack and Preacher. And about how many more stars there were out here. The mountains; the air, so clean and sharp it almost took you by surprise. About the people who came to the doctor bringing things, like tons of food, a lot of which went right across the street to the bar where Preacher used it in his creations; about how Jack refused to take a dime from either Doc or Mel for food or drink. Anyone who cared for the town had a free meal ticket over there.

"But it's very rural. Doc put in a call to the county social services agency, but I gather we're on a waiting list—they may not figure out foster care for who knows how long. Frankly, I don't know how the old doc made it without any help all these years."

"People nice?" Joey asked. "Other than the doctor?"

"The ones I've met—very. But the main reason I called, besides letting you know that I'm safe, is to tell you I'm on the old doc's phone—the cell just isn't going to work out here. I'll give you the number."

"Well," Joey said, "at least you sound okay. In fact, you sound better than you have in a long time."

"Like I said, there are patients. Challenges. I'm a little keyed up. The very first day, I was left alone here with the baby and the key to the drug cabinet and told to see any patients who wandered in. No training, nothing. About thirty people came—just to say hello and visit. That's what you hear in my voice. Adrenaline."

"Adrenaline again. I thought you swore off."

Mel laughed. "It's a completely different brand."

"So—when you wrap it up there, you'll come to Colorado Springs?"

"I don't have any better ideas," Mel said.

"When?"

"Not sure. In a few days, hopefully. Couple of weeks at the outside. But I'll call you and let you know when I'm on my way. Okay?"

"Okay. But you really do sound…up."

"There's nowhere around here to get highlights.

Some woman in town does hair in her garage, and that's it," Mel said.

"Oh, my God," Joey said. "You'd better wrap it up before you get some ugly roots."

"Yeah, that's what I was thinking."

Wednesday, Appointment Day, came and Mel watched the baby and saw a few patients with only minor complaints. One sprained ankle, a bad cold, another prenatal exam, a well-baby check and immunizations. After that there were a couple of walk-ins—she stitched up a laceration on a ten-year-old's head and Doc said, "Not bad." Doc made two house calls. They traded off babysitting to walk across the street to Jack's to eat. The people she met at the bar and those who came into the doctor's office were pleasant and welcoming. "But this is just temporary," she was careful to explain. "Doc doesn't really need any help."

Mel put in an order for more diapers with Connie at the corner store. The store was no bigger than a minimart and Mel learned that the locals usually went to the nearest large town for their staples and feed for animals, using the store merely to grab those occasional missing items. There were sometimes hunters or fishermen looking for something. They had a little of everything—from bottled water to socks. But only a few items of each.

"I heard no one's turned up for that baby yet," Connie said. "I can't think of anyone around here who'd have a baby and give it up."

"Can you think of anyone who'd have a baby without any medical intervention of any kind? Especially since there's a doctor in town?"

Connie, a cute little woman probably in her fifties,

shrugged. "Women have their babies at home all the time, but Doc's usually there. We have some isolated families out in the woods—hardly ever show their faces for anything." She leaned close and whispered, "Strange people. But I've lived here all my life and have never heard of them giving up their children."

"How long do you expect the social services intervention to take?"

Connie laughed. "I wouldn't have the first idea. We run into a problem, we usually all pitch in. It's not like we ask for a lot of outside help."

"Okay, then, how long before you get in a new supply of disposable diapers?"

"Ron makes his supply run once a week, and he'll do that tomorrow morning. So, by tomorrow afternoon, you should be fixed up."

A teenage girl came into the store carrying her book bag—the school bus must have just dropped off. "Ah, my Lizzie," Connie said. "Mel, this is my niece, Liz. She just got here—she's going to stay with me for a while."

"How do you do?" Mel said.

"Hey," Liz said, smiling. Her full, long brown hair was teased up high and falling seductively to her shoulders, eyebrows beautifully arched over bright blue eyes, eye makeup thick, her glossy lips full and pouty. Little sex queen, Mel found herself thinking, in her short denim skirt, leather knee-high boots with heels, sweater tugged over full breasts and not meeting her waist. Belly-button ring, hmm. "Need me to work awhile?" Liz asked Connie.

"No, honey. Go to the back and start your homework. Your first day was good?"

"Okay, I guess." She shrugged. "Nice to meet you," she said, disappearing into the store's back room.

"She's beautiful," Mel said.

Connie was frowning slightly. "She's fourteen."

Mel's eyes grew wide as she mouthed the words silently. Fourteen? "Wow," she whispered to Connie. The girl looked at least sixteen or even seventeen. She could pass for eighteen.

"Yeah. That's why she's here. Her mother, my sister, is at the end of her rope with the little hot bottom. She's a wild one. But that was in Eureka. Not so many places to go wild around here." She smiled. "If I could just get her to cover her naked body, I would feel so much better."

"I hear ya," Mel laughed. "May the force be with you." *But I'd consider birth control,* Mel thought.

When Mel had her meals at the bar, if there was no one around she knew, like Connie or her best friend Joy, or Ron or Hope, she would sit up at the bar and talk to Jack while she ate. Sometimes he ate with her. During these meals she learned more about the town, about summer visitors who came for hiking and camping, the hunters and fishermen who passed through during the season—the Virgin was great for fly fishing, a comment that made her giggle. And there was kayaking, which sounded like fun to her.

Ricky introduced her to his grandmother who made a rare dinner appearance. Lydie Sudder was over seventy and had that uncomfortable gait of one who suffered arthritis. "You have a very nice grandson," Mel observed. "Is it just the two of you?"

"Yes," she said. "I lost my son and daughter-in-law in an accident when he was just a little thing. I'd sure worry about him if it weren't for Jack. He's been looking out for Ricky since he came to town. He looks after a lot of people."

"I can sense that about him," Mel said.

The March sun had warmed the land and brought out the buds. Mel had a fleeting thought that seeing this place in full bloom would be glorious, but then reminded herself that she would miss it. The baby—little Chloe—was thriving and several different women from town had stopped by to offer babysitting services.

She realized that she'd been here over a week—and it had passed like minutes. Of course, never getting more than four hours of sleep at a stretch tended to speed up time. She'd found living with Doc Mullins to be more bearable than she would've thought. He could be a cantankerous old goat, but she could give it back to him just as well, something he seemed to secretly enjoy.

One day, when the baby was asleep and there were no patients or calls, Doc got out a deck of cards. He shuffled them in his hand and said, "Come on. Let's see what you got." He sat down at the kitchen table and dealt the cards. "Gin," he said.

"All I know about gin is that you mix it with tonic," she told him.

"Good. We'll play for money," he said.

She sat down at the table. "You plan to take advantage of me," she said.

"Oh, yes," he confirmed. And then with a smile so rare, he began to tell her how to play. Pennies for points, he told her. And within an hour she was laughing, winning, and Doc's expression was getting more sour by the minute, which only made her laugh harder. "Come on," she said, dealing. "Let's see what you got."

The sound of someone coming through the front door

temporarily stopped the game and Mel said, "Sit tight, I'll see who it is." She patted his hand. "Give you time to stack the deck."

Standing just inside the front door was a skinny man with a long graying beard. His overalls were dirty and the bottoms frayed around filthy boots. The edge of his shirt sleeves and collar were also frayed, as though he'd been in these particular clothes a very long time. He didn't come into the house, probably because of the mud he tracked, but stood just inside the door twisting a very worn felt hat.

"Can I help you?" she asked him.

"Doc here?"

"Uh-huh. Sure. Let me get him for you."

She fetched Doc to the front door and while he was chatting with the man, she checked on Chloe. When Doc finally came back to the kitchen, he was wearing a very unpleasant expression. "We have to make a call. See if you can rustle up someone to keep an eye on the baby."

"You need my assistance?" she asked, perhaps more hopefully than she wished.

"No," he said, "but I think you should tag along. See what's on the other side of the tree line."

Chloe stirred in her bed and Mel picked her up. "Who was that man?"

"Clifford Paulis. Lives out in the woods with some people. His daughter and her man joined them a while back. They have regular problems. I'd rather you just see."

"Okay," she said, perplexed.

After a few phone calls had been placed with no success, the best they could do for the baby was take her across the street to Jack's with a few diapers and a bottle. Mel carried her little bed while Doc managed the baby in one arm and his cane in the other hand, though Mel had offered to make two trips.

"Are you sure you'll be all right?" she asked Jack. "You might have to change her and everything."

"Nieces," he said again. "I'm all checked out."

"How many nieces, exactly?" she asked.

"Eight, at last count. Four sisters and eight nieces. Apparently they can't breed sons. Where are you off to?"

"I'm not sure."

"Paulises'," Doc said. And Jack whistled.

As they drove out of town, Mel said, "I don't have a good feeling about this. Seems everyone knows about this family except me."

"I guess you deserve to be prepared. The Paulises live in a small compound of shacks and trailers with a few others—a camp. They stay out of sight and drink a lot, wander into town very rarely. They keep a supply of pure grain alcohol on hand. They're dirt-poor, miserable folk, but they haven't given Virgin River any trouble. Clifford says there was a fight last night and there's some patching up to do."

"What kind of fight?"

"They're pretty gritty folk. If they sent for me, it must've been a good one."

They drove a long way into the woods, the dirt road a narrow, bumpy, one lane before it finally broke open into a clearing around which were, as Doc had said, two shacks and a couple of trailers. Not mobile homes, but camper shells and an itty-bitty trailer that had seen better days, along with an old wheelless pickup truck up on blocks. They circled an open area in the middle of which was a crude brick oven of sorts. There were tarps stretched out from the campers and shacks with actual furniture under them. Not outdoor furniture but household—tables and chairs, old sofas with the stuffing popping out. Plus old tires, a couple of small trucks, unidentifiable junk, a wringer washer lying on its side. Mel peered into the trees and blinked to clear her vision. There appeared to be a semitrailer, half buried in the ground with camouflage tarps over the top. Beside it was, unmistakably, a gas-powered generator.

Mel said, "Holy shit."

"Help if you can," Doc said. "But try not to talk." He peered at her. "That'll be hard for you."

Doc got out of the truck, hefting his bag. People started to drift into the clearing—not from within their homes, such as they were, but more like from behind them. There were just a few men. It was impossible to tell their ages; they all looked like vagrants with their dirty and worn dungarees and overalls. They were bearded, their hair long and matted, like real sad hillbillies. Everyone was thin with sallow complexions; they were not enjoying good health out here. There was a very bad smell and Mel thought about bathroom facilities. They would be using the forest; and it smelled as if they didn't get far enough from the camp. Their facilities were minimal. It was like a little third-world country.

Doc nodded to people as he pressed forward, getting nods back. He'd obviously been here before. Mel followed more slowly. Doc ended up in front of a shack outside of which Clifford Paulis stood. Doc turned to make sure Mel was with him, then entered.

She felt their eyes on her, but they kept their distance. She wasn't exactly afraid, but she was nervous and unsure and hurried behind Doc to enter the shack with him.

There was a small table inside with a lantern on it. Sitting on short stools at the table were a man and a woman. Mel had to stifle a gasp. Their faces were swollen, cut and bruised. The man was perhaps thirty, his dirty blond hair short and spiky, and he twitched and jittered, unable to sit still. The woman, maybe the same age, was holding her arm at an odd angle. Broken.

Doc put his bag on the table and opened it. He pulled out and put on his latex gloves. Mel followed suit, but slowly, her pulse picking up. She had never worked as a visiting nurse, but knew a few who had. There were nasty hovels all around the poorer sections of L.A. where paramedics might be called, but in the city if you had a situation like this, you'd notify the police. The patients would be brought to the emergency room. And in the event of domestic violence, which this clearly was, these two would both be booked into jail right out of the E.R. When there's an injury in a domestic, no one has to press charges besides the police.

"Whatcha got, Maxine?" he said, reaching out for her arm, which she extended toward him. He examined it briefly. "Clifford," he called. "I'm gonna need a bucket of water." Then to Mel he said, "Get to work on cleaning up Calvin's face, see if sutures are required, and I'll attempt to set this ulna."

"Do you want a hypo?" she asked.

"I don't think we'll need that," he said.

Mel got out some peroxide and cotton and approached the young man warily. He lifted his eyes to her face and grinned at her with a mouth full of dirty teeth, some of which appeared to be rotting. In his eyes she saw that his pupils were very small—he was full of amphetamine, higher than a kite. He kept grinning at her and she tried not to make eye contact with him. She cleaned some of the cuts on his face and finally said, "Wipe that look off your face or I'll let Doc do this." It made him giggle stupidly.

"I'm going to need something for the pain," he said.

"You already had something for the pain," she told him. And he giggled again. But in his eyes there was menace and she decided not to make any more eye contact.

Doc made a sudden movement that slammed Calvin's arm onto the table, hard, gripped by Doc's arthritic hand. "You never do that, you hear me?" Doc said in a voice more threatening than Mel had heard before, then slowly released Calvin's forearm while boring through him with angry eyes. Then Doc immediately turned his attention back to Maxine. "I'm going to have to put this bone right, Maxine. Then I'll cast it for you."

Mel had no idea what had just happened. "You don't want an X-ray?" she heard herself ask Doc. And her answer was a glare from the doctor who'd asked her to try not to talk. She went back to the man's face.

There was a cut over his eye that she could repair with tape, no stitches required. Standing above him as she was, she noticed a huge purple bump through the thinning hair on the top of his head. Maxine must have hit him over the head with something, right before he broke her arm. She glanced at his shoulders and arms through the thin fabric of his shirt and saw that he had some heft to him—he was probably strong. Strong enough at least to break a bone.

The bucket of water arrived—the bucket rusty and dirty—and momentarily she heard Maxine give out a yelp of pain as Doc used sudden and powerful force to put her ulna back into place.

Old Doc Mullins worked silently, wrapping an Ace bandage around her arm, then dipping casting material into the bucket, soaking it and applying it to the broken arm. Finished with her assignment, Mel moved away from Calvin and watched Doc. He was strong and fast for his age, skilled for a man with hands twisted by arthritis, but then this had been his life's work. Casting done, he pulled a sling out of his bag.

Job done, he snapped off his gloves, threw them in his bag, closed it, picked it up and, looking down, went back to the truck. Again, Mel followed.

When they were out of the compound she said, "All right—what's going on there?"

"What do you think's going on?" he asked. "It isn't complicated."

"Looks pretty awful to me," she said.

"It is awful. But not complicated. Just a few dirt-poor alcoholics. Homeless, living in the woods. Clifford wandered away from his family to live out here years ago and over time a few others joined his camp. Then Calvin Thompson and Maxine showed up not so long ago, and added weed to the agenda—they're growing in that semitrailer. Biggest mystery to me is how they got it back in here. You can bet Calvin couldn't get that done. I figure Calvin's connected to someone, told 'em he could sit back here and watch over a grow. Calvin's a caretaker. That's what the generator is about—grow lights. They irrigate out of the river. Calvin's jitters don't come from pot—pot would level him out and slow him down. He's gotta be on something like meth. Maybe he skims a little marijuana, cheats the boss and trades it for something else. Thing is, I don't think Clifford and those old men have anything to do with the pot. They never had a grow out there before that I know of. But I could be wrong."

"Amazing," she said.

"There are lots of little marijuana camps hidden back in these woods—some of 'em pretty good size—but you can't grow it outside in winter months. It's still the biggest cash crop in California. But even if you gave Clifford and those old boys a million dollars, that's how they're going to live." He took a breath. "Not all local growers look like vagrants. A lot of 'em look like millionaires."

"What happened when you grabbed his arm like that?" she asked.

"You didn't see? He was raising it like he was going to touch you. Familiarly."

She shuddered. "Thanks. I guess. Why'd you want me to see that?"

"Two reasons—so you'd know what some of this country medicine is about. Some places where they're growing are booby-trapped, but not this one. You should never go out to one of those places alone. Not even if a baby's coming. You better hear me on that."

"Don't worry," she said with a shudder. "You should tell someone, Doc. You should tell the sheriff or someone."

He laughed. "For all I know, the sheriff's department's aware—there are growers all over this part of the world. For the most part, they stay invisible—it's not like they want to be found out. More to the point, I'm in medicine, not law enforcement. I don't talk about the patients. I assume that's your ethic, as well."

"They live in filth! They're hungry and probably sick! Their water is undoubtedly contaminated by the awful, dirty containers they keep it in. They're beating each other up and dying of drink and...whatever."

"Yeah," he said. "Doesn't make my day, either."

She found it devastating, the acceptance of such hopelessness. "How do you do it?" she asked him, her voice quiet.

"I just do the best I can," he said. "I help where I can. That's all anyone can do."

She shook her head. "This really isn't for me," she said. "I can handle stuff like this when it comes into the hospital, but I'm no country practitioner. It's like the Peace Corps."

"There are bright spots in my doctoring, too," he said. "Just happens that isn't one of them."

She was completely down in the dumps when she went back to the grill to collect the baby. "Not pretty out there, is it?" Jack said.

"Horrid. Have you ever been out there?"

"I stumbled across them a couple years ago when I was hunting."

"You didn't want to tell anyone?" she asked. "Like the police?"

"It isn't against the law to be a bum," he said with a shrug.

So, she thought—he didn't know about the semitrailer. Doc had said it showed up not long ago. "I can't imagine living like that. Can I use your bathroom? I want to wash up before I touch the baby."

"Right back off the kitchen," he said.

When she got back she picked up Chloe and held her close, breathing in the clean, powdery scent.

"Fortunately, you don't have to live like they do," he said.

"Neither do they. Someone should do an intervention

out there, get them some help. Food and clean water, anyway."

He picked up the baby bed to carry it across the street for her. "I think they've killed too many brain cells for that to work," he said. "Concentrate on the good you can do and don't gnaw on the hopeless cases. It'll just make you sad."

By early evening, Mel was coming around. She took her dinner at the bar, laughed with Jack and even Preacher cracked the occasional smile. Finally, she put her small hand over Jack's and said, "I apologize for earlier, Jack. I never even thanked you for watching the baby."

"You were kind of upset," he said.

"Yeah. I surprised myself. It's not as though I haven't seen plenty of bums and street people. They were frequent clientele at the hospital. I didn't realize before today that in the city we'd clean 'em up, straighten 'em out and hand 'em off to some agency or another. In the back of my mind I probably always knew they'd be back picking out of trash cans before long, but I didn't have to see it. This was very different. They're not going anywhere and they're not getting any help. It's been down to Doc. Alone. Takes a lot of courage to do what Doc does."

"He does more than a lot of people would do," Jack said.

She smiled. "This is rough country."

"It can be," he said.

"Not a lot of resources out here."

"We do pretty well with what we've got. But you have to remember, the old boys in that little camp don't seem to want resources so much as to be left alone," he said. "I know that's hard to stomach, but most of this area is the opposite—thriving and healthy. Did that trip out into the woods make your desire to get out of here even more desperate?"

"It sure opened my eyes. I thought small-town medicine would be peaceful and sweet. I never thought it had that other side—as hopeless as some of our worst inner city problems."

"Don't know that it is," he argued. "The sweet and peaceful will far outnumber the hopeless. I swear on it. You're welcome to see for yourself and call me a liar. But you'd have to hang around."

"I made a commitment to stay till the baby is placed," she said. "I'm sorry I can't promise more."

"No promises necessary. Just pointing out the options."

"But thank you, for taking care of the baby for me."

"She's a good baby," he said. "I didn't mind at all."

After she'd gone back to Doc's, Jack said to Preacher, "You okay here? I'm thinking about a beer."

Preacher's bushy black brows shot up in surprise, but he didn't say it. Didn't say, "Another beer? So soon?" He finally said, "I'm okay here."

Jack knew that if he didn't say anything at all to Charmaine for a few weeks, she wouldn't know there was anything to be said. He also knew that despite the fact Mel had captured his thoughts, it didn't mean anything would ever happen, didn't mean she'd make it even another week in Virgin River. That wasn't really the point. The issue was that it was wrong to go to Charmaine at all, ever, if he wasn't into Charmaine. It was a point of honor with him. Even though he never thought in terms of commitment, he certainly didn't think in terms of using someone.

Then there was another matter. A fear that he'd be having sex with Charmaine and behind his closed eyes, see another face. That couldn't happen. That would insult both women.

When she saw him walk into her tavern, her first reaction was one of pleased surprise and she smiled at him. Then she immediately realized how unprecedented this visit was and her smile vanished.

"Beer?" she asked him.

"Talk?" he answered. "Can Butch cover for you for ten minutes?"

She actually took a step back. She knew what was coming and sadness seeped into her brown eyes. Her face actually fell. "Is that all it's going to take?" she asked. "Ten minutes?"

"I think so. There isn't too much to say."

"There's someone else," she said at once.

"No. There isn't. Let's take a table." He looked over his shoulder. "That one over there. Ask Butch."

She nodded and turned from him. While she spoke to Butch, Jack moved to the table. Butch took the bar and Charmaine joined Jack. He reached across and took her hands. "You've been a wonderful friend to me, Charmaine. I never for one second took that for granted."

"But…"

"My mind is on other things," he said. "I won't be coming to Clear River for a beer anymore."

"There can only be one thing," she said. "Because I know you. And you have needs."

He'd thought about this long and hard on the way over, and it wasn't in his mind to lie to her. But there wasn't anyone else. Mel wasn't someone else—and might never be. Just because she'd taken over his consciousness didn't mean it would ever materialize into something more. She might stick to her word and leave Virgin River at the first opportunity, and even if she didn't, you don't show your hand this early in the game. His reason for breaking this off wasn't just about having Mel, but about not misleading Charmaine. She was a good woman; she had been good to him. She didn't deserve to be strung along while he waited to see what the other woman was going to do.

The cabin in Virgin River might be ready, but Mel sure wasn't. The baby at Doc's was keeping her in town for now, but it was impractical to think of her caring for Chloe out at the cabin—there was only the one Plexiglas incubator, no car seat for traveling back and forth, no phone. Of course, it was no punishment to have her living right across the street. But he wanted her in the cabin he'd renovated, he wanted that real bad.

Charmaine was so right—he had needs. But somehow when he looked at this young Mel, he knew it would never be like this—an arrangement for sex every couple of weeks. Jack had absolutely no idea what it might become, but he already knew it was going to be more than that. He had a very long history of not getting hooked up, so this disturbed him. The chances were real good he was casting adrift in a sea of sheer loneliness. Because Mel had complications. He had no idea what they were, but that occasional sadness in her eyes came out of the past, something she was trying to get over.

But he wanted her. He wanted all of her; he wanted everything with her.

"That's the thing," he said. "I have needs. And right now I think what I need is completely different from what I've needed in the past. I could easily keep coming here, Charmaine. I sure don't suffer, you're awful good to me. But the past two years when I've been here, I've been here completely. It shouldn't be any other way."

"The last time was different," she said. "I knew something was wrong."

"Yeah, I'm sorry. It's really the first time my head wasn't connected to my body. You deserve better than that."

She lifted her chin and gave her hair a toss. "What if I said I didn't care?"

God, he felt so bad doing this. "I do," was all he could say.

She got teary. "Okay, then," she said bravely. "Okay, then."

When he left he knew it was going to be a while before he felt all right about what he'd just done. That business about playing it fast and loose, about having no ties or commitments, that wasn't really how it was. All that no commitment bullshit meant was that you didn't talk about it, you never took it to the next level. He had had a contract of sorts with Charmaine, even if it wasn't a formal one, a legal one, even if it was pretty casual in the give-and-take department. She had stuck to the contract; he had just broken it. And let her down.

Five

In the mornings, after the baby had that first really early feeding and was settled back to sleep, Mel liked to take her coffee out to Doc's front porch and sit on the steps. She found she enjoyed watching this little town wake up. First the sun would create a kind of golden path through the tall pine trees onto the street, slowly lighting it. The sound of doors opening and closing could be heard. A Ford truck drove slowly from the east to the west down the street, tossing out papers— the *Humboldt News*. She liked getting the paper early— though it was hardly akin to the *L.A. Times*.

Soon the kids started to emerge. The bus picked them up at the far west end of the main street. Those in town would walk or ride their bikes down the street and gather there, chaining their bikes to trees in someone's front yard. That would never happen in the city— someone just allowing their yard to be used as a bike lot while the kids were in school. She saw Liz come out of Connie's house right next to the store; Liz sashayed across the street, book bag slung over one shoulder, bottom swaying seductively. Boy howdy, Mel was thinking. That girl's advertising like mad.

Cars and trucks began to drop off the more rural kids. It was not yet seven—a long day for these country kids—driven to the bus stop, ride the bus for who knows how long since there was no school in Virgin River, then back to town, back to the farm or ranch. The kids who gathered there, probably thirty, ranged in age from five to seventeen and the mothers of the younger ones stood around chatting while they waited for the bus. Some of them held their coffee cups and laughed together like old, old friends.

Then it would come, the bus, driven by a big happy woman who got off, said hello to the parents, herding each one of the kids on board.

Jack came out of the bar, fishing rod in one hand, tackle box in the other. He put his gear in the back of his truck and lifted a hand to her. She waved back. Out to the river for some fishing. Not long after, Preacher was sweeping off the front porch. When he looked up, he lifted a hand, as well.

What had she said about this little town? That it didn't resemble the pictures she'd seen? In the early morning the town was lovely. Rather than looking old and tired, the homes looked sweet and uncomplicated. They were unfussy clapboards in a variety of colors— blue, light green, beige with brown trim. Connie and Ron's house, right next to the corner store, was the same yellow with white trim as their store. Only one house on the street had been painted recently, a white house with dark green shutters and trim. She saw Rick come out of that house, sprint across the porch, jump down to the street and into his little white truck. It was a safe-looking street. Friendly homes. No one walked out of their homes to see another person and fail to greet, wave, stop and talk.

A woman came out from behind the boarded-up church down the street and seemed to be walking unevenly toward her. As she neared, Mel stood up. "Hello," she said, holding her coffee cup in both hands.

"You the nurse?" she asked.

"Nurse practitioner and midwife, yes. Can I help you with something?"

"No," she said. "I heard about you is all."

The woman's eyes were drawn down sleepily, as though she had trouble staying awake, with dark circles under them. She was a large woman, maybe five-ten, and rather plain, her greasy hair pulled back. It was possible she was sick. Mel stuck out a hand. "Mel Monroe," she said.

The woman hesitated a minute before accepting a handshake. She wiped her palm down her pant leg first, then reached out. Her grip was strong and clumsy, her nails dirty. "Cheryl," she said in response. "Creighton." She pulled her hand back and put both her hands in the pockets of baggy pants. Men's pants, it looked like.

Mel stopped herself before saying, *Ahh. That would be the Cheryl who was supposed to clean the cabin; the Cheryl Hope suspected was drinking again.* Which would explain her sallow complexion and weary eyes, not to mention all the little broken blood vessels in her cheeks. "Sure I can't do anything for you?"

"No. They say you're leaving right away."

"Do they now," she said with a smile. "Well, I have a few things I made a commitment to see through first."

"That baby," she said.

Mel tipped her head to one side. "Hardly anything goes unnoticed around here. Do you know anything about the baby, or her mother? I'd like to find the woman w—"

"So you could go sooner? Because if you want to go—I could take care of the baby…"

"You have an interest in the baby?" she asked. "May I ask why?"

"I just mean to help. I like to help out."

"I really don't need much help—but I sure would like to find the baby's mother. She could be sick, giving birth alone like that."

Mel chanced a glance toward the bar and noticed that Preacher had stopped sweeping and watched. At that same moment, Doc came out of the house. "Cheryl," Doc said.

"Hey, Doc. Just telling the nurse here—I could help out with that baby. Watch her for you and stuff."

"Why'd you want to do that, Cheryl?"

She shrugged. "Jack told me about it."

"Thanks. We'll sure keep you in mind," Doc said.

"'Kay," she said with another shrug. She looked at Mel. "Nice meetin' you. Explains a lot, now I see you." And she turned and walked back the way she'd come.

Mel looked up at Doc and found him frowning. "What was that all about?" she asked him.

"Seems like she wanted to see what you look like. She tends to follow Jack around like a lovesick puppy."

"He shouldn't serve her."

"He doesn't," Doc said. "Jack's a generous guy, but not a foolish one. Giving Cheryl booze would be like throwing kerosene on a fire. Besides, she can't afford Jack's place. I think she gets some of that rotgut they keep out in the woods."

"That's going to kill her."

"Unfortunately."

"Can't somebody help her?"

"She look to you like she wants help?"

"Has anyone tried? Has Jack—"

"Jack can't do anything for her," Doc said. "That would put an awful lot of useless ideas in her head."

He turned around and went back into the house. Mel followed him and said, "Do you think it's possible she gave birth?"

"Anything's possible. But I doubt it."

"What if we checked her? It would be obvious."

Doc looked down at her and lifted one snowy brow. "Think I should call the sheriff? Get a warrant?" And he walked off toward the kitchen.

What an odd little town, Mel found herself thinking.

While the baby napped, Mel took a break and wandered down to the store. Connie poked her head out of the back and said, "Hey, Mel. Can I get you something?"

"I just thought I'd look at your magazines, Connie. I'm bored."

"Help yourself. We're watching our soap, if you want to come back here with us."

"Thanks," she said, going to the very small book rack. There were a few paperbacks and five magazines. Guns, trucks, fishing, hunting and *Playboy*. She picked up a paperback novel and the *Playboy* and went to the back where she'd seen Connie.

A parted curtain hung in the doorway to the back room. Inside, Connie and Joy sat in old canvas lawn chairs in front of the small desk, coffee cups in hand, their eyes focused on a small TV that sat on a shelf. The women were complete physical opposites—Connie being small and trim with short hair dyed fire-engine-red, and Joy must be easily five-nine and two-fifty, very plain with her long, graying hair pulled back into a ponytail, her face round and cheerful. They were an odd pair and it was said they'd been best friends since they were kids. "Come on back," Joy said. "Help yourself to coffee if you want."

On the television a very pretty woman looked into the eyes of a very handsome man and said, "Brent, I never loved anyone but you! Ever!"

"Oh, she is such a liar!" Connie said.

"No, she's not—she didn't love any of them. She just screwed 'em all," Joy said.

On the TV: "Belinda, the bab—"

"Brent, the baby is yours!"

"The baby is Donovan's," Joy told the TV.

Mel leaned a hip against the desk. "What is this?"

"Riverside Falls," Connie said. "Brent and the slut Belinda."

"This is what Lizzie is going to be doing if Connie can't get her out of those slutty clothes."

"I have a plan," Connie said. "As she grows out of her clothes and I replace them, we're going to get a more conservative wardrobe."

Joy laughed loudly. "Connie, it looks like she already grew out of them!"

The camera pulled back and Mel saw that the couple on screen were in bed together, their naked bodies barely concealed by a sheet. "Whew," she said. "Soaps have come a long way."

"You ever watch any soaps, honey?" Connie asked.

"Not since college. We watched *General Hospital.*" Mel put down her magazine and book on the desk and helped herself to a cup of coffee. "We used to get our patients to keep an eye on it for us. I had one long-term care patient—an old guy—and I used to give him his bath at two every afternoon and we'd watch it together."

"There is only one man left on this show that Belinda

hasn't done—and he's seventy. The patriarch." Connie sighed. "They're going to have to bring in some new talent for Belinda."

Back on TV, Belinda bit at Brent's lip, then his chin, then slipped lower in the bed and disappeared under the sheet. All three women in the back room leaned toward the TV. The lump in the sheet that was Belinda's head went lower and momentarily Brent threw back his head and let a delicious moan escape.

"My God," Mel said.

Connie fanned her face.

"I think that's her secret weapon," Joy said. And the program cut to commercial.

Connie and Joy looked at each other, giggled and got up out of their chairs. "Well, not much has changed since yesterday. That baby's gonna be in college before it gets out who the daddy is."

"I'm not even sure it is Donovan's. She was with Carter, too."

"That was a long time ago—it couldn't be his."

"How long have you two been watching this soap?" Mel asked.

"Oh, God, fifteen years?" Connie answered by way of a question.

"At least."

"You find a magazine, honey?"

Mel made a face and held up the *Playboy*.

"My, my," Connie said.

"I'm not too interested in trucks, fish, guns or game," she said. "Don't you ever get any others in?"

"If you tell me what you want, I'll have Ron pick 'em up on his next run. We only carry what we sell."

"Makes sense," she said. "I hope I haven't just

snatched up some poor guy's *Playboy* that he's looking forward to."

"Don't you worry about it," Connie said. "Hey, there's a little potluck at the bar tonight for Joy's birthday. Why don't you come on over?"

"Aw, I don't have a present!"

"We don't do presents, honey," Joy said. "Just come and party."

"Well, happy birthday anyway, Joy. I'll check with Doc," she said. "What time? If I can come, should I bring something for the potluck?"

"We'll get over there about six, and no, don't you worry about bringing anything. I don't guess you do any cooking at Doc's and we have the food covered. Nothing new on that baby, huh?"

"Not a peep."

"Damnedest thing," Joy said. "Bet whoever's it is came from another one of the towns."

"I'm starting to think that, too," Mel said. She pulled some bills out of her pocket to pay for her stuff. "Maybe I'll see you later, then."

On her way back to Doc's she passed the bar. Jack was sitting on the porch with his feet up on the rail. She wandered over. Sitting beside him was a fishing tackle box full of beautiful feathery flies. Small pliers, scissors and a razor blade were sticking out of the tackle box, as well as little plastic envelopes that contained colorful feathers, silver hooks and other paraphernalia.

"Break time?" he asked her.

"I've been on break all day, except for a little diaper changing and feeding. The baby's asleep, there aren't any patients and Doc is afraid to play gin with me. It turns out I can beat his socks off."

Jack laughed. He leaned forward and peered at the

book and magazine. He looked at her face and raised an eyebrow. "Little light reading?" he asked.

She lifted the magazine. "It was either this or guns, trucks, hunting or fishing. You want to borrow it when I'm through?"

"No, thanks," he laughed.

"You don't like naked women?"

"I love naked women—I just don't feel like looking at pictures of them. It seems like you'd get enough of that in your line of work," he said.

"Like I said, the choices were pretty limited. I haven't seen one of these in years, but when I was in college my roommates and I used to laugh ourselves stupid at the advice column. And they used to have some interesting stories. Does *Playboy* still run fiction?"

"I have absolutely no idea, Melinda," he said, grinning.

"You know what I've noticed about this town? Everyone has a satellite dish and at least one gun."

"A couple of items that seem to be necessary. No cable TV out here. You shoot?" he asked.

"I hate guns," she said with a shudder. "Try to imagine the number of gunshot deaths in a trauma center in L.A." She shivered again. *He has no idea,* she thought.

"The guns around here aren't the kind people use on each other. Hardly a handgun in the town, although I have a couple, just because I've had them for a long time. This is rifle and shotgun country—used for hunting, euthanizing a sick or wounded animal, protection from wildlife. I could teach you to shoot, so you'd be more comfortable with guns."

"No way. I hate to even be around them. All these guns I see in the gun racks in the trucks—are they loaded?"

"You bet. You don't take a minute to load your rifle

if a bear is charging you. Bear fish in the same rivers we do."

"Whew, fishing just took on a whole new meaning. Who shot all the animals on the walls in the bar?" she asked.

"Preacher got the buck. I caught the fish and shot the bear."

She was shaking her head. "How can you get any satisfaction out of killing innocent animals?"

"The buck and fish were innocent," he admitted. "But that bear wasn't. I didn't want to shoot her, but I was working on the bar and she was poking around right back there, maybe looking for trash. Bear are scavengers—they'll eat anything. It was a real dry summer. Her cub wandered too close to me and riled her up. Pissed her off. She must have gotten the idea I was going to interfere with the cub. So…?"

"Aw. What happened to the cub?"

"I locked him in the bar until Fish and Game could come out for him. They relocated him."

"That's too bad. For her. She was just being a mother."

"I didn't want to shoot that bear," he said. "I don't even hunt bear. I carry repellent—sort of a pepper spray. That day the repellent was in the truck, but the rifle was handy. I wouldn't have shot her, but it kind of got down to her or me." He grinned at her. "City girl," he said.

"Yeah, I'm just a city girl. With no dead animals on my walls. Think I'll keep it that way."

Friday night, big night in Virgin River. There were more than the usual number of cars parked around the bar, though the people Mel knew best would have walked over. Mel had said to Doc, "There's a potluck for Joy's birthday at Jack's tonight. I assume you're going over. Maybe later, if you could spell me for a half hour, I can just drop in and wish her a happy birthday."

Doc scoffed at that idea. All he wanted was to go collect his one whiskey of the day, have a bite to eat and turn in. So Mel fed and settled the baby while he was across the street. She fluffed her hair and put on a little lipstick, ready for what she expected to be a fairly dull evening, but an evening with a few friendly faces nonetheless. It was seven-thirty before Chloe slept and she was able to leave. "I won't be long," she told Doc.

"I'm not going anywhere," he said. "Dance till dawn for all I care."

"Will you call me if you need me?" she asked Doc.

"Hardly ever have a party in this town," he said. "You should take advantage of it. I know how to change and feed. Been doing it a lot longer than you."

When she walked in, she found the place nearly full of people. The jukebox, which was hardly ever playing, provided background music. Country. Jack and Preacher were behind the bar, Ricky was busy bussing tables. She looked around until she found Joy.

"Sorry to be showing up so late, Joy. The baby didn't really want to settle down tonight." She plucked her sweater away from herself and gave a little sniff. "I think I might smell like cheese."

"You're fine—and there's still plenty of food left so grab yourself a plate."

A few tables had been pushed together to line a wall and upon them, dish after casserole dish of delicious-looking food. Right in the center was a sheet cake practically covered with candles. After she'd put some food on her plate, people started wandering over to say hello and chat. She greeted Fish Bristol, noted fisherman in these parts, and his wife, Carrie. Harv, who was found in the bar almost every morning, was a lineman for the telephone company, but before getting out on the road he had his breakfast at Jack's. "My wife can't be bothered to get out of bed just to cook breakfast," he said with a laugh. She noticed that Liz was tucked away in the corner, looking miserably bored, her long, shapely legs crossed, her short skirt just barely covering her privates. Mel gave her a wave, coaxing a very small smile out of Liz. Mel was introduced to a sheep rancher and his wife, Buck and Lilly Anderson—Buck, tall and skinny and balding and Lilly, short and round and rosy cheeked. "Any news on that baby?" Lilly asked.

"Nothing," she said.

"Is she a good baby?"

"Oh, God, she's perfect. An angel."

"And no one's asked if they can take her? Adopt her?"

"I haven't even heard from social services yet," Mel said.

Connie brought a friend over to introduce. "Mel, this is Jo Fitch. She and her husband live on the end of the street—the biggest house there."

"I'm so glad to finally meet you," Jo said. "No one expected such a young, pretty girl. We—"

Before Jo could finish she was joined by a man who slipped an arm about Jo's waist and, while swirling a drink in his glass, boldly looked Mel up and down and said, "Well, well, well…so this is our little nurse? Ohh, nurse, I'm not feeling so good!" And then he treated himself to a great big laugh.

"My husband, Nick," Jo said. If Mel wasn't mistaken, she said it somewhat nervously.

"How do you do," Mel said politely, deciding that he'd had a bit too much to drink. She turned to Connie and said, "Everything is so delicious."

"So, nurse Melinda—how do you like our little town?" he asked her.

"Please, just call me Mel," she said. "It's great. You're very lucky."

"Yep," he said, looking her over again. "We really got lucky. Where do I sign up for an examination?" And he laughed at himself some more.

It came back to her then—Jo Ellen and that husband of hers. This was the guy. He'd been slapped down by more than one woman, Hope had said. He couldn't possibly be more obvious. "Gosh, excuse me just a second, I'll be right back. I need something to drink."

He grabbed her arm and said, "Let me—"

She shook him off firmly, smiling all the while. "No, no. You wait right here," and she scooted away as fast as she could. On her way to the bar she stopped to say hello to Doug and Sue Carpenter, frequent visitors at Jack's. She met the elder Fishburns—Polly's mother and father-in-law. When she got to the bar and hopped up on a stool in front of Jack, setting her plate down, she didn't have his attention right away. He was looking into the crowded room, frowning.

Finally he looked at her. "Could I have a beer?" she asked him.

"Sure," he said.

"You don't look too happy," she observed.

His expression relaxed. "Just keeping an eye on things," he said. "Having fun?"

"Hmm." She nodded, taking a sip. "Have you eaten this stuff? It's almost as good as Preacher's. These country women can cook!"

"That's why most of them are—how should I put it? Robust?"

She laughed at him. Leaving her beer for a moment,

she ate a little more off her plate. "Yet another reason for me to get back to civilization."

She stayed there for a moment longer, then he was beside her again. Nick. "I waited," he said.

"Oh, Nick. Sorry—but I have to mingle. I'm new in town you know." And off the stool she leaped, beer in her hand, leaving the plate behind.

As Nick made to follow, he found his wrist clamped down on the bar. Jack looked into his eyes darkly. "Your wife is waiting for you over there."

"Be a sport, Jack," Nick said, laughing.

"You'd better behave yourself," Jack warned.

Nick laughed heartily. "Now, Jack—you can't have all the pretty girls to yourself. I mean, come on, man! All our wives are hot for you—cut a guy some slack." And he made his escape.

Jack watched closely from behind the bar. He was able to serve drinks and draw drafts without taking his eyes off the room. Nick seemed to follow Mel around like a smitten puppy, sidling up as close as possible, but Mel was quick. She'd go around to the far sides of tables to crouch to speak to people, get other men between her and Nick, slip across the room as if there was someone she just had to see, always leaving Nick in her dust. Preacher was behind the bar with him and at a point said, "Want me to give him a little advice before he gets his nose broken?"

"No," Jack said flatly. Jack was thinking that breaking his nose was going to feel very good. If Nick put one hand on her, he was going to come apart.

"Good," Preacher said. "I haven't been to a good bar fight in years."

In keeping an eye on things, he saw Connie's young niece stand up and walk over to the buffet, stick her finger into the icing on the cake and then into her mouth, slowly, so slowly pulling her finger back out while glancing over her shoulder at Rick—and his boy Ricky froze at one of the tables where he was picking up glasses. Jack saw him see her; saw Ricky almost tremble for a moment, mouth open slightly, eyes wide, taking her in—those long legs, full breasts. *Oh, boy,* Jack thought.

Someone lit the candles on the cake and everyone got up from their tables and came from the edges of the room to gather round, sing and watch Joy knock herself out trying to blow out fifty-three of them.

Mel stood at the rear of the crowd; Jack's eyes were back on her. Jack scowled blackly as Nick came up behind her. He couldn't see what was happening through the crowd, but he noted that a smile grew on Nick's face just as Mel's chin rose up, her eyes grew round and startled and she threw a panicked look in Jack's direction. Jack pushed himself off the bar and was making fast tracks to the other side when Mel reacted.

Mel felt a hand run over her bottom and inch between her legs. She was stunned for a moment, disbelieving. Then her instincts kicked in and shifted her beer to her other hand, threw an elbow back into his gut, brought that same elbow up under his chin, swept his legs out from under him with one booted foot, lifting him off his feet to send him crashing to the floor, flat on his back. She put her foot on his chest and glared into his eyes. "Don't you *ever* try anything like that again!" All this without spilling a drop of her beer.

Jack froze at the end of the bar. *Whoa,* he thought. Damn.

A second passed. Then Mel looked around the now silent room in some embarrassment. Everyone was shocked and staring. "Oh!" she said, but her foot still held Nick on his back. Nick who, it seemed, couldn't draw a breath, just lay there, stunned. She removed her foot. "Oh…" she said.

A laugh broke out of the crowd. Someone clapped. A woman yelped approvingly. Mel backed away somewhat sheepishly. She ended up at the bar, right in front of Jack. Right where she felt safest. Jack put a hand on her shoulder and glared in Nick's direction.

Mel felt awfully sorry for Jo Ellen. What's a woman from a town this size supposed to do with an obnoxious husband like that? Once Jo peeled him off the floor and took him home, the party became much more fun, and the jokes were fabulous. Several men asked her to arm wrestle and she had clearly become a hero to the women.

The stories of Nick's antics were both shocking and entertaining. Once, when he was feeling invincible and couldn't resist a breast, he'd been coldcocked by a woman. Up till tonight that was the most legendary putdown he'd suffered. He'd collected a number of slaps, but by some miracle had not yet been beat to a pulp by an angry husband; he was apparently regarded as a pathetic joke. It seemed that when there was some kind of community or neighborhood party, like tonight, he'd have a couple of pops and get frisky, take chances that, by the light of day, he managed to keep under control. His reputation was firmly established.

"And yet you keep inviting him," Mel observed to Connie.

"It's just us here, kiddo. We're kind of stuck with each other."

"He should be told that if he can't mind his manners, he won't be included anymore."

"The problem with that is it would leave Jo out—and she's good people. I feel a whole lot sorrier for Jo than any of the women he pesters," Connie said. "Makes her look like a damn fool. We can pretty much take care of ourselves." She patted Mel's arm. "And you, girl—I doubt he's going to give you any more trouble."

At nine o'clock the party abruptly ended. It was as though someone had rung a bell—all the women gathered up their dishes, men stacked up plates and picked up trash, goodbyes were being said and people were filing out the door. Mel was at the back of the group, following, when Jack called her. "Hold up," he said. So she went back and jumped up on the stool. He put a cup of coffee in front of her. "Did I call you a city girl?" he asked with a smile.

"I didn't even know I could still do that," she said, accepting the coffee.

"Mind if I ask how you learned that?"

"It was a long time ago—when I was in my last year of college. There had been some rapes around the campus and a bunch of us went to a self-defense instructor together. To tell you the truth, I was never sure that would work in a real situation. I mean, with an instructor, mats on the floor, everything rehearsed and knowing exactly what to expect—that's one thing. But I wasn't sure I could react the same way if a real rapist jumped out from behind a parked car."

"Now you know. He never saw it coming."

"Yeah, that worked to my advantage, too." She sipped her coffee.

"I didn't see what he did," he said. "I could tell by the stupid grin on his face and the shocked look on yours that something happened."

She put her cup on the bar. "Major butt grope," she

said. And she noted that Jack's expression went instantly dark; mean, narrowed eyes, deep frown. "Whew, easy, buddy, it wasn't your butt. I saw you making a move— what were you about to do?"

"Way too much," he said. "I don't like seeing something like that in my bar. I was watching him all night. The second he saw you, it was a target lock-on."

"He was a giant nuisance, but I'm pretty sure he'll leave me alone now," she said. "It was kind of funny the way the party just suddenly stopped like that. Did someone look at their watch or something?"

"Livestock don't give days off," he said.

"Neither do babies," she said, getting off the stool.

"I'll walk you," Jack said.

"You don't have to, Jack. I'm okay."

He came around the bar anyway. "Indulge me. It's been an interesting night." He took her arm, telling himself he was just being gentlemanly but, in fact, if he saw the chance, he was going to get his lips on hers. He'd been wanting to kiss her for days.

They walked across the porch and down the steps, out into the street. There were no streetlights, but the moon was high and full and cast a soft glow over the town. There was a light on in the upstairs bedroom at Doc's. Jack stopped right in the middle of the street. "Look, Mel. Look at that sky. You can't find that anywhere else on earth. All those stars, that moon—the clear black sky. That belongs to us."

She looked up at the most gorgeous sky imaginable, with more stars than she thought existed. He stepped behind her and with his hands on both of her upper arms, he gently squeezed.

"You just can't see this in the city. In any city."

"It is beautiful," she said softly. "I admit, this is beautiful country."

"It's majestic. One of these days, before you pack it in and run for your life, I'd like to show you some things. The redwoods, the rivers, the coast. It's almost time for whale watching." She leaned back against him and couldn't deny it felt pretty good to be shored up by Jack. "I'm sorry about what happened tonight." He leaned down and inhaled the scent of her hair. "I was really impressed with how well you handled it—but I'm sorry he… I hate that he touched you like that. I thought I had an eye on him."

"Too quick for me. Too quick for you," she said.

He turned her around and looked into her eyes. He thought he saw an invitation there in her upturned face and he lowered his.

She put a hand on his chest. "I have to go in now," she said, a little breathless.

He straightened.

"We both know I couldn't throw you," she said, smiling weakly.

"You'll never have to," he said. But he still held her arms, so reluctant to let go.

"Good night, Jack. And thanks for everything. Despite Nick—I had a good time."

"Glad to hear it," he said. And he let go.

She turned, and with her head down, went the rest of the way alone.

He stood in the street until she was inside, then headed back to the bar. On his way, he saw Ricky's truck parked right in front of Connie's house. Well, damn—the boy sure didn't waste any time. Ricky didn't have a mom or dad and his grandmother wasn't well. Jack had been looking out for him for a long time and he knew this day would come eventually—they'd have to have *the* talk. But not tonight. Tonight Jack would have that talk with himself.

Preacher had the chairs upside down on the tables and was sweeping up. Jack walked right by him at a good clip. "Where you going in such a hurry?" Preacher asked.

"Shower," he said miserably.

It was because Connie and Ron liked Ricky so much that they had no problem with him staying out in front of the house talking with Liz for a few minutes. They trusted him, he knew this. But maybe they shouldn't because if they knew what one look at Liz had done to him, they'd lock her up.

She leaned against the porch, crossed her legs in front of her, pulled a cigarette out of her purse and lit it.

"What are you doing that for?" he asked her.

"Got a problem with it?" she said, blowing out smoke.

He shrugged. "Makes your mouth taste like shit," he said. "No one's going to want to kiss you if you smoke."

She smiled at him. "Someone wants to kiss me?" she asked.

He took the cigarette out of her hand and tossed it. Then he grabbed her around the waist and brought her onto his lips. *Yeah,* he thought. *Makes your mouth taste bad, but not bad enough.*

She curved right to him and of course it happened to him. Happened all the time these days. When she opened her mouth and pressed harder against him, it happened even more. Holy God, he was dying. He could feel her full, hard breasts against his chest and right now all he wanted was to palm one. Against her lips he said, "You shouldn't smoke."

"Yeah."

"It'll cut your life short."

"We wouldn't want that."

"You're beautiful," he said. "Really beautiful."

"So are you."

"Guys aren't beautiful. You want a ride to school Monday?"

"Sure. What time?"

"Pick you up at seven. What class are you?"

"Freshman," she said.

It stopped happening to him real fast. "Four…fourteen?" he asked her.

"Yeah. And you're…?"

"Ah… A junior. Sixteen." He backed away a little. "Damn. Holy God."

"Did I just lose my ride?" she asked, tugging her sweater down a little bit, which only made her boobs pop out more.

He smiled at her. "Nah. What the heck, huh? See you Monday morning." He started to walk away, then turned back abruptly and decided on another kiss. Deep and strong. Long. And then another, still longer. Maybe deeper. She sure didn't feel fourteen.

Six

One morning, Doc left the house early, before break-fast, to make a call. He hadn't been gone long when Lilly Anderson came to the office to see Mel. Lilly was in the same general age group with Connie and Joy and most of the other women Mel had met—late forties to early fifties. She was pleasantly round with a soft, kind face and lots of short, curly brown hair strung with gray. She wore no makeup and her skin was perfect, blemish-free ivory with pink cheeks and a sweet dimpled smile. The moment Mel met her at the potluck, she'd sensed a safe, nurturing way about her. Mel instantly liked her, trusted her. "You still have that little one, that baby?" Lilly asked.

"I do," Mel said.

"I'm surprised no one has come forward, wanting to take her in, adopt her."

"I'm kind of surprised by that, too," Mel said.

"Perfect healthy little baby," she said. "What about all those people who want to adopt healthy babies? Where are they?"

Mel shrugged. "Maybe it's just a matter of social services getting their ducks in a row—I understand they're busy and small towns like this get put on the back burner."

"I haven't been able to stop thinking about her. I thought, well, maybe I could help out," Lilly said.

"That's nice of you," Mel said. "Do you live nearby? Because sometimes it's nice for me and Doc to get a break for a few hours. Especially if we have patients."

"We're ranchers—I'm on the other side of the river, but it's not so far. Thing is, I already raised six young-sters—had my first at only nineteen and my baby is eighteen now and already married. But I have room at the house, what with the kids gone off on their own. I could take in the baby until something permanent is ar-ranged for her. I even have those old baby things stored in the barn. Maybe I could be a foster parent. Buck, my husband, he says it would be okay."

"That's very generous, Lilly, but I'm afraid we couldn't pay you anything."

"I wouldn't need pay," she said. "It's just a neighborly thing. We help out when we can. And I do love babies."

"Let me ask you something—have you any idea who might've had this baby?"

She shook her head and looked terribly pained. "You have to ask yourself, what kind of woman would give up her baby? Maybe some young girl in trouble, no one to help her. I raised three daughters and by the grace of God, none had to pass that way. I have seven grand-children already."

"That's the beauty of starting early," Mel said. "Your grandchildren come along while you're still young enough to enjoy them."

"I'm blessed," she said. "I know this. I can only imagine that whoever left her must have been desperate, so desperate." Mel thought Lilly might have even briefly had tears in her eyes.

"Well, I'll take your offer to Doc and see what he says. You're sure? Because I can give you some formula and diapers, and that's all."

"I'm sure. And please tell Doc I'd be more than happy to do it."

When Doc returned an hour later, Mel told him the story. His white eyebrows shot up in surprise and he rubbed a hand over his head. "Lilly Anderson?" he asked. He seemed to be considering this idea with some consternation.

"Does something about that worry you, because we can make do here a while longer…"

"Worry me? No." He collected himself. "Surprises me, is all." And he shuffled off to his office.

She followed him. "Well? You didn't have an answer."

He turned back toward her. "Can't think of a better place for that infant than Lilly's," he said. "Lilly and Buck are good people. And they know what to do with a baby, that's for sure."

"You don't need time to think about this?" she asked.

"I don't," he said. "I was hoping a family would turn up." He peered at her over his glasses. "Seems like maybe you need some time to think about it."

"No," she said, somewhat tremulously. "If you're okay, I'm okay."

"Think it over, just the same. I'll walk across the street and see if anyone's willing to play cribbage. Then, if you're of a mind, we'll take her out to the Anderson ranch."

"Okay," she said. But she said it very quietly.

Jack was painfully, embarrassingly aware that Mel had only been in town three weeks, and he could think of little else. Fact was, from the moment he looked at her in the dim light of the bar that first night, he wanted to sit right down at that table with her and get to know her.

He saw her every day, and given their meals together and long conversations, he knew himself to be her closest friend at the moment. And yet there was much about herself she was concealing. She was open about having lost her parents young, her close relationship with her sister and sister's family, her nursing career, the crazy and chaotic life at the hospital, but it was as though there was a block of time missing. *Him,* Jack thought. The one who devastated her and left her hurt and lonely. Jack would drive him away, given half a chance.

He wished he knew what it was that had hooked him so quickly, so thoroughly. It wasn't just her beauty, though that was evident. True, there weren't any pretty, single women around town, but he hadn't been lonely. And Mel hadn't been the only sexy woman he'd laid eyes on in the past few years. He was hardly a hermit; he'd been to lots of the other towns, the coastal towns, to night spots. There'd been Clear River.

But Mel had some aura that had him all worked up. That tight little body, full breasts, compact bottom, rosy lips, not to mention some real sexy brains—it was all he could do to keep from breathing heavy in her presence. When she had those moments when whatever plagued her was forgotten, and she smiled or laughed, her whole face brightened up. Her blue eyes danced. He'd already dreamed of her; felt her hands all over his body, felt her beneath him, felt himself inside of her, heard her soft moans of pleasure and bam! He awoke to find himself as alone as ever, bathed in sweat.

Jack was already turned on before Mel dropped Nick on his ass, but if he hadn't been, that sure would have sealed the deal. She was a dynamo. Gorgeous, feminine little thing with one helluva punch. Whoa. Damn.

The vulnerability in her eyes warned him he'd better be very, very careful. One wrong move and she'd jump in that little BMW and shake the dust of Virgin River off the soles of her shoes, the town's medical needs notwithstanding. He reminded himself constantly that this was one reason he hadn't sprung the cabin on her yet. Walking away from her last week after Joy's party had been one of the hardest things he'd ever done. He had wanted nothing so much as to crush her to him and say, *It's going to be all right—I can make it all right, all good. Give me a chance.*

Doc and Preacher sat at a table in the bar, playing cribbage. Jack put a slice of Preacher's apple pie on a plate, covered it with Saran wrap and left the bar to walk across the street. No cars or trucks at Doc's except Doc's truck and that little BMW parked on the side. *All clear,* he thought, his pulse picking up. He opened the front door and looked around; no one. He thought to go tap on the office door, but a sound from the kitchen led him there instead.

The baby in her little Plexiglas bed on wheels sat near the warm stove and Mel was at the table, her head down, resting on her folded arms. And she sobbed. He rushed to her; he put the pie on the table and was down on one knee at the side of her chair, all in one movement. "Mel," he said.

She lifted her head, her cheeks chafed and pink. "Dammit," she said through her tears. "You caught me."

His hand was on her back. "What is it?" he asked gently. *Now,* he thought. *Now she'll tell me about it, let me help her through it.*

"I've found a home for the baby. Someone came in and offered to take her and Doc endorses it."

"Who?" he asked.

"Lilly Anderson," she said, large tears spilling over. "Oh, Jack. I let it happen. I got attached." And she leaned against his shoulder and wept.

Jack forgot everything. "Come here," he said, pulling her out of the chair. He traded places with her and pulled her down on his lap. She encircled his neck with her arms, her face buried in his shoulder, crying, and he gently stroked her back. His lips were on her soft hair. "It's okay," he whispered. "It's okay."

"I let it happen," she said into his shirt. "Stupid. I knew better. I even named her. What was I thinking?"

"You gave her affection," he said. "You were so good to her. I'm sorry it hurts." But he wasn't sorry, because he had his arms around her and it felt as he knew it would, her little body, warm and solid, against his. She was light as a feather on his lap, her arms around his neck like ribbons, and the sweet, fragrant smell of her hair coiled around his brain and tightened, addling his thoughts.

She lifted her head and looked into his eyes. "I thought about taking her," she said. "Running away with her. That's how crazy I am. Jack, you should know—I'm totally nuts."

He wiped the tears from her cheeks. "If you want her, Mel, you can try to adopt her."

"The Andersons," she said. "Doc says they're good people. A good family."

"They are. Salt of the earth."

"And that would be better for her than a single mother who works all the time," she said. "She needs a real bed, not this incubator. A real family, not a midwife and an old doctor."

"There are lots of different kinds of families."

"Oh, I know what's best." Then the tears began to flow again. "It's just so hard." And she laid her head back on his shoulder. His arms tightened around her and hers tightened around his neck. He closed his eyes and just rested his cheek against her hair.

Feeling these strong arms around her, Mel let herself sink into a good, heartfelt cry. She was fully aware of him, but what really mattered to her at the moment was that for the first time in almost a year of crying, she wasn't alone. Someone was holding her and she felt protected. There was the comfort of strength and warmth, and she welcomed it. His chambray shirt was soft against her cheek and his thighs hard beneath her. He had a wonderful scent of cologne and the outdoors and she felt safe with him. His hand stroked her back and she was aware that he softly kissed her hair.

He rocked her gently as she continued to dampen his shirt. Minutes passed and her weeping slowed to a sniffle, then a murmur. She lifted her head and looked at him, though she said nothing. His brain went numb. He touched her lips softly with his, gently, tentatively. Her eyes closed as she allowed this and his arms tightened around her as he pressed more firmly against her lips. Hers opened and his breath caught as he opened his own and felt her small tongue dart into his mouth. His world reeled and he was lost in a kiss that deepened, that moved him, that shook him.

"Don't," she whispered against his mouth. "Don't get mixed up with me, Jack."

He kissed her again, holding her against him as

though he would never let her go. "Don't worry about me," he said against her lips.

"You don't understand. I have nothing to give. Nothing."

"I haven't asked you for a thing," he said. But in his mind he was saying, *You're mistaken. You are giving, and taking—and it feels damn good.*

All Mel could think, in the abstract, was that her body for once wasn't hollow and so empty she ached. She drank it in, the feeling of being connected to something. To someone. Anchored. So wonderful to have that human contact again. In her soul she had forgotten how, but her body remembered. "You're a good man, Jack," she said against his lips. "I don't want you to be hurt. Because I can't love anyone."

All he said was, "I can take care of myself."

She kissed him again. Deeply. Passionately. For a long minute; two minutes, moving under his mouth with heat.

And the baby fussed.

She pulled away from him. "Oh, man, why'd I do *that?*" she asked. "That's a mistake."

He shrugged. "Mistake? Nah. We're friends," he said. "We're close. You needed some comfort and— and here I am."

"That just can't happen," she said, sounding a little desperate.

He took charge, feeling his own sense of desperation. "Mel, stop it. You were crying. That's all."

"I was kissing," she said. "And so were you!"

He smiled at her. "You are so hard on yourself sometimes. It's okay to feel something that doesn't hurt once in a while."

"Promise me that won't happen again!"

"It won't if you don't want it to. But let me tell you something—if you do want it to, I'm going to let you. You know why? Because I like kissing. And I don't beat myself up about it."

"I'm not doing that," she said. "I just don't want to be stupid."

"You're punishing yourself. I can't figure out why. But," he said, lifting her off his lap and putting her on her feet, "you get to call the shots. Personally, I think you secretly like me. Trust me. And I think for a minute there, you also liked kissing me." He grinned at her. "I could tell. I'm so smart that way."

"You're just desperate for a little female companionship," she said.

"Oh, there are females around. That has nothing to do with anything."

"Still—you have to promise."

"Sure," he said. "If that's what you want."

"It's what I need."

He stood up and looked down at her. He had warned himself of this and stupidly ignored his own warnings. He had to renew that trust. Fast. He lifted her chin with a finger and looked into her pretty, sad eyes. "Would you like me to take you and Chloe to the Anderson ranch? If I promise not to kiss you anymore?"

"Would you?" she said. "I want to take her, to see where she'll live. And I don't think I want to be alone."

Jack knew it was imperative that Mel regain her sense of control. He went back to the bar to get his truck and poked his head in. "Doc, I'm going to drive Mel and the baby out to the Andersons'. You okay with that?"

"Sure," the old boy said, not looking up from his game. When Mel had the few amassed baby things packed up, he took her. They had no car seat, so she held the baby—and she got a little teary. But once they had traversed the long road up into the hills and were passing through the fenced pastures of grazing sheep, he could see that she was pulling herself together.

Lilly Anderson brought them into her home—a simple house that spoke of the abundance of life. The floors and windows were shining from the housekeeping attention they received; there were folded quilts on the ends of sofas and draped over chairs, crewel pictures on the walls, the smell of freshly baked bread, a pie cooling on the counter and dozens of pictures of children, of family, a collection that spanned many years. A wicker bassinet stood ready for Chloe. Lilly made Mel tea and they sat at the kitchen table and talked while Jack went with Buck to the corral where his grown sons had begun the spring shearing.

"I'll be honest with you, Lilly. I got pretty attached to her."

Lilly reached across the table for her hand. "It's perfectly understandable. You should come out here often, hold her, rock her. You should stay close."

"I don't want you to go through that—when someone finally comes for her."

Lilly got tears in her eyes in sympathy with the tears Mel was showing. "You must be such a tender heart," Lilly said. "Don't worry, Mel—now that I'm a grandma, lots of little ones pass through here and don't stay. But while she's here, promise you won't be a stranger."

"Thank you, Lilly. For understanding. My women and their babies—it's what I live for."

"It shows. We're so lucky to have you with us."

"But I'm not staying, you know...."

"You should think about that. This isn't a bad place."

"I'll hang around long enough to be sure things are working out for Chloe. And I'll try to make it a few days before I'm back to cuddle her," Mel said.

"You come every day if you like. Twice a day."

It wasn't long before Mel joined Jack at the fence and stood watching the shearing. "You'll have to come back for the lambing in a few weeks," Buck said. "We like to shear before the lambing—it's easier on the sheep."

When they left the ranch, Jack drove around the hills of Virgin River. He didn't say anything—he just let her see the beauty of the green fields, the high hills, grazing livestock. He took her for a little stretch along Highway 299 through a piece of the redwoods that, despite her morose mood, caused her to gasp in awe. The sky was still and blue, the breeze light and cool, but in the tallest trees it was dark except for those blinding flashes of bright sun that broke through. He could tell she was getting better, if slowly, quietly.

It was like this place was divided into two worlds— the dank and dark world of the deep forest where life was bleak and poor, the people desperate. And this world, the national forest of redwoods, the first-rate campgrounds, the hills and valleys where the fields were lush and plentiful, where health and contentment abounded.

Jack drove down a tree-canopied road toward the widest curve in the Virgin River, pulled the truck up to the edge and parked. There were two men in the river, waders held by suspenders, wearing tan fishing vests with many pockets and wicker creels held by shoulder straps, casting out into the water. The arcs of their lines were like a ballet, so graceful, so rhythmic.

"What are we doing?" she asked.

"I wanted you to see a few things before you cut and

run. This is where a lot of the town and visitors like to fish, where I mostly fish. When the winter rains come, we come out here to watch the salmon leap up over the natural waterfalls to return to their home creeks to spawn. It's really something to see. Now that the baby is at the Andersons', I'll take you to the coast if you like. Pretty soon the whales will be migrating north to cooler waters for the summer. They'll travel close to the coastline with their new calves and it's incredible."

She watched the fishermen cast and reel in, then there was a catch. A good-size brown trout.

"During a good season, fish is the main staple on the menu at the bar," he said.

"Most of it you catch yourself?" she asked.

"Me and Preacher and Ricky. The best way to make work into play. Mel," he said, his voice soft. "Look downstream. There…"

She squinted and then sat back with a gasp. Poking their heads out of the brush at the side of the river on the other side was a mother bear and her cub.

"You were asking about the bear. Black bear. The cub looks young. They're just giving birth and coming out of hibernation. Have you ever seen anything like that?"

"Only on the Discovery Channel. The fishermen don't see her?" she asked.

"I'm sure they see her. She won't bother them and they won't bother her. But they carry bear repellent just in case. And they'll have a rifle in the truck—but if she gets too close they'll just reel in their lines and sit in their trucks until she leaves." He chuckled. "Watch while she eats their fish."

She watched in fascination for a moment, then said, "Why'd you bring me here?"

"Sometimes, if something's eating me up—I can

come out here, or drive into the redwoods, or go up on the knoll where the sheep are grazing, or maybe out to a pasture where the cows roam, and just sit awhile. Just connect with the earth. Sometimes that's all I have to do."

One elbow sticking out of the window, wrist of the other hand balanced on the top of the steering wheel, Jack just watched the fishing—the men and the bear. The men were so intent on their sport that they had never even turned around at the sound of the truck pulling into the clearing.

They were quiet. Jack had no idea what she might be thinking, but he thought, *Don't turn and run just because you got kissed. Things could be worse.*

After about twenty minutes, he started the truck. "I have something to show you. You're in no hurry, are you?"

"Doc's in town," she said. "I guess not."

Jack eventually pulled into the clearing where Hope McCrea's cabin sat. It was perfectly obvious he'd like her to reconsider leaving. But she never expected him to do what he had done. As they pulled up to the cabin and parked, she looked at him in surprise.

"My God," she said. "How did you do this?"

"Soap," he said. "Wood. Paint. Nails."

"You shouldn't have, Jack. Because—"

"I know—because you're not staying. I've heard that at least a hundred times over the past couple of weeks. That's fine. You'll do what you have to do. But this is what you were promised and I thought you ought to have the option."

Straight ahead of her was the little A-frame cabin with a new, strong, wide porch, painted red. Two white Adirondack chairs sat on the deck and four white pots holding red geraniums sat on the porch rails in the corners. It was beautiful. She was afraid to go inside. Did this mean that if it were lovely, she'd be forced to stay? Because she knew it was going to be lovely.

Wordlessly, Mel got out of the truck. She slowly walked up the steps to the house, aware that Jack had not gotten out of the truck behind her. He was letting her go alone. She pushed open the door, which no longer stuck. Inside, the wood floors gleamed, the countertops sparkled. The windows, previously so grimy you couldn't see out, were so clean it seemed possible there was no glass. The window that had been boarded up was replaced. The appliances were spotless, the furniture had been so vigorously vacuumed or shampooed that the colors were now bright because there was no dust. There was a new area rug on the floor.

She wandered into the bedroom. A new comforter replaced the old and she could tell without even checking under the covers that a fat, firm mattress had been purchased and that the nasty soiled one was gone. The brightness of the sheets indicated these were not Hope's hand-me-downs, but newly purchased linen. On the floor beside the bed, a wide, thick rug. In the bathroom, new towels and accessories. The shower glass had been completely replaced and the tiles had been scrubbed to such a high sheen that even the grout was immaculate. There was the faintest smell of bleach; not a spot or stain remained. She loved the bright towels, alternating red and white. The rugs were white; the trash can, glass and tissue dispenser were red.

There were two bedrooms downstairs and a small, open loft upstairs at the peak of the A-frame—only large enough for a bed and maybe a small dresser. Both of them had been scoured clean, but they were empty of furniture. Back in the living room, she saw the fire had been laid and a fresh pile of wood sat at the side of the hearth. The books in the bookcases were dust free, the trunk that could be used as a coffee table had been polished with lemon oil. The cupboards shone with oil, as well. She opened one of them and saw there were new ceramic dishes to replace the dingy Melmac that had been there before. Graying old plastic was replaced with glass. A wine rack on the counter held four bottles.

Inside the refrigerator, which also gleamed, there were a few staples. A bottle of white wine was chilling, a six-pack of good beer. There was milk, orange juice, butter, bread, lettuce and other salad items. Bacon and eggs. Sandwich items—lunch meat, cheese, mayo, mustard. On the kitchen table, which wore a pretty new tablecloth, sat a festive ceramic bowl holding fresh fruit. In the corner of the counter, a set of four thick, round white candles. She lowered her face and sniffed. Vanilla.

She left the house, pulling the door closed behind her and went back to the truck. It made her melancholy, all that he'd done. This was not what she'd expected, either. Mel had come to terms with the fact that she'd made a mistake. Now that she'd accepted that, she was ready to move on. As soon as they could spare her.

"Why did you do this?"

"It was promised to you," he said. "You're under no obligation."

"But what did you hope?" she asked.

"The town needs you. Doc needs help, you can see that. I hoped you'd give it a chance. A few more weeks, maybe. Just to see if it worked for you. I think the Virgin River folks have already made it clear—it works for them."

"Did you do this hoping it would force me to the terms of Hope's one-year contract?" she asked him. "Because as the place was, we were at an impasse. She couldn't hold me to it—she hadn't met the terms."

"She will not force that contract," he said flatly.

"But yes, she will."

"No. She will not hold you to that contract. Guaranteed. I'll see to it. This is just for you—not leverage for Hope."

She shook her head sadly. "You can see I don't belong here," she said softly.

"Aw. I don't know, Mel. People belong wherever they feel good. It can be a lot of different places. For a lot of different reasons."

"No, Jack, look. Look at me. I'm not a camper—I'm a shopper. I'm really not one of those homespun country midwives. I'm so citified, it's scary. I feel so out of place here. It's as if I'm not like anyone. They don't make me feel that way, but I can't help it. I shouldn't be here, I should be at Nordstrom's."

"Come on," he laughed.

She lowered her face into her hands and massaged her eyes. "You just don't understand. It's complicated, Jack. There's more to this than you realize."

"Tell me. You can trust me."

"That's just it—one of the reasons I agreed to come here is so I wouldn't have to talk about it anymore. Let's say I made a crazy decision. An insane decision. The *wrong* decision. This isn't for me."

"It wasn't just burnout, was it?" he asked her.

"I got rid of everything that tied me to L.A. and ran for my life. It was a panicked, crazy, irrational decision," she said. "I was hurting all over."

"I assumed as much. A man, maybe. A heartache or something."

"Close enough," she said.

"Believe me, Mel. This is as good a place as any to work through a heartache."

"You?" she asked him.

"Yeah, in a manner of speaking. But I didn't come here in a panic. I was looking for a place like this. Good fishing and hunting. Remote. Uncomplicated. Clean air, decent values, hardworking people who help each other out. It serves."

She took a deep breath. "I don't think it's going to work for me in the long-term."

"That's okay—no one asked you to make a long-term commitment. Well, no one except Hope, but no one really takes her seriously. But you shouldn't rush out of here with the same panic as you rushed in. It's a healthy place. It's a loving place. Who knows? You might find it helps you get through…whatever."

"I'm sorry. I'm such a downer sometimes. I should be so thankful. Grateful. And instead—"

"Hey, easy," he said, throwing the truck into gear to take her back to town. "I blindsided you. You had it in your head that you could use the excuse of having no decent housing. And now Chloe isn't holding you here. But I figured, you don't have to stay at Doc's now, and if someone's going to give birth in your bedroom there, maybe it's time you have your own place. If you want it, that is."

"Are there bears out here?" she asked.

"It might be best if you kept your trash indoors, and drive it into town to put in the Dumpster. Bears so like garbage."

"Oh, for the love of God!"

"We haven't had a bad bear scare in ages." He reached across the console and squeezed her hand. "Just give yourself a break. Work on your particular heartache. And while you do, take the occasional temperature. Give a pill now and then. No one's holding you hostage."

She watched him as he drove. That strong profile. He had a solid square face, straight nose, high cheekbones, bristle of stubble on his cheeks. He was a hairy guy; she noticed that he shaved his neck down to the top of his chest and she found herself wondering what was under his shirt. She remembered Mark's complaints of his receding hairline, which did nothing to detract from his boyish good looks. But this man, Jack, wasn't boyish. He had the hard good looks of a woodsman. And, though his hair was cropped short in that military buzz, it was so thick that it looked as if it should be thinned. The big hands on the steering wheel were calloused— he worked hard. The guy was dripping in testosterone.

What was this magnificent man doing locked away in a little town of six hundred, where there were no women for him? She wondered if he had the faintest clue about her—that she had no heart. He had just given so much and she had absolutely nothing to give. Nothing. She was hollow inside. If she weren't, a man like Jack would appeal to her.

This was the worst thing about grief, she thought as she walked back to Doc's house. It emptied you. She should be flattered and pleased with what had been done for her in the renovating of the cabin. She should be thrilled that a man like Jack was interested in her, because clearly he was. But instead she was sad. She had lost the ability to be moved by these acts of kindness. Instead, it made her feel depressed and alone, because she didn't feel up to the task of receiving gifts and kindnesses graciously. She couldn't respond to a handsome man's interest. She couldn't be happy. Sometimes she asked herself if she was paying some tribute to Mark's memory by hanging on to the sadness of losing him.

Ricky worked at the bar after school every day and some weekends, whenever Jack wanted him. He dropped Liz at the store after school, then parked behind the bar next to Jack's and Preacher's trucks. As he was going in, Jack was coming out. "Grab your gear," Jack said. "We're going to run out to the river, see if we can make a catch."

"There isn't anything out there now," Ricky said. The good catch was in the fall and winter, dwindling by spring, starting to pick up again in summer.

"We'll cast a while," Jack said. "See what you got."

"Preacher coming?" Ricky asked, going to the storeroom in the kitchen to get his rod, reel and waders.

"Nah. He's busy."

Jack remembered the first day he'd met Ricky. The kid had been thirteen and had ridden his bike up to the cabin that would become the bar. Skinny and frecklefaced with the most engaging grin and sweetest disposition. He let him hang around, help with the carpentry during the renovation if he could pay attention. When he found out it was just Ricky and his grandma, Lydie, he kind of took him under his wing. He'd watched the boy grow tall and strong; Jack taught him to fish, shoot. Now he was damn near a man. Physically, he didn't have far to go, but mentally and emotionally, sixteen was still just sixteen.

At the river's edge, they cast their lines a few times and then it came. The real reason for fishing when there were few fish. "You and I should have a little talk, I think," Jack said.

"About?"

Jack didn't look at him. He just cast in long beautiful arcs. And said, "About all the places you can put your dick that aren't statutory."

Ricky snapped his head around and looked at Jack's profile. Jack turned his head and met the boy's eyes.

"She's fourteen," Jack said.

Ricky looked back at the river, silent.

"I know she doesn't look fourteen. She's fourteen."

"I haven't done anything," Ricky said.

Jack laughed. "Oh, gimme a break. I saw your truck over at Connie's the first Friday night she was in town—you moved on her fast. You want to stick with that story?" He reeled in and turned toward Ricky. "Listen, son, you have to keep your head. You hear me, Rick? Because this is dangerous ground you're on. She's a little hottie—"

"She's a sweet girl," Rick said defensively.

"You're already hooked," Jack said, hoping they weren't already doomed. "How hooked?"

Ricky shrugged. "I like her. I know she's young, but she doesn't seem that young, and I like her."

"Okay," Jack said, taking a breath. "Okay, maybe we should talk about the things you can do to avoid putting your sixteen-year-old swimmers in contact with her fourteen-year-old eggs. Hmm?"

"You don't have to," Ricky said, casting. And casting pretty badly.

"Aw, Jesus. You're already involved. Physically, huh?" Rick didn't answer and Jack thought, who knew what they were up to. Jack remembered only too well the things experimental kids could do to get a little satisfaction without going all the way. It was a frickin' art form. Problem was, it just didn't last, and the closer you got, the greater potential for slip-ups. Sometimes it made more sense to decide you were going all the way with good birth control in place, rather than risk an accident. But man, you should be older. Older. "Aw, Jesus." Jack took a breath. He dug down into his waders, down into the pocket of his jeans. He pulled out a fist full of condoms. "This is tough, Rick, because I don't want you to use these on her, and I don't want you not to. I'm stuck here. Help me out, will you?"

"It's okay, Jack. I'm not going to do her. She's four-teen."

Jack reached out and tousled his hair. Those freckles had given way to the stubble of a young beard; he wasn't skinny anymore. The work he did at the bar plus the pastimes of hunting and fishing, not to mention chores for his grandma, had bulked the kid up and his shoulders and arms were muscled. Handsome kid, he thought. Real grown-up. He had a lot of responsibility—he worked hard, maintained his grades, did every physical thing around his grandma's house that needed doing. With Jack's supervision, Rick had painted her house. All that built toward creating a solid, reliable man—one who shouldn't get shot in the foot by a teen-age pregnancy.

"So, how old were you?" Ricky asked him.

"'Bout your age. But the girl was much older."

"Much?"

"Way older than Lizzie. Older than me. Smarter than me." He handed Rick the condoms and although Rick's cheeks took on a dark stain, he accepted them. "I know you're at that age—I was that age once. You know what the problem is. She might not look so young, but she's got a long way to go yet. Huh?"

A shiver went through Ricky and Jack caught it. Well, it's not as though he had been oblivious to Lizzie's rather over-matured charms. Thus the talk. "Yeah," Ricky said, a little breathless.

"Let's be sure you know some things," Jack said. "You know that old business about pulling out in time— you know that doesn't work. Right? And trying to not put it all the way in? Useless. First of all, if you can do that, you're a stronger man than I am, and even if you can, it's not good enough—you can still get her pregnant. You know these things, right?"

"Of course I know that."

"Rick, you understand, if there's no backing out of this relationship with her and if there's a strong potential for it to get more serious rather than less, you might have to be the one to take charge. Draw a line in the sand—insist on birth control at least. You got a midwife in town—there's help available. For Liz. I think she's too young to be having sex, personally. But I *know* she's too young to be pregnant. You with me here, buddy?"

"I told you, I have it under control. But thanks, Jack. I know you just want me to do the right thing."

"Which includes not getting caught off guard. If it's getting close, you get her fixed up. Double protection— hers and yours. You have to use the head with the brain in it. Believe me, I've seen more than one good man go down because he was thinking with his dick." He watched Ricky's chin lower as he looked down and he knew. Liz was irresistible to him. He was fighting for his life. His pants were on fire.

"Yeah," Ricky said. "I hear ya."

"You make sure you always have a condom, okay?

It's your responsibility to keep her safe, son. If you use even one condom, Rick, you get her to Mel. Right away."

"Do we have to talk about this anymore?"

Jack grabbed the boy's arm and felt solid biceps in his grasp. Damn, Ricky was nearly six feet and still growing. "You wanna be a man, son? You have to think like one. It's not enough to just feel like one."

"Yeah," he said. Then, "By the way, it's not statutory unless I'm over eighteen."

Jack laughed in spite of himself. "Too smart for your own goddamn good, aren't you?"

"I hope so, Jack. Holy God, I hope so."

Seven

Mel talked to Joey at least every other day, sometimes every day. She would place the call from Doc's when she had a free minute and Joey would call her back so it wasn't on his nickel. She sent her digital pictures of the renovation of the cabin from Doc's computer and Joey, being an interior decorator, was fascinated by all the building and refinishing Jack had done. Then Mel told Joey that she was going to stay a little longer. A few weeks. At least long enough to be sure Chloe was doing well with Lilly. She loved the little cabin and wanted to see Polly through her delivery.

She didn't tell Jack. But by her daily presence at the grill, he came to realize that she was giving it a chance, and he couldn't hide the fact that it pleased him.

She and Doc played gin, Mel walked down to the store in time to watch the soap with Connie and Joy, and spent a large amount of time at the bar. Joy, who was not a librarian, was the person who opened up the little library on Tuesdays—and Mel was always there. It was about ten by twelve feet, crammed with books, mostly paperbacks with the stamps from secondhand stores inside the covers. It was the only entertainment Mel had when she went home at night.

Mel learned that Lydie Sudder had poor general health when Doc sent her down to the Sudder house to deliver diabetic testing supplies, insulin and syringes. Lydie, beside being diabetic and arthritic, had a weak heart, but Mel was surprised to find that the little house she shared with Ricky was very well kept and nicely furnished; Lydie somehow managed to keep up with things. She got around slowly, but her smile was kind and her manners delightful. Of course, she wouldn't let Mel out of the house without tea and cookies. She was still there, visiting with Lydie on the front porch, when Ricky came home from school, driving up in his little white truck.

"Hey, Mel," he said. He leaned down and kissed his grandmother's cheek. "Hi, Gram. I'm going to work if you don't need anything."

"I'm just fine, Ricky," she said, patting his hand.

"Call me if you need me," he said. "I'll bring you something of Preacher's later."

"That would be nice, honey."

The boy went inside to drop off his books, then out again, jumping off the porch steps and back into his truck to drive the whole block to the bar. "I guess a man can't be separated from his wheels," Mel observed.

"That appears to be the case." Lydie laughed.

The next day she sat at the grill at lunchtime with Connie. "I haven't heard you say you're leaving for days now," Connie said. "Something change on that score?"

"Not a great deal," Mel said. "But since Jack went to such a lot of trouble to work on that cabin, I thought I owed it to him to give it a few weeks. I can deliver Polly's baby."

Connie glanced at the bar where Jack was setting up lunch in front of a couple of fishermen. She gave a nod in his direction. "Bet that makes Jack real happy."

"He seems to think the town can use me, even if Doc doesn't think so."

Connie laughed at her. "Girl, you need glasses. The way Jack looks at you, I don't think it's about Doc. Or the town."

"You don't see me looking back in any particular way, do you?"

"You should. There isn't a woman within a hundred square miles wouldn't leave her husband for him."

"Even you?" Mel asked with a laugh.

"I'm different," she said, drinking her coffee. "I married Ron when I was about seven." She took a drink of her coffee. "But okay—if he begged me, I'd leave Ron for him."

Mel laughed at her. "It is pretty strange that no one's latched on to him."

"I heard he was seeing a woman in Clear River. Don't know how serious it is. Might be nothing."

"Do you know her? The woman he's seeing?"

She shook her head, but lifted one curious brow at Mel's obvious interest. "He's private, isn't he? Doesn't let anything slip. But he can't hide those looks he sends your way."

"He shouldn't waste his time," she said. *I'm not available,* she didn't add.

In her new abode, Mel had put her own favorite books on the shelves—all of which she had already read and reread—and Mark's picture on the table beside the bed. Each night she told him how much she missed him. But she cried less. Maybe because of the way Jack looked at her. The soothing way he talked to her.

The house Mel sold in L.A. was almost four thousand square feet and it had never seemed too big; she had loved the spaciousness of the rooms. Yet the cabin, maybe twelve hundred square feet total, felt right. Like a cocoon. It hugged her.

One of her favorite parts of the day was at the end, before she drove out to her new cabin. She would go to the bar for a cold beer and some chips or cheese and crackers. Once in a while she had dinner, but she didn't mind being by herself at her cabin where there was now food in the cupboard.

Jack put her cold beer in front of her. "We have macaroni and cheese tonight," he said. "I can talk Preacher into putting a slice of ham with that."

"Thanks, but I'm going home for dinner tonight."

"You're cooking?" he asked.

"Not exactly," she said. "I cook things like sandwiches. Coffee. The occasional fried egg. And takeout."

"A modern woman." He laughed. "But that place is working out for you?"

"It's wonderful, thanks. And I need the quiet. Did you know Doc snores like a freight train?"

He chuckled. "Doesn't surprise me."

"I picked up a little gossip about you. That you're seeing a woman in Clear River?"

He didn't look all that surprised. He lifted his brows and his coffee mug. "Seeing? That sounds a little delicate for this crowd."

"I was glad to hear you have someone in your life."

"I don't," he said. "Ancient history. And I wasn't exactly seeing her. It was a lot more basic than that."

Somehow, that made her smile. "Sounds like maybe you had some kind of arrangement."

He sipped from his mug and gave a shrug. "It was—"

"Wait," she said, laughing. "You don't owe me any explanation."

He put both hands on the bar and leaned toward her. "We had an understanding. I went to her place once in a while. For an evening. Nothing deep. No love affair. Casual sex, Mel, between consenting adults. When I realized it didn't work for me, we parted as friends. I'm not with a woman."

"Well, that's kind of too bad," she said.

"It's not necessarily a permanent condition," he said. "That's just how it is right now. Want a slice of pie to take home?"

"Yeah," she said. "Sure."

Mel had been in Virgin River four weeks. In that time, patients and friends dropped by frequently. Some had a little cash for medical services, a few had insurance, but the majority had produce from their farms, ranches, orchards, vineyards or kitchens. The latter, knowing that a single loaf of bread or pie probably didn't cover the cost of an exam and treatment or medication, tended to stop by with a little something even when they were well. The unprepared food—a bushel of apples or nuts, canned or fresh fruit, vegetables, berries, lamb shank or veal, would go right over to Preacher, who could make good use of it, later feeding some of it to Mel and Doc. In some ways, it was like a commune.

That usually left Doc and Mel with more food than they could use, especially since they were getting most of their meals at Jack's. Mel packed up a box of some stuff that was likely to go bad soon—some eggs, bread, sliced ham and a brick of cheese, a pie, apples and nuts. A carton of orange juice she'd picked up from Connie. She put the box in the passenger seat of Doc's old truck before she asked him, "Could I borrow your truck for a couple hours? I want to drive around some and I don't really trust the BMW. I promise, I'll be real careful with it."

"My truck? I can't see you in my truck," he said doubtfully.

"Why not? I'll gas it up, if that's what you're worried about."

"I'm worried about you driving it off a cliff and leaving me with that piece of shit you call a car."

She pursed her lips. "Some days, you're more than I can take. Really."

He picked up his keys and flipped them at her. She caught them. "Don't hurt the truck. As God is my witness, I will never be caught driving that foreign job."

She drove his truck out of town and the minute she was on the winding mountain roads, in the trees, driving up up up and then down down down over the mountain, her heart started to beat a little wildly. She was afraid, plain and simple. But she'd been haunted for two weeks and couldn't live with the feeling. And that brought a plan into focus.

She surprised herself by remembering where Clifford Paulis's camp was. She wondered if she was driven by some psychic energy. Her sense of direction in the hills, through the trees, was perfectly lousy. But—before long she was there, recognizing the nearly invisible old logging road that led to their compound. She drove in, made a big turn inside the opening so that she was pointed toward the way out, and then got out of the truck. She stood right beside the driver's door and yelled, "Clifford!"

No one appeared immediately, but in a few moments a bearded man came out from around a camper shell that had been pulled off a pickup and she recognized him as one of the men she'd seen on her last visit. She crooked her finger at him, beckoning him to her. He shuffled slowly toward her and as he neared, she reached back into the truck and pulled out the box. "I thought maybe you guys could use this," she said. "It was going to waste at the clinic."

He looked at her dumbly.

"Go ahead," she said, pushing the box toward him. "No strings. Just a little neighborly gesture."

He seemed to take the box reluctantly. He looked inside.

She dazzled him with her prettiest smile. When he smiled back, his teeth were god-awful, but she didn't react. After all, she'd seen people like him before. But before, she'd call one agency or another, hand them off, clear her charts. It was different out here.

She got in the truck and put it in gear to leave. In the rearview mirror she saw him hurrying toward that camper shell, and a couple of guys had come out from behind and joined him. It made her heart feel better. Good.

When she got back to town, she returned the keys to Doc, who sat behind his desk in his cramped office. "I guess you think I don't know what you did," he said. She lifted her chin in some defiance. "I thought I told you—stay away from there. It isn't an innocent place and no one knows what might happen."

"You go," she said.

"And I told you not to."

"Did we have some understanding? That I was going to follow your nonmedical orders? Because I don't recall that in my personal life, I'm obligated to do everything you tell me."

"Guess you're not obligated to use your brain in your personal life, either."

"I filled your truck up with gas, you old pain in the ass."

"I didn't get caught in that piece of shit foreign job of yours, you obstinate little strumpet."

And she laughed at him so hard, tears came to her eyes and she had to leave, laughing all the way back to her cabin.

It was a bright and sunny afternoon when Mel went to Doc's office. She tapped lightly and stuck her head in. "Do you have any idea what's taking social services so long to do something about Chloe?" she asked him.

"Certainly don't," he said.

"Maybe I should do a follow-up—give them a call."

"I said I'd take care of it," he answered, not looking up.

"It's just that—you know—I got attached. I didn't mean to, didn't intend to, but there it is. I'd hate for Lilly Anderson to go through that withdrawal. It doesn't feel good."

"She's raised a passel of kids. She knows the score."

"I know, but…" She stopped talking as she heard the front door open. She leaned out of his office and looked down the hall. Right inside the door stood Polly. She seemed to be holding her belly up with her hands and instead of that usual glow on her cheeks, she looked just a bit pale. Nervous. Right behind her was a young man in almost identical overalls, holding a small, worn suitcase. Mel looked back at Doc and said, "Showtime."

Polly wasn't even sure how far apart the pains were. "It feels like one big one," she said. "Mostly down real low."

"Okay, let's just go upstairs and get settled."

"Can Darryl come?"

Mel reached over and took the suitcase from Darryl. "Of course. That would help a lot. I'm going to concentrate on you." She took Polly's hand. "Come on."

Once upstairs, she had Polly sit in the rocker while she went about the business of getting a bed ready with the plastic mattress protector and clean sheets. "Good timing, Polly. My cottage was ready at the same time my littlest patient went out to Lilly Anderson's ranch to stay. I'm all moved out and you, Darryl and the baby can have the whole room."

"Arrrgggghhhh," Polly answered, grabbing her belly and leaning forward. There was a slightly muffled sound that preceded the soft dripping of amniotic fluids onto the floor.

"Oh, Polly!" Darryl exclaimed. He looked suddenly stricken. Embarrassed.

"Well," Mel said, looking over her shoulder. "That should speed things up. Just stay put until the bed's ready and I can help you change."

A half hour later Polly sat up in the hospital bed, not terribly comfortable on a couple of towels, her green hospital gown stretched over her belly. Mel had changed into a pair of scrubs and Nikes she'd packed for just such an event. If this were L.A., the anesthesiologist would be on his way to check her and discuss the epidural, but this was the country, no anesthesia here. Doc came around right after Mel had given Polly a pelvic to see how far she had dilated, and then upon noting Darryl's pallor, he said, "Young man—let's you and me wander across the street and have a drop of courage."

"Darryl, don't leave me!" Polly begged.

"He'll be right back, and I won't leave you," Mel

promised. "But sweetheart, you're only at four centi-meters—it's going to be a while."

Good to her word, Mel stayed at her side. She wasn't sure what she had expected the situation to be like, but was admittedly surprised by a few things. One—Doc Mullins stayed out of her way and let her have the case even though Polly had been his patient. Two, he took on the job of watching Darryl in case it became neces-sary to take the lad out of the room. Doc was staying up long after his usual bedtime. And, the few times Mel wandered out of the patient's room through the night to fetch supplies or a fresh cup of coffee, she looked across the street to see the lights were on and the Open sign lit at Jack's. He kept the bar open all night.

Polly's labor intensified slowly as the hours ticked by, but she remained stable and progressed normally. Mel had her up walking, squatting, getting gravity on their side. She had Darryl hold her forward while she rocked her hips side to side and at three thirty in the morning, Polly began to push. The girl was most comfortable on her side, so Darryl and Mel joined forces to help her deliver in that position. Mel had Polly lie on her side in the fetal position, the leg beneath her tucked up and under while Polly and Darryl together lifted the upper leg to clear the field of birth. It was a big first baby and Polly couldn't have managed that position, pushing for so long, without a good assistant. It was important that the mother have whatever control she could, trusting her body; it made the whole experience so much more beautiful. Darryl held up pretty well despite the fact that it was difficult to watch his young wife in pain, and the sight of blood, even though he'd slaughtered his share of pigs, was clearly tough on him.

At four-thirty Polly's baby emerged after an hour of

pushing. Mel cut the cord, wrapped the baby and passed him to his father. "Mr. Fishburn," she said to Darryl, "there is another Mr. Fishburn in the family. Please help Polly get your son situated on her breast—it'll help her deliver the placenta and slow the bleeding."

This was so much more like a scene from *Gone with the Wind* than the type of midwifery Mel had known in a large, well-equipped city hospital. While Doc checked over the newborn, Mel cleaned up the mother with soap and water and changed her sheets and bedclothes.

By six-thirty in the morning, physically exhausted but wired on caffeine, Mel's work was done. The baby would reside in the room with Polly, and Darryl could have the other bed if he wanted it. It took them both about sixty seconds to fall into a deep sleep. Mel washed her face, rinsed her mouth with a little mouthwash, let her hair out of the clip that had held it on top of her head and went looking for Doc.

"Go to bed, Doc," she said. "It was a long night. I'll keep the office open."

"No, sir," he said. "I don't sleep in daylight, and you did all the work. I'll keep an eye on the Fishburns. Go to your place."

"I'll make a deal with you. I'll go take a nap and come back in early afternoon to spell you."

"That'll do," he said. Then, peering over his glasses, added, "Not bad. For a city girl."

The sun was just peeking over the mountains, bathing the little town in pinkish-beige rays. The April air was cold. She pulled her wool jacket around herself and sat on Doc's front porch, feeling exhilarated, and perhaps a little too wound up for sleep right away.

Polly had done well, for a mere girl. No Lamaze training for those two, and no drugs. There had been some powerful grunting, groaning and straining; Darryl had grunted along with his wife with such sincerity, it was lucky he didn't mess his pants. Nice, big, eight-pound country baby. There was nothing in this world like pulling a squalling infant from its mother's womb; no panacea for a breaking heart could do more. This didn't throw Mel into a stupor of longing or depression because this was her life's work—what she loved. And she loved it so much more when the couple was happy and excited, the baby robust and healthy. Holding the baby she had just delivered, handing it to its mother and watching it suckle hungrily—it was like seeing God before you.

She heard a loud thwack. And another. She had no idea what time Jack's usually opened. It was only six-thirty. Another loud thwack, coming from his place.

She went down the porch stairs and across the street. Behind the bar there was a big brick barbecue. Wearing boots, jeans and a flannel shirt, and hefting a heavy ax, Jack was splitting logs on a tree stump. She just stood there watching him for a moment. Thwack, thwack, thwack.

He looked up from his chore to see her leaning against the side of the building, pulling her jacket tight over turquoise scrubs. She had no idea that what made him grin at her was the huge toothy smile she wore. "Well?" he said, leaning the ax against the tree stump.

"Baby boy. Big baby boy."

"Congratulations," he said. "Everyone is okay?"

She walked toward him. "They're better than okay. Polly did great, the baby is strong, healthy, and Darryl is expected to recover." And then she laughed, throwing her head back. Nothing, nothing was more satisfying than coming out of a delivery with one-hundred-percent success. "My first country birth. Harder on Mom than on me. In the city, it's always an option to just roll over, bare your spine and labor in comfort from an epidural. Women out here are made of steel."

"I've heard that," he said with a laugh.

"Know what Doc said? 'Not bad for a city girl.'" She reached for his hand. "Did you stay open all night?"

He shrugged. "I nodded off by the fire a couple of times. But you never know when someone might need something. Boiling water. Ice. A stiff drink. You want some coffee?"

"God, I think it would make me barf. I've had enough coffee to jangle even the nerves of a caffeine junkie." Uncharacteristically, she wrapped her arms around his waist and hugged him. This man had become her closest friend. "Jack, it was wonderful. I had forgotten how wonderful. I haven't delivered a baby in, gee, almost a year, I think." She looked up into his eyes. "Damn, we did a good piece of work. Me, Mom and Dad. Damn."

He smoothed a little hair off her forehead. "I'm proud of you."

"It was so awesome."

"See? I knew you'd find something here to sink your teeth into." He reached down, crossed his arms under her bottom and lifted her straight up so that her face was even with his.

"Nowwww, what did we decide?" she asked, but her tone was teasing. Her smile was playful.

"We decided that I would not kiss you."

"That's right."

"I haven't," he said.

"Maybe we should have talked about this," she added, but she certainly didn't struggle. In fact, this seemed oddly right. Celebratory. Like being picked up and swung around after the win of a big game. And that was how she felt—as though she'd just scored a touchdown. Arms resting on his shoulders, she clasped her hands behind his head.

"We further decided that if you kissed me, I would let you," he said.

"You're fishing."

"Does this look like fishing to you?"

"Begging?"

"Doing exactly as I've been told. *Waiting.*"

What the hell, she thought. Absolutely nothing could feel better after the night she'd just spent than to plant a big wet one on this guy—a guy who'd keep his business open all night just in case they needed something. So she laid one on him. She slid her lips over his, opening them, moving over his with wicked and delicious intent, getting her tongue involved. And he did nothing but hold her there, allowing this.

"Did you not like that?" she asked.

"Oh," he said. "Am I allowed to respond?"

She whacked him softly in the head, making him laugh. She tried it again, and this time it was much more interesting. It made her heart beat faster, made her breathe hard. *Yes,* she thought. *It is okay to feel something that doesn't hurt sometimes.* This wasn't because she was grief-stricken or needy, this was because she was victorious. And all she could think about at the moment was his delicious mouth.

When their mouths came apart, she said, "I feel like a total champ."

"You are," he said, enjoying her mood more than she would ever guess. "God, you taste good."

"You don't taste that bad," she said, laughing. "Put me down now," she instructed.

"No. Do it again."

"Okay, but only one more, then you have to behave."

She planted another one on him, thoroughly enjoying his lips and tongue, the strength of the arms that held her. She refused to worry about whether this was a mistake. She was here, she was happy for once, and his mouth felt as natural to hers as if she'd been kissing him for years. She let the kiss be a little longer and deeper than she thought prudent, and even that made her smile.

When it was over, he put her on her feet. "Whew," she said.

"We don't have nearly enough births in this town."

"We have another one in about six weeks. And if you're very, very good…"

Ah, he thought. *That gives me six weeks.* He touched the end of her nose. "Nothing wrong with a little kissing, Mel."

"And you won't get ideas?"

He bellowed. "You can make me behave, it turns out. But you can't keep me from getting ideas."

April waned and May brought out the early spring flowers; foxgloves and Queen Anne's lace grew wild along the roads. Australian Fern blanketed the earth beneath the big trees. Every week or ten days, Mel borrowed Doc's truck, took a little lip from him, and delivered a box of food to the Paulis camp that would otherwise go to waste. Doc would have no part of it and scolded her. She ignored him indignantly and that alone made her feel good. It made her heart pound wildly as she went, and beat with satisfaction as she returned to Virgin River.

The cabin was turning out to be a haven for Mel. She purchased a small TV on which she got terrible reception. If she were staying, she'd get a satellite dish, but she was only committed to a few more weeks. And one day she came home from the clinic to find she had a telephone in her kitchen and bedroom. Jack spoke to Harv, telephone lineman for the county, and had stressed Mel's occupation as midwife to get her phone installed ahead of schedule. He got another kiss for that—behind the bar where no one could see. Okay, two or three kisses. Deep and long. Strong and delicious.

Living and sleeping in the cabin in the woods was as restful and peaceful as anything Mel had known in almost a year. She woke in the early mornings, in time to see the sun slowly creeping over the tall pines, to hear the birds singing. She liked to get a cup of coffee and go out on that new, strong porch and enjoy the clean morning air, still cold on early spring mornings.

It wasn't yet 6:00 a.m. when she opened her front door and there, before her, were at least a dozen deer, grazing contentedly on the grass, bushes and ferns at the edges of her clearing. She took note of the freckled fawns—it was spring and time for birthing of all sorts.

She went for her digital camera and snapped a few sneaky shots. Then she loaded the pictures onto her laptop and dialed up the internet, which took forever, but there was nothing faster out here. After she had sent the pictures to Joey, she called her.

"Go online," she told her sister. "I've sent you something amazing."

"What is it?" she asked.

"Just hurry," Mel said. "You're going to love it."

There was only a short wait as Joey could get online and download in seconds as opposed to the length of time it took Mel. She heard her sister gasp. "Deer!" she said.

"In my front yard," Mel said. "Look at the babies. Aren't they adorable?"

"Are they still there?"

"I'm looking out my kitchen window at them right now," she said. "I'm not leaving the house until they're done with breakfast. Isn't that the most wonderful thing you've ever seen? Joey, I'm staying a little longer."

"Oh, Mel—no! I want you to come here! Why are you staying?"

"Joey, I'm delivering another baby pretty soon. After that last one, I can't resist. It just isn't like in the hospital where everything's so sterile and artificial and there's a surgeon and anesthesiologist right down the hall. It's just me and her, getting the job done. So pristine and wonderful and natural. So country—like Doc taking Mom's twenty-year-old husband across the street to the bar for a shot of courage so he can be a less nervous assistant."

"Oh, lovely," Joey said sarcastically, causing Mel to laugh.

"It was fantastic," Mel said. "There's another pregnant woman in town and I'm thinking of staying for her, too. The cabin is just great—you saw the pictures."

"I saw. Mel, are you dressed for the day?"

"Yeah…?"

"Look at your feet. Tell me what's on your feet."

She sighed. "My Cole Haan boots. I love these boots."

"They cost over four hundred dollars!"

"And they're starting to look like crap, too," she said. "If you only knew where I've been…"

"Mel, you're not one of them. Don't get them depending on you. Come to Colorado. We can accommodate your shoe fetish and you can find a good job here—close to us."

"I sleep so well here," she said. "I was afraid I'd never sleep well again—it's probably the air. It's so unbelievable, it almost wears you out—by the end of the day the bed feels so good. The pace is slower. I've needed a slower pace."

"Are you that busy? With patients?" Joey asked.

"Not that much. They're very sparse, actually. We only make well-visit appointments on Wednesdays and the rest of the week they either wander in with one complaint or another, or Doc goes to them. I go along most of the time. Or people wander in to talk, or drop off a pie, or some fresh baked dinner rolls. But the women—the pregnant ones—are so relieved after one look at my hands, compared to Doc's."

"What do you do with yourself?"

"Well," she said, laughing, "every day I walk down to the corner store to watch a soap with Connie and Joy, two middle-aged best friends who have been watching televised adultery on *Riverside Falls* for about fifteen years. The side comments are more interesting than the show."

"Gawd," she said.

"I go out to the Anderson ranch and hold the baby—Chloe. She's thriving there, and so is Lilly. More and more I know that was the right thing to do, and it just fell in my lap. Sometimes I take some of our leftover food out to this bunch of bums in the forest—they look so thin and hungry, but Doc says they'll probably bury us all. I stop by the bar to see if anyone's playing cribbage. If I can reel him in, Doc and I play gin—but it's hard to catch him in the mood. He taught me to play and now he can't beat me. Penny a point—I'm funding my retirement."

"So—when do you think you're going to get over this break from sanity?"

"Oh, I don't know. Just let me think about it. I've only been here a couple of months—it's not an eternity."

"But I hate to think of you rotting away in some dinky town, watching the soaps and growing bad roots."

"I could visit Dot in that garage where she does hair…"

"Ugh. Aren't you lonely, honey?"

"Not so much. At the end of the day, if nothing's going on, we go to the bar—Doc has his one whiskey of the day and I get a cold beer. There are always people around. We eat dinner—someone usually says, come over and sit with us. There's great gossip, that's the cool part about small towns where everyone knows everyone's business. Except, apparently, who gave birth to little Chloe. I just count it lucky that no woman who suffered post-partum hemorrhage or infection turned up. And also—no word from social services."

"I miss you so much. This is about the longest we've been apart in years… Why do you sound happy?"

"Do I? Maybe because everyone around me is happy. They let me know they're glad I'm here, even if my presence isn't medically saving this town." She took a breath. "I still feel out of place a lot, but I think I'm more content than I've been in eleven months and three days. I might finally be detoxing from the adrenaline."

"Promise me you're not going to stay in that godforsaken place, alone, watching soaps and drinking beer."

Mel's voice became soft. "It's not godforsaken, Joey. It's…" She struggled for a word. "It's breathtaking. Oh, the architecture leaves something to be desired—most of the houses and buildings are small and old and could use paint. But the countryside is wondrous. And I'm not lonely—I have a town. I've never had a town before."

Ricky and Liz were going to the spring dance at the high school. Except they didn't. It gave Rick a twinge of guilt because he knew in his heart that Connie and Ron trusted him. And probably they shouldn't.

The thing about living in a small town in the midst of dozens of small towns separated by forests was there were a million secluded places to park and make out. He always had a condom in his pocket, one that he was determined not to have to use, but he had it just the same. He hadn't even needed Jack to supply him—he was on top of that. He felt protective toward Liz; he didn't want to get her into trouble. What they were doing was working, even if it was getting them pretty worked up.

And they were doing plenty. It got off to a roaring start. Lots of deep kissing, heavy petting, incredible rubbing. They'd done a lot of bumping and grinding on the outside of clothes, but now they were getting right down to the skin, deeper than skin, but not going all the way. They were catching on real fast. It hadn't taken them long to figure out how to have orgasms without penetration, for which Rick was sublimely grateful. Even so, he wanted more. Wanted it real bad, and so did she. He was about ready to have the big talk with her, but he knew he had to save it for the clear light of day, not the dark of night while they were pawing each other in the cab of his little truck.

He loved making her feel good; she really wanted to please him. He hadn't imagined it could be this wonderful—holding someone, loving them, touching them, giving these feelings, receiving them. Nothing had prepared him for how you could be swept away by it all; it was as though the sheer pleasure had a life of its own.

He had moved over to the passenger seat and held her on his lap, kissing her, hard and hot while she squirmed around deliciously.

His hand wandered under her short skirt and met with... *Nothing.*

"Oh my Jesus," he whispered.

"Surprise," she said, grinding on his lap. Then her hand went there, feeling him through his clothes, making him nearly cry out.

She scooted forward on his lap a little. He slid back in the seat slightly, knowing that she would now take him in her small hand. He lived for that. As she opened his pants to free him, he massaged her with his fingers of one hand, fondling her breast with the other, drowning in her mouth, holding her tight against him. She was moving roughly against his hand, wriggling, reaching desperately for her special moment, when suddenly she shifted her weight slightly. She was straining toward him, he was straining toward her, her hands went to his shoulders, his hands grabbed her bottom, her knee went across his lap and she was over him. She moved down, he moved up and they were suddenly disastrously, wondrously, exquisitely merged. She came right down on him. He lifted right up into her; she was all around him. It was a whole new world, a lot better than a hand. He couldn't breathe.

"Holy God, Liz," he whispered. "Oh my Jesus."

She was oblivious, pressing furiously into his lap, on a mission.

"Liz. Lizzie. No. Lizzie. Holy God. Holy Jesus."

He was half trying, half hoping to fail to lift her off him, to get out of her, when it happened for her and the sensation of her body squeezing around him, clenching in hot spasms as she moaned her ecstasy, caused him to lose his mind. He thought he might have been momentarily unconscious. He lost all will. And that wasn't all he lost. He blew it—erupted inside of her with the force of a volcano. Right after he thought *Ahhhh,* he thought *Oh, fuck. Way to go, genius.*

She collapsed into his arms and he held her, stroking her back as she calmed. As he calmed. As they caught their collective breath. Finally he said, "That could have been a huge mistake."

"Oh-oh," she said. "Oh-oh. Now what?"

"Well, I sure as hell can't reel it back in," he told her. "If I'd known that was going to happen… Liz, I have a condom, for Christ's sake."

"I didn't know that."

"Well, I didn't know we were going to do that."

"I didn't know, either." She sniffed. "I'm sorry." She dropped her head to his shoulder and cried. "I'm sorry, Rick."

"No. I'm sorry. Okay, baby, take it easy. Can't do anything about it now. Shh." He held her and she rested against him, close in his arms. He kissed her cheeks and lips until her tears stopped. Then he took her open mouth again. God, her mouth was hot. And after a little while, as he held her, he began to grow firm again, and he was still there, inside. Without meaning to, without planning to, he began to pump his hips up and down again, driving himself into her. And she pushed into his lap. What the hell—the damage was done, he thought. And he said, "Can't do anything about it now…"

Eight

There were no patients in the morning and Mel took the opportunity to drive over to Clear River for gas, there being no service station in Virgin River. She took the pager with her so that Doc could call her back if something happened, but hardly anything ever happened.

Every time she went to one of the little surrounding towns she looked in particular at the women, wondering where Jack might have gone once in a while for "something a little basic." It didn't take her long to realize that he probably had his pick, and that there were plenty of attractive women around these towns.

She thought she might like to get something like a salt lick or some kind of feed for the edge of her property to draw the deer, so went to the very small strip mall on the main drag. As she passed the hardware store, she saw a window display of shears mounted on pegboard. They ranged in size from tiny scissors to clippers with six-inch, thick, curved blades. She stared at them, frowning, for a long time.

"Help you?" a young woman in a green store apron asked.

"Hmm. What do you do with those?"

"Roses," she said, smiling.

"Roses? I haven't seen that many roses around."

"Oh, you're not looking hard enough," she said, grinning.

"Hmm. Well, I'm looking for something that would draw deer," Mel said.

"Like a doe call? But hunting season is months away."

"God, I wouldn't shoot at them! I like seeing them in my yard in the early morning. Can you tell me where to find that?"

"Um, if you want deer in your yard, you're the only one. Just plant some lettuce or a couple of apple trees. With deer, if you don't want them in your produce, you can hardly keep them away."

"Oh. If I throw some lettuce out there, will that work? Because I don't garden."

The woman tilted her head and smiled with eyes that frowned. "Where you from?"

"Los Angeles. Concrete jungle."

"I mean, now."

"Up in Virgin River. Kind of back in the woods, you know…"

"Listen, don't try the lettuce, okay. Because there are also bear. Just keep your food indoors and don't press your luck. If you get deer, you get deer." Then she looked down and said, "Nice boots. Where can I get a pair like that?"

Mel thought a second, then said, "Can't really remember. Target, I think."

Rather than going back to Doc's, she drove out to the river. She saw that there were six anglers in the river, and that one of them was Jack. She pulled up, parked and got out to lean against the front of her car to watch. He looked over his shoulder at her, smiled a hello, but went back to his sport. He'd pull out some line and let it slack, then gracefully cast out, the line reaching behind him in a large S before sailing smoothly out over the river, touching down on the top of the water as lightly as a leaf floating lazily down from a tree. And again, and again.

She loved to watch the arc of the lines, the whir of them going out, the clicking of them reeling in. They seemed almost synchronized, choreographed, the air above the water filled with flying lines. The men, in waders and vests, would walk around the swirling shallow waters while fish jumped now and then in the river. If there was a catch, the fish would either be released or go in the creel dangling from a shoulder strap.

After a peaceful interlude, Jack came out of the river with his rod and reel in hand. "What are you doing out here?"

"Just watching."

"Want to try?"

"I don't know how," she said.

"It's not very hard—let's see if I can scrounge some boots or waders." He went to his truck and dug around in the back. He came up with some huge rubber hip boots. "This'll keep you dry—but you won't be able to wade too far out."

She stepped into them. His legs were so much longer than hers that he had to fold them down twice at the top of her thighs, not an unpleasant sensation. They were so big that she had to shuffle rather than walk, dragging them along. "I won't be able to run for my life, either," she said. "Okay, what do I do?"

"It's all in the wrist," he said. "Don't worry about

aim so much as a nice clean arc and a little distance—
getting you into the deeper part of the river where the
fish are more plentiful." He took her hand, led her to the
water's edge and showed her his casting. "Don't snap
it hard, just roll it off nice and easy. Give it a little arm,
but don't throw your body into it."

He handed her the rod, showed her where to unlock
the reel. She gave it a try and the fly plunked down right
in front of her. "How's that for distance?"

"We're going to have to work on that," he said. He
stepped behind her and guiding her hand, helped her
cast. Twenty-five feet, maybe. Probably a fourth of the
distance he could achieve, and her fly came down hard,
making a splash. "Hmm, better," he said. "Reel her in,
slowly."

She brought it back and repeated the process, this
time without his hand guiding hers. "Good," he said.
"Watch your footing—there are spots where you can
drop, trip, slip off a rock. You wouldn't want to fall in."

"I wouldn't want to," she said, casting again. That
time she flicked her wrist too hard and the hook flew
back behind them, whooshing past their heads. "Oops,"
she said. "Sorry."

"It's okay, but be careful. I'd hate to have that thing
pulled out of the back of my head. Here," he said. He
stood behind her and put a hand on her hip. "Don't
throw your body into it—just use your arm and wrist—
and go easy. You'll get the distance. Eventually."

She did it again, and it was good. A nice, graceful
arc, a respectable distance into the river. A fish jumped
out where her fly had landed. "Oh, he's a big one."

"Brown trout—a beauty. You get him today and
you'll show up all of us."

Something slithered past her feet and she jumped

with a gasp. "Lamprey eel," he said. "They like to suck the roe and fluids out of the salmon."

"Ew. Charming." She cast again. And again. This was fun. Now and then Jack would take her wrist and cast with her, reminding her of the wrist action. The other hand stayed on her hip, holding her still. "I like this," she said. Then she had a hit and reeled in a fish. It wasn't a very big fish, but it was a fish. And she'd caught him by herself.

"Not bad," he said. "Take it off the hook carefully."

"I don't know how," she said.

"I'll show you, but then you have to do it. If you're going to fish, you're going to take the fish off the hook. Like this." He demonstrated, sliding his hand from the fish's head to his wriggling body, holding it firmly, disengaging the hook cautiously. "His mouth is okay. We're going to let him grow into a civilized meal," he said, tossing the fish back.

"Aw," she said.

"You got lucky. Come on," he said, turning her back to the river. He stood behind her, holding her body straight and still with that large hand on her hip, his other hand guiding her wrist. She cast again, reeled in again.

"Jack, are there an awful lot of roses around here in summer?" she asked.

"Hmm? I don't know. Sure, some."

"I stopped by the hardware store this morning and they had this huge display of rose clippers. All sizes. I guess I've never noticed anything like that before…"

When she brought in her line, he turned her around slightly. He frowned. "Rose clippers?"

"Uh-huh. From little tiny ones to great big ones with curved blades and leather grips."

"Where?"

"Clear River. I went over for gas and—"

"Mel, those aren't rose clippers. Well, I guess you could use 'em for that. More likely, they're for marijuana harvests. Little ones for manicuring buds, big ones for cutting down plants."

"Naw. Come on."

He turned her back toward the river. "There are towns around here that stock a lot of the stuff illegal growers need. Clear River's one. What were you doing at the hardware store?"

"I thought I'd pick up something that would invite the deer to my yard, like a salt lick or feed or something, but—"

He turned her back to face him again. "Salt lick?"

"Well, cows like that, right? So I thought…"

He was shaking his head. "Mel, listen—don't do anything to invite wildlife to your yard. You might get some unfriendlies. Okay? Like maybe a buck who's more interested in rutting than having his picture taken. Or a bear. Understand?"

"Rutting?" She frowned.

He smiled patiently and touched the end of her nose. "Making love."

"Oh. Sure. Okay," she said, turning back to the river. Casting again.

"Rose clippers." He laughed. "I think you're getting the hang of this," he said.

"I like it. I'm not sure about that getting the fish off the hook part."

"Come on, don't be a sissy."

"Well…"

"You have to catch one first," he said.

"You just watch. I'm precocious."

Mel lost all track of time as she worked the rod, sending the colorful fly out across the water, bringing it back slowly. Again and again she cast, noting, too, that Jack kept his hand on her hip and now and then ran his other hand down her arm to her hand to guide her. "Come on," she kept telling the fly. "I'm ready!"

"Keep your voice down," he said softly. "This is a peaceful sport."

Again and again she would cast her line. She wasn't skilled by any means, but she was getting it out there, and doing so prettily. At least, she thought so.

She felt that hand that had been on her hip slide stealthily around her, holding her at her waist, pulling her just slightly back against him. "You're distracting me," she said, casting again.

"Good," he said, lowering his lips to her head, inhaling.

"Jack, there are *people!*"

"They could care less," he said, holding her against him.

She looked around and saw that what he said was true—the other fishermen didn't even glance their way. Their lines were flying around in gentle, beautiful arcs. They didn't even look at each other. *Okay,* she thought. *This feels good. I like the hand, the arm around me. I can manage this.*

Then she felt his lips on her neck. "Jack! I'm fishing!"

"Okay," he said hoarsely. "I'll try not to bother you too much."

He pulled her just a little harder against him and began to nibble at her neck. "What *are* you doing?" she asked, laughter in her voice.

"Mel, please… Can't we go somewhere and just make out for a while?"

"No!" she laughed. "I'm *fishing!*"

"If I promise to take you fishing after...?"

"No! Now behave yourself!" But she was smiling because it was pretty heady having this big tough guy turn weak and desperate just from the taste of her neck. She concentrated on her casting while he concentrated on her neck, his arm tight around her waist. Ahh... Nice. Very nice.

After a few more minutes passed, he let go of her with a tortured moan, walked back to his truck and laid himself over the front, arms outstretched wide, head lying on the hood. She looked over her shoulder at him and chuckled. Brought him to his knees, she thought. Big tough marine. Ha!

She treated herself to a few more casts, then turned and shuffled in those great big boots back to Jack. She leaned the rod against the truck and pulled her feet out of the rubber boots. He lifted his head and looked at her through narrowed eyes. "Thanks, Jack. I have to go. It's time for my soap." She treated him to a conciliatory peck on the cheek. "Maybe we can do this again sometime."

As she drove back to town, she got to thinking—a few weeks ago, she was absolutely certain there was nothing in her that allowed her to respond to a man. To Jack. Now she wasn't so sure. A little contact, a little kissing—deep kissing—it felt good. It made her forget sometimes that she had nothing to give. In fact, it made her wonder if maybe she was wrong about that. Going somewhere to make out for a while didn't sound like a bad idea. She was going to give that more thought.

She poked her head into Doc's and found him on the computer and said, "Anything?"

"Nope," he said.

"Okay, I'm going to the store. Need anything?"

"Nope," he said again.

She checked her watch, found herself hoping she hadn't missed the beginning. When she walked into the store, Joy stood in the curtained doorway and said, "Mel! Thank God!"

The panicked look on her face sent Mel rushing to the back room. Leaning forward in the lawn chair, her hand gripping the front of her sweatshirt and breathing shallowly was Connie. Mel kneeled down. "What is it?" she asked.

"I don't know," she said weakly. "I can hardly breathe."

"Joy, get me a bottle of aspirin. Pain?" she asked Connie.

"My back," she said.

Mel put a hand between her shoulder blades. "There?"

"Yeah."

Joy handed her a brand-new aspirin bottle off the shelf and Mel ripped it open, shaking one out into her palm. "Swallow this quickly." Connie did so and Mel asked, "Pressure in the chest?"

"Yeah. Oh, yeah."

Mel got up, grabbed Joy's hand and pulled her out of the back room. "Run for Doc. Tell him it might be her heart. Hurry."

Mel went back to Connie. She took her pulse and found it fast and irregular. She had grown clammy and her respirations were rapid and shallow. "Try to relax and breathe slowly. Joy has gone for Doc."

"What is it?" she asked. "What's happening?"

Mel noticed that Connie's left arm dangled at her side, probably in pain, while she gripped her shirt with her right hand and tried to pull it away from her body, as though to relieve the pressure in her chest. If Mel had speculated on a heart attack for one of these two women, she'd have bet on Joy who was overweight and probably had high cholesterol. Not Connie who was petite and didn't even smoke.

"I'm not sure," Mel said. "Let's wait for Doc. Don't talk, just stay calm. I'm not going to let anything happen to you."

A tense couple of minutes passed before Joy, breathless, came flying through the door with Doc's medical bag and rushed to Mel's side. "Here," she said. "He said try the nitro and get an IV started. He'll be right here."

"Okay, then." She dug around in the bag, found the nitro tablets and shook one out of the bottle. "Connie, hold this under your tongue."

She did as she was told while Mel got the blood pressure cuff and stethoscope out of the bag. Connie's pressure was high, but within seconds some of the pain was easing. The nitro might be working. "That better?"

"A little. My arm. I can hardly move my arm."

"Okay, we'll take care of that." She snapped on a pair of gloves. She pulled the rubber strap around Connie's upper arm and started searching for a good vein, slapping her inner arm with two fingers. She tore open the package containing the IV needle and inserted it slowly. Blood eased up the clear tube and dripped on the floor. Mel then capped it off because she had no tubing or bag of fluid.

A moment later she heard a sound she didn't recognize and looked out of the back room to see old Doc wheeling a squeaky old gurney into the store. He left it in the store aisle and picked up a bag of Ringer's solution from its bed, handing it to Mel, while he toted a small portable oxygen canister. He put the cannula around Connie's neck and into her nostrils while he asked, "What've we got?"

As Mel hooked up the tubing to the needle and the Ringer's to the tube, she said, "Elevated pressure, diaphoretic, chest, back and arm pain... I gave her an aspirin, and the nitro."

"Good. How's that pill working, Connie?"

"A little," she said.

"Here's what we're going to do. Put her on the gurney in the back of the truck, you beside her holding the Ringer's and monitoring her pressure, and if you think we have to stop for any reason, you bang on the window. The black bag goes with you—you have oxygen, a portable defibrillator in the truck bed, and I want you to draw an eppie and atropine right away, to have ready." He went back to the gurney, pushed it into the very narrow space in the back room and lowered it. He shook out and spread a large, heavy wool blanket over the sheet and said, "Okay, Connie."

Managing the IV bag and tubing, Mel supported Connie under the arm so that she could be transferred from her chair to the lowered gurney. Doc lifted the back slightly so that she wouldn't be lying flat, then wrapped the blanket around her and strapped her in. He put the oxygen canister on the gurney between Connie's legs, then said to Mel, "Have Joy hold up the bag of Ringer's while we get her out of here."

"Shouldn't we wait for an ambulance?"

"Not the best idea," he said while together they lifted the gurney to its former upright position. As they rolled out of the store, Mel once again in control of the IV bag, Doc said, "Joy, as soon as we get out of here I want you to call Valley Hospital and ask them to get a cardiologist to meet us in E.R. Tell Ron to meet us at Valley." Doc and Mel released the legs on the gurney and slid it in the back of the truck. Doc took off his heavy wool coat and draped it over Connie. As he would have headed for the driver's door of the truck, Mel grabbed his sleeve.

"Doc, what the hell are we doing?"

"Getting her there as fast as possible," he said. "In you go. You're going to be cold."

"I'll manage," she said, climbing into the truck bed beside Connie.

"Don't bounce out," Doc said. "I don't have time to stop and pick you up."

"Just drive carefully," she said, already dreading those narrow, curving roads and sheer drops, squeaking by big logging trucks, not to mention the darkness and drop in temperature as they passed through the towering trees.

He jumped in, pretty spry for seventy, and put the truck in gear. He made a wide turn in the street, Mel in the back of the truck, holding the Ringer's above Connie's head because there was no IV stand on this old gurney. As they drove out of town, Jack was just returning. But Mel's attention was focused on Connie. She balanced the bag of Ringer's on the gurney above Connie's head, and dug around in Doc's black bag for syringes and vials, drawing her drugs quickly despite the hectic driving and bouncing. She capped the syringes and took up the IV bag again.

Just don't arrest, Mel kept thinking. Just to be safe, she used one hand to open the portable defibrillator case, having it handy to be switched on if necessary. It was the kind used on commercial airlines; rather than paddles, there were patches that adhered to the chest. Rather than bare Connie to the cold before it became necessary, she decided not to attach the patches to her chest. Then, with one hand over her head, she leaned her body close across Connie's to keep her warm.

She had to give Doc a lot of credit for fancy driving. He managed to move down the mountain at a pretty fast clip, braking suddenly for the sharp curves and picking up speed for the straightaways while avoiding potholes and bumps. Mel was freezing, but Connie was taking steady breaths and her pulse was even and slower, when from the sheer fright and the ride in the back of the truck, it should probably be racing.

"That Doc," she said breathlessly into Mel's ear. "He sure is bossy."

"Yeah," Mel said. "Try to rest."

"Oh, sure," she whispered.

Mel had to switch the arm that held the Ringer's several times, she got so sore. And even when she stayed low in the bed of the truck, the wind was chilling her to the bone. May in the mountains, under the shade of huge, towering trees, was not warm. She tried to imagine doing this in winter, and she got colder. Her cheeks were numb, her fingers nearly without feeling.

After just over an hour ride, they pulled into a parking lot in front of a small hospital where two med techs and a nurse stood ready in the parking lot, waiting with their own gurney.

Doc jumped out of the truck. "Take her on my gurney—I'll get it later."

"Good," one said, pulling the gurney holding Connie out of the back of the truck. "She have any meds?"

"Just an aspirin and a nitro tab. Ringer's TKO."

"Gotcha," he said. "Emergency staff standing by," and off they went, running with the gurney across the parking lot.

"Let's go, Melinda," he said, moving a little more slowly now.

Mel began to realize that waiting for emergency transport could have been a tragic mistake—it could have turned that trip into three hours. As she waited with Doc in the emergency room, she learned that Valley Hospital was small but efficient, serving the needs of many small towns. They were capable of labor and delivery, C-sections when the infant and mother were not at major risk, X-rays, ultrasounds, some general surgeries, lab work and outpatient clinic, but if something as serious as emergency heart surgery or major surgery were required, a larger hospital was needed. It was a while before the doctor finally came out. "We're going to run an angiogram—I think we're looking at blockages. She's stable for the moment, but they may be considering bypass surgery as soon as possible. We'll transport her by helicopter to Redding for that. Has her next of kin been notified?"

"He should be here any minute. We'll wait for him here."

Within ten minutes, Connie was wheeled past them and down the hall. Another ten minutes brought Ron with Joy into the emergency room doors. "Where is she? Is she all right?" Right behind them were Ricky and Liz, straight from school.

"They've taken her for an angiogram—it's like an X-ray of blood vessels. Based on what that test tells them, they'll decide whether or not she needs surgery. Let's go to the cafeteria and get a cup of coffee and I'll try to explain it to you—then we'll go see how they're doing on that test."

"God, Doc, thank you," Ron said. "Thank you for getting her help."

"Don't thank me," he said. "Thank Melinda. She saved Connie's life."

Mel's head jerked toward him in surprise.

"It was her fast action—that aspirin and calling for help—not to mention her ride in the back of my pickup, that I believe allowed us to get her to the hospital so fast."

It was nine o'clock before Mel and Doc got back to town, and of necessity they both headed for Jack's, more than a little grateful he had stayed open. And she knew he'd stayed open for them. Doc asked for his whiskey and Mel said, "I think I better have one, too. Maybe something a little smoother than that."

Jack poured her a Crown Royal. "Long day?" he asked.

"Shew," Doc said. "We spent most of it waiting for a decision. Connie's going to have bypass surgery in the morning. We waited around until they transported her to Redding."

"Why didn't we just take her to Redding?" Mel asked. Both men laughed. "What? I looked at the map before I even came up here. It's just over a hundred miles of highway."

"It's about a hundred forty, Mel," Jack said. "Narrow, two-lane, over the mountains. Would take about three hours to cross at best from Eureka. Probably closer to four. Coming from Virgin River—five."

"Jesus," she moaned.

"I think Ricky is taking Liz to her mother's for the night while Ron and Joy will make the long drive to Redding to spend the night at Connie's bedside. They're a little on the nervous side," Doc said.

"No doubt," Jack said. "I saw you flying out of town.

I couldn't tell who you had in the back—I just saw Mel hanging on for dear life."

Doc took a sip. "She came in kinda handy."

"What would you have done without a little help?" she asked him.

"I probably would've thrown Joy back there. But who knows if we'd have gotten that far. You know how great one little aspirin is for a heart attack?"

"Hmm." Mel took a sip of her drink and let her eyes slowly drift closed appreciatively.

"Connie's going to be all right?"

"Oh, better than all right," Doc said. "People go into that surgery a little gray around the gills and they give them nice fresh, clear arteries to float their oxygen through and they come out rosy cheeked and brand-new."

Mel took another sip. "Oh, God, I didn't think I'd ever be warm again."

"You want me to light the fire?" Jack asked her.

"No, just let me drink this. Tell Doc I caught a fish today."

"She did," he said. "Wasn't much of a fish, but she caught it herself. Even if she couldn't take it off the hook without help."

Doc peered at her over his specs and she lifted her chin a bit defiantly. "Careful, Melinda," he said. "You could become one of us."

"Not likely," she said. "Not until you at least get a camper shell. We'd have been better off in the back of my BMW."

"You'd have been better off," Doc said. "That piece of shit isn't big enough for a patient having a heart attack and a practitioner trying to keep her alive."

"I'm not going to fight with you for saying that,"

she said. "Because you at least called me a practitioner and not a nurse. You seem to be coming around, you old fart." She looked up at Jack. "We keeping you up?"

"Nah," he said, chuckling. "Take your time. In fact, I'll join you." He reached behind him and selected a bottle, tipping it over a glass. He lifted it in a toast to both of them. "Good team work, amazingly. Glad everything's okay."

Mel was exhausted, most of which came from the ride and long afternoon of tensely waiting at the hospital. Connie, she realized without much surprise, was more than a patient to her—she was a friend. And when you do this kind of work in this kind of place, your patients are almost always your friends. Must be hard to maintain objectivity. On the other hand, success was that much more gratifying. Fulfilling.

It wasn't like this in L.A.

Doc finished his whiskey and got up. "Nicely done, Melinda. We'll try to have a dull day tomorrow."

"Thank you, Doc."

After the doctor left, Jack said, "Sounds like maybe the two of you have started to bond or something."

"Or something," she said, sipping.

"How was that trip to Valley Hospital?"

"Like Mr. Toad's wild ride," she said, making him laugh a little. She pushed her glass toward him and he gave her another splash of Crown.

"You want ice or water with that?" he asked her.

"No, this is good. Very good, in fact."

She sipped her drink rather too quickly. She looked up at him, tilted her head to one side, then inclined it toward the glass.

"You sure? Because I think maybe that's enough.

Your cheeks are flushed and I can tell, you're not cold anymore."

"Just a tish."

A tish was what she got—a couple of swallows.

"Thanks for taking me fishing," she said. "Sorry you didn't get in my pants again."

A large surprised laugh escaped him. She was getting a little tiddly. "That's okay, Melinda. Whenever you're ready."

"Aha! I knew it!"

"Like it's been hard to tell."

"You're so transparent." She downed the rest of her drink. "I'd better get going. I'm completely shot." She stood up and nearly fell down. She grabbed at the bar to right herself and Jack came around to her side. He put an arm around her waist. She looked up at him with watery eyes and said, "Damn. I forgot to eat."

"Let me make you some coffee," he suggested.

"And ruin this perfectly good buzz? Hell, I've earned it." She took a step and wavered. "Besides, I don't think it'll make me sober. Probably just wide-awake drunk."

Jack tightened his hold around her and laughed in spite of himself. "All right, Mel. I can put you in my bed and take the couch…"

"But sometimes I have deer in my yard in the morning," she said, a little whiny. "I want to go home. They might come back."

Home. That sounded good to Jack, that she thought of that cabin as her home. "All right, Mel. I'll take you home."

"That's a relief," she said. "Because I'm pretty sure I already can't drive. Even on a straight and undangerous road."

"You're a lightweight," he said.

They took a couple of steps and her legs buckled a second time. He gave a sigh and bent to lift her into his arms. She patted his chest. "It's good that you're strong," she said. "You're good to have around. It's like having my own personal valet."

He chuckled under his breath. Preacher had gone upstairs for the night so he turned off the Open sign and managed to get his keys out of his pocket without dropping her. He locked the front door and took her down the steps and around to the back of the bar where he kept his truck. He put her in and she managed, though with some difficulty, to buckle her seat belt. When he got in and started the truck she said, "You know something, Jack? You've turned out to be my very good friend."

"That's nice, Mel."

"I really appreciate this. Boy, whew. I'm sure not much of a drinker. I think I'm a one-beer girl. Two if I've had a side of beef and an apple pie."

"I think you've assessed the situation correctly."

"If I ask for the good stuff again, be sure to ask me if I've had food."

"Sure will," he said.

She laid her head back on the seat. Within five minutes, it lolled. And Jack spent the rest of the drive wondering a couple of things. One—what if she roused enough as he was taking her inside to invite him to stay? That would be okay, wouldn't it? Even though she was just a "tish" disadvantaged? Or—what if she didn't rouse and he just lay down beside her to be there in case she woke and decided it was time? That would be okay. Or maybe he could just wait on her couch, in case she needed anything…like sex. Then if she woke up during the night he'd be there. He'd be ready. He'd *been* ready.

He played a dozen scenarios in his mind. He would

carry her to her room and she would wake and say, "Stay with me tonight." He really didn't have the strength to say no. Or, she would wake and he would kiss her and then she would say, "Okay." Or morning would come, he would already be there and she would say, "Now, Jack." Whoo boy. He was getting a little warm.

But she was still asleep when he pulled up in front of her cabin. He unbuckled her and lifted her out of the truck. He whacked her head on the door frame. "Ow!" she yelled, her hand going to her head.

"Sorry," he said. And thought to himself, *Foreplay that was* not.

"S'okay." She laid her head back on his shoulder.

Now, he thought, *I should stay to be sure she doesn't have a concussion. And that she doesn't need sex for it. Or just to be there in case she did...*

He carried her across the porch, through the door to her room and, flipping on the light, laid her on the bed. Without opening her eyes she said, "Thank you, Jack."

"You're welcome, Melinda," he said. "Your head okay?"

"What head?"

"Okay. Let's get your boots off."

"Boots. Off." She lifted a leg, making him laugh. He pulled the boot off. The leg dropped and the other one came up. He pulled that one off and the leg dropped. Then she curled into a cute little package, pulling the quilt around her. He looked down at her and saw that it was lights out for Melinda. Then he saw the picture.

Something hit him, and it didn't feel particularly good. He picked up the picture and looked at the man's face. *So, you're the guy,* he thought. He didn't look like a bad guy—but clearly he had done something to Mel. Something she was having trouble getting beyond. Maybe he'd left her for another woman—but that seemed impossible to imagine. Maybe he left her for a man. *Oh, please let it be so—I can make that better— just give me five minutes.* Or maybe he looked harmless but had been an impossible asshole and she'd broken off with him, but still loved him helplessly. And here she had his picture right there, to be the last face she saw before falling asleep at night.

At some point she was going to give Jack a chance to make that picture go away, but it wasn't going to be tonight. Probably just as well. If she woke to find him there, either in her bed or ready to be, she would put the blame on Crown Royal. He wanted it to come from desire—and he wanted it to be real.

He scribbled a note. *I'll be back for you at 8:00 a.m. Jack.* He left it by the coffeepot. Then he went to his truck to get something he'd purchased earlier in the day. He brought the leather case holding the dismantled fly fishing rod and reel and the waders into the house and left them by the front door. And went home.

At 8:00 a.m. he was back in front of her cabin and what he saw made him smile. All the disappointing thoughts that had plagued him the night before vanished. She was sitting in her Adirondack chair in her new waders, idly casting her fly into the yard. A steaming cup of coffee rested on the wide chair arm beside her.

He got out of the truck, grinning. "You found it," he said, walking to the porch.

"I *love* it! Did you get this for me?"

"I did."

"But why?"

"When we go fishing, I need to stand beside you.

Not in back of you, smelling your hair and feeling you against me. You need your own stuff. How do they fit?"

She stood up and turned around for him. "Perfect. I've been practicing."

"Getting any better?"

"I am. I'm sorry about last night, Jack. I had been tense and hungry and freezing all day and it really hit me."

"Yeah. It's okay."

"I should keep this in my trunk, huh? In case we have a light day at Doc's and can just sneak off and fish."

"Good idea, Mel."

"Let me put my gear away," she said happily.

And he thought—*Just give me time. I'm going to get that picture put in storage.*

Ricky hadn't been around the bar the week right after Connie's heart attack, hanging close to the family in case they needed him for anything. When he did come into the bar, it was late and there were only two men at a table and Preacher behind the bar. Ricky sat up at the bar, his eyes downcast.

"How's everybody doing?" Preacher asked.

He shrugged. "Connie's doing pretty good I guess. They sent Liz back to her mom's in Eureka."

"Eureka isn't the end of the world, man. You can visit her."

Ricky looked down. "Yeah, but…probably shouldn't," he said. "She was…she was the first girl I felt that way about." He looked up. "You know. *That* way."

The two men at the table stood and wandered out of the bar. "Close call?" Preacher asked him.

"I wish. Holy God," Rick said, shaking his head. "I thought I had it under control."

Preacher did something he'd never done before. He drew a couple of cold drafts and put one in front of Rick, one in front of himself. "Tough call, that control thing."

"Tell me about it. This for me?"

Preacher lifted an eyebrow. "I thought maybe you might need it right about now."

"Thanks," he said, lifting the glass. "She doesn't look like a kid, but she's just a kid. She's way too young."

"Way," Preacher agreed. "You got a handle on it now?"

"Oh, yeah," he said. "Now that it's too late."

"Welcome to the world." Preacher drank half his draft.

Rick just looked into his. "It's just that I'd die if anyone got hurt, you know. If I hurt her. If I let you and Jack down."

Preacher put his big hands on the bar and leaned toward Rick. "Hey, Ricky, don't worry about letting us down. Some things are just nature, you know? You're a human being. You do the best you can. Try to think ahead next time, if you get my drift."

"I do now."

Jack came into the bar from the back. He noticed right away that Ricky and Preacher had beers and that Ricky wore a troubled expression. "Do I need to toast anything?" He poured himself a glass of beer.

"I'm pretty sure that's a no," Ricky said.

"Ricky here, if I'm reading him right, has entered the world of men. And wishes a little bit he hadn't."

"Instead of giving me a handful of rubbers, you should've had me laminated," he said to Jack.

"Oh, boy. You gonna be okay, buddy?" Jack asked. "She gonna be okay?"

"I don't know. When am I gonna know? How am I gonna know?"

"A month," Jack said. "Maybe less. Depends on her cycle. You're going to have to ask her, Rick. If she got her period."

"I'm gonna die," Ricky said miserably.

"Okay then. Let's toast to your continued good luck. Since you got, you know, lucky."

"Right now I gotta wonder why they call it that," Ricky said.

Nine

The grass grew tall in the pastures, the ewes fat with lambing imminent. The cows were ready to calve and Sondra Patterson was almost to term.

Sondra was expecting her third child, and the first two had come to her quickly and easily, so she and Doc claimed. She had decided to have this one at home, as she had the first two. This would be the first home birth for Mel, and she looked forward to it with nervous delight.

May aged bright and sunny—and brought with it a bunch of men in pickups and campers. There was a great deal of horn-honking at the bar in the afternoon and Mel looked out to see this gathering descend on Jack's. She watched as he came out on his porch and greeted them with bear hugs and shouts and whistles.

"What's going on?" she asked Doc Mullins.

"Hmm. I think it's another Semper Fi reunion. Jack's old buddies from the Marine Corps. They come up here to hunt, fish, play poker, drink and yell into the night."

"Really? He never mentioned that." *And,* she thought, *is this my cue to be scarce?* Because that after-work beer, the occasional kiss, had become the best part of her day. She was further bewildered by the fact that he hadn't tried anything more. And yet, if he had, she would have worried about the consequences. She shouldn't be involved with anyone, even Jack. Not until she was sure she could handle it. Thing was, she just couldn't bring herself to give up that little bit of kissing. She was sure that Mark would understand. If their situations had been reversed, she told herself, she would.

But with the marines in town, there would be none of that.

Doc seemed to have no inclination to stay away, and at the end of the day he took himself over to the bar. "Coming?" he asked her.

"I don't know… I don't want to distract anyone from their reunion…"

"I wouldn't worry about that," he said. "The whole town looks forward to seeing these boys."

She went with him and found that of course Doc was greeted by these visiting men as if they were old friends. Jack dropped a possessive arm around Mel's shoulders and said, "Boys, meet Mel Monroe, new nurse midwife in town. She's been working with Doc. Mel, meet Zeke, Mike Valenzuela, Cornhusker—Corny for short, Josh Phillips, Joe Benson, Tom Stephens and Paul Haggerty. There will be a test later—no name tags."

"Doc, you are a fine and smart gentleman," Zeke said, grinning, reaching for her hand, obviously under the impression Doc had hired her rather than resisted her. "Miss Monroe, it's an honor. An honor."

"Call me Mel," she said.

The noise with which they descended on her was invigorating. The next surprise for her, and perhaps it shouldn't have been, was that Preacher was one of them.

And of course they drew Rick in as though he were a younger brother.

Mel learned that Preacher had served under Jack when he was just a kid of eighteen in the first conflict in Iraq—Desert Storm—it turned out he was much younger than he looked. During that same time a cop from L.A. by the name of Mike Valenzuela and a builder from Oregon by the name of Paul Haggerty also served with them, but the two latter marines, being reservists, were called up for the latest Iraq conflict, again with Preacher and Jack, who were still on active duty at that time. The others, all reservists, were called up for Iraq where they were united in Baghdad and Fallujah. Zeke was a fireman from Fresno; Josh Phillips, a paramedic, and Tom Stephens, a news helicopter pilot—were both from the Reno area. Joe Benson was an architect from the same Oregon town as Paul Haggerty—Paul often built Joe's houses. And Corny, another firefighter, came the farthest, from Washington state, but he was born and raised in Nebraska, thus the nickname.

Jack was older than these men by four years or more, the next oldest in the crowd being Mike at thirty-six. Four of them were married with kids—Zeke, Josh, Tom and Corny. Mel was fascinated by the way they talked about their women with lusty smiles and glittering eyes. No jokes about the old ball and chain here. Rather, they sounded as though they couldn't wait to get home to them.

"How's Patti doing?" someone asked Josh.

He curved his hands over his flat belly to indicate a pregnant tummy and grinning boastfully, said, "She's ripe as a tomato. I can hardly keep my hands off her."

"If she's ripe as a tomato, I bet you get slapped

down like crazy," Zeke laughed. "I got another one on Christa."

"No way! I thought she said you were through!"

"She said that two kids ago—but I snuck one more by her. She's cooking number four. What can I say— that girl's been lightin' my fire since high school. You should see her, man. She's lit up like a beacon. Nobody cooks 'em like Christa. Whew."

"Hey, buddy, congratulations, man! But I don't think you know when to quit."

"I don't. It's like I can't quit. But Christa says she's all done with me. She said after this one, snip snip."

"I think I can go one more," Corny said. "Got my girls. I feel a boy coming on."

No one could better appreciate this kind of enthusiasm for pregnant women than a midwife. Mel was loving it. Loving them.

"Yeah, I've heard that a lot," Jack said. "Eight nieces later, no one got their boy. My brothers-in-law have run through all their chances, I think."

"Maybe you're packin' a boy, Jack."

"I don't even kid myself about that," he laughed.

Jack was among the five single men with Preacher, Mike, Paul and Joe. Confirmed bachelors, Mel was warned. They loved women, but couldn't be caught. "Except Mike," Zeke said. "He gets caught regular." Mel learned that Mike was twice divorced and had a girlfriend back in L.A. who was trying to be wife number three.

The camaraderie was engaging, electrifying. These guys were tight, it was real easy to see. Mel didn't exactly rush away—she had fun. Other folks from town who frequented the bar seemed, like Doc, to be acquainted with this band of brothers and dropped in to partake of the reunion, every bit as welcoming of them as Jack and Preacher had been.

As she left that evening, Jack broke away from his buddies to walk her to her car. "Oh, now there will be talk," she said.

"There's already talk, but around here, what do you expect? Listen, Mel, you shouldn't stay away on account of them—they're a good bunch of guys. But let me tell you what the agenda will be. There will be lots of beer and poker, fishing all day. They'll stay in their campers, make too much noise and fill the place up with cigar smoke. Preacher will have something on the stove every day. And I sense a lot of fish coming our way. Preacher's got a stuffed trout that will knock you down, it's so good."

She put a hand against his chest. "Don't worry about it, Jack. You just enjoy yourself."

"You're not going to ignore me for five days, are you?"

"I'll come by after work for a beer, but you know I like my cabin, my peace and quiet. Have fun. That's the important thing."

"These are great guys," he said. "But I have a feeling they're going to get in the way of my love life."

She laughed at him. "Your love life is pretty bleak, as a matter of fact."

"I know. I keep trying to spool it up. And now them," he said, giving his head a jerk in the direction of his bar, which seemed to be throbbing from the noise and laughter within. He put his hands on her waist. "Kiss me," he said.

"No," she said.

"Come on. Haven't I been perfect? Haven't I followed all your rules? How can you be so selfish? There's no one around—they're busy drinking."

"I think you should go back to your reunion," she said, but she laughed at him again.

Boldly, he picked her up under her arms and lifted her high, holding her above him, slowly lowering her mouth to his. "You're shameless," she told him.

"Kiss me," he begged. "Come on. Gimme a little taste."

It was simply irresistible. He was irresistible. She grabbed his head in her hands and met his lips. She opened hers, moving over his mouth. When he did this to her, she thought of nothing but the kiss. It consumed her deliciously. She allowed his tongue, he allowed hers, and she reached that moment when she wanted it to never end. It was so easy to become lost in his tenderness, his strength.

And then, inevitably, it had to end. They were standing in the street, after all, though it was almost dark. "Thank you," he said. He put her on her feet and behind them, a raucous cheer erupted. There, on the porch at Jack's, stood eight marines and Rick, their tankards raised, shouting, cheering, whistling, cat-calling.

"Oh, brother," she said.

"I'm going to kill them."

"Is this some kind of marine tradition?" she asked him.

"I'm going to kill them," he said again, but he kept his arm around her shoulders.

"You realize what this means," she said. "These little kisses are no longer our little secret."

He looked down into her eyes. The shouts had subsided into a low rumble of laughter. "Mel, they are not little. And since it's leaked," he said, grabbing her up in his arms, lifting her up to him again, her feet clear of the ground, and planted another one on her, to the excited shouts of the old 192nd. Even with that riot in the background, she found herself responding. She was growing addicted to the perfect flavor of his mouth.

When it was done she said, "I knew it was a mistake to let you get to first base."

"Ha, I haven't even thrown out the first pitch yet. You're invited to go fishing with us, if you like."

"Thanks, but I have things to do. I'll see you tomorrow night for a beer. And I'll get myself to my car. I'm not going to make out in front of them for the next week."

A little local research revealed to Mel that there was an ultrasound machine in Grace Valley, about thirty minutes away in northern Mendocino county. She had a long chat with one of the town doctors, June Hudson, and they worked out a deal for the use of the ultrasound—the deal was that June would provide this service out of the goodness of her heart. "The ultrasound was donated," she said. "Women from at least a half dozen surrounding towns make use of it."

Mel arranged to bring Sondra in for a screening that day but Sondra insisted on baking six dozen cookies that she would leave at the Grace Valley clinic. "Are you sure your husband can't come along? It's really something to see," Mel said.

"It would have to be him and the kids," Sondra said. "And I'm really looking forward to getting away for a few hours."

The two of them set out for Grace Valley, driving down through the foothills and along back roads that led them past farms, pastures, vineyards, ranches, flower fields and through a few towns that were not even specs on a map. Sondra, having lived in this part of the country all her life, was able to give Mel a running commentary on where they were, whose ranch was whose, what kind of crops were being grown—mostly alfalfa and silage for the cattle—orchards of fruit and nuts, and the inevitable lumber harvesting. It was a gorgeous day, a beautiful drive, and when they entered the town, Mel was instantly impressed by the shiny clean appearance of the place.

"It's kind of brand-new," Sondra said. "A flood nearly wiped them out not long ago and they did a lot of rebuilding and painting. You can still see the high water marks on some of the big old trees."

There was a café, a service station, a big church, the clinic and lots of well-kept little houses. Mel pulled up to the clinic and got out. Inside she was immediately faced with Dr. Hudson, a trim woman in her late thirties, dressed much like Mel. She was clad in jeans and boots, chambray shirt with a stethoscope around her neck. She smiled and stuck out her hand. "It's such a pleasure, Ms. Monroe," she said. "I'm delighted you're working with Doc Mullins—he's due a little assistance."

"Please, call me Mel. You know the doctor?"

"Sure. Everybody knows everybody."

"How long have you been in Grace Valley?" Mel asked.

June laughed. "I've been here all my life. Except for medical school." June stuck her hand out toward Sondra. "This must be Mrs. Patterson."

"I've brought you cookies," she said. "It's really generous of you to do this for me. I never had one with the other two kids."

"It's a very convenient precaution," June said, gladly taking the box of cookies. She opened it up, inhaled deeply and said, "Oh, these are sinful looking." Then looking back at Sondra and Mel she said, "If you knew how many people from the neighboring towns helped us rebuild after the flood, then you'd know generosity.

Come on, let's see what we've got. Then if you have time, we can go grab a bite to eat at the café."

Over the course of the next hour, they determined that Sondra would give birth to a baby boy, the baby was already in position and there was nothing to indicate there would be complications. They met Dr. Stone, a drop-dead gorgeous blond man June referred to as a city-boy transplant. At the café, they met June's father, the town doctor before her, and he asked after Old Mullins, who couldn't be any older than Doc Hudson. "He still as ornery as ever?" Doc Hudson wanted to know.

"I'm softening him up," Mel said.

"So, what's your story?" June asked over lunch. "How long have you been in Virgin River?"

"Just a couple of months. I came up here from L.A., looking for a change, but I admit, I wasn't prepared for country medicine. I took all of our resources and hospital technology for granted."

"How do you like it so far?"

"It has its challenges. There are aspects of rural living that I think might be growing on me," Mel said. "But I'm not sure how long it's going to work out for me. My sister is in Colorado Springs, married with three children, and she really wants Aunt Mel nearby." She took a bite of a delicious hamburger and said, "I don't want to completely miss out on her kids' childhoods."

"Oh, don't say that," Sondra said.

"Not to worry," she said, patting her hand. "I'm not going anywhere before you deliver, which from the look of things is going to be real soon." She laughed and added, "I just hope we don't have to pull off to the side of the road on our way home today."

"I hope you'll stay on," June said. "It'll be nice to have you so close by."

"Close by? It took us over a half hour of twisting, turning and inching past logging trucks, just to go one way! And I bet it's not twenty miles!"

"I know," June said. "It's just over fifteen miles. Isn't it great that we're neighbors?"

Before they were done with lunch a man came into the café carrying a baby. He reminded Mel just slightly of Jack—equal in height, muscled, rugged-looking in his jeans and plaid shirt, fortyish and handling a baby with ease. He bent, gave Dr. Hudson a kiss on the cheek and handed over the baby. "Meet Jim, my house husband. And our son, Jamie."

All the way back to Virgin River Mel was thinking, *I didn't feel so out of place today.* She loved June and John Stone. Even old Doc Hudson was a kick. After she dropped Sondra off at her farm and drove back into town, it seemed as though the town was cuter somehow. Not quite the falling-down little burg she'd first thought. It seemed oddly like home.

She pulled up in front of Doc's house and noticed as she did so that the men were just getting back to Jack's from fishing all day. She went into the house to find Doc in the kitchen assembling something at the kitchen table. It looked as though he'd gotten himself a new bag. "Doc Hudson sends his regards, as do June and John. What are you up to?"

He put a couple of things in the bag and pushed it toward her. "Time you had one of your own," he said.

It was fun to watch the marines load up their gear and head for the river in the early morning. Mel waved to them from her spot on Doc's front steps where she took her morning coffee, and though they'd been up half the night playing poker and drinking, they seemed full of energy and enthusiasm. They'd shout and wave, and whistle at her. Flirt. "Oh, baby, you are so beautiful in the morning," Corny yelled across the street. His reward was a playful whap on the back of the head from Jack.

They were barely gone when a large, dark SUV pulled into town, driving slowly down the street. To Mel's surprise, the driver stopped in front of Doc's. The door opened, but the engine continued to run. A man got out and stood in the street next to the open door, half-hidden. He was a tall guy, broad-shouldered. He wore a black ball cap and his hair curled out beneath it. "This doctor make house calls?" he asked.

Mel stood up. "Someone's sick?" she asked.

He shook his head. "Someone's pregnant," he answered.

She felt a smile reach her lips. "We can make house calls, if necessary. But it's a lot more convenient to do prenatal checks here in the clinic. We see well patients on Wednesdays."

"You Doc Mullins?" he asked, his eyes crinkling doubtfully.

"Mel Monroe," she said with a chuckle. "Family nurse practitioner and midwife. Doc hasn't been doing much women's health since I got here. Where does your wife plan to have the baby?"

He shrugged. "That's up in the air."

"Well, where do you live?"

He tilted his head. "She's on the other side of Clear River. Almost an hour from here."

"We have a hospital room here. Is it a first baby?"

"I think so, yeah."

She laughed. "You think so?"

"It's the first one I've been around for," he said. "She's not my wife."

"Sorry," Mel said. "I made an assumption. Bring the lady in for a prenatal checkup," Mel said. "I can show her our room and talk to her about her options."

"How about if she has it at home?" he asked.

"Well, that's an option, too," Mel said. "But really, Mr....?" The man didn't respond as he should, with his name. He just stood there, big in his denim jacket, tall in his boots. Serious. "Really, the person having the baby needs to be involved in the discussion. Want to make an appointment?"

"I'll call," he said. "Thanks." And he got in the SUV and proceeded out of town.

She found herself chuckling; she'd never had a consultation go quite like that. She hoped the man would confer with the pregnant woman about where she'd like to give birth.

The marines left at the end of the week and the town quieted down, but after getting to know them, she was actually sorry to see them go. While the boys were in town, Preacher was a lot more animated, laughing easily, scowling so much less. And each one of them grabbed her and hugged her goodbye, like she was part of their family.

Mel found herself looking forward to having Jack to herself again, but it was not to be. Jack was oddly morose and somewhat distant. He didn't lift her off the ground or pester her for kisses, and for someone who had resisted and complained of the inadvisability of same, she was disappointed. Bereft. When she questioned his strange mood, he said, "I'm sorry, Mel. I think the boys wore me out."

When she went to the bar for lunch, Preacher reported that Jack was fishing. "Fishing?" she said. "Didn't he get enough of that last week?" To which Preacher merely shrugged.

Preacher didn't seem particularly worn out. He presided over the bar with the help of Ricky, polishing glasses, serving food, bussing tables and partaking of the occasional game of cribbage. "What's the matter with Jack?" Mel asked.

"Marines. They take their toll," he replied.

Four days later, a week ahead of schedule, Mel got the call from the Patterson farm that it was time. Given the fact that Sondra reported easy, quick births and had already been experiencing contractions through the night, Mel went immediately.

Babies are odd—they do as they please. Having a history of short labors didn't necessarily mean they would all be that way. With the support of her mother, mother-in-law and husband, Sondra labored hard through the day. Finally in the early evening, the little boy arrived. He didn't emerge with a lusty cry and Mel had to suction, stroke and cajole him into the world. Sondra bled a little too much and the baby wasn't interested in nursing right away. Even Sondra quickly knew the difference between this and her previous two experiences.

Getting a slower than usual start in the world doesn't necessarily mean trouble, and the baby's heart, respirations, coloring and cry caught up right away. Still, Mel stayed a bit longer than she ordinarily might have. She rocked the baby for three hours past the time she felt everything was fine, playing it extra safe.

It was ten at night by the time Mel finally decided to give them back their lives, their family, that it was perfectly safe to leave them. "And I'm wearing my pager," she said. "Don't hesitate, if you think anything is amiss."

Instead of going right back to her cabin, she went into town. If Jack's was dark and closed up, she'd go home. But the light was on in the bar, though the Open sign was not lit.

When she pushed open the door, she was greeted by a most unexpected sight. Preacher was behind the bar, a steaming cup of coffee in front of him, but Jack sat at a table with his head down on his arms. In front of him was a bottle of Scotch and a shot glass.

When Preacher saw her enter, he said, "Throw the latch on that door, Mel. I think this is enough company."

She did so, but the look on her face was completely nonplussed. She walked over to Jack and put a hand on his back. "Jack?" she asked. His eyes briefly opened and then rolled back in their sockets and closed again. His head lolled and one arm fell off the table and dangled at his side.

Mel went to the bar, hopped up on a stool in front of Preacher and said, "What's the matter with him?" Preacher shrugged and made a move to reach for his coffee mug, but before he could connect with it, Mel virtually lunged across the bar, grabbed the front of his shirt in her fist and said, hotly, "What's the *matter* with him?!"

Preacher's black brows shot up in surprise and he put up his hands as if being arrested. Mel slowly let go of his shirt and sat back on the stool. "He's drunk," Preacher said.

"Well, no kidding. But there's something wrong with him. He's been different all week."

Again the shrug. "Sometimes when the boys are here, it dredges things up. You know? I think he's having some remembering of things not so good."

"Marine things?" she asked. Preacher nodded. "Come on, Preacher. He's the best friend I have in this town."

"I don't think he'd like me talking."

"Whatever this is, he shouldn't go through it alone."

"I'll take care of him," Preacher said. "He'll snap out of it. He always does."

"Please," she implored. "Can't you guess how much he means to me? I want to help, if there's any way I can."

"I could tell you some things, but they're very ugly things. Not for a lady to hear."

She laughed a little. "You can't imagine the things I've seen, much less heard. I worked in a trauma center for almost ten years. It could get pretty ugly at times."

"Not like this."

"Try me."

Preacher took a deep breath. "Those boys that come up every year? They come to make sure he's okay. He was their sergeant. My sergeant. Best sergeant in the marines. He's been in five combat zones. The last one, Iraq. He was leading a platoon into interior Fallujah and one of the boys stepped on a truck mine. Blew him in half. Right away we were pinned down by sniper fire. Our boy who stepped on the mine, he didn't die right away. Something about the heat of the explosion—it must've cauterized arteries and vessels and he didn't bleed out. Didn't have pain, either—it must have done something to his spine. But he was fully conscious."

"My God."

"Jack ordered everyone to take cover in the buildings, which we did. But he sat with his man. He wouldn't leave him. Under sniper fire, leaning against a fat tire on an overturned truck, he held him and talked to him for a half hour before he died. Kid kept telling Jack to go, take cover, that it was okay. You know he didn't go. He'd never leave one of his men behind." He took a drink of coffee. "We saw a lot of stuff back there that will give you nightmares, but that's the one that sometimes gets to him. I don't know what hits him harder—the kid's slow death or the visit he paid his parents to tell them all the things he said before he went."

"And he gets drunk?"

"Fishes a lot. Maybe goes into the woods and camps awhile to get his stability back. Sometimes he'll try to drink it away, but that's pretty rare. First, it doesn't work too well and second, he feels like crap afterward. But it'll be okay, Mel. He always comes out of it."

"Jesus," she said. "I guess everyone has baggage. Gimme a beer."

He poured one from the tap and put it before her. "So maybe the thing to do is just let him be awhile."

"Is he going to wake up soon?"

"No. He's tanked. I was just about to carry him to bed when you walked in. I'll sleep in the chair in his room, just in case."

"In case of what?"

"In case he's not just drunk. In case he gets sick or something. He carried me down a road in Iraq—about a mile. I'm not letting anything happen to him now."

She drank some of her beer. "He's carried me a little, too," she said. "I don't think he knows it, though."

They sat in silence for a little while. She drank about half her beer. "I'm trying to get a picture of him carrying you," she said. "Must've looked like the ant and the rubber tree."

He surprised her with a chuckle.

"How'd he get you to come here? To this little town?"

"He didn't have to talk me into it. I kept in touch with him when he got out, and when I got out, I came up. He said I could stay and help around the bar if I wanted to. I wanted to."

A noise behind her made her turn. Jack fell off the chair and crashed to the floor, sprawling there.

"Nightie-night time," Preacher said, coming around the bar.

"Preacher, if you'll get him to his room, I'll stay with him."

"You don't have to do that, Mel. Could be unpleasant. You know?"

"Not a problem," she said. "I've held many a bucket, if it comes to that."

"Sometimes he cries out."

"Sometimes, so do I."

"Is it what you want?"

"It is. I want to."

"You really do care about him, then?" he asked.

"I said so, didn't I?"

"Well, okay. If you're sure."

Preacher crouched and pulled Jack upright. Hands under his armpits, he got him to a limp standing position, then putting a shoulder to his midsection, hoisted him over his shoulder in a fireman's carry. Mel followed him to Jack's bedroom.

She'd never been in Jack's quarters. It was set up like a little efficiency apartment with two means of entry—either through the kitchen behind the bar or the back door that led out to the yard. It was L-shaped, the bedroom being in the short end of the L and the living area larger. There was a table with two chairs by the window and while there was no kitchen, there was a small refrigerator.

Preacher put Jack on the bed and unlaced and removed his boots. "Let's get the jeans off," she said. To

Preacher's dubious look, she said, "I assure you, I've seen it all." She undid the leather belt and unsnapped the jeans. Mel took the right pant leg, Preacher took the left and they pulled, leaving him in his boxers. Mel unbuttoned his shirt and rolling him from side to side, removed it. She took the clothes to his closet. Hanging on a peg just inside the door was a holster with a hand-gun in it and it made her gasp. She hung the pants and shirt over the gun.

Preacher was staring down at Jack, clad only in box-ers. "He's gonna kill me for this," Preacher said.

"Or thank you," she supplied, giving him a small smile. "If my pager goes off, I'll come for you." She pulled the comforter over Jack.

"Or if you have any problems," the big man said.

When Preacher had gone, Mel pulled off her boots and in stocking feet, she poked around a little. He had a roomy bathroom with cupboards and drawers. She opened one and found that he kept underwear and socks in there. Towels were stored there, as well, and remem-bering that first day in Virgin River, she sniffed one. Downy, like he had said.

The closet was a medium-size walk-in. There was a small laundry room with cabinets in addition to the washer and dryer. The bathroom and laundry room had doors that closed, but the bedroom was in full view of the living room.

Looking around, it was so obviously Jack. Very mas-culine; very functional. He had a leather couch and big leather chair. There was a television on the facing wall and beside it, a glass-and-wood gun case filled with ri-fles, the key dangling from the lock. There was a heavy wood coffee table and a side table between the sofa and chair with a lamp on it. The walls were of rough-hewn wood and there were only two framed pictures on the side table. A family photo showing all of them, Jack, four sisters, four brothers-in-law, eight nieces, one silver-haired father as large as Jack. Beside it, a rather older portrait of his mother and father.

She picked up the family photo. This was a family of strong good looks, the men all tall and handsome, the women trim and pretty, the girls adorable—the youngest just little, like three or four, the oldest a teen. She thought Jack the best looking of them all, and he stood in the middle of the group, an arm around a sister on each side.

She took the throw off the couch, wrapped it around herself and curled up in the large chair. Jack hadn't moved a muscle. Eventually she, too, nodded off.

Somewhere in the night, sounds came from Jack's bed. He was fitful, rolling around, muttering in his sleep. Mel went to the bed, sat on the edge and touched his brow. He grumbled something unintelligible and curled toward her, grabbing her and pulling her into the bed. He rested his head against her. She took his head in the crook of her arm and lay down beside him. "It's okay," she said to him. And he quieted at once, draping an arm over her.

She pulled the comforter over them both and snuggled up to him. She sniffed the pillow—Downy. Who was this guy? she found herself asking. Looks like Paul Bunyan, runs a bar, has all these guns, and cleans and launders like Martha Stewart.

In his sleep, he pulled her closer. His breath smelled of Scotch. *Whew,* she thought. She put her face against his hair, which smelled of his musk combined with the wind and trees. She inhaled deeply; she'd already begun to love his particular scent and the taste of his mouth. She had wondered what was under the shirt—a nice mat of brown hair on his chest and a couple of tattoos. On his upper left arm an eagle, globe and anchor, almost as big as her hand. On the upper right, over a ribbon, the words:

SAEPE EXPERTUS,
SEMPER FIDELIS,
FRATRES AETERNI

She couldn't resist, she rubbed her hands over the mat of hair on his chest and over his smooth shoulders. She pulled him close. Within minutes, she had fallen back to sleep, cradling Jack in her arms, his arm comfortably embracing her.

In the dim light of early morning, Jack awakened with a pounding head. He turned his face to the side and the first thing he saw were Mel's golden curls against the pillow next to him. She clutched the covers under her chin, sleeping soundly. He raised himself up on an elbow and looked down at her face. Her pink lips were parted in sleep; sooty lashes lay against her cheek. He lifted a soft curl off the pillow and held it to his face, inhaling. Then he leaned toward her and lowered his lips to gently touch hers.

Her eyes came open. "Morning," she whispered sleepily.

"Did we do it?" he asked.

"No," she said.

"Good," he said.

She smiled at him. "I didn't expect you to say that."

"When we do it, I want to remember it. I don't even know why you're here."

"I stopped by the bar for a beer just about the time Preacher was scraping you off the floor. Headache?"

"It went away the minute I saw you. I must have had one too many."

"Did it work? Did you scare away all the demons?"

He shrugged. "It got you in my bed. If I'd known it was that easy, I'd have gotten plastered weeks ago."

"Lift the covers, Jack," she said.

He did so. There he was, boxer clad and sporting quite a healthy morning erection. And there she was, fully clothed. "Don't look down," he said, dropping the comforter. "You have me at a *huge* disadvantage." She laughed at him. "We could do it now," he suggested. He felt the texture of her hair between his thumb and finger. "I'll treat you real, real good." He grinned.

"No, thank you," she declined.

"Did I try anything?" he wanted to know.

"No." She laughed. "Why?"

"I drank enough so that could have been really humiliating. Assault with a dead weapon."

She ran her fingers over the tattoo. "I sort of expected this," she said.

"Rite of passage. I bet every young marine wakes up with a splitting head and a little remembrance of the Corps."

"What does this mean?" she asked, running her fingers over the words on the other arm.

"Often tested, always faithful, brothers forever." He touched her cheek. "What did Preacher tell you?" he asked her.

"That the boys come up here and stir up some of your roughest memories of the wars you've been in. But I suspect that now and then you'd have those memories anyway, whether they came or not."

"I love those boys," he said.

"And they're devoted to you. So—maybe it's worth a little discomfort now and then. Friendships like that don't come cheap."

Ten

Jack was back to his old self. It was either the Scotch or the fact that he woke up to a pretty blonde in his bed. He bet on the blonde.

He never did ask Preacher precisely what he had told Mel. And he didn't ask Mel to be more specific. It didn't really matter. What did matter was that he had bonded with Mel on a new level that night without planning to. That she knew he was tortured over something terrible from his past and instead of shying away, stayed with him, willing to take it on—it had meant something. She had held him while he tossed and turned against a mean-spirited ghost. After that, she yielded more willingly to those kisses. He was definitely ready to move ahead with her.

They were the current talk in Virgin River, which gave Jack a strange satisfaction. For a man who didn't want to be tied down to a woman, a man who tended to keep his woman in the shadows, he found himself wanting everyone to know they were a couple. And he worried that she would make good on her threats to leave before he could convince her to stay forever.

Jack took Mel to the coast to whale watch and they

talked all the way there and back, but on the high cliffs above the ocean, they held hands, quiet, while the great fleet of behemoth mammals swam by, jumping out of the water and landing with an enormous splash. Their own guard of dolphins escorted them to the north. She let him kiss her for a long time that day. Many times. Then if his hand wandered she said, "No. Not yet." And that gave him hope. Not yet meant it was on the agenda.

He was completely smitten. Jack was forty and this was the first time that he had a woman in his life he couldn't imagine giving up.

Mel called her sister. "Joey," she said quietly, in almost a whisper. "I think I have a man in my life."

"You found a man in that place?"

"Uh-huh. I think so."

"Why do you sound so…strange?"

"I have to know something. Is it okay? Because I'm not even close to being over Mark. I still love Mark more than anything. Anyone."

Joey let out her breath slowly. "Mel, it's all right to get on with your life. Maybe you'll never love anyone as much as you loved Mark—but then maybe there will be someone else. Someone next. You don't have to compare them, honey, because Mark is gone and we can't get him back."

"Love," she corrected. "Not past tense. I still *love* Mark."

"It's all right, Mel," Joey said. "You can go on living. You might as well have someone to pass the time with. Who is he?"

"The man who owns the bar across from Doc's clinic—the one who fixed up the cabin, bought me the fishing pole, got my phone installed. Jack. He's a good man, Joey. And he cares about me."

"Mel… Have you…? Are you…?"

There was no answer.

"Mel? Are you sleeping with him?"

"No. But I let him kiss me."

Joey laughed sadly. "It's okay, Mel. Can you really think otherwise? Would Mark want you to wither away, lonely? Mark was one of the finest men I've ever known—generous, kind, loving, genuine. He'd want you to remember him sweetly, but to get on with your life and be happy."

Melinda started to cry. "He would," she said through her tears. "But what if I can't be happy with anyone except Mark?"

"Baby sis, after what you've been through, would you settle for some marginal happiness? And a few good kisses?"

"I don't know. I just don't know."

"Give it a go. Worst case—it takes your mind off your loneliness."

"Is that wrong? To use someone to take your mind off your dead husband?"

"What if you put that another way? What if you *enjoyed* someone who took your mind off your dead husband? That could pass for happiness, couldn't it?"

"I probably shouldn't be kissing him," she said. And she cried. "Because I just can't stay here. I don't belong here. I belong in L.A. with Mark."

Joey sighed heavily. "It's only kissing, Mel. Just take it one kiss at a time."

When they hung up the phone, Joey said to her husband, Bill, "I have to go to her. I think she might be heading for a crisis."

* * *

Mel had started thinking about the past more—that morning that the police came to the door to tell her that Mark was dead. They had worked the swing shift together at the hospital the night before. They'd taken their lunch hour together in the cafeteria. But Mark was on call and the E.R. was busy, so he stayed through the night. It happened when he was on his way home.

She had gone to the morgue to view him. Left alone with him for a little while, she took his cold, lifeless body into her arms, his chest riddled with three perfect holes, and wept until they dragged her away.

She had a video in her mind—one that ran from the pictures of Mark lying on the floor at the convenience store, the police at her door at dawn, through the funeral, those nights that she cried literally through the entire night, right up to the long days of packing up his things and the long months of not being able to part with them. She saw the film in her head as if from above, curled into a fetal position in her bed, grabbing herself around the gut as though she'd been run through by a knife, crying hard, loud tears. Cries so loud that she thought the neighbors would hear and call for help.

Rather than just telling his picture that she loved him, she began carrying on long, one-sided conversations with his flat, lifeless face. She would tell him everything she'd done all day and it would inevitably end with, "I still love you, damn you," she would exclaim harshly. And urgently, "I still love you. I can't stop loving you and missing you and wanting you back."

Mel had always thought that Mark was the kind of lover, the kind of husband, who would find a way to contact her from beyond, because he was so devoted. But there had never been any evidence that he'd crossed back. When he went, he went all the way. He was so gone, it left her feeling desolate inside.

She woke up crying three days running. Jack had asked her if anything was wrong, if there was anything she wanted to talk about. "PMS," she told him. "It'll pass."

"Mel, have I done anything?" He wanted to know.

"Of course not. Hormones. I swear."

But she was starting to think that the brief reprieve she seemed to have experienced lately was now officially over and she was on her way back to the darkness of grief and longing. Back to the stark loneliness.

Then something happened to jar her out of it. She returned from her short walk to the corner store to watch her soap with Joy and a recovering Connie to see a rented car in front of Doc's. When she went inside she was face-to-face with her sister's bright smile. Mel gasped, dropped her bag and they swooped together, lifting each other off the ground, laughing and crying at once. When the crazy moments had passed, still holding Joey's hand, Mel turned toward Doc to make a formal introduction. But before she could, Doc said, "Kind of scary, there being two of you."

Mel ran her hand over Joey's shiny and smooth brown hair. "Why are you here?" she asked.

"You know. I thought you might need me."

"I'm okay," she lied.

"Just in case, then."

"That's so sweet. Do you want to see the town? Where I live? Everything?"

"I want to see the man," Joey whispered in Mel's ear.

"We'll do that last. Doc? Can I have the afternoon?"

"I certainly wouldn't be able to stand having the two of you yakking and giggling around here all day."

Mel rushed on Doc and gave him a kiss on his with-ered cheek, which the old boy quickly wiped off with a grimace.

Mel's spirits were high and she didn't think about Mark for a little while. She took Joey to all her favorite places, beginning with her cabin in the woods, which Joey thought was charming, if a little in need of her professional decorator's touch. "You should have seen it when I arrived," Mel laughed. "There was a bird's nest in the oven!"

"God!"

Then they went to the river where there were at least ten men in waders and vests, angling. A couple of them turned and waved to her. "The first time I was here, Jack brought me and we saw a mama bear and her cub, right downriver, fishing. First and last bear I've ever seen. I think I'd like to keep it that way. The next time I came, I fished. I fly fished—not as good as what they're doing, but I actually caught a fish. I have my own gear in the trunk."

"No way!"

"Way!"

Next, to the Anderson ranch to visit little baby Chloe and see the new lambs. Buck Anderson lifted a couple of little lambs out of the pen and handed one to each woman.

Mel stuck her finger in a lamb's mouth and he closed his little eyes and sucked, making the women say, "Aww...."

"I raised six kids—three boys and three girls—and each and every one of them smuggled a lamb into their bedroom to sleep in their beds. Keeping the livestock out of the house was a lifetime chore," he told them.

Mel drove her sister down Highway 299 through

the redwoods and took great pleasure in her oohs and ahhs. They got out and walked through Fern Canyon, one of the filming sites of Spielberg's *The Lost World*. She showed her the back roads of Virgin River, the green pastures, fields of crops, craggy knolls, towering pines, grazing livestock, vineyards in the valley. "If you're going to stay awhile and I can pry myself away from Doc, I'll take you to Grace Valley to meet some of my newer friends. They have a larger clinic there, complete with EKG, a small surgery and ultrasound."

Then, as the dinner hour approached, so did a heavy and cool summer shower and they ended up at Jack's, where the drop in temperature had prompted the laying of a friendly fire. Word had apparently gotten out, because the bar was busier than usual—so untypical of a rainy night. Some of her favorite people were present. There was Doc, of course, and Hope McCrea. Ron brought Connie for a little while and where Connie went these days, Joy was nearby with her husband, Bruce. Darryl Fishburn and his parents stopped by and she introduced Darryl as the daddy of her first Virgin River baby. Anne Givens and her husband were there, a couple from out on a big orchard—their first baby was due in August. Preacher treated Joey to his rare smiles, Rick was his usual grinning, adorable self, joking about how the whole family must be gorgeous, and Jack charmed her thoroughly. When he went to the kitchen to get their dinners, Joey leaned close to Mel and said, "Holy crap, is he a hunk or what?"

"Hunk," Mel confirmed.

They were served a delicious salmon-in-dill-sauce dinner, which Jack ate with them, and Mel regaled her sister with tales of country doctoring, including the two births she had attended on her own.

It was a little after seven when Doc's pager sent him to the phone in Jack's kitchen. Then he dropped by Mel's table. "Pattersons called. The baby seems to be having trouble breathing and is getting a little pale and blue around the gills."

"I'm going with you," Mel said. She stood and told Joey, "I delivered that baby and he had a slow start. If I'm late, can you find the cabin?"

"Sure. Want to give me a key?"

Mel smiled at her sister. She kissed her cheek. "We don't use too many keys around here, sugar. It's open."

Mel rode with Doc in his truck, just in case some of the dirt roads had gotten soft from the rain. She didn't want her BMW stuck in the mud.

They found Sondra and her husband in a state of panic, for the baby did seem to be wheezing. His respirations were accelerated and shallow, but he had no temperature. After a little oxygen, he cleared right up, which did nothing to tell them what was wrong. Mel rocked him for a good long while. Doc sat at the kitchen table and talked to the Pattersons, drinking coffee. "He's too young for something like asthma. Might be some kind of allergic reaction, a symptom of an infection, or it could be more serious—a problem with his heart or lungs. Tomorrow you're going to have to take him over to Valley Hospital to the outpatient clinic for tests. I'll write down the name of a good pediatrician."

"Is he going to be all right through the night?" Sondra asked tearfully.

"I expect so, but I'll leave the oxygen. You can drop it off tomorrow. It wouldn't hurt to spell each other and stay awake, just in case. If you have any problems or you're worried about him, call me. That little foreign thing of Mel's isn't worth a crap on these roads in the rain. Besides, Melinda has company from out of town."

Two hours later, Doc was ready to take Mel back to her sister.

By eight o'clock, all the patrons had left Jack's except Joey. Jack had sent Ricky home, Preacher was cleaning up the kitchen, and he brought Joey a cup of coffee and sat down with her again. He asked about her kids, what her husband did, how she liked living in Colorado Springs, and then, "She didn't know you were coming."

"No, it was a complete surprise. Though it shouldn't have been."

"Your timing couldn't be better. Something's been eating at her."

"Oh," Joey said. "I guess I thought you knew what was going on. Because she said that you and she…" She stopped and looked into her coffee cup.

"We what?" he asked.

Joey raised her eyes and smiled sheepishly. "She said you kiss."

"Every time she'll give in a little."

"In a place like Virgin River, does that make you a couple?" she asked.

He sat back in his chair, willing the bar to stay empty. "Yeah, something like that," he said. "With a big hunk of something missing."

"Look, I don't know that I have the right…"

"To tell me who ripped her heart out and crushed it under the heel of his boot?" he finished for her.

"Her husband," Joey said bravely, lifting her chin.

That caused Jack to sit up straighter. Joey hadn't said *ex*-husband. "What did he do to her?" he asked, a definite angry edge to his voice.

Joey sighed. *In for a penny, in for a pound,* she thought. If Mel hadn't told him, she didn't want him to know. She was going to be pissed. "He got himself murdered in an armed robbery that he happened into by accident."

"Murdered," Jack said weakly.

"He was an emergency room doc. He'd worked an all-nighter and stopped into a convenience store for milk on his way home in the morning. The robber panicked and shot him. Three times. He died instantly."

"God," Jack said. "When?"

"A year ago. Today."

"God," he said again. He leaned an elbow on the table and rested his head in his hand. He massaged his eyes. "She knows it was today?"

"Of course she knows. She's been heading for it. Painfully."

"In L.A.," he said. It wasn't a question. "And to think I wanted to punch him in the face a few times for hurting her."

"Look, I feel kind of funny about this. Disloyal. One of the things that drew her here was that no one knows. No one looks at her with pity. No one asks her fifteen times a day how she's doing, if she's lost more weight, if she's sleeping yet… I guess I thought she'd have told you, since…"

"She's holding back," he said. "Now I know why."

"And I let it out. I don't know whether to be guilty or relieved. Someone who cares about her out here should know what she's been through. What she's going through." She took a breath. "I didn't think she'd make it a week here."

"Neither did she." Jack was quiet for a minute and then said, "Can you imagine what kind of courage it took for her to chuck her big job in L.A. and come to this little town, to work with a man like Doc Mullins? She told me a little about what it was like there—city medicine, she called it. A battle zone, she said. She thought it was going to be real dull and boring here. Then she ends up riding to the hospital with a patient in the back of an old pickup, over these roads, holding an IV bag over her head, freezing. Christ, I could've used her in combat."

"Mel has always been tough, but Mark's death really derailed her. That's why she did this—she started being afraid to go to the bank, the store."

"And she hates guns," he supplied. "In a little town where everyone has a gun because they have to."

"Oh, jeez. Look, it's no secret—I begged her not to do this—I thought it was crazy and way too drastic a change," Joey said. "But something about this seems to be working for her. What she calls country doctoring. Or maybe it's you."

"She has these spells," he said. "When she's so sad. But it passes and there is such a brightness inside her. You should have seen her the morning after she delivered her first baby at Doc's. She said she felt like a champ. I've never seen anyone so lit up." He chuckled at the memory, but there was a morose tone to his laugh.

"You know what—I think I'm going to call it a night. Go back to Mel's and hang out until she gets home, so I can be there for her."

"Let Preacher drive you," he said. "These roads at night, in the rain, can be treacherous if you don't know them. The first night Mel drove out to the cabin, she slid off a soft shoulder and had to be towed out."

"What about Mel?" she asked.

"Doc might just take her straight home—he has no

respect for that little car of hers. Or she could come here for her car—she's pretty good on these roads now, but if she has any worries about it, I'll drive her out. Fact is, it wouldn't surprise me if she was out at Patterson's half the night, so don't worry. She hates leaving a sick patient. But I'll wait up." He went to the bar and got a piece of paper. "Call me if she shows up at the cabin. Or if you need anything," he said, writing down his number.

It was nearly ten by the time Mel walked into the bar. She saw Jack at the table by the fire, but frowned when she looked around and didn't see Joey. "Where's my sister?" she asked. "Her car's out front."

"I had Preacher take her home in the truck. Her first night in town she shouldn't have to deal with those roads in the rain."

"Oh. Thanks," she said. "I'll see you sometime tomorrow, then."

"Mel?" he called. "Sit with me a minute."

"I should go to Joey. She came all this way…"

"Maybe we should talk. About what's been going on with you."

She had been on this precipice for days, teetering on the fine edge of losing it. The only thing that seemed to take her mind off the violent event that changed her life was work. If she had a patient or an emergency, she could lose herself in it. Even the day with her sister, showing Joey the town, the lambs, the beauty, took her away a little bit. But it just kept coming back, haunting her. A picture of him lying on the floor bleeding out could float in front of her eyes and she'd have to pinch them closed, praying she wouldn't break down. There was no way she could sit down and talk about it.

What she needed right now was to get out of here, go home and have a good hard cry. With her sister, who understood.

"I can't," she said, her words little more than a breath.

Jack stood up. "Then let me drive you home," he said.

"No," she said, holding up a hand. "Please. I need to just go."

"Why don't you just let me hold you. Maybe you shouldn't be alone."

So, Mel thought. She *told* him! She closed her eyes and held up a hand as if to ward him off. Her nose became red, her lips pink around the edges. "I really want to be alone. *Please,* Jack."

He gave his head a nod and watched her leave.

Mel went down the porch steps to her car, but she didn't make it. It hit her before she could get there. She was nearly doubled over by the sudden crushing pain of memory, of loss. The emptiness came back, draining her of all good feelings and filling her up with the horrific unanswerable questions. *Why, why, why? How can this happen to a person? Even if I'm not good enough to deserve better, Mark was! He should have lived to be an old man, to save lives and treat people with the brilliance and compassion that made him one of the best emergency room doctors in the city!*

She had made it all day without falling apart, but now in the dark, in the cold night rain, she felt as though she was going to collapse to the ground and just lie there in the mud long enough to perish, to be with him. She stumbled toward a tree and grabbed the trunk, embracing it, holding herself up and holding on at the same time. The cries that came out of her were loud and wrenching.

Why couldn't we at least have had a baby? Why

couldn't even that small thing have worked in our favor? Just to have a piece of him to live for...

Inside, Jack paced back and forth in the bar, feeling his own helplessness because he couldn't do anything for her. He knew all about the crushing pain of loss; even more about the difficulty of getting beyond it. He hated that she'd left without at least letting him try to comfort her.

Frustrated, he opened the door to go after her. There sat her BMW, right in front of the porch, but she wasn't in it. He squinted to look into the car, but then he heard her. Sobbing. Wailing. He couldn't see her. He stepped out onto the porch, went down the steps into the rain. And then he saw her—holding on to the tree, the rain drenching her.

He ran to her, embracing her from behind, holding the tree with her, holding her against the tree. Her back heaved with her cries, her cheek pressed against the rough bark. The sound of her anguish broke his heart; no way could he let her go, no matter what she said about being alone. This crying made her weeping over baby Chloe look like a mere rehearsal. She was wracked. She started to crumble to the ground and he put his arms under hers and held her upright as the rain soaked them.

"Oh God, oh God, oh God," she howled. "Oh God, oh God, oh God!"

"Okay," he whispered. "Let it go, let it out."

"Why, why, why?" she cried in the night, her breath coming in jagged gasps. Her whole body jerked and shook as she cried. "Oh, God, *why?*"

"Let it all out," he whispered, his lips against her wet hair.

She screamed. She opened up her mouth, tipped her

head back against him and screamed at the top of her lungs. He hoped she wouldn't wake the dead, the sound was so powerful. But he only hoped she wasn't heard so that no one would disturb them and stop this purging. He wanted to do this with her. He wanted to be there for her. The scream subsided into hard sobbing. Then more quietly, "Oh, God, I can't. I can't, I can't."

"It's okay, baby," he whispered. "I've got you. I won't let anything happen to you."

Her legs didn't seem to hold her up anymore; he was keeping her upright. He had the passing thought that no amount of emotion he had ever expelled in his lifetime could match this. It was almost phenomenal in its strength, this pain that gripped her. What had he thought? That his few days of brooding, a good drunk, had been demonstrative of his pain? Ha! He held in his arms a woman who knew more about gut-wrenching pain than he did. His eyes stung. He kissed her cheek. "Let it go," he whispered. "Get it out. It's okay."

It was a long time before she began to cry more softly. Fifteen minutes, maybe. Twenty. Jack knew you don't stop something like this until it's over. Till it's all bled out. They were both soaked to the skin when her breath started coming in little gasps and hiccups. It was a long time before she pushed herself away from the tree and turned toward him. She looked up at his rain soaked face, hers twisted with pain, and said, "I loved him so much."

He touched her wet cheek, unable to tell the tears from the rain. "I know," he said.

"It was so unfair."

"It was."

"How do I live with it?"

"I don't know," he answered honestly.

She let her head drop against his chest. "God, it hurt so much."

"I know," he said again. Then he lifted her in his arms and carried her back into the bar, kicking the door closed behind him. He took her to his room in the back, her arms looped around his neck. He put her down on the big chair in the sitting room. She sat there, shivering, her hands tucked between her knees, her head down, her hair dripping. He went for a clean, dry T-shirt and towels and came back to her, kneeling in front of her. "Come on, Mel. Let's get you dry."

She lifted her head and looked at him with eyes that were both terribly sad and exhausted. She was listless. Spent. And her lips were blue with cold.

He peeled off her jacket, tossing it on the floor. Then her blouse. He was undressing her like one might a baby, and she didn't resist. He wrapped a towel around her and keeping her covered, reached beneath and undid her bra, slipping it off without exposing her. He pulled the T-shirt over her head, holding it for her arms, and once it covered her to her thighs, he yanked out the towel. "Come on," he said, pulling her upright. She stood on shaky legs and he unbuttoned and pulled down her trousers before sitting her back down. He removed her boots, socks and pants; he dried her legs and feet with the towel.

Though still drenched himself, he used the towel to attempt to dry her curling hair, blotting the locks between folds of the towel. He wrapped the throw from the couch around her shoulders, then went to his bureau and found a pair of clean, warm socks. He rubbed her cold feet vigorously, warming them, and put on the socks. When she looked up at him, some sanity had seeped into her eyes, and this made him smile a small smile. "Better," he said softly.

He went to the cupboard in his laundry and brought out a decanter of Remy Martin and two glasses. He poured her a small amount of the brandy, neat, and took it to her, kneeling in front of her. She took a sip and then in a voice both weak and strained, she said, "You're still wet."

"I am," he said. "Be right back."

He went to his closet and quickly stripped off his clothes, pulling on only a pair of sweatpants, leaving his chest bare and his wet clothes in a pile on the floor. He poured himself a little brandy and went to her. He sat forward on the sofa at a right angle to her, putting the palm of his hand against her cheek and was pleased to note that she had already warmed. She turned her face against his hand and kissed the palm. "I've never been taken care of like this," she said.

"I've never taken care of anyone like this," he said.

"It seemed like you knew exactly what to do."

"I guessed," he said.

"I crashed," she said.

"It was a helluva crash. If you're going to go down, go down big. You should be proud." And then he smiled.

He held her hand as it lay on her lap while she lifted her brandy to her lips with the other hand, trembling a bit. When it was gone, he said, "Come on. I'm putting you to bed."

"What if I cry all night?"

"I'll be right here," he said. He pulled her hand and led her to his bed, holding up the covers so that she could slip in. He tucked her in as if she were a little girl.

Jack dealt with the wet clothes, spinning the water out of them and putting them in the dryer. When he checked on Mel, she was asleep, so he went back into the little laundry and behind closed doors, called Joey. "Hi," he said. "I didn't want you to worry. Mel is with me."

"Is she okay?" Joey asked.

"She is now. She had a meltdown. Out in the rain, it was awful. I don't think she has another tear in her, at least for tonight."

"Oh, God," she said. "That's why I came! I should be with her now…"

"I got her in some clean, dry clothes and put her to bed, Joey. She's asleep and I—I'll watch over her. If she wakes up and wants to go home, I'll take her, no matter what time it is. But for now, let's let her sleep." He inhaled deeply. "She's had it."

"Oh, Jack," Joey said, "were you with her?"

"I was. She wasn't alone. I was able to… I held her. Kept her safe."

"Thank you," Joey said, her voice small and shaky.

"There's nothing more to do right now but let her rest. Have a glass of wine, get some sleep and try not to worry about Mel. I'm not going to let anything happen to her."

With only a dim night-light in the room, Jack pulled a chair from his table near to the bed. His feet planted on the floor, his elbows resting on his knees and the rest of his Remy clutched in his hands, he watched her sleep. Her hair curled across his pillow and her pink lips were parted slightly. She made little noises in her sleep—little hums and purrs.

I have a high-school education, he thought. *She was married to a medical doctor. A brilliant, educated man. An emergency room hero, made even more perfect in death. How do I compete with that?* He reached out and lightly touched her hair. *There's no way,* he thought. *I'm sunk. And my heart hasn't beat the same since she walked into town.*

He was in love with her. This man who had never been in love in his life. Not once. As a kid, a young man, he'd thought himself in love a couple of times, but it hadn't felt like this. Lust, he was familiar with that. Wanting a woman was something he knew quite well— but wanting to take care of a woman so that she would never hurt, never want, never be afraid or lonely—he had no experience with that. There had been beautiful women in his past; intelligent women, clever women, women with wit and courage and passion, but as far as he could remember, never one like Mel; never before a woman who had everything he'd ever wanted. *And it just figures,* he thought. *I'm stupid in love with a woman who isn't available to me. She's still in a relationship, albeit a relationship that was no longer viable.*

Didn't matter. He'd held her while she was wracked with the pain of losing someone else. She had a lot to get over, to get past. Even if he stood by her and waited for that to happen, it didn't mean she could fall in love with him. Still, he had no choice. He was into her all the way.

He finished the brandy, putting aside the glass, but he didn't leave her. He watched her, occasionally succumbing to the temptation to softly, carefully, touch the silkiness of her hair. When she sighed contentedly in her sleep, he found himself smiling, pleased that she had found some peace. At some point he realized that he knew how she felt—once you know how much you love someone, no one else would do.

He looked down at the floor. *I'll be here for you, Mel,* he thought. *It's the only place I want to be.* When he raised his head, her eyes were open and she was looking at him. He stole a glance at the bedside clock and was surprised to see that two hours had passed.

"Jack," she said in a whisper. "You're here."

He smoothed her hair back from her face. "Of course I am."

"Kiss me, Jack. When you kiss me, I can't think of anything else."

He leaned toward her and touched her lips with his for a soft kiss. Then more firmly, moving over her mouth, feeling her lips open and her small tongue enter. Her hand crept around to the back of his neck to pull him closer, and his kiss became hungrier, deeper.

"Come in here with me," she whispered. "Hold me. Kiss me."

He pulled back slightly, but she wouldn't let go of his neck. "I'd better not."

"Why?"

He laughed a little. "I can't just kiss you, Mel. I'm not a machine. I won't want to stop."

She pulled the covers back for him. "I know," she said in a breath. "I'm ready, Jack. I don't want to hurt anymore."

He hesitated. What if she called out another man's name? What if the morning came and she was sorry? He had fantasized about this, but he wanted it to be the beginning of something, not the end.

Then you better make it good for her, he told himself. *You'd better leave her wanting more.* He slipped in beside her, pulling her into his arms, devouring her mouth with a kiss so hot and powerful she melted to him with a whimper. Her arms went around him, holding him as she yielded to his lips, his tongue. His sweatpants, so loose and soft, left nothing to the imagination and he was instantly hard against her. She moved against him, rubbed against him, inviting him. With a large hand on her bum, he held her there.

Jack rolled with her, bringing her on top of him. He grabbed the bottom of the T-shirt that covered her and raised it, pulling it over her head. When he felt her breasts against his bare chest, he said, "Ahh." Her breasts were soft and full in his big hands, her nipples hard. Running his hands along her ribs to her hips, he found that she still wore her thong panties; he slid them lower and she wiggled out of them. Her skin was so delicate, so smooth, he worried that his hands were too rough for her, but by her soft and eager moans, she was not unhappy with the sensation.

Holding her lips with his, he rolled with her again, so that they lay on their sides, and he took a moment to free himself from those sweats. Her hand wrapped around him, causing his breath to catch in his throat, and he thought, *Better not leave your boots on this time, buddy. You better do it for her.* And he concentrated, because he'd never wanted to please a woman more than tonight.

Feeling her against him like this made it very difficult to slow down, to wait, but by sheer dint of will he managed. He took his leisure of her, employing a slow hand that fondled her breasts. His mouth followed, drawing on one nipple then the other. She arched toward him greedily, spreading her legs, throwing one over his hip, urging him closer. He slipped a hand down and touched her in her soft center, bringing a passionate moan from her. He touched her deeply, and learned that he wasn't the only one feeling a little desperate. She was ready for him. Starving. "Mel," he said in a throaty whisper.

"Yes," she answered. "Yes."

He turned her onto her back and held himself over her. He captured her mouth with his and entered her in one long, slow, deep, powerful stroke that caused her to gasp and rise against him urgently. With one hand under her bottom and the other still caressing a place that turned her sighs to moans, he began to move within her. The heat of her nearly drove him out of his mind, but he held on. He was determined that her needs would come before his own. He moved steadily, pushing and pulling, and within moments her breathing came harder and faster, her body straining toward his, reaching for satisfaction. He was more than happy to deliver it, pushing into her, rubbing against her. And then he felt those hot spasms of fulfillment, heard her cry out in ecstasy and he held her fast, pressing himself into her. In that moment of blinding pleasure, she bit down on his shoulder; sweet, welcome pain. And he hung on with all the strength he could muster, saving himself, and finally she weakened beneath him and the clenching spasms that surrounded him slowly subsided. Her body relaxed and her breathing began to slow. Her pants became sighs and her kisses came soft and sweet against his lips.

Mel stroked his back, tasted his mouth, her body still quivering from a thundering climax. She felt the muscles of his shoulders and back at work as he held himself up enough to keep from crushing her with his weight. When he released her mouth and looked into her eyes, she saw in his a smoldering fire that was not even close to being extinguished. She put her palm against his cheek. "Oh, Jack," she said, breathless.

His name on her lips brought him such pleasure, he felt himself expand somewhere inside his chest, as if his heart grew just a little bit. He lowered his lips and sucked gently at hers. "Are you all right?" he asked softly.

"You were right there. You know exactly how all right I am," she said. "It's been a long, long time."

"It's never going to be that long again," he whispered. "Not ever again."

He began to move down her body with his lips and tongue, kissing and nibbling, tasting in slow, delicate strokes. He ran a tongue around each nipple until they were hard little pebbles, perfect for his mouth. He slid lower, until he had moved down over her flat belly. He gently parted her legs and buried his face in her, hearing her gasp above him. No longer delicate, he went to work on that prominent, erogenous knot in her center. He felt her moving her hips against his mouth and when her breathing became rapid and labored once more he rose, slowly kissing his way up her body. "God, you're sweet," he whispered against her lips. "You taste like heaven." He slid into her again, filling her, moving in long deep strokes that became powerful thrusts that brought her to yet another shattering climax. Again she cried out and he covered her open mouth with his. Swept away, she couldn't be quiet, and that thrilled him. Every sound, every wild cry gave him joy. He held her as she collapsed beneath him, spent.

Jack felt her small hands on his back, her lips on his neck, and her breathing inevitably slowed and came under control. To his surprise he heard the sound of her soft laughter. He rose above her and looked at her smile. "You lied to me," she said. "You are a machine."

"I just wanted to make you happy," he said. "Are you happy?"

"I've been happy a couple of times. What can I do so that you can join me?"

He laced his fingers through hers and holding her hands, stretched her arms up above her head, holding them there. "Baby, you don't have to do anything but be present."

He lowered his mouth to hers, kissed her deeply and began to move inside her once more, pumping his hips. She lifted her knees and tilted beneath him, bringing him deeper, and he could feel her begin to move in concert with him. She wrapped her legs around his waist and he followed the rhythm she set in place. He rocked with her, slow and steady, deep and long, hanging on to control until he heard her moaning and sighing rise again, her tempo increased, and finally the noises she made, already familiar to him, already beautiful to him, told him she was reaching for yet another orgasm. He had expected her to be passionate, but the heat and power of her passion amazed him, and it filled a need in him. And this time, when she clenched around him and pleasure stole her breath away, he let himself go and matched her. Surpassed her. For a moment, through the powerful pulsing, he felt light-headed. His eyes watered. And he heard it again. "Jack!"

"Ah, Mel… Ah, baby," he whispered, kissing her, loving her.

He gently caressed her as she calmed. "Jack," she whispered. "I'm sorry…"

"What do you have to be sorry about?" he asked in a whisper.

"I think I bit you."

He laughed, a deep throaty sound. "I think you did. Is that a habit of yours?"

"I must have been a little out of control…"

He laughed again. "I take the blame," he said. "That was all part of the plan."

"Ohh," she said. "I might've lost my mind there for a while."

"Yeah," he whispered. "I love it when that happens."

"You were taking a big chance, driving an already crazy woman out of her mind like that…"

"Nah, you were in good hands. You were always safe." He kissed her softly. "Would you like to rest now?"

"Maybe for a little while," she answered, her hands gentle on his face.

He gathered her close to him, holding her. Their naked bodies entwined, they spooned. He kissed the back of her neck as she lay on his arm. His face rested against her soft, fragrant hair, one arm over her and cupping her breast. Very soon he could hear the sounds of her even breathing, her sleep. He closed his eyes and relaxed with her in his arms, finding sleep himself.

Sometime in the dark of night he opened his eyes to find she had rolled over to face him, her hands boldly caressing him. He kissed her and asked, "Have you slept?"

"I did," she said. "And woke up wanting you. Again."

"I guess it's pretty obvious, the feeling is mutual."

Mel woke in the early morning and to her surprise, there was a song in her head. She was humming along with Johnny Mathis in her sleep. "Deep Purple." Her music was back.

She rolled over to find the bed beside her empty. She could hear the sound of Jack splitting logs in the backyard. She rinsed her mouth and rubbed his toothpaste against her teeth. A light blue, long-sleeved denim shirt hung on a hook in his closet and she put it on, sniffing the collar, smiling at his scent on it. It more than covered her; she was drowning in it. She went to the back door and stood watching him heft the ax and bring it down. Thwack. The air was clear and sharp; the rain was gone and the huge trees were washed clean. She watched him heft the ax again, and bring it down. His shirtsleeves were rolled up to the elbows and his biceps rippled under the weight and force of the ax.

Then he looked in her direction. She lifted a hand toward him and smiled.

He dropped the ax at once and came to her. As he stood before her, she put her hand on his chest. He ran the back of a knuckle against her pink cheek. "I think I roughed you up a little with whiskers."

"Yeah. Don't worry about it. I like it. It feels right. Natural. Good."

"I love the way you look in my shirt," he said. "I love the way you look out of my shirt."

"I think we have a little time," she said.

He swooped her up into his arms, kicking the door closed behind him, and bore her gently to the bed.

Eleven

The morning air was cool and foggy as Mel drove to her cabin. The front door was open, letting in the crisp June morning air. She kicked off her muddy boots on the porch and when she went inside found Joey sitting on the sofa, a quilt wrapped around her, a steaming cup of freshly brewed coffee on the table beside her.

Joey lifted a side of the quilt for Mel and Mel went to her, cuddling beside her, resting her head on Joey's shoulder. Joey pulled the quilt snugly around them both. "You okay, baby sis?" Joey asked.

"I'm okay. I lost it last night." She turned her head and looked up at her older sister. "Why didn't I see that coming? You did."

"The anniversary of deaths has a reputation," she said. "Even if you don't remember the exact date— it'll sneak up on you and knock the wind out of you."

"It sure did," she said, laying her head back down on Joey's shoulder. "I knew what day it was. I just didn't expect such a dramatic event."

Joey stroked Mel's hair. "You weren't alone, at least."

"You just wouldn't have believed it, even if you'd seen it. I was completely out of control, standing in the rain, screaming. I screamed for a long time. He just held me and let me. He kept telling me to let it out. Then he took care of me like you would a stroke victim. Undressed me, got me into dry clothes, gave me a brandy and put me to bed."

"I think Jack must be a very good man…"

"Then I invited him into bed with me," Mel said. Joey said nothing. "We made love all night long. I've never had so much sex in my life. I mean—never."

"But you're all right," she said, and it was not a question.

"When I lifted the blanket for him, all I could think was, this will numb me. Rub out the pain, give me escape."

"It's okay, sweetie."

Mel looked at Joey again. "It didn't exactly work that way," she said. "Maybe if he'd been average, I could've closed my eyes and just gone to a happy place. But he's not average. Holy shit, he's astonishing."

Joey laughed a little, sentimentally. Sisters. They had talked about sex since they were teenagers. Laughed about it, told dark secrets about it. With Mark's death, Joey had feared these kind of talks would never happen again.

"All he wanted was for me to have pleasure. Wild, blinding, crazed pleasure."

Again Joey laughed. "Did it work?"

"Oh, yeah," she said in a breath. Then she turned and looked at her sister. "Do you think he just felt sorry for me?"

"Well, you were there. Do you think that?"

Mel smiled. "I don't care," she said. "I just hope he feels sorry for me again, real soon."

Joey smoothed the curly hair away from her sister's

pretty brow. "I'm glad you have this in your life again."
And then she giggled, and so did Mel.

"How did this happen, Joey? That I went from wanting to die, to wanting Jack? Wanting him so much I
was almost a maniac? Wouldn't you think that would
be impossible? That I wouldn't be able to even think
like that?"

Joey took a breath. "I think when your emotions
reach a pitch like that, it follows suit. You just feel everything more intensely. I think it makes stupid sense,
actually. Haven't you ever noticed that some of the best
sex seems to follow a big fight? I'm pretty sure I conceived Ashley on the same night I told Bill that if I
didn't just leave him, I'd at least never speak to him
again."

Giggles.

"I haven't even asked you how long you can stay,"
Mel said.

"I can stay as long as you want me to, but a truly kind
sister would pack up and get out of your hair right now."

"No," she said, shaking her head. "I've missed you
so much." She smiled. "It's a sacrifice I'm willing to
make for you."

Joey hugged her close. "A few days, then. If you're
sure."

"I'm sure."

"Mel?"

"Huh?"

Joey revisited a topic from their earliest discussions
on this subject, reaching back to their high-school and
college days. "Do you think there's any truth to that old
wives' tale that you can tell from the size of a man's
foot?"

"Uh-huh."

"So. What size boot do you think Jack wears?"

Giggles.

"Twenty-seven," Mel said.

Mel took Joey with her to Doc's that very morning. Joey cozied up in the kitchen with a book while Mel and Doc saw a few patients. The three of them had lunch together at the house, then the girls went to Grace Valley where they visited June and John at the clinic. There were no patients scheduled for the next day and Doc wore his pager while he went to the river to fish, so Joey and Mel drove all the way to the coast, having lunch in the adorable little Victorian town of Ferndale.

They visited the shops—there were things that Joey thought would be perfect for Mel's cabin—a throw for the sofa, some accent pillows, a wall clock, colorful place mats. They stopped off and bought a small barbecue for the yard and wooden salad bowls. A vase that would complement the table. On the way home they went to the market and bought some groceries and fresh flowers.

It seemed like a quick beer at Jack's was in order and they went into the bar arm in arm, laughing because Mel had whispered, "If I catch you looking at his crotch, I will slap you." Which almost guaranteed Joey was going to find the temptation irresistible. Then they invited him to come out to the cabin for dinner, and he not only eagerly accepted, he brought a six-pack.

They told stories from their childhood and teenage years that had him laughing right along with them till almost midnight.

When Jack was getting ready to leave, Joey slipped discreetly away so Mel could say good night to him in private. Outside, on the porch, with only the filtered light from inside the cabin, Jack stepped down a step so that he could be eye-to-eye with Mel. She draped her arms over his shoulders while he encircled her waist with his large hands. She leaned toward him and teasingly nibbled at his lower lip.

"You told her everything," he said.

"Nah," she said, shaking her head.

"She keeps looking at my crotch," he said.

Giggles. "Not everything," she said. "I kept the more delicious stuff to myself."

"Have you been all right?" he asked, drawing his brows together in concern. "Any more tears?"

"Completely all right." She smiled.

"I miss you already, Mel."

"It's only been a couple of days…"

"I missed you after a couple of hours."

"You're going to be a lot of trouble, aren't you? Demanding, imposing, insatiable…"

He covered her mouth in a searing kiss that answered the question. She yielded happily, holding him closely. *Ah,* she thought. *This is such a wonderful, powerful, sexy man.* She never wanted it to end, but at length it had to. "I have to go," he said in a husky voice. "Either that, or carry you into the woods."

"You know, Sheridan… This place is growing on me."

He gave her a little peck on the lips. "Your sister is great, Mel." He gave her another. "Get rid of her," he said. Then with a whack on the butt, he turned and left her.

When he got to his truck and opened his door, he turned to look at her. He stood there for a long time. Then he slowly lifted his hand. And she did the same.

Jack was sweeping off the porch at the bar the next morning when he saw Joey and Mel walk out of Doc's house and embrace at Joey's car. Then Mel walked back inside and to his surprise, Joey came over to the bar.

"I'm going to shove off," she said to him. "I thought I'd beg a cup of coffee from you on my way out of town. Mel has a couple of patients this morning, or she'd have come with me. So we said our goodbyes."

"I'd be glad to buy you breakfast," he said.

"Thanks, I've had a little something already. But I'm not going to pass up your coffee. And I wanted a moment. To talk. To say goodbye."

"Coming up," he said. He leaned the broom against the wall and held the door for her. She jumped up on a stool and he went behind the bar to serve her coffee. "It was great meeting you, Joey. And spending a little time."

"Thanks. You, too. But mostly, thanks for what you've done for Mel. For taking care of her, looking out for her..."

He poured himself a mug. "I think you know—you don't have to thank me. I'm not doing anybody any favors."

"I know. Still... Just so you know, it's easier for me to leave her here, knowing that she isn't all alone."

It was on his mind to tell her that he hadn't felt like this since he was sixteen. All steamed up, crazy in love, willing to take a lot of chances for just one chance. But what he said was, "She won't be alone. I'll keep an eye on things."

She sipped her coffee. She seemed to struggle with something. "Jack, there's something you should keep in mind. Just because the crisis seems to have passed doesn't mean... Well, there could still be some struggles ahead for her."

"Tell me about him," Jack said.

Joey was startled. "Why?"

"Because it might be a long time before I can ask Mel. And because I'd like to know."

She took a deep breath. "Well, you have every right to ask. I'll do my best. But the only thing that allows the rest of us to hold it together as well as we do is because Mel has been so fragile. It *was* like losing a brother. It *was* losing a brother. We all loved Mark."

"He must have been one helluva guy."

"You have no idea." She sipped more of her coffee. "Let's see—Mark was thirty-eight when he died, so that made him thirty-two when he met Mel. They met at the hospital. He was the senior resident in the emergency room and she was charge nurse on the swing shift. They fell in love right away, moved in together a year later, married a year after that and had been married four years. I think the most characteristic things about Mark were his compassion and sense of humor. He could make anyone laugh.

"And he was the one doctor you wanted in Emergency when there was a crisis that required the family be handled with kindness, with sensitivity. Our whole family loved him right off. His entire staff adored him."

Jack didn't realize that he chewed absently on his lower lip.

"It's hard to remember that he wasn't perfect," she said.

"You'd be doing a guy a big favor by telling me one or two things that made him less than perfect," he said.

She laughed at him. "Well, let's see. He clearly loved Mel very much and he was a good husband, but she used to say that his first wife was the E.R. It's that way with doctors anyway, and I don't think it was much more than an irritation—she was a nurse and knew the score.

But they fought about his long hours, about him going into the hospital even when he wasn't on call. There were lots of times they had plans and he didn't show up. Or he'd leave early and she'd take a cab home."

"But that's how it is," Jack said. Marines left their families behind to do the country's work abroad. While a part of him wished that Mel had hated her husband for frequently abandoning her for work, there was another part that held a grudging respect for a woman who knew the ways of the world and held strong through them.

"Yeah. I don't think it threatened their marriage, not really. He'd get absorbed in his work and miss entire conversations. She said she sometimes thought she was talking to a wall. But of course, Mark being Mark, he'd apologize and try to make it up to her. I'm sure if he hadn't died, they'd have stayed married for fifty years."

"Come on, Joey," he said. "Didn't he drink too much, smack her around, cheat on her?" he asked hopefully. So hopefully that it made Joey laugh.

She dug around in her purse, pulled out her wallet and flipped through the pictures until she came to one of Mel and Mark. "This was taken about a year before he died," she said.

It was a studio portrait, husband and wife. Mark had his arm around her and they were both smiling— carefree. Her eyes twinkled; so did his. A doctor and a nurse midwife—brilliant, successful people—they had the world by the balls. Mark's face was familiar to Jack, having seen the picture beside her bed. But he looked at this with new eyes, knowing what he knew. Mark was not bad looking—and this was the only context under which Jack would allow himself to make such an assessment of another man. Short, neat brown hair, oval face, straight teeth. He would have been thirty-seven in the picture, but he looked much younger—he had a baby face. He did not look unlike many of the young marines Jack had taken into battle with him.

"A doctor," Jack said absently, staring at the picture.

"Hell, don't be intimidated by that," Joey said. "Mel could easily have been a doctor. She holds a bachelor's in nursing and post-grad degree in family nurse practitioner with a certification in midwifery. She's got a brain bigger than my butt."

"Yeah," he said. That Joey's butt wasn't big was not the point she was making.

"They had as many arguments as any couple," Joey said. "Vacations brought out the worst in them—they never wanted to do the same things. If he wanted to golf, she wanted to go to the beach. They usually ended up going somewhere he could golf while she lay on the beach, which might sound like a reasonable compromise, except for one thing—they weren't spending the vacation together. That used to piss her off," she added. "And Mel, pissed off, is unbearable.

"And," Joey went on, "he was lousy with money. Paid absolutely no attention. His focus had been purely on medicine for so long, he'd forget to pay bills. Mel took over that job right away to keep the lights from being turned off. And he was pretty anal about tidiness—I'd eat off the floor of his garage in a second."

Such urban, upper-class problems, Jack found himself thinking.

"Not an outdoorsman, I guess," Jack said. "No camping?"

"Shit in the woods?" she laughed. "Not our man, Mark."

"Funny that Mel would come here," he said. "It's rugged country. Not too refined. Never fancy."

"Um, yeah," Joey said, looking into her coffee cup. "She loves the mountains, loves nature—but Jack, you need to know something…this was an experiment. She was a little crazy and decided she wanted everything different. But it isn't her. Before Mark died, she must have had subscriptions to a dozen fashion and decorating magazines. She loves to travel—first class. She knows the names of at least twenty five-star chefs." She took a breath and looked into his kind eyes. "She might have a fishing pole in her trunk right now, but she's not going to stay here."

"Rod and reel," he said.

"Huh?" Joey asked.

"Rod and reel, not a fishing pole. She really likes it."

"Take care of your heart, Jack. You're a real nice guy."

"I'll be okay, Joey," he said, smiling. "She'll be okay, too. That's the important thing, isn't it?"

"You're amazing. Just tell me you understand what I'm telling you. She might have run from that old life, but it's still inside her somewhere."

"Sure. Don't worry. She was good enough to warn me."

"Hmm," Joey said. "So, what do you do for vacation?" she asked him.

"I'm on vacation every day," he said, smiling.

"Mel said you were in the Marine Corps—what did you do then? When you had leave?"

Well, he wanted to say, *if I wasn't recovering from some wound and we were in country, I'd get drunk with the boys and find a woman. A far cry from flying first-class to the islands to tan on the sandy beach or snorkel in the bay.* But he didn't say that; it was another life. One he left behind. People do that, he thought briefly and hopefully; leave another life behind and move on to something new. Different. "If I had a long leave, I'd visit the family. I have four married sisters in Sacramento and they live for the opportunity to boss me around."

"How nice for you," she said with a grin. "Well, you have any more questions? About Mel? Mark?"

He didn't dare. More information about the sainted Mark might do him in. "No. Thanks."

"Well, then, I'm going to get going—I have a long drive and a plane to catch."

She jumped off the stool and he came around the bar. He opened his arms to her and she happily gave him a robust hug. "Thanks again," she said.

"Thank you," he returned. "And Joey, I'm sorry for your loss."

"Jack. You don't have to compete with him, you know."

He put an arm around her and walked her out onto the porch. "I can't," he said simply.

"You don't have to," she said again.

He gave her shoulders a final squeeze and watched as she walked across the street to where her car sat at Doc's. She gave one last wave as she drove out of town.

Jack couldn't help but spend way too much time trying to picture Mel's life as it had been with Mark. He saw an upscale home and expensive cars. Diamonds as birthday gifts and country club memberships. Trips to Europe; to the Caribbean to unwind and relax from the high stress of city medicine. Dinner dances and charity events. The kind of lifestyle that even if Jack could fit into it, he wouldn't want to.

The upscale life wasn't alien to him—his sisters lived in that world very well. They and their husbands were educated, successful people; they had grappled with finding the best schools so their girls would be likewise. Donna, the oldest at forty-five, was a college professor, married to a professor. Jeannie, the next at forty-three, was a CPA married to a developer. Then there was Mary, thirty-seven, a commercial airline pilot married to a real estate broker—they were the country clubbers. His baby sister and the most bossy—and his favorite—was Brie, almost thirty, a county D.A. married to a police detective. He was the only one in the family who had gone into the military as an enlisted man—as a mere boy—educated only through high school. And found that what he had a gift for was physical challenge and military strategy.

He wondered if Joey was right, that Mel couldn't possibly be happy here for long in this dinky little town full of ranchers and blue-collar types, without a five-star chef within three hundred miles. Maybe she was just too classy for this backwoods life. But then an image of the Melinda he'd fallen in love with would float into his mind—she was natural and unspoiled, tough and sassy, uninhibited and passionate, stubborn. Perhaps it was a premature worry—he'd hardly given her a chance. It was always possible she'd find things here to love.

He didn't see her all that day. He never left the bar, just in case she came by for a sandwich or cup of coffee, but she didn't. It wasn't until almost six that she showed her face. As she walked in, he felt that sensation that had become so common for him lately—desire. One look at her in those tight jeans and he was in agony. It took willpower to keep himself from responding physically.

There were people present—the dinner crowd and about six fishermen from out of town—so she said hello to everyone she knew on her way to the bar. She jumped up on a stool and, smiling, said, "I wouldn't mind a cold beer."

"You got it." He fixed her up a draft. Now this woman, looking like a mere girl really, asking for a beer and not a champagne cocktail, this did not fit the picture he'd had earlier of the country club set, the diamonds, the charity dinner dances. Still, seeing her in a fitted, strapless black dress—he could manage that. It made him smile.

"Something's funny?" she asked.

"Just happy to see you, Mel. Going to have dinner tonight?"

"No, thanks. We were busier than I thought we'd be all morning, so I fixed Doc and I something to eat at around three. I'm not hungry. I'll just enjoy this."

The door opened and Doc Mullins came in. A couple of months ago he'd have sat at the other end of the bar, but no more. He was still as grouchy as he could manage, but he took the stool next to Mel and Jack poured him a short bourbon. "Dinner?" he asked the doctor.

"In a minute," he answered.

The door opened again and in came Hope. She had finally discarded the rubber boots in favor of tennis shoes—just as muddy. She sat on Mel's other side. "Oh, good, you're not eating," she said, pulling a pack of cigarettes out of her pocket. "Jack?" she asked, requesting her usual Jack Daniel's.

"Jack coming up, neat," he said, pouring.

Hope puffed and asked, "So, how'd your sister like your little town?"

"She had a good time, thanks. Though she expressed some concern about the state of my roots."

"Get that old codger to give you a day off and go over to Garberville or Fortuna and get a do."

"You have nothing but days off anymore," Doc grumbled.

"That's an interesting statement coming from someone who didn't want any help around here," Mel teased. Then to Hope she said, "You know big sisters. She just wanted to make sure I hadn't gotten myself into anything that held the potential for disaster, and now that she's convinced I'll live, she can go back to her family with a clear conscience. What have you been doing with yourself, Hope?" Mel asked. "I haven't seen much of you."

"Just the garden, from morning till night. I plant and grow, the deer come in and eat it. I need to round up Jack's marines and get 'em all out there to pee a border around the property."

Mel sat back. "That works?"

"Hell, yeah. Better than anything."

"Well, live and learn," she said. Mel finished her beer. "I'm going home," she stated flatly, getting off her stool.

Mel was barely out the door when she felt Jack come up behind her. He took her arm and walked with her to her car. Once there she turned to him and said, "Think you can find your way out to that little cabin?"

He leaned down to kiss her and groaned. It was happening to him again. "I'll be right there," he said.

"Take your time. Give me a head start so I can wash Hope's cigarette out of my hair. Go finish serving dinner."

He lowered his lips to her neck. "I'm going to walk back in there and yell 'Fire!'"

She laughed at him and pulled away. "I'll see you later," she said. And got in her car to leave.

Mel drove home knowing that he was starving and wouldn't be long. He was the most sexually driven man she'd ever known. But there were a couple of things she wanted to do. When she got home, she put her medical bag by the front door and went to the bedroom. She sat on the bed, picked up Mark's picture and held it. She looked into his kind eyes and mentally said to him, "You know I love you, and I know you understand." And then she slipped it into the drawer.

Then she went to the shower to freshen up.

Jack went back behind the bar and made sure everyone was taken care of. He brought Doc his dinner, said good night to Hope as she left, then went for Preacher. "It's thinning out," he said. "I'm going out to Mel's," he added, knowing Preacher would have his tongue cut out before he'd tell anyone. As if anyone needed telling. When Jack and Mel were in the same room, the air warmed up. People glanced at them knowingly. "You can reach me there if you need me. Don't need me."

"I'm good," Preacher said. "Ricky and I can handle things."

Jack might've driven a little too fast down the curving, tree-canopied road, but he was dying for her. He parked and went to the porch, sitting in one of the Adirondack chairs to pull off his boots. Inside, he heard the shower running and called out so he wouldn't frighten her. "Mel?"

"I'll be out in a minute," she called back.

But he was already out of his shirt, his hands on his belt buckle. He left a trail of clothes through the living room to the bathroom. The glass of the shower was steamed and inside was her small naked form in the mist. He slowly opened the door and stood there looking at her in all her glistening beauty. God, she was so perfect. She reached a small, inviting hand in his direction and he stepped in with her.

"You didn't take your time," she said against his lips.

"I tried," he admitted.

"I wanted to freshen up for you."

He covered her mouth with his, but his hands were all over her, running up and down her smooth, soft back, over her bottom, caressing her breasts, digging into her wet hair, down her neck and over her shoulders, down her arms to entwine his fingers with hers. He trembled, he wanted her so badly. And her hands were on him, running over his chest, around to his back, filling her hands with the hard muscles on his butt, and finally over his flat belly and down to his swollen erection, causing him to say, "Ohh... Mel..." before capturing her lips anew.

His fingers wandered lower to examine her, gently probing. It made him swell with some kind of erotic pride to find that she was slick and as anxious as he. This woman didn't need much warming up. This mutual need, this had become the best part of his life. He lifted her up. Her arms went around his neck, her legs around his waist and he settled her upon him, entering her slowly, firmly. He turned with her in his arms, bracing a shoulder against the shower wall. Then he began to move her upon him, lifting her up and down. Her sighs became quickened breaths, her legs tightened around him.

Mel hung on to his shoulders and neck, her mouth on his, their tongues hot and desperate as they devoured each other. The sensation of his arms and shoulders at work as he held her caused her blood to boil and she felt her desire rising and rising to a wonderful pitch that soon erupted into bliss.

Jack loved nothing so much as bringing her that crazy moment and feeling her tighten around him.

When she cried out, he held her closer, if possible. He reached himself as far inside her as humanly possible and the storm of his own wild climax shook him to his core.

She held on to him, he on to her, while they calmed, their breathing slowly returning to normal. She nibbled at his lip and said, a little breathlessly, "I didn't know that was even possible. Being with you... It's an adventure."

"You do something to me. You drive me out of my mind."

"Good. You do good work, brainless." And then she laughed and touched his shoulder. "You have a little bruise..."

"I love that little bruise..."

"Let's dry off and meet in the bed."

"You don't have to ask me twice. But please, don't move just yet. This part is dicey." He held her a moment longer and then, carefully and slowly, lifted her up and away from him, setting her down on her feet in the shower. They showered off, dried off. Mel needed a little extra time to dry that golden mane of hers— emerging roots and all. Jack went to the bedroom and sat on the bed. It was gone—the picture. He wasn't an idiot, he knew that only the picture was gone, not the memories. Still, it made him smile to himself. He settled himself in her bed and waited impatiently.

When she came to the bedroom, she reached for the light and he said, "Leave it on, Mel." Without questioning him, she slid into the bed beside him. Lying on his side, he rose up, his head braced on his hand. "There are a couple of things we should talk about. The other night wasn't about talking."

"Oh-oh," she said, suddenly on edge. "Is this the

part where you explain about casual sex and consenting adults?"

"No," he said. "Not at all. Just details. I want you to know something—there have been…women. You know? Mel, I'm forty. I've never been celibate. I always wore a condom. Always. Plus, the marines were ridiculous about medicals, including tests for STDs. But if you'd like me to be tested…"

"I tend to be cautious…"

"Done. And then, we didn't talk about birth control, and I don't want to be irresponsible. This comes a little after the fact—I'm sorry."

"You're okay," she said. "I've got that covered. But, if you're so used to putting on the condom, what happened the other night?"

He shrugged. "I didn't have anything handy, and the only thing on my mind was making sure everything was good. It started out as such a bad night for you and Jesus, I didn't want you to regret it. I guess I went a little crazy. But I can be prepared in the future. Just say the word."

"And tonight?" she asked.

"I apologize—in the pocket of those jeans on the living room floor, there's… Sorry. I was so ready to be with you. I was out of my head, Mel. It doesn't have to be like that every—"

She put a finger on his lips, smiled and whispered, "I like it like it is. When you're a little crazy." She looked up into his eyes. "Ordinarily, I would have thought of the condom, but I guess the state I was in…well. If you'll just take care of that screening, I'm sure we'll be all right. Have there been an awful lot of women?"

He made a face. A frown. "More than I like."

"Any really special ones?" she asked.

"You're going to think I'm lying. No."

"What about the woman in Clear River?" she asked.

"Mel, we were only sleeping together. No, not true—I never spent a night. She didn't come to Virgin River. I never thought I'd be embarrassed about that."

"You don't have to be embarrassed. You're a grown-up."

"It wasn't like this. This feel casual to you?" he asked her.

"Actually, it feels a little intense."

"Good," he said. "Everything about this is different. I hope you understand that."

"You're not just sleeping with me?" she asked, teasingly.

"I *am* sleeping with you," he said, running his hand over her smooth shoulder and down her arm. He gave her a sweet, short kiss. "It's not just sex. It's everything. It's special."

She laughed at him. "Are you *seeing* me?" she teased.

"Yeah," he said. "It's a first for me."

"So, in some ways, you're just a virgin from Virgin River."

"In this, I am."

"That's very sweet."

"This is madness, I want you all the time. I feel like a kid."

"You don't act like a kid," she said.

"Melinda—I have had more erections in the last week than I've had in the last decade. Every time you walk by, I have to concentrate on something else. This hasn't happened to me since I was sixteen, when anything from a beer commercial to a geography assignment could put me in agony. It was almost laughable, if it wasn't just so ridiculous."

"Raging hormones," she said with a laugh. "You are an amazing lover."

"I'm not doing this alone," he said. "You're pretty amazing yourself. Damn, baby. We fit together real nice."

"Jack—does everyone in town know?"

"They'd be guessing. I haven't said anything."

"Somehow, I don't think you have to."

"We could try to keep it quiet, if that works better for you. I could manage to not look at you like I'm going to have you for dessert, if that's what you want."

"It's just that…well, you know. I have these issues."

"I know. I held you through some major issues. And I do understand that it's going to take more than a little sex to resolve all that." He grinned. "Good sex."

"*Very* good sex."

"Oh, yeah…" he agreed breathlessly.

"Just so you know. I'm still all screwed up. I don't want to disappoint you. Jack, I don't want to hurt you."

He ran a hand down her body, lightly brushing her soft, warm skin. "Mel, this doesn't hurt." He smiled. "It feels real, real good. Don't worry about me." He gave her a light kiss. "You want to try to keep this… us…quiet? Private?"

"Think it would work?"

"There's probably no point in pretending," he said. "It's your call."

"Oh, what the hell," she said. "It isn't against the law, is it?"

He leaned over her and kissed her more deeply. "It probably should be." He kissed her again.

In the early morning as dawn was just beginning to streak through the cabin windows, Jack was stirred awake by the soft sound of slightly off-key humming. He found Mel nestled into the crook of his arm, her breath tickling his chest. She was purring, humming, her lips moving slightly, as though singing. It might've troubled him if her expression had been sad or disturbed. But she was smiling. She snuggled closer, throwing a leg over his. And this sleepy little music, contented, drifted out of her.

He could count on one hand the number of times he'd spent the entire night in bed with a woman. And already, he couldn't imagine waking up alone. He pulled her closer knowing he'd never been happier in his life.

Twelve

Rick called Liz every couple of days, although he wanted to call her seven times a day. His pulse always picked up when he dialed, then the sound of her voice made it race.

"Lizzie, how you doing?" he'd ask.

"I miss you," she would always say. "You said you'd come over."

"I'm going to. I'm trying. But with school and work… So, how are…things?"

"I just wish I was there, instead of here." Then she'd laugh. "Funny, I hated my mother for making me go to Aunt Connie's, and now I hate her for making me stay here."

"Don't hate your mom, Liz. Don't."

Then they'd talk for a while, about kids, about school, about Virgin River and Eureka, just mundane stuff. She never volunteered any information about the feared pregnancy.

Rick was dying a million deaths. He was terrified something had gone wrong and she was caught with a baby on that one and only night. But almost worse than that, he wasn't sure what was happening to him, in his head, in his body. He dreamt about her, wanted to feel his arms around her, wanted to smell her hair and kiss her lips. He wanted her breast in one hand, but he also wanted to have her riding beside him in that little truck on the way to and from school, cracking jokes, laughing, holding hands.

This phone call was no different than the others had been. Then she asked, "Why don't you come to Eureka?"

He drew a heavy breath. "I'll tell you the truth, Liz— I'm afraid to. You and me, we get pretty worked up."

"But you have those rubbers..."

"I told you before, that's not enough. You have to get something, too. Pills or something."

"How'm I gonna do that? I don't even drive. You think I should say to my mom, 'Hey, I have to get some birth control—me and Ricky want to do it'?"

"If you were here, you could see Mel. Maybe you can talk your mom into a visit to Virgin River." But even as he said that, he cringed. And flushed so hot he thought he might faint. Was he really suggesting to a fourteen-year-old that she get herself fixed up so they could have sex? In the cab of a truck?

"I don't know," she said softly. "I think I would hate that. I don't think I could tell someone who's like, grown-up. Could you?"

He already had; Preacher and Jack both knew. But he said, "I could if it was this important."

"I don't know," she said. "I'll think about it."

If you couldn't stop dreaming about a girl, if you constantly thought about the way her hair felt against your cheek, if you couldn't get the softness of her skin out of your mind, did that mean you loved her? If you felt a little better after every time you talked to her, heard her laugh, did that mean anything, or were you just this horny sixteen-year-old boy? He knew he was that—the thought of getting inside her again almost made steam come out of his ears. But there was other stuff. He could talk to Liz; he could listen to her. *Wanted* to listen to her. He could almost go into a trance when she told him about something as boring as algebra. If he had one drop of courage, he'd ask Jack—what is love and what is sex? When are they the same thing?

Finally he asked, "Any news about being pregnant, Lizzie?"

"You mean…?"

"Yeah, I mean that." Silence answered him. She was going to make him say it, once again. Every time he asked, his gut clenched just from forming the words, words alien to a boy. "Did you get your period?" he asked, grateful she couldn't see the color of his cheeks.

"That's all you really care about."

"No, but I care about it a lot. Liz, baby, if I got you in trouble, I'm gonna want to die, okay? I just want the scare over, that's all. For both of us."

"Not yet—but that's okay. I told you—I'm not regular. And I feel fine. I don't feel like anything's different."

"I guess that's something," he said.

"Ricky, I miss you. Do you miss me?"

"Ohh, Liz," he said in an exhausted breath. "I miss you so much it scares the hell out of me."

Mel made a few phone calls the following week, then asked Jack if he could pry himself away from the bar for a full day to run some errands with her. She wanted to drive into Eureka, she said. And she didn't want to go alone. Of course he said he could—he did anything she asked of him. He offered to drive, but she told him she'd like to take her car, put the top down and enjoy the sunny June weather.

When they were underway, she said, "I hope this wasn't too presumptuous of me, Jack. I made myself an appointment at the beauty shop and one for you at the clinic—that testing you offered."

"I was going to run over to the coast, to the Naval Air Station there, but this is just as convenient. I meant it when I offered. I want you to feel safe."

"I'm not worried, really. It's just a precaution. And if anything turns up, I'll get screened. I wouldn't put you at risk, you understand. But the last seven years, it was only..." She stopped.

"Your husband," he finished for her. "You can say it. That was your life. That *is* your life. We have to be able to talk about it."

"Well," she said, gathering herself up again. "Then, I've made arrangements to test-drive a vehicle and I'd like your opinion. A vehicle that doesn't get stuck in the mud."

"Really?" he said, surprised. "What kind of vehicle?"

She stole a glance at him, so neatly folded up in the front of her BMW, his knees sticking up so high it almost made her laugh. "A Hummer," she said.

He was speechless. Finally he said, "I guess you know what they cost."

"I know," she said.

"Hope's paying you better than I would've guessed."

"Hope's paying me practically nothing—but it also costs me practically nothing to live. Especially with that end-of-the-day cold beer on the house every night. No, this is my own investment."

He whistled.

"I have a little money," she said. "There were…there was…"

He reached across the console and put a hand on her thigh. "It's all right, Mel. I didn't mean to pry."

"You didn't pry!" she exclaimed. "You don't even ask, which is amazing to me. Here it is—there were investments. Retirement. Insurance. I sold the house at a ridiculous profit. And then there was a wrongful death suit—pending. It'll settle. The little scumbag came from money. Jack, I have plenty of money. More than I really need." She glanced over at him. "I'd appreciate it if that went no further."

"No one even knows you're widowed," he told her.

She took a deep breath. "So—I had a long talk with June Hudson, the doctor in Grace Valley. I asked her what she'd do to turn an all-wheel-drive vehicle into a makeshift ambulance, and I have quite a shopping list. If it works out I'll have a vehicle that can not only get me and Doc all over valley and into the hills, but get our patients to the hospital when we need to, without me sitting in the back of a pickup, holding an IV bag up in the air."

"That's a lot to do for a little town like Virgin River," he said, and he said it very quietly.

He'd done a lot for the little town, too, she thought. He renovated a cabin into a bar and grill, served meals at low prices all day long. Drinks were cheap and it served more as a gathering place than a profit-making establishment. He probably didn't need Ricky in there, but clearly he was a surrogate father. And Preacher— there was no question he was looking out for him, as well. But then, it probably didn't take much for Jack to get by, either—he'd done most of the renovation work himself, collected a retirement from the military and surely eked out a modest but completely adequate income from the place. And at the same time, enjoyed his life.

Mainly what Jack did for the town was sit at the center of it, helping anyone who needed anything. Anyone who served the needs of the town, like Doc or Mel, and lately the occasional sheriff's deputy or highway patrol officer ate free. He'd do repairs, babysit, deliver meals and absolutely never went for supplies without phoning up little old ladies like Frannie and Maud, to ask if they needed anything. He'd done that with her, too. Behaved as though it was his mission to serve her needs.

"That little town has accidentally done a few things for me, too," she said. "I'm starting to feel like I might live after all. A lot of that is because of you, Jack."

Jack couldn't help himself. He said, "You're staying."

"For the time being," she said. "Another baby is coming at the end of summer. I live for those babies."

One of these days, he said to himself, *I'm going to tell her. Tell her I love her more than I thought I could love a woman. Tell her that my life started when she walked into town. But not yet.* He didn't want to back her into a corner and make her feel she had to either say she loved him, too, or run.

"Well, Mel, as it happens, I've driven a ton of Hummers."

She glanced at him with surprise, for she hadn't even thought of that. "Of course you have!" she said. "I had forgotten that!"

"I'm also a passably good mechanic. Born of necessity."

"Good then," she said. "You'll be a bigger help than I realized."

The first items on the agenda were her hair and his

blood tests. Mel was very appreciative of the fact that her seventy-five-dollar cut and highlights seemed to be more than adequate. Either she'd been countrified or ripped off in L.A.

After that they went to a used car lot where there was one ridiculously high-priced used Hummer. It was a repo, had only twenty thousand miles on it, and seemed to be in good condition. Jack looked at the engine and had them put it up on the lift so he could examine the axle, frame, shocks, brakes and whatever else he could see. They took it out and it drove well, but the price was out-of-sight. Sixty thousand and it wasn't loaded.

Except—Mel had a sweet little BMW convertible trade-in and cash. It took only a couple of hours to bring that price into range and Jack was able to pridefully explore another aspect of Mel's character—she was a hardheaded, master negotiator.

Next they went to the hospital supply where they had the back of the Hummer outfitted with some emergency equipment, from a defibrillator to an oxygen tank. Some medical supplies had to be ordered and would be delivered to Virgin River within a couple of weeks. Then they drove it back down the highway and up the mountain pass to Virgin River. "You don't want anyone to know where this came from," Jack said to Mel. "How are you going to explain it?"

"I'm going to say that I used to work with a lot of rich, bored doctors in L.A. and hit them all up for donations for the town."

"Ah," he said. "If you leave?" He just couldn't make himself say "when."

"Maybe I'll actually call some of those rich, bored doctors I really do know, and hit them up for a donation," she said. "But let's not put the cart before the Hummer."

He laughed. "Let's not."

Mel and Jack took the Hummer back to the bar where they did a little show-and-tell with the dinner crowd who would waste no time spreading the word to the rest of the town. Doc Mullins, as if he was annoyed by this unnecessary addition to the town, grumbled that his old truck had worked just fine. But Mel countered his comments by telling him that he would have to get checked out in the new vehicle the very next morning. It soon became apparent that his fit of pique was obviously contrived and he was even caught smiling once or twice as he looked it over. Ricky talked her out of a spin and Preacher stood on the porch, arms crossed over his massive chest, grinning like a schoolgirl.

When Mel called June Hudson the next morning to tell her about the new vehicle, June suggested they get together at her home the next Sunday for a casual dinner of burgers and hot dogs. "If I bring some potato salad and beer, may I bring a friend?" Mel asked. She told herself she asked because this little picnic was comprised of couples, except for June's dad, old Doc Hudson, and she didn't want to feel oddly alone. But really it was because she had found she didn't much like being away from Jack.

"So," Jack said, grinning, "are you bringing me out of the closet?"

"Just for the day," she answered. "Because you've been very good."

June had the kind of adorable country house that Mel had fantasized about when planning her escape from the city—wide porch, bright paint, cozy furnishings, right up on a knoll from which she had a view of the valley. Part of her decor was comprised of needlepoint pillows and quilts—June was a master stitcher. She seemed to have the perfect country doctor life—her husband, Jim, to back her up and help with the baby; an ornery father butting in all the time and supportive and delightful friends in John and Susan Stone.

Susan was a nurse, so she and Mel compared notes. Plus, Susan and John were transplants from the city and she was candid about how it took her a while to appreciate the slower pace and get used to the absence of amenities in Grace Valley. "I used to go to the day spa down the street for a facial and eyebrow wax," she said. "Now it's a major undertaking just to buy groceries." Susan was also very, very pregnant. She was continually pressing on her lower back, pushing her belly forward.

The women sat on the porch. June rocked in the porch swing and nursed her baby, Susan fidgeted, trying to get a throw pillow to sit right against her lower back, while out in the yard the men stood around the Hummer, each one with a beer, occasionally looking inside or under the hood.

"That's quite an attractive man you brought along," June observed.

Mel glanced out at them. Jim and Jack were about the same height and weight and both wore their uniforms of jeans, plaid or denim shirts and boots. John, just a bit shorter at a very respectable six feet, was not quite as casually dressed in his khakis and polo, but a damn fine specimen. "Look at them," Mel said. "They look like an ad for *Virility Magazine*. Mother Nature's best work."

"Mother Nature is twisted," Susan said, squirming. "If she had any compassion, we'd have six-week pregnancies." She winced. "I bet it's really Father Nature. The creep."

"Uncomfortable, huh?" Mel asked.

"I'm going to have back labor again, I just know it. It's such a nice day to be so pregnant."

"This is nice, June. Thank you," Mel said. "It's so relaxing, low stress, for me if not poor Susan. Does everybody in the valley have such simple, uncomplicated lives?"

June surprised her by laughing, after which Susan joined in. Sydney, Susan's seven-year-old, burst through the door, blond curls flying, and ran down the steps with Sadie, June's collie chasing her into the yard. She ran to her dad and hung on his leg for a minute, then continued racing around the yard with the dog in pursuit, the collie trying to herd her back to the group.

"Something's funny?" Mel asked.

"Things haven't exactly been uncomplicated around here. A couple of years ago I was pretty sure I'd never get married, much less have a baby."

This caused Mel to scoot to the edge of her chair. "It seems like you and Jim have been together forever."

"He came into my clinic late at night a little over a year ago, looking for help with a comrade's gunshot wound. Jim's now a retired law enforcement officer. When I met him, though, he was skulking around the countryside, working some case—and in the dark of night he'd sneak into my bedroom. I kept him my little secret for quite a while—until my tummy started to grow."

"No way."

"Oh, yeah. No one in town knew I even had a man in my life, and then suddenly I'm pregnant. And not a little pregnant—by the time I realized it, I was already pretty far along. We've only been married a few months. We didn't get it done before the baby came."

"In a small town like this?" Mel was flabbergasted.

"People were decent about it. I mean, we did have a flood, lost our preacher for a while, there was a huge drug raid out in the woods, one thing after another. And probably because they all took to Jim so quickly. But my dad almost had a stroke."

"And maybe because Jim moved right into your house and wouldn't let you out of his sight until you agreed to marry him," Susan added.

"I had been single a long time," June said. "I was a little nervous about the whole thing. I mean, we hadn't even been together all that long—and my God, not very often. I don't know how it happened," June said. "But it sure happened fast."

"No—you know how it happened," Susan said. "This," she said, petting the giant mound that would soon be screaming to be changed, "is the great mystery. We had to try for a long time to get Sydney. We needed a little help, in fact. I just don't get pregnant."

Maybe in time Mel would join in, share her secrets. For now, though, she just wanted to hear theirs.

"John and I were having a big fight," Susan said. "We were barely speaking. I had him sleeping on the couch—he was such an ass. By the time I forgave him and let him back in bed with me, he was packing quite a punch." She giggled. Her eyes twinkled.

"At least you're married," June put in.

"Tell us about your man," Susan said.

"Oh, Jack's not my man," she said automatically. "He is the first friend I made in Virgin River, however. He runs a little bar and grill across the street from Doc's— as much a meeting place as a restaurant. They don't even have a menu—his partner, a big scary-looking guy named Preacher who turns out to be an angel—cooks up one breakfast item, one lunch item and one dinner item every day. On an ambitious day, they might have two items—maybe something left from the day before. They run it on the cheap, fish a lot and help out around town wherever needed. He fixed up the cabin I was given to stay in while I'm there."

The women didn't say anything for a moment. Then Susan said, "Honey, I have a feeling he doesn't think of you as a friend. Have you seen the way he looks at you?"

She glanced at him and as if he could feel her gaze, he turned his eyes on her. Soft and hard all at once. "Yeah," Mel said. "He promised to stop doing that."

"Girl, I'd never make a man stop doing that to me! You can't possibly not know how much he—"

"Susan," June said. "We don't mean to pry, Mel."

"June doesn't mean to pry, but I do. You mean to say he hasn't…?"

Mel felt her cheeks flame. "Well, it isn't what you think," she said.

June and Susan burst out laughing, loud enough to cause the men to turn away from their conversation and look up at the porch. Mel laughed in spite of herself. Ah, she had missed this—girlfriends. Talking about the secret stuff, the private stuff. Laughing at their weaknesses and strengths.

"That's what I thought," Susan said. "He looks like he can't wait to get you alone. And do unspeakable things to you."

Mel sighed in spite of herself, her cheeks growing hotter. *He can't,* she almost said. *And ohh…*

June took the baby off her breast and put him on her shoulder to burp him. The group of men seemed to turn as one and head for the porch, Jim first. "Sounds like trouble up here," he said. He reached for the baby and took over the burping.

John lowered his lips to Susan's forehead and gave her a kiss. His other hand ran smoothly over her belly. "How are you doing, honey?" he asked solicitously.

"Great. Right after dinner, I want you to get it out of me."

He handed her his beer. "Here, have a slug and mellow out."

Jack stood behind Mel and put his hand on her shoulder. Without even realizing it, she reached up and stroked his hand.

"I'll start the grill," old Doc Hudson said, going through the house.

They all sat around a picnic table in the backyard, talking about their towns, their cases. Mel got some tips from John on home births—he explained that he was an OB before doing a second residency in family practice. He'd never done a home birth in Sausalito, but once he'd arrived in Grace Valley he'd become the local midwife. He liked the hospital but couldn't convince all the women to leave their homes to deliver. Small-town stories were told, laughter was shared, and too soon it was growing dark.

As Jack and Mel were leaving, Mel took an opportunity to speak with June about the baby—Chloe. She expressed her concern that they still hadn't heard anything from social services.

June was frowning. "It's true that the county has a lot of ground to cover, but they're usually pretty good. One of my closest friends is a social worker, although she's in Mendocino county. I could run this by her— get her impression."

"Maybe you should. Especially if you think this is irregular," Mel said.

"I'll do it, and give you a call. Meanwhile, if you consider the baby your patient, you can assess the situation. See if you can find out anything. Doc Mullins is smarter than he lets on," June said. "He's a crafty old devil. Find out if he's got something up his sleeve."

Mel hugged June while Jack waited at the car. "Thank you. For everything. It was a perfect day."

Driving back to Virgin River, Mel was lost in one of the most serene moods she'd felt in a long time. Her connection to this place had deepened with the new friendships, and no small part of that was their acceptance of Jack.

"You're awfully quiet," Jack observed.

"I had such a good time," she said dreamily.

"Me, too. Nice people, your friends."

"They liked you, too. Did you know that Jim is a former cop?"

"I got that, yeah."

"And John and Susan came up here from the city a couple of years ago. And Elmer—the old doc—he's a riot. I'm so glad we did that."

They drove in companionable silence until they neared Virgin River. Jack said, "What do you want to do tonight? My place?"

"Would you be terribly hurt if we took a night off?"

"Whatever you need, Mel. Just so long as nothing's wrong."

"Nothing's wrong. In fact, I've never felt more right with the world. I just thought I'd go home, shower off the picnic and get a good night's sleep."

"It's up to you." He reached across the front seat and

grabbed her hand. "It's always up to you." He drew her hand to his lips and pressed a soft kiss into her palm.

He pulled up to the bar and they traded places so she could drive home. After a kiss good-night, she left him there and went out to the cabin.

As she entered the clearing in front of her home, the first thing she noticed was a big, dark SUV parked in front of her cabin. The driver, the big nameless man with the ball cap and hair that curled beneath it was leaning against the passenger door. When she pulled up, he straightened and slipped his thumbs in his front pockets. She recognized him and the vehicle at once. This was the big guy who'd stopped by Doc's several weeks ago, and what flashed through her mind was "someone's pregnant." Then she took note of his side-arm—a big gun, with straps holding the holster to his thigh. But his hands stayed away from it.

In a place like this, she was never sure how to feel about a person toting weapons. If she'd seen this in the city, she'd have ducked for cover. But out here, it didn't necessarily mean anything. She could play it safe and make a run for it, though she didn't handle the Hummer so well yet. Besides, the man had already approached her in the clear light of day to ask about a delivery. She pulled up, keeping her headlights on him, and he seemed to straighten expectantly, stepping away from the SUV. She opened her door and stepped out. "What are you doing out here?"

"That baby's coming," he said.

No matter what the circumstances, the same thing seemed to happen to her when she heard that—she stopped thinking of herself and began to concentrate on the work at hand, the mother and child. "That was pretty quick," she said.

"No. I was pretty slow," he said. "She kept it to herself for a long time and I didn't realize she was this ready, this—look, I need you to come. To help."

"But why are you here? Why didn't you go into town, to the doctor's office? I almost didn't come home tonight…"

"Lucky for me you did. I couldn't go to town, couldn't run the risk of someone wanting to come with you, or someone telling you not to come with me. Please, let's go."

"Where?"

"I'll take you," he said.

"No. I'll follow you. I'll just go inside, make a call and—"

He took a step toward her. "We can't do it that way. It'll be better for all of us if you don't know exactly where you are. And really, it has to be just you."

"Oh, gimme a break," she said with a short laugh. "You expect me to get in that car with you? Without knowing you or where we're going?"

"That's the general idea, yeah," he said. "She thinks she's doing this alone, having the baby. But I'd rather you come with me, in case… What if there's a problem? Huh?"

"I can call Doc Mullins, maybe he'll go with you. I don't make a habit of getting in a vehicle with a stranger to be driven to some mysterious birthing…"

"Yeah, I wish it was mysterious. I wish it wasn't happening, but it is. I don't want to have to do this at all— but I also don't want anything stupid to go wrong that we could prevent. I don't want any unnecessary trouble. You should probably be there. In case."

"This your baby?" she asked him.

He shrugged. "Yeah, could be. Probably."

"I don't even know there *is* a baby coming. I've never seen the mother," Mel said. "What if there is no baby?" she said.

He took a tentative step toward her. "What if there is?" he asked.

She looked around her. It was obvious if he wanted to hurt her, he wouldn't need to take her anywhere. He wouldn't even need to draw that weapon. They were completely isolated. He could take ten short steps toward her, whack her across the jaw and it would be done.

He spread his arms wide. "I just have to keep the place covered. It's a place of business, all right? Could we please go get that baby born? I'm not kidding, it freaks me out. She says she's been hurting all day. And there's blood."

"A lot of blood?"

"What's a lot? Not puddles, but enough to make me get in the truck and come for you. Pronto."

"You have a gun," she pointed out to him. "I hate guns."

He rubbed a hand along the back of his neck. "Protection for you," he said. "I'm just a businessman, but there's some crazy people stuck out there in the woods. I'm not going to let anything happen to you—that would make my life way too complicated. I don't want any attention from the sheriff. We really gotta go. There's a baby coming. Real soon."

"Oh, shit," she said. "Don't do this to me."

"I'm doing something to you? I'm asking. That's all. I want to get a baby born without anything stupid and wrong happening to the baby or the mother. Get me?"

"Why didn't you just take her to the hospital?" she asked him.

"She works for me, okay? And she has warrants. They ID her at a hospital and she's going to jail. You can't take care of a baby from jail. That's why it's gotta be this way."

"Look, go get her and take her to town, to Doc's. We'll do it there and no one will ask any questions about—"

"I'm telling you, there isn't *time!*" he shouted. The look on his face was desperate and he took a pleading step toward her, arms wide, palms out. "It's gonna happen soon, and we're almost an hour from her! We might not make it as it is!"

She took a deep breath. "We should take the Hummer…"

"Can't," he said. "Can't leave my vehicle here in case someone comes looking for you and finds only my truck. Sorry."

"I'll get my bag," Mel said reluctantly.

She grabbed her bag out of the Hummer and got in his SUV. He held a black sash in his hand. "You should blindfold," he said.

"Get real," she answered. "I'm not doing that. Hurry up. If she's been hurting all day, just hurry up."

"Put it on. Come on."

"So I won't see what? Where we're headed? I'm from L.A., buddy. I've been here three months and I can hardly get myself to town in the daylight along these mountain roads. It's pitch-black. Just move it—I'm never going to be able to tell anyone where we went." And more softly, "Besides, I wouldn't. The only thing that would make me do that is if I needed to find you, or her, to save a life."

"This some kind of trick?" he asked.

"Oh, please. Now stop scaring me. I might panic

and throw myself out of the car, and then where would you be?"

He put the SUV in gear and peeled out of the drive and headed east. "I hope you're not lying to me, setting me up. Because after this is taken care of, you don't have to see me again. Unless…?"

"Setting you up?" She laughed. "Did I come to *your* house? You want to just get this baby born on your own?" she asked him.

"I never did anything like this before," he said, his voice solemn and serious. "If I'd known there was a baby coming, I would've taken her somewhere. Somewhere out of this county. But I didn't know. Just do your thing, I'll pay you, and we'll be done. Okay?"

"We'll be done?" she asked. "These babies that no one expects? Sometimes they last about ninety years! After labor and delivery, there's stuff to do! Children to raise!"

"Yeah," he said tiredly. Focused on the road he whirled the SUV around the tight turns, gunned the engine when the road was straight. But the straightaways were short, always followed by more tight turns. Most of the time the speedometer read about twenty miles per hour. He used not only his headlights, but the lights mounted on his roof. It was a long, silent spell before he said, "I'll take care of what they need. After the baby's here, when she's up to it, there's a sister she can go to in Nevada."

"Why's this all so secret?" Mel asked. She looked at his profile and saw him grin largely. He had a slight bump in his nose. Under the bill of his ball cap his eyes crinkled when he smiled like that, and she noted that while he was rugged and scruffy, he was not unattractive.

"Jesus, you're something, you know that? Just go with it, little girl."

"How'd you know where I live?" she asked him.

He laughed. "I hope you don't think you're hiding out there, miss. Because everyone knows where the new midwife lives."

"Oh, great," she said under her breath. "That's just great."

"It'll be okay. Nobody wants you hurt or anything. That would just bring a whole heap of trouble on a whole lot of people." He stole a glance at her. "Someone like you goes missing, three counties go tearing up the hills. That's bad for business."

"Well," she said softly, "I guess I should be honored." She looked over at him. "Why am I not feeling so honored yet?"

He shrugged. "I guess this is all new to you."

"Yeah," she said. "Boy howdy."

They rode silently for a while, twisting around the mountain roads, up and over, down and around. "How'd you get yourself into this mess?" she asked him.

He shrugged. "Just one of those things. Let's not talk about this anymore."

"She better be okay," Mel said.

"That's what I'm thinking. Jesus, she better be okay."

Mel thought again about all the help available in a big city—lots of people. Not the least of whom was law enforcement—real handy. Cops parked right inside the hospital all the time. Right now, it was just her. Before her, it had been just Doc. If a woman was having a baby out in the middle of nowhere and there was only one midwife in the area, what were the options?

Mel began to tremble. What if they were too late and something wasn't right—what if things turned nasty?

She wasn't sure how long they'd been on the road. Definitely over a half hour. Maybe forty-five minutes. The man took a left turn down a one-lane dirt road that seemed to stop at a dead end. He got out and pushed open what appeared to be a gate made entirely of bushes and they drove through, down a potholed, washboard road thickly enshrouded by big trees. At the end, the powerful lights on the roof of his SUV illuminated a small building and an even smaller trailer. There were lights on inside the trailer.

"This it is. She's in there," he said, pointing at the small trailer.

That's when she knew, and was amazed that she hadn't understood sooner. She—who was so cynical about the crusty side of big city medicine—was totally naive about the pretty mountains and what she had thought was benign small-town life. The house and trailer were buried beneath the trees, camouflaged by the tall pines, and right between the two was a generator. This was why everything was so secret, why there was a gun for protection—he was a grower. Further, this was the reason he'd hire someone to work for him who had felony warrants, the only kind that could get you sent straight to jail—because that's who you could get to sit out in the woods and watch over a crop like this.

"Is she alone in there?" Mel asked.

"Yeah," he said.

"Then I need your help. I'll need you to get me some things."

"I don't want any part of—"

"You better just do as I say, if we're going to salvage this situation," she said, her voice sounding more authoritative than she felt inside. She rushed to the trailer, opened the door, stepped up and in. Five steps took her through a little galley and into what passed for a bedroom, a berth, upon which a young woman writhed beneath a sheet soiled with blood and fluids.

Mel put a knee on the bed, placed her bag beside her knee and opened it, dropped her jacket off her shoulders onto the floor behind her, and there was a transformation within her, taking her from scared and uncertain to driven and focused. Confident. "Easy does it," she said gently. "Let's have a look." Over her shoulder she said, "I need a large, empty pan or bowl, some towels or blankets—soft as possible—for the baby. A pan of warm water for cleanup. Ah…" she said, lifting the sheet. "All right, sweetheart, you have to help me. Pant like this," she instructed, demonstrating while she put on her gloves. "No pushing. More light!" she yelled over her shoulder.

The baby was crowning; another five minutes and Mel would have missed the whole thing. She heard the man moving around behind her and suddenly a saucepan appeared beside her bag. Then there were a couple of towels and an overhead light flicked on. Mel made a mental note to add a flashlight to the articles in her bag.

The woman grunted weakly and the baby's head emerged. "Pant," Mel instructed. "Do *not* push—we have a cord situation. Easy, easy…" She gently tugged on the ropey, purplish cord, pulling it from around the neck, freeing the baby. She hadn't been in the trailer for five minutes, but it was the most critical few minutes of this infant's life. She slipped a gloved finger into the birth canal and gently eased the baby toward her. Cries filled the room before the baby was completely born; the strong, healthy cries of a newborn. Her heart lifted in relief; this was a strong baby. Suction was not even necessary.

"You have a son," she said softly. "He looks beautiful." She looked over the raised knees of her patient and saw a young woman of perhaps twenty-five years at most, her long, dark hair damp from perspiration, her black eyes tired but glowing, and a very small smile on her lips. Mel clamped and cut the cord, wrapped the baby and made her way around the narrow space to the woman's head. "Let's put this baby on the breast," she said softly. "Then I can deal with the placenta." The woman reached for her baby. Mel noticed that sitting beside her on the bed was a large basket, ready to receive the baby. "This is not your first," Mel said.

She shook her head and a large tear spilled down her cheek as she took her son. "Third," she said in a whisper. "I don't have the other ones."

Mel brushed the damp hair back from her brow. "Have you been out here alone?"

"Just the last month or so. I was here with someone, and he left."

"Left you, out in the woods in a trailer, in advanced pregnancy?" Mel asked softly, running a finger over the baby's perfect head. "You must have been so scared. Come on," she said, giving the woman's T-shirt a tug. "Let the baby nurse. It'll make a lot of things feel better." The infant rooted a little bit, then found the nipple and suckled.

Mel went back to her position, donned fresh gloves from her bag and began to massage the uterus. She heard the trailer door close behind her and glanced over her shoulder. On the short counter in the galley she saw a dishpan of water.

Mel's patient was able to direct her to supplies from newborn diapers to sterile wipes. She found clean sheets and peri-pads, washed up the baby and mother, then sat on the edge of the bed for a long while, holding the baby.

Her patient reached over and held Mel's hand a couple of times, giving a grateful squeeze, but they didn't talk. An hour after the birth, Mel looked in the refrigerator. She rummaged around for a glass and poured the woman some juice. Then she brought a plastic container of water near the bed. She checked her patient's bleeding, which was normal. She got her stethoscope out of the bag and listened to the baby's heart, then the mother's. Coloring was good, respirations normal, mother exhausted and the baby, sleeping contentedly. All was complete.

"Tell me something," Mel said. "Is the baby going to have drug issues?" The woman just shook her head, letting her eyes close. "All right—there's a small clinic in Virgin River. I work with the doctor there. He won't ask you about yourself or the baby, so you have nothing to worry about. He likes to say he's in medicine, not law enforcement. But you both should be looked at to be sure everything is okay."

Mel picked up her jacket off the floor. "Is there anything else I can get for you?" she asked her patient. The woman shook her head. "Plenty of fluids tonight, for the breast milk." Then she went around the narrow space to the head of the bed and leaned down, placing a small kiss on her head. "Congratulations," she whispered. Then wiped a couple of tears gently from her patient's cheeks. "I hope everything works out for you and the baby. Be very safe and careful."

"Thank you," the woman said softly. "If you hadn't come…"

"Shh," Mel shushed. "I came. And you're fine."

Mel realized, not for the first time, that it didn't matter if her patient was a happily married Sunday-school teacher who'd been waiting years for her first baby, or a felon handcuffed to the bed—a birth was the great equalizer. In this vulnerable state, mothers were mothers, and it was her passion to serve them. Helping a baby safely into the world, its mother accomplishing the experience with health and dignity, was the only thing that mattered. Even if it meant putting herself at some risk, she was bound to do what she could. She couldn't control what became of a mother and child after she left them, but when called upon for this, she was unable to refuse.

Her chauffeur was waiting at the SUV as she came out. He opened the passenger door for her. "They're okay?" he asked anxiously.

"They seem to have come through very well, considering. I guess you don't live there with them?"

He shook his head. "That's why I didn't see she was pregnant. I only come around sometimes and I dealt mostly with her man. I guess he left her when—"

"When he realized you'd dealt with her a little, too?" Mel finished for him. She shook her head and got into the car. When he was in beside her she said, "I want two things from you, and the way I see it, you owe me. I want you to go back there tonight, stay with them, so you can get them to the hospital if anything goes south in the night. If there's any real heavy bleeding, or if the baby has problems. Don't panic—they seem good— but if you don't want to take any unnecessary chances, that's what you do. Then, in a couple of days, two to four days, bring them to the clinic to be checked over. Doctor Mullins in Virgin River won't ask any questions, and all I care about right now is that they stay healthy." She looked over at him. "You'll do that?"

"I'll get it done," he said.

She leaned her head back against the seat and let her eyes close. The hard and fast beating of her heart now was not from fear, but from the rapid decompression of adrenaline that always followed an emergency. It left her feeling weak, a little shaky, slightly nauseous. If the conditions had been different, she might have felt even more alive than before the birth. This one, however, had been rife with complications.

When he pulled up in front of her cabin, he held out a wad of bills toward her. "I don't want your money," she said. "It's drug money."

"Suit yourself," he said, putting it in the front pocket of his jacket.

She stared at him for a second. "If you'd left her to deliver herself, if I hadn't gone with you, that baby wouldn't have— You understand about the cord, right? Wrapped around his neck?"

"Yeah, I get that. Thanks."

"I almost didn't go with you. Really, there's no reason I should have trusted you."

"Yeah. You're a brave little girl. Try to forget my face. For your own sake."

"Listen, I'm in medicine, I'm not a cop," she said. Then she gave a weak huff of laughter. She'd been used to having the backup of LAPD, but tonight it had been down to her. There was no backup. And if she hadn't been there, it could have been down to Doc, who was seventy. What was going to happen five years from now? To her chauffeur she said, "Now keep it in your pants or use protection—I don't really feel like doing business with you again."

He grinned at her. "Tough little broad, aren'tcha? Don't worry. I'm not looking to have that kind of trouble again."

She got out of the SUV without comment and walked toward her porch. By the time she neared her front door, he had turned around and driven out of the clearing. She sank into the porch chair and sat in the dark. The night sounds echoed around her; crickets, an occasional owl, wind whirring through the tall pines.

She wished she could just go inside, undress and go to bed alone, but she was wired and out of courage for the night. After a moment, when she could no longer hear the engine of his big SUV, she went down the stairs to the Hummer. She drove into town and parked behind the bar, next to Jack's truck. The sound of the engine and car door must have awakened him, because a light went on and the back door to his quarters opened. He stood in the frame, a dim light behind him, wearing a pair of hastily pulled on jeans. She walked right into his arms.

"What are you doing here?" he asked softly, pulling her inside and closing the door.

"I went out on a call. A baby. And I didn't want to go home. Didn't want to be alone after that. It was a close one, Jack."

He slipped his hands inside her jacket to hold her closer. "Did everything work out okay?"

"Yes," she said. "But there wasn't very much time. If I'd been five minutes longer getting there… The cord was around his neck." She shook her head. "But I did get there. And he's a beautiful baby."

"Where?" he asked, smoothing her hair over her ear.

"The other side of Clear River," she said, remembering what the man had said when he pulled up to the front of Doc's clinic. In truth, she had no idea where they'd gone. He could've driven around in circles for all she knew.

"You're trembling," he said, pressing his lips to her brow.

"Yeah, a little. Coming down from the experience."

She tilted her head to look up at him. "Is it okay that I'm here?"

"Of course it is. Mel, what's wrong?"

"The mother was going to deliver herself, but the father got nervous and came for me." She shivered. "I thought I had some wild experiences in L.A.," she said with a weak laugh. "If you'd told me a year ago that I'd go out to some poor trailer in the woods, in the middle of the night to deliver a baby, I would have said, never gonna happen."

He rubbed a knuckle along her cheek. "Who was it?"

She shook her head. If she told him she didn't have the first idea, he'd flip. "They're not from around here, Jack. He dropped by Doc's a while ago, looking for someone who could handle a birth. I can't talk about patients unless they say it's okay, but these patients, I didn't even ask. They weren't married or anything. She lives in a crappy little trailer by herself. It's a pretty horrid situation for her." And she thought, *I'm doing things out here in the mountains that I never, in a million years, thought I could do. Terrifying, impossible, dangerous things. Exhilarating things that no one else would do. And if no one had, there'd be a dead baby. Possibly a critical mother.* She leaned her head against Jack's chest and took a deep, steadying breath.

"He called you?" Jack asked.

Damn. Bold-faced lies to straight questions were so hard for her. "He was waiting at the cabin. If I'd stayed the night here with you, I'd have missed him and that baby wouldn't have made it."

"Did you tell him where to find you after hours?"

She shook her head before she thought about her answer. "He must have asked someone," she said. "Everyone in Virgin River knows where I live. And probably half the people in Clear River."

"God," he said, tightening his arms around her. "Did it ever occur to you that you could have been at risk?" he asked her.

"For a minute or two," she said. She looked up at him and smiled. "I don't expect you to understand this—but there was a baby coming. And I'm glad I went. Besides, I wasn't in trouble. The mother was."

He let out a slow, relieved breath. "Jesus. I'm going to have to keep a much closer eye on you." He kissed her brow. "Something happened tonight. Something you're not telling me. Whatever it was—never, never let that happen again."

"Could we get in bed, please? I really need you to hold me."

Jack was sitting on the porch of the bar, tying off flies, when a familiar black Range Rover pulled slowly into town and parked right in front of Doc's. He sat forward on the porch chair and watched as the driver got out, went around to the passenger door and opened it. A woman carrying a small bundle got out of the car, walked up the porch steps to enter the clinic and Jack's heart began to pound.

When the woman entered Doc's, the man went back to his SUV and leaned against the hood, his back to Jack. He took out a small pen knife and began to idly clean under his nails. Because of the kind of guy this was, Jack knew he had seen him sitting there, on the porch. He would have observed everything worth seeing when he came into town; he'd know every escape route, any threat. Today, coming into town with a woman and new baby, Jack would bet there wouldn't be contraband of any kind in that vehicle and if he had weapons, they'd be registered. And…his license plate was splattered with mud so it couldn't be read. Lame trick. But Jack remembered it; he'd memorized it the first time this guy had come to town.

So, he hadn't come to Virgin River for a couple of drinks a while back. He'd come to see if there was medical assistance here. Mel had said that the delivery that shook her up had occurred on the other side of Clear River and there was no doctor or clinic in that town. Grace Valley and Garberville were just a little farther away, but there were more people around.

It was a little over a half hour before the woman came out, Mel walking behind her. The woman turned and shook Mel's hand; Mel squeezed her upper arm. The man helped her into the car and drove slowly out of town.

Jack stood and Mel met his eyes across the street. They were on their respective porches and, even from the distance, she could see the deepening frown gather on his face. Then he walked over to her.

She slipped her hands into the pockets of her jeans as he approached. When he was near, he put one foot up on the porch steps and leaned his forearms on his bent knee, looking up at her. The frown was not angry, but definitely unhappy. "Doc know what you did?" he asked her.

She gave a nod. "He knows I delivered a baby, if that's what you mean. It's what I do, Jack."

"You have to promise me, you're not going to do that again. Not for someone like him."

"You know him?" she asked.

"No. But he's been in the bar and I know what he is. The problem isn't him bringing a woman to the doctor, you know. It's you being on his turf. It's you going with him in the middle of the night. Alone. Just because he says—"

"I wasn't threatened," she said. "I was asked. And he had been by the clinic before, looking for a doctor, so he wasn't a complete stranger."

"Listen to me," Jack said firmly. "People like that aren't going to threaten you in your clinic or my bar. They like to keep a real low profile. They don't want their crops raided. But out there," he said, giving his chin a jerk toward the mountains to their east, "things can happen. He could've decided you were a threat to his business and—"

"No," she said, shaking her head. "He wouldn't let anything happen to me. *That* would be a threat to his business—"

"Is that what he told you? Because I wouldn't take his word for that." He shook his head. "You can't do that, Melinda. You can't go alone to some illegal grower's camp."

"I doubt there will be a situation like that again," she answered.

"Promise you won't," he said.

She shook her head. "I have a job to do, Jack. If I hadn't gone—"

"Mel, do you understand what I'm telling you? I'm not going to lose you because you're willing to take stupid chances. Promise me."

She pursed her lips and merely lifted her chin defiantly. "Never…never suggest I'm stupid."

"I wouldn't do that. But you have to understand—"

"It was down to me. There was a baby coming, there really was, and I had to go because if I hadn't it could've been disastrous. There wasn't time to think about it."

"Have you always been this stubborn?" he asked.

"There was a baby coming. And it doesn't matter to me who the woman is or what she does for a living."

"Would you have done something like that in L.A.?" he asked, lifting an eyebrow.

She thought for just a moment about how life had changed since leaving L.A. After being picked up by a gun-carrying illegal grower and delivering a baby back in the woods, shouldn't she be packing? Running for her life? Unwilling to ever be put in a position like that again? Instead, she was doing a mental inventory of what was in Doc's refrigerator, wondering if it wasn't about time to take a few things out to Paulis's camp. It had been a couple of weeks since she'd last done that.

Although she really didn't want a repeat of the scenario with the grower, something about the experience got her attention. When she'd left L.A., they didn't have any trouble filling her job. There were ten people who could do what she did, and do it just as well. In Virgin River, and the surrounding area, it was her and Doc. There just wasn't anyone else. There was no day off or week off. And if she had hesitated even long enough to fetch Doc to go with her, that baby wouldn't have made it.

I came here because I thought life would be simpler, easier, quieter, she thought. *That there would be fewer challenges, and certainly nothing to fear. I thought I'd feel safer, not that I'd have to grow stronger. Braver.*

She smiled at him. "In L.A. we send the paramedics. You see any paramedics? I'm in this little town that you said was uncomplicated. You're a big liar, that's what you are…"

"I told you, we have our own kind of drama. Mel, you should listen to me—"

"This is a real complicated place sometimes. I'm just going to do my job the best I can."

He stepped up onto the porch, put a finger under her chin and lifted it, gazing into her eyes. "Melinda, you're getting to be a real handful."

"Yeah?" she asked, smiling. "So are you."

Thirteen

Mel didn't tell Doc where she was going, just that there were a couple of people she wanted to look in on. He asked her, since she was out, to stop and check on Frannie Butler, an elderly woman who lived alone and had high blood pressure. "Make sure she has plenty of medicine and that she's actually taking it," he said. He popped an antacid.

"Should you be having so much heartburn?" she asked him.

"Everyone my age has this much heartburn," he answered, brushing her off.

Mel got Frannie's blood pressure out of the way first, though it wasn't quick. The thing about house calls in little towns like this was it involved tea and cookies and conversation. It was as much a social event as medical care. Then she drove out to the Anderson ranch. When she pulled up, Buck came out of the shed with a shovel in his hand and an astonished look on his face when he saw the Hummer. "Who-ee," he said. "When did that thing turn up?"

"Just last week," she said. "Better for getting around the back roads than my little foreign job, as Doc calls it."

"Mind if I have a look?" he asked, peering into the window.

"Help yourself. I'd like to check on Chloe. Lilly inside?"

"Yup. In the kitchen. Go on in—door's open." And he immediately stuck his head in the driver's door, taken with the vehicle.

Mel went around back. Through the kitchen window she could see Lilly's profile as she sat at the kitchen table. The door was open and only the screen door was closed. She gave a couple of quick raps, called out, "Hey, Lilly," and opened the door. And was stopped dead in her tracks.

Lilly, too late, pulled the baby blanket over her exposed breast. She was nursing Chloe.

Mel was frozen in place. "Lilly?" she said, confused.

Tears sprang to the woman's eyes. "Mel," she said, her voice a mere whisper. The baby immediately started to whimper and Lilly tried to comfort her, but Chloe wasn't done nursing. Lilly's cheeks were instantly red and damp; the hands that fussed with her shirt and held the baby were shaking.

"How is this possible?" Mel asked, completely confused. Lilly's youngest child was grown—she couldn't possibly have breast milk. But then she realized what had happened. "Oh, my God!" Chloe was Lilly's baby! Mel walked slowly to the kitchen table and pulled out a chair to sit down because her knees were shaking. "Does everyone in the family know?"

Lilly shook her head, her eyes pinched closed. "Just me and Buck," she finally said. "I wasn't in my right mind."

Mel shook her head, baffled. "Lilly. What in the world happened?"

"I thought they'd come for her—the county. And that someone would want her right off. Some nice young couple who couldn't have a baby. Then she'd have young parents and I—" She shook her head pitifully. "I just didn't think I could do it again," she said, dissolving into sobs.

Mel got out of her chair and went to her, taking the fussing baby, trying to comfort her. Lilly laid her head down on the tabletop and wept hard tears.

"I'm so ashamed," she cried. When she looked up at Mel again she said, "I raised six kids. I spent thirty years raising kids and we got seven grandkids. I couldn't imagine another one. So late in my life."

"Wasn't there anyone you could talk to about this?" Mel asked.

She shook her head. "Mel," she wept. "Country people… Small-town country people know that once you talk about it… No," she said, shaking her head. "I was sick when I realized I was pregnant and forty-eight years old. I was sick and a little crazy."

"Did you ever consider terminating the pregnancy?"

"I did, but I couldn't. I just couldn't. I make no judgment, but it isn't in me."

"What about arranging an adoption?" Mel asked.

"No one in this family, in this town for that matter, would ever understand that. They'd have looked at me like I killed her. Even my friends—good women my age who would understand how I felt, could never accept it if I said I didn't want to raise another child, my own child. I didn't know what else to do."

"And now what do you intend to do?" Mel asked.

"I don't know," she wailed. "I just don't know."

"What if they come now—social services? Lilly, can you give her up?"

She was shaking her head. "I don't know. I don't think so. Oh, God, I wish I had a chance to do it over."

"Lilly—how did you conceal your pregnancy? How did you give birth alone?"

"No one pays much attention—I'm overweight. Buck helped. Poor Buck—he didn't even know till it was almost time—I kept it from him, too. Maybe we can adopt her now?"

Mel sat down again, still jiggling the baby. She looked down at Chloe, who was burying her fist in her mouth, squirming and fussing. "You don't have to adopt her, you gave birth to her. But I'm awful worried about you. You abandoned her. That must have almost killed you."

"I watched the whole time. Till you and Jack came to the porch. I wouldn't let anything happen to her. It was terrible hard, but I felt like I had to. I just didn't know what else to do."

"Oh, Lilly," Mel said. "I'm not sure you're okay yet. This is just too crazy." She passed the baby back to Lilly. "Here, nurse your baby. She's hungry."

"I don't know that I can," she said, but she took the baby. "I might be too upset."

"Just hook her up—she'll do the work," Mel said. When the baby was again at the breast, Mel put her arms around Lilly and just held them both for a few minutes.

"What are you going to do?" Lilly asked, her voice a quivering mess.

"God, Lilly, I don't know. Do you understand that doctors and midwives protect your confidentiality? If I'd been here when you'd discovered your pregnancy, you could have trusted me with your secret. You could have trusted Doc, or Dr. Stone in Grace Valley. The people in the family planning clinic keep confidential records—they would have helped. But…" She took a breath. "We're also bound by laws."

"I just didn't know where to turn."

Mel shook her head sadly. "You must have been so scared."

"I haven't ever been through anything as difficult in my life, Mel. And me and Buck, we've had some real hard times holding this family and ranch together."

"How did you keep the breast-feeding from your kids? I assume they're around quite a bit—and don't your boys work the ranch with Buck?"

"I give her a bottle if anyone's around, and I nurse her when we're alone."

"Even though you planned to let her go, you nursed her? You didn't have to do that."

Lilly shrugged. "It seemed like the least I could give her, after what I did. I'm sorry. I'm so, so sorry. You just don't understand what it's like—spending your whole life raising kids—and then having another one on the way when you're a grandmother. Me and Buck—we've struggled with money our entire marriage! You just don't understand."

"Oh, Lilly, I know you were terrified and desperate. I can imagine. But I'm not going to kid you, this is complicated."

"But will you help us? Will you help Chloe?"

"I'll do what I can—but those laws…" She sighed. "I'll do whatever I can," she said gently. "We'll find a way to sort this out. Just let me think."

Not long after, when Mel was sure that Lilly was calmed down and safe, Mel left her. She'd been with her about forty minutes, but Buck was still combing the Hummer with envious eyes. "Helluva ride, Mel," he said, grinning.

"Buck, go in the house and comfort your wife. I just walked in on her nursing your daughter."

"Oh, boy," he said.

It was on the ride back to town that Mel realized Doc Mullins was onto this. In fact, he might've given birth to it, so to speak. He'd always said the mother would turn up, and she had. Weeks ago when Mel had told him that Lilly had offered to take in the baby, his eyebrows had shot up in surprise. He hadn't expected it to be Lilly. He had *never* called social services. And yet, he never brought her into the conspiracy.

By the time she got back to his house it was after four and she was steamed up pretty good. Doc was seeing a patient who was coughing and hacking like a dying man. She had to wait. And while she waited, she began to seethe. When the man finally left with a butt full of penicillin and a pocket full of pills, she faced him down. "Your office," she said flatly, preceding him in that direction.

"What's got your dander up?" he asked.

"I went to the Andersons'. I walked in on Lilly nursing the baby."

"Ah," he said simply, limping around her to sit behind his desk, his arthritis obviously kicking up again.

She leaned her hands on the desk and got in his face. "You never called social services."

"Couldn't see the need. Her mother came for her."

"What do you plan to do about the birth certificate?"

"Well, when we get this straightened out a little better, I'll sign and date it."

"Doc, you can't pull this shit! That baby was abandoned! Even though her mother came back for her, it might still be considered a crime!"

"Settle down. Lilly was a little overwrought is all. She's fine now—I've been keeping an eye on it."

"At the very least, you could have told me!"

"And have you go off half-cocked like this? Snatch up that baby and turn her in? That woman was at the end of her rope—and turned out all she needed was a little time to cool down, come to her senses."

"She should've seen a doctor."

"Aw, Lilly had all her kids at home. She'd have come in if she was sick. Fact is, if Lilly had turned up any sooner—I'd have insisted on examining her, just to be safe. By the time she came around, it was obvious she was in good health."

Mel fumed. "I can't work like this," she said. "I'm here to give good, sound medical care, not run around in circles trying to guess what you're dreaming up!"

"Who asked ya?" he threw back.

She was stunned quiet for a moment. Then she said, "Shit!" And she turned to leave his office.

"We're not done here," he bellowed. "Where are you going?"

"For a beer!" she yelled back.

When she got to Jack's it was impossible for her to hide the fact that she was all riled up, but she couldn't talk about it. She went straight to the bar without saying hello to anyone.

Jack took one look at her and said, "Whoa, boy."

"Beer," she said.

He served her up and said, "Wanna talk about it?"

"Sorry. Can't." She took a drink of the icy brew. "Business."

"Must be sticky business. You're pissed."

"Boy howdy."

"Anything I can do?"

"Just don't ask me about it, because I'm bound by confidentiality."

"Must be a doozie," he said.

Yeah, a doozie, she thought.

Jack slid an envelope across the bar to her. She looked at the return address—it was from the clinic in Eureka he had visited. "Maybe this will brighten your mood a little. I'm clear."

She smiled a small smile. "That's good, Jack," she said. "I thought it would come out like that."

"Aren't you going to look?" he asked.

"No," she said, shaking her head. "I trust you."

He leaned forward and put a light kiss on her brow. "Thanks, that's nice," he said. "You go ahead and sulk in your beer. Let me know if you need anything."

She began to calm down with her beer. It was probably a half hour later that Doc Mullins came into the bar and sat on the stool beside her. She glared at him, then focused again on her glass.

Doc raised a finger to Jack and he set up a whiskey. Then wisely, left the two of them alone.

Doc had a sip, then another, then said, "You're right. I can't leave you out of the loop like that if you're going to help take care of the town."

She turned and looked at him, one eyebrow lifted. "Did you just apologize to me?"

"Not quite, I didn't. But in this one instance, you're right. I'm just used to acting on my own, is all. Meant no disrespect."

"What are we going to do?" she asked him.

"You're not going to do anything at all. This is on me. If there's any malpractice involved, I don't want it on you. You were always prepared to do the right thing.

I wanted to do the right thing, too—but I had a different right thing in mind."

"I think she should be examined. I can do it or we can make her an appointment with John Stone."

"I'll call John," Doc said, taking another sip of his whiskey. "I want you away from this for now."

"And this time, you'll actually make the call?"

He turned and regarded her, glare for glare. "I'll call him."

Mel just concentrated on her beer, which had gone warm and dull.

"You do a good job, missy," he said. "I'm getting too old for some things, especially the babies." He looked down at his hands, some fingers bent, knuckles swollen. "I can still get things done, but these old hands aren't good on the women. Better you take care of women's health."

She turned toward him. "First a partial apology. Then a partial compliment."

"I apologize," he said without looking at her. "I think you're needed here."

She let out her breath slowly. She knew how hard that was for him. She took another deep breath and put her arm around his shoulders. She leaned her head against him.

"Don't go soft on me," she said.

"Not a chance," he returned.

Jack had no idea what had passed between Mel and Doc, but she said they were going back to the clinic and would have a bite to eat together there. He assumed they had issues to work out. Then she promised to come back to the bar before going home.

He served quite a few people at six. By seven the

crowd was thinning and there were only a few people there when the door opened. Charmaine. She'd never come to Virgin River before; he'd let her know that he wanted to keep those two parts of his life separate. She wasn't wearing waitress clothes tonight, so her intention was pretty obvious. She wore a nice pair of creased slacks, a crisp white blouse with the collar folded on the outside of a dark blue blazer. Her hair was down and full, makeup thick but perfect, heels. It pleased him to be reminded that she was a handsome woman, especially so when she didn't wear those tight clothes that drew attention to her large breasts. She looked classy. Mature.

She sat up at the bar and smiled at him. "I thought I'd drop by and see how you've been," she said.

"Good, Char. You?"

"Great."

"How about a drink?" he asked.

"Sure. Yes. How about a Johnny Walker, ice. Make it a good Johnny."

"You got it." He set her up with a black label—he didn't have any blue. Too pricey for his usual crowd. In fact, he didn't move much of the black label. "So, what brings you to my neighborhood?"

"I wanted to check in. See if things are the same with you."

He looked down for a second, disappointed. He had hoped not to have to do this again, and certainly not here. This was no place to discuss their relationship, such as it had been. He looked back into her eyes and simply nodded.

"No change, then?"

He shook his head, hoping he could leave it at that.

"Well," she said, taking a sip of her drink, "I'm sorry

to hear that. I was hoping that maybe we could… Never mind. I can tell by the look on your face—"

"Char, please. This isn't the right time or place."

"Take it easy, Jack, I'm not going to push. Can't blame a girl for checking it out. After all, what we had was pretty special. To me, anyway."

"It was special to me, too. I'm sorry, but I had to move on."

"So—you still insist there's no one else?"

"There wasn't at the time. I didn't lie to you. I've never lied to you. But now—"

Just as he said that, the door swung open and Mel came in. Her expression earlier had been angry, but now it was subdued. Tired. And she did something she had never previously done. Rather than jumping up on a stool and asking for a beer, she came around the bar. To Charmaine he said, "Excuse me just one second." He met Mel at the end of the bar.

Mel immediately put her arms around his waist and hugged him, laying her head on his chest. His arms went around her, as well, returning the gesture, painfully aware that Charmaine was burning a hole in his back with her eyes.

"Today was trying," Mel said softly. "Doc and I had a come-to-Jesus meeting about how we're going to work together, if we're going to work together. It was harder than I thought. Emotionally draining."

"Are you all right?" he asked.

"I'm fine. Might I have one of those nifty little Crowns? I've eaten and I promise to only have one, with ice, and you're welcome to take me home tonight. If you want to."

"You're kidding, right? I'm scared to death to let you go home alone. Who knows what you'll do, who you'll take a ride with." He put a small kiss on her brow and turned her around so she could go to the front of the bar. He didn't make eye contact with Charmaine, but rather fixed the drink and put it before Mel. By now she was on a stool at the very end of the bar. "You'll have to give me a minute."

"Sure," she said. "Take your time. I just want to unwind."

"Unwind away." He went back to Char.

The expression in Charmaine's eyes was one of hurt, but at least there was clarity.

"I think I understand," she said, taking another sip of her drink.

He reached for her hand and held it. "Charmaine, I wasn't lying. Doesn't really matter now, I guess, but I'd like it if you believed I was telling the truth. There wasn't anyone else."

"But you wanted there to be."

He nodded, helplessly. He glanced at Mel. She was watching them. Her expression was perplexed and unhappy.

"Well. Now I understand," Charmaine said, pulling her hand away from his. "I'm going to take off. Leave you to your business."

She plunked down a twenty-dollar bill, insulting a former lover who would buy her a drink. She whirled off the bar stool and headed for the door. Jack grabbed that twenty and went down to the end of the bar. "Mel, I'll be right back. Stay put."

"Take all the time you need," she said, but she didn't say it happily.

Just the same he followed Charmaine outside. He called to her and she stopped once she got to her car.

He caught up with her and said, "I'm sorry it worked out like this. I wish you'd just called."

"I'm sure you do." She had moist eyes, as though any minute there might be tears. "I see now," she said.

"I'm not sure you do. This is… It's very recent," he said.

"But she was on your mind?"

He took a breath. "Yeah."

"You love her," she said.

He nodded. "Oh, yeah. Big time."

She laughed hollowly. "Well, who'd guess. Mr. No-Attachments."

"I didn't mean to mislead you, Char. That's why I broke it off, because I knew if Mel gave me half a chance, I'd find myself with two women, and I wouldn't do that to either one of you. I'd never deliberately…"

"Aw, take it easy, bub. She's young, she's pretty—and you're a goner. Now I know. I just wanted to be sure."

He grabbed her hands, pressing that twenty into one. "You can't believe I'd let you buy a drink in my bar."

"Old lovers drink on the house?" she asked sarcastically.

"No," he said. "Good friends drink on the house." He leaned toward her and kissed her forehead. "I'm sorry if I hurt you. I didn't mean to." He took a deep breath. "I never saw it coming."

She sighed. "I understand, Jack. I miss you, is all. I hope it all works out for you, but if it doesn't…"

"Char, if this doesn't work, I won't be worth a damn."

She chuckled. "Okay, then. I'll take off. Good luck, Jack." She got in her car, backed out and drove away. He watched until she was gone, then went back inside.

He stood behind the bar, facing Mel. "I'm sorry about that."

"What was that?"

"An old friend."

"Clear River?"

"Yeah. Just checking up."

"Wanting another run at you?"

He nodded. "I made it clear…"

"What did you make clear? Huh, Jack?"

"That I'm off the market. I tried to do that kindly."

Her expression softened somewhat. She smiled a little and put the palm of her hand against his cheek. "Well, I guess I can't bitch about that. Your kindness is one of your best features. But tell me something, cowboy. Is she going to keep showing up here?"

"No."

"Good. I don't like competition."

"There isn't any, Melinda. There never was."

"There better not be. Turns out I'm a very selfish woman."

"I broke it off with her before I even held your hand."

She lifted an amused eyebrow. "That was optimistic of you. You could have ended up with no one."

"A chance I was willing to take. The other way—I didn't want to take that kind of chance. It could have seriously messed up what I wanted. And I wanted you." He smiled at her. "You're being a pretty good sport about this," he said.

"Hey. I know why she was here. I wouldn't give you up at the point of a gun. Wanna take me home? Spend the night?"

"Yeah," he said with a smile. "I always want to."

"Get permission from your bald guy then. I want you to prove yourself to me tonight. Again." Then she grinned.

July came in sunny and warm with a bit of occasional rain. Jack was sitting out on the porch when Rick showed up for work. He came in earlier in the day during summer when there was no school—sometime between breakfast and lunch. It was the peculiar look on his face that caused Jack to say, "Hold up, pardner. How you doing?"

"Good, Jack," he said.

"Pull up a chair. I haven't wanted to ask, but it's been on my mind. You and Liz."

"Yeah," Ricky said, leaning against the porch rail rather than sitting. "Must show all over me, huh?"

"Something's showing. Everything okay?"

"Yeah, I guess." He took a breath. "I kept after her to let me know if we were all clear, you know? And when she finally said it was okay, she wasn't pregnant or anything, I told her that I thought maybe we should cool it. It killed her."

"Whooo," Jack said. "Rough."

"I feel like the biggest dog."

"I guess you had your reasons."

"I tried to explain—it's not that I don't like her. A lot. I really like her a lot. I'm not just saying that. And it's not just because of what we did. You know."

"I get that, yeah," Jack said.

"Can I tell you something?"

"It's all up to you, bud."

"I really like the girl a lot. I maybe even love her, if that doesn't sound too stupid. But it turns out it's a little too hot for me to handle, and I don't want to screw up my life and her life because of that. That one time— Jack, I did *not* see that coming. I think it's best for her and me to put some miles between us. Does that make me a wimp?"

Jack felt a slow smile spread across his lips. "Nah. That makes you a person with a brain."

"I feel like a damn dog. But Jack, that girl—she just does it to me. Holy God. I get close to that girl and I have no brain at all."

Jack sat forward in his chair, leaning toward Rick. "There will be times when too hot to handle will work right into your plans, Rick. But you won't be sixteen anymore. You need to be smart. Sounds like you're being smart. I'm sorry you and the girl are having a hard time with this."

"I hope you're right about this. Because I feel like shit. Plus, I miss her like mad. And not just that... I miss *her*."

"Ricky, buddy, you are too young to be a daddy. I'm sorry this hurts, but sometimes you have to do the difficult thing. And she's just too frickin' young to be put in that position. Someone has to be a grown-up. You're doing the right thing. If she's the right girl, it'll keep."

"I don't know," he said, shaking his head sadly.

"Let the girl get a little older, pal. Maybe you can check back with her later."

"Or maybe not, Jack. I think I hurt her real bad. I might not get another shot."

"Do yourself a favor. Don't keep going back to the scene of the crime. It'll just buy you trouble."

Mel began to glow in the brightness of summer. She had a patient in her last trimester with a first baby and first babies were so much fun. This couple, unlike Polly and Darryl, unlike the sad and anonymous couple in the woods, had been trying for a baby for quite a while, so they were filled with anxiety and excitement. Anne and Jeremy Givens were in their late twenties and had been married eight years. Jeremy's dad owned a large orchard, and Jeremy and Anne lived on the land with the extended family. The baby would come before the apple crop.

Jack and Mel had solidified a couples' friendship with June and Jim, and John and Susan. They spent more time in Grace Valley and the other couples came to Virgin River twice—once to Mel's little cabin for dinner, once to Jack's bar. On the last visit Susan announced that she wouldn't be leaving town again, unless she could use the twisting, bumpy, thirty-minute drive to start labor. She was about to pop. Jack invited Jim, Elmer Hudson and a friend of Elmer's, Judge Forrest, to fish with him and Preacher in the Virgin, and their catch was good. It made her almost as happy that the men were friends as it did that she had these women friends in her life.

Given the time she was spending with her girlfriends, Mel had opened up a little, but just a little. She admitted she was in a relationship with Jack and that he was the best thing that had happened to her in Virgin River. "It looks like you were made for each other," Susan said. "Kind of like June and Jim—barely acquainted and like old soul mates."

To Joey she reported, "I never sleep by myself anymore. It feels more natural to have him near. And Joey—it's so nice not to be alone anymore." She didn't dare tell her sister that after going out to a marijuana grow to deliver a baby, Jack would hardly let her out of his sight. She smiled secretly; there was always a bright spot to everything.

"Do you get any sleep?" Joey asked.

Mel laughed. "I sleep very well, every night. But Joey," she said, shivering, "I've never known anything like this. Every time I look at him, I just want to get undressed."

"You deserve it, Mel."

"He asked me to do something that has me a little tense—he's going to Sacramento for his youngest sister's birthday—a gathering of the whole family. And he wants me to go."

"Why would that make you tense? You sprung me on him and it went very well. He's crazy about me," she added with a laugh.

"I'm not worried that they won't like me. I'm worried they might make more of this than there is."

"Ah," Joey said. "Holding back a little?"

"Not on purpose," she answered. "For some reason I just can't stop feeling that I'm married to someone else."

"Oh, Mel—go! That other guy—the one you still feel married to? He's not going to get in the way of this. In fact, if he's watching, he's probably glad you have someone special to warm up your nights."

"If he's watching," she said, "I'm blushing."

Jack convinced her. All the way to Sacramento, she was nervous as a cat. "I just don't want your family to think we're in a serious relationship."

"Aren't we?" he asked her. "Aren't you?"

"You know there's no one else in my life," she said. "I'm completely monogamous. I just need time… You know…"

"Man," he said, laughing. "This figures."

"What?"

"All those years I made sure the woman I was seeing at the time knew I couldn't be tied down… There are women out there, Mel, who would think I'm getting just what I deserve right now."

"You know what I mean. It's just my issues…"

"I'm waiting out the issues. And I'm serious about that."

"You're very patient with me, Jack. And I appreciate it. I just don't want them to get the wrong idea. And we will sleep in separate bedrooms at your dad's."

"No," he said firmly. "I'm over forty years old. I sleep with you every night. I told my dad that one bedroom would be just fine."

She sighed heavily. Nervously. "Okay then. But we're not doing it at your dad's." And he laughed at her.

It was so much hotter in Sacramento in July than in Virgin River. Hotter even than L.A. in July—Sacramento was located on an inland valley and had no ocean breezes to cool the land.

Sam Sheridan still lived in the house where he'd raised his five children—a spacious ranch-style home in the suburbs with a lush yard, pool and a big kitchen. When Mel met him, she looked into the eyes of an older version of Jack—a man of the same height and girth with thick, steel-gray hair, a big smile and a powerful handshake. Jack and Sam embraced like brothers, so happy to be together.

The three of them had a nice evening with steak cooked on the backyard barbecue and red wine. The men insisted on cleaning up the dishes, so Mel took her glass of wine and wandered around the house a little bit. She found herself in what passed as Sam's study, or office or bragging room. There was a desk, a TV, computer, bookshelves and wall upon wall of pictures and awards. All his daughters in their wedding dresses, all his granddaughters, ranging in age from five to eighteen, but the thing she hadn't given any thought to at all were the pictures she would see of Jack. Pictures she had never seen around Jack's room—a marine wearing rows of ribbons. Jack and his various squads and platoons, Jack and his parents, Jack and generals. Jack and the guys who came to Virgin River for their Semper Fi reunions. And cases of medals. She didn't know much about military awards, but there was no mistaking three purple hearts and silver and bronze stars.

She reached out and gently ran her fingers over the glass case that held the medals. Sam came up behind her and put his hands on her shoulders. "He's a hero," he said softly. "Many times over."

She looked over her shoulder at Sam. "You'd never know that from talking to him," she said.

"Oh, I know." He laughed. "He's modest."

"Dad," Jack said, coming into the room, drying a wineglass with a dish towel. "I told you to put all that shit away."

"Ha," Sam said, just ignoring his son, turning his back on him. "This one is from Desert Storm," he told Mel. "And this—Bosnia. There were downed fighter pilots—Jack and his unit went into a hot zone and pulled them out. He got shot in Afghanistan, but still managed to get his squad out of danger. And this one—the latest Iraq conflict—he saved six men."

"Dad…"

"Your dishes done, son?" he asked without turning around, dismissing Jack.

Mel looked up at Sam. "Do you think this bothers him? The memories?"

"Oh, I'm sure some of them do. But it never bothered him enough to keep him from going back, time and again. They might've sent him anyway, but every bit of training and fighting—he volunteered. This boy has been awarded medals by many generals and one president. He was the marines' best—and I'm damn proud of him. He won't keep the medals with him. He'd put 'em in storage or something. I have to keep them here to keep them safe."

"He's not proud of this?" she asked.

Sam looked down at Mel. "Not the medals so much as the men. He was committed to his men, not military awards. You didn't know this about my son?"

"I knew he was in the marines. I met some of his friends. These guys," she said, pointing at a picture.

"He's a leader of men, Melinda," Sam said. He glanced over his shoulder and seeing that his son was gone, said, "He tends to act embarrassed that he was only a high-school graduate when his sisters—and their husbands for that matter—all hold college degrees, and even some post-graduate degrees among them. But I think the man has accomplished more, done more good and saved more lives, than many a man or woman with more education. And if you know him, you know he's very intelligent. If he'd gone to college, he'd have excelled there, as well, but this was his path."

"He's so gentle," she heard herself say.

"He is that. I've seen him with each one of my granddaughters, handling them like they're nitro and might blow up if he makes a wrong move. But he is not gentle when he's in the fight. This man is not just a marine. He's a highly decorated hero. His sisters and I stand in awe."

"It must have been hard for you, when he was in combat."

"Yes." He looked at the pictures and medals with a wistful expression on his face. "You can't imagine how much his mother and I missed him. Worried about him. But he did what he was driven to do. And he did it well." Sam smiled. "We'd better get back to the kitchen. He gets surly when I brag."

When Mel got up the next morning, Jack was not beside her. She heard him talking with his dad in another room; she heard them laughing, so she showered and dressed before joining them. She found them in the dining room, paperwork spread out all over the table.

"Board meeting?" she asked.

"Something like that," Sam said. "So, son, everything look okay to you?"

"Great. As usual." He stuck out his hand and shook his father's. "Thanks, Dad. Appreciate it."

Sam gathered up the papers, clutched them in a stack atop an accordion file and left the room.

"My dad was an agent for a brokerage firm before he retired. While I was in the marines, I'd send him money from time to time. He's been investing for me for twenty years."

"I didn't think a marine made a lot of money," she said.

"Not really." He shrugged. "But if you're single and you keep re-upping and going to war, there are bonuses, incentives, combat pay, promotions. My buddies—most of them—had those benefits eaten up by housing, braces on kids' teeth, the usual. I always lived cheap and saved. My dad," he said, "he always made that such an issue while I was growing up."

"Smart man," she said, and she wasn't speaking of Sam.

Jack grinned. "You thought I was making a killing on that little Virgin River bar?"

"I figured you didn't need to. With a military retirement and low cost of living…"

"Nah. That aside, I'm set," he said. "If the bar burns to the ground, all I have to do is support Preach for the rest of his life. And I'd like to make sure Ricky gets an education. That's about it." He reached for her hand. "Otherwise, I have everything I need."

That afternoon the rest of the family descended on the Sheridan home—four sisters and their husbands, eight nieces. As they came, one family at a time, they flung themselves on Jack. His sisters ran to him, hugging and kissing him. His brothers-in-law embraced him fondly. He picked up each one of his nieces and hugged them like they were his daughters, spun them around, laughed into their pretty faces.

Mel wasn't sure what she had expected them to be like. Having seen the family picture in his room and those around the house, she knew they were a good-looking family; good genes. His sisters were very different from each other, but each was svelte, lovely, smart. Donna, the oldest, was very tall, probably five-ten, with short, frosted hair, Jeannie was nearly as tall, quite thin and chic, Mary was next tallest at perhaps five-five, but so trim and fragile-looking it was hard to imagine her handling a big commercial jet. Donna and Jeannie each had three daughters, Mary had two. And then there was Brie, the baby, celebrating her thirtieth birthday. She was the only sister who did not yet have children. She was just about the same size as Mel with long light brown hair that fell down her back almost to her waist— a little bitty thing who put away hardened criminals for a living. And their men, like Jack and Sam, were big guys, the nieces, each one beautiful.

Jack's sisters brought some of Mel's closest friends with them—Ralph Lauren, Lilly Pulitzer, Michael Kors and Coach. Each one of them had a strong sense of style, but what was more obvious than their collective taste in fashion was their warmth and humor. They all met Mel with delight, eschewing the offered handshake and immediately embracing her. It was a very physical, affectionate family. Every time Mel stole a look at Jack he had his arms around a sister or niece, frequently dropping kisses on their heads or cheeks. Just as frequently he would seek out Mel and put a possessive arm about her shoulders or waist. And to her surprise, so would Sam, as though they'd been close for years.

All Brie had wanted for her birthday was to have the family together and her brother home. "He's not so very far away," Mel said. "Don't you get to see him often?"

"Not nearly often enough," Brie said. "Jack has been essentially gone for twenty-three years. Since he was seventeen."

It was a loud day, filled with laughter and good food. Sam took care of the meat while the sisters brought delicious side dishes. After dinner, the kids took off to watch DVDs on the big screen or jump in the backyard pool or play video games on Grandpa's computer. It was just the adults sitting around the patio tables and they told stories about Jack that almost made him blush.

"Remember, Dad, when you were giving away Jack's bed and were going to surprise him with a new bigger one because he'd gotten so tall? So heavy?" Immediate laughter from everyone—Mel was the only one not intimate with this story. "A friend of the family wanted the bed for one of his younger kids. He was a respected member of the PTA…"

"Aw, you act like he was the frickin' preacher or something," Jack protested.

"And when they pulled off the mattress, Jack's private library was exposed for all eyes to see," Donna said, and everyone howled.

"I'd been raising girls," Sam said. "I completely forgot what boys were doing when they were supposed to be doing homework."

"At least it was good, solid, decent girlie magazines and not pictures of women in bras from Sears catalogs," Jack said in his defense. "Fine, upstanding, naked women!"

"Here, here," the brothers-in-law intoned.

"You know," Mel said, "I've noticed there's only one bathroom besides the master bath in this house…"

Immediate noise erupted—shouts, laughter, whistles, jeering. "We used to have the biggest fights over the bathroom," one of the women said.

"I wasn't in that," Jack insisted.

"You were the *worst!*" it was accused.

"Plus, when he got the bathroom, he'd stay in there for hours! He wouldn't give it up until all the hot water was gone!"

"Mom had to give him a timer for his shower—so the rest of us could get clean, too. Of course, he just ignored it. And Mom would say, 'Now, now, I know Jack's trying.' Because Jack was her little precious."

"I started showering at night—it was the only way," Donna said.

"Speaking of nights—do you know what he used to do to us at night? Mary and I had the same bedroom, and it was crammed to the ceiling with our stuff. Jack and one of his friends used to sneak in when we were asleep and tie strings to our fingers and toes and connect the strings to stuff around the room, so when we turned over in our sleep—everything came crashing down around us!"

"That's nothing," Jeannie said. "I used to come home from school and find all my stuffed animals with nooses around their necks, hanging from my bed canopy!"

"They act like they never did anything to me," Jack said.

"Do you remember the time we were all in the family room, all five of us, and Mom came into the room with a bunch of condoms in her hand and said, 'Guess what I found floating in the washer? Jack, I imagine these must belong to you.'"

Wild laughter erupted and Jack got all stirred up. "Yeah, but they weren't mine, were they? Because mine were right where I'd left them! I suspect Donna!"

"I was a feminist," Donna declared.

"Mom would never have believed it—Donna was her pride and joy!"

"Donna was screwing around!"

"I can't take these stories," Sam said, standing up and going for a beer, making them all laugh.

"It's okay, Dad," Donna yelled. "I don't need birth control anymore!"

When it was time to clean up and the sun had set, the men went off somewhere and three of the sisters insisted that the birthday girl and the guest relax while they did the work. Mel was left with Brie. They sat at the patio table by candlelight.

"My brother has never brought a woman home before," Brie said.

"After watching him with his family—all these females—it's so hard to imagine. He's completely comfortable with women. He should have been married years ago. He should have a big family of his own," Mel said.

"It just never happened," Brie put in. "I blame it on the marines."

"When I first met him, I asked him if he'd ever been married and he said, 'I was married to the marines, and she was a real bitch.'" Brie laughed. "Have you visited him in Virgin River?" Mel asked.

"Not en masse," she said. "But we've all gotten up there at one time or another. The guys like to fish with Jack and Preacher. Dad will go up there for as long as a couple of weeks at a time—he loves that little bar of Jack's."

"Jack seems to have found his niche, his happy place," Mel said. "I've only been there a little over four months, and my adjustment hasn't been that easy. I'm used to big-city medicine where you can get anything you want, and fast. This is a whole new game. And I had to drive for two hours to get a decent haircut and frost job."

"What made you choose Virgin River?" Brie asked her.

"Hmm. The flip side of big-city medicine—I'd had it with the chaos and crime. As I told Jack, I left the E.R. not just because I felt drawn to midwifery, but I thought I could get away from having half my patients brought in by the police. And guess what? The first woman I ever delivered had multiple felony warrants and was being arrested when she went into labor. She was handcuffed to the bed when I examined her prior to delivery." She chuckled. "I was looking for something smaller and simpler." She laughed. "I got smaller, but simpler? Little towns like Virgin River have their own challenges."

"Like?"

"Like how about loading a critical patient in the back

of a pickup truck and speeding down the mountain, hanging on for dear life, trying to get her to the hospital before she goes into cardiac arrest. Man, did I ever lust after that big, chaotic emergency room that day. And there's always the adventure of having your services requested by a big, gun-toting drug farmer in the middle of the night... Um, if you tell Jack that version of the story, there's going to be a scene."

Brie laughed. "He doesn't know?"

"Not some of the details. He was very pissed that I went alone to an unknown location with a man who was basically a stranger."

"Holy smoke."

"Yeah, well, it's a good thing I did. There were complications with the delivery. But I don't think that will cheer up Jack too much." She shrugged. "Jack's protective. Of everyone."

"Have you found your niche?" Brie asked.

"I kind of crave a trip to Nordstrom's," Mel said. "I wouldn't mind a facial and leg wax, either. On the other hand, I didn't realize I could get by on so little. So simply. There's something about that... It's freeing, in a way. And there's no question, it's beautiful. Sometimes it's so quiet, your ears ring. But when I first got there, I thought I'd really screwed up big—it was so much more rugged and isolated than I expected. The mountain roads terrified me, and Doc and I manage in that clinic with the most rudimentary equipment. The cabin I was promised, rent free for a year, was horrible. In fact, my first morning there the porch collapsed and dumped me into a deep, freezing mud puddle. The cabin was so filthy, I was on my way out of town—running for my life—when a medical emergency stopped me and I reluctantly stayed a few days that turned into a couple of weeks."

"That turned into a few months…" Brie observed.

"Jack renovated the cabin without being asked, while I stayed at Doc's house," Mel said. "About the time I was going to make a break for it, he showed it to me. I said I'd give it a few more days. Then my first delivery occurred and I realized I should give the place a chance. There's something about a successful delivery in a place like Virgin River where there's no backup, no anesthesia… Just me and Mom… It's indescribable."

"Then there's Jack," Brie said.

"Jack," Mel repeated. "I don't know when I've met a kinder, stronger, more generous man. Your brother is wonderful, Brie. He's amazing. Everyone in Virgin River loves him."

"My brother is in love with *you*," Brie said.

Mel shouldn't have been shocked. Although he hadn't said the words, she already knew it. Felt it. At first she thought he was just a remarkable lover, but soon she realized that he couldn't touch her that way without an emotional investment, as well as a physical one. He gave her everything he had—and not just in the bedroom. It was in her mind to tell Brie—*I'm a recent widow! I need time to digest this! I don't feel free yet—free to accept another man's love!* Her cheeks grew warm and she said nothing.

"I realize I'm biased, but when a man like Jack loves a woman, it's a great honor."

"I agree," Mel said quietly.

Late, in the dark of night, as he held her in his arms in the bed in his father's house, she said, "You have the most wonderful family."

"They love you, too."

"It was such fun watching you all together. They're ruthless—you don't have a secret left!" And she laughed.

"I told you. No slack here."

"But what fun, to have all that history, all those hysterical stories."

"Oh—I listened to you and Joey for a few days. You didn't grow up deprived." He kissed her neck. "I'm just glad you had fun. I knew you would." He kissed her neck again, nuzzling closer.

"Your sisters are all so put together," she said. "Very classy, very sharp. I used to dress like that, before I moved to a place where you're overdressed in good jeans. You should have seen my closet in L.A.—it was huge, and bulging."

He pulled the T-shirt she wore up and over her head. "I like what you're wearing right now. In fact, I find you overdressed in this thong."

"Jack, I thought we decided, we're not going to do it in your father's house…"

"No, you said you weren't going to." He slipped the thong down. "I'm thinking of going after that G-spot again…"

"Oh, God," she said, weakening. "We shouldn't. You know how we get…"

He rose above her and grinned into her eyes. "Want me to get a sock for your mouth?"

Susan Stone delivered her son in August—a robust eight-pounder. She went to Valley Hospital, had a stunning delivery and was home in Grace Valley in forty-eight hours. It was in Mel's mind to give her some time alone with her baby, but both John and June called and urged her to come the next Sunday afternoon, the baby not yet a week old.

Jack would not be left behind. He brought the beer and cigars.

Susan was very fit for a woman who had just delivered, but still she stayed on the couch, bassinet nearby, and let her friends fuss over her. In typical country fashion, women brought food so that the new parents wouldn't have to be bothered with cooking. Mel was surprised to see such an air of celebration and atmosphere of an open house so soon after bringing a baby home.

There was another couple present, a very pregnant Julianna Dickson and her husband, Mike. John dropped an arm around Julianna's shoulders and said to Mel, "This one is legendary—she could never seem to wait for the doctor. June and I finally got to attend one of her births—it was the last baby, and it was sheer luck. She delivers with about fifteen minutes' notice. This is number six. We're going to admit her tomorrow and induce."

"Don't let the baby hear you say that," Julianna said. "You know what always happens."

"Maybe we should go over there right now?"

"Maybe you should strap yourself to me and keep one hand on my stomach."

The women gathered in the living room around Susan with cups of coffee and cake. John plucked the baby out of his bassinet to show him off. As Jim already had baby Jamie in his arms, John offered the baby to Jack. And he willingly, happily took him into his arms. He cooed at the little bundle.

Mel's eyes warmed as she watched him.

"You're pretty good at that for a bachelor," John said appreciatively.

"Nieces," he said.

"Eight of them," Mel added.

Jack jiggled and the baby sent up a loud wail. "I guess you're not that good," John said.

"Jack did fine. He's hungry," Susan said, reaching for the baby.

"Okay—there's going to be breast-feeding," John said. "We should find something to do."

Jack pulled cigars out of his breast pocket and immediately a very grateful hum of approval sounded. Jim handed Jamie off to June and left the women and babies in the house to go outside and indulge.

"They're going to stink," Julianna said.

"To high heaven," June agreed.

"At least they're out of our hair." Susan settled the newborn onto her breast and Mel watched with longing. "Mel," she said, "how'd it go in Sacramento? With Jack's family?"

"Oh, they're fantastic," she said, coming back to herself again. "Four sisters who tell every secret he'd ever dream of keeping, and eight nieces, all beautiful, all in love with their uncle Jack. It was delightful. So, Susan—how was your labor? Back labor, like you predicted?"

"Epidural," she said with a grin. "Piece of cake."

"I've never had time for one of those," Julianna said somewhat wistfully, smoothing a hand over her round tummy.

"You and Julianna are awful close to the same due date," Mel observed.

They all laughed. "I might've neglected to mention— the big fight John and I had before this little conception? It happened at a night of cards with Julianna and Mike."

"We were both so furious with our husbands—they

had both been banished. Apparently we let them both into bed at about the same time." More laughter. Julianna rubbed her swollen tummy. "I meant to stop doing this…"

"What in the world happened?" Mel wanted to know.

"Long story short—they had a couple of beers and started in on working women. I wanted to work alongside John and June in the clinic, but John wanted me to stay home, mind my own business and clean house. And make sure he had one of those solid country meals in front of him when he got home. Now, I come from the part of the world where a salad with some chicken strips is a dining delight."

"Mike, on the other hand, thought it was wonderful that I *didn't* work. With five kids and a farmhouse to run," Julianna said.

"Oh, brother," Mel said.

"They were made to suffer very appropriately," June put in. "No conversation, no sex. Perfect discipline for idiots."

"How'd it turn out?" Mel asked.

"Well, when I'm not nine months pregnant or post-partum and nursing, I run the clinic."

"And very well, at that."

"But a side effect was… Well, as you can plainly see—we had been knocked up. You might not want to drink the water around here," Susan advised.

"No kidding," said June, propping Jamie on her shoulder.

I drank the water, Mel almost said.

Nursing done, Susan passed the baby to Mel. She smiled gratefully and took the little guy. His rosy round face was contented in sleep; little baby noises escaped him.

The women talked about their labors, about their

men, and they brought Mel into the conversation very well with questions about her midwifery experiences. June went to the kitchen for the coffeepot and refilled them all while Mel happily cuddled with the newborn. Her breasts actually ached as she held him. *Hormones are amazing,* she found herself thinking.

On the way back to Virgin River, Jack said, "Your friends throw a nice little party."

"Don't they?" she replied, reaching across the truck's front seat to hold his hand.

"All these babies," Jack said. "Everywhere you look."

"Everywhere."

He pulled up in front of her cabin. "I'll shower off the cigars," he said.

"Thanks," she answered. "It actually makes me a little nauseous."

"I'm sorry, honey. I didn't realize."

"No big deal. But I'll be glad to loan you the shower. And meet you in the bed. I'm suddenly exhausted."

Mel was just pulling up to the clinic in the morning when beside her an old pickup was pulling into the next parking spot. She recognized the man at once—Calvin. She hadn't seen him since that first time, when she treated his facial wounds. He jumped out of the truck as she got out of the Hummer. His hands were plunged into his pockets and he seemed to nearly vibrate with the jitters. She suddenly realized something—the man who took her to deliver his baby in the backwoods, also a grower, didn't seem to be on anything. This guy was wired. High. She'd never have gotten in a truck, in the middle of the night, with Calvin—baby or no baby. She further realized that without a plan of any kind, she could get hurt if she refused such a request from Calvin. He was pretty scary, and clearly unstable.

Before she could even address him, he said, "I need something. Back pain."

"What do you need?" she asked calmly, very practiced in handling his type back in the city.

"Pain medicine. I need something for pain. Fentanyl, maybe. OxyContin. Morphine. Something."

"Did you hurt your back?" she asked, trying to avoid his eyes as she proceeded to Doc's front porch. He was jerking and tweaking, and upright rather than sitting on a low stool, she became aware of his size. He was almost six feet and broad-shouldered. It was clear he'd gotten his hands on something not depressive. Maybe methamphetamine, as Doc had earlier suspected. He wanted a narcotic to bring him down. The pot from his garden must not be doing it for him.

"Fell off a ledge out there. Might've broke it. It'll be okay, but I need a little medicine."

"Fine. You'll have to see Doc," she said.

His feet moved nervously. He pulled a hand out of his pocket and grabbed at her sleeve and she jerked out of his reach.

Jack, coming from her cabin arrived behind her and was just pulling into town as Calvin made that move and for a split second she almost felt sorry for him. Jack accelerated, screeched to a stop within inches of Doc's porch and was out of the truck in one second. "Get away from her!" he shouted.

The guy backed away, but just a little bit. He looked at Mel. "I just need something for the pain in my back," he said.

Jack reached into his truck and had his hand on his rifle. The look in his eyes was frightening. "I'm okay," she said to Jack. Then to the twitchy young man, "I don't prescribe the kind of drugs you're looking for. We leave that to the doctor. And he'll want an X-ray, undoubtedly."

The guy stared at her, then grinned stupidly. "You ain't got no X-ray."

"There's one at Valley Hospital," she said.

Jack pulled the rifle off the rack and held it at his side for a moment. Then he kicked the truck door closed and came up onto the porch to stand beside Mel. He put an arm around Mel and pulled her against him. "Want to see the doctor?" he asked Calvin, rifle in hand.

"Hey, man," he laughed nervously. "What's your deal, man?" He backed away with his hands up, palms facing Jack. "Take it easy. I'll go to the valley," he said. He jumped off the porch, not bothering with the steps. *Must be some back pain,* she thought. He got in the old pickup, started it, put it in gear and drove away. But he didn't go toward the valley—he went toward the woods.

"You know him?" Jack asked.

"He was at that camp Doc and I went to a few months ago. When you watched the baby for us. You remember…"

"Paulis's?"

"Uh-huh. Did you have to do that?" Mel asked. "He really hadn't done anything threatening."

Jack glared after the departing truck. "Yeah," he said. "I had to. He's wrong. He's just wrong."

Fourteen

Every August before school started, the Andersons played host to a huge late-summer picnic at their ranch. Everyone they knew in Virgin River and even some folks from surrounding towns showed up. Buck had a huge canvas tent he erected in the pasture outside the corral, barbecues were set up, people provided tables and chairs. The Bristols brought their miniature horses and set up pony rides. Jack always donated a couple of kegs while Preacher whipped up some of his best potato salad in a tub so big it looked as if it would feed a third-world nation. There were barrels of lemonade and iced tea, ice chests full of sodas and, in the afternoon, homemade ice-cream makers were brought out of trucks and SUVs, and the hand cranking began.

The barn floor was swept clean and a small band was set up for country dancing. There were children everywhere, running from one end of the ranch to the other, from corral to hay loft.

Mel had looked forward to the picnic as a chance to hold Chloe for a while, and also to do something she hadn't done before—meet the rest of the Anderson family. She had a passing acquaintance with two of the three sons who worked the ranch with Buck, and one of the daughters had come to Doc's for a prenatal exam, but otherwise, they were strangers to her.

But not strangers for very long. Each one of them, the sons, the daughters, their spouses and children, greeted her as the person who had given them Chloe. The baby was passed around from Anderson to Anderson, cuddled, swept up in the air, kissed, tickled. Even the little ones—Lilly and Buck's seven grandchildren—ran to Chloe to snuggle her as if she were their newest sweet puppy. Buck was pretty busy around the barn and barbecues, but from time to time he was near the picnic tables or food tables and she would catch a glimpse of him holding Chloe comfortably on his hip.

The Andersons were wonderful, homespun, authentic people with nothing but tons of love in their hearts. Just like Lilly; sweet, nurturing and tender. The sun was beginning to lower in the late afternoon sky when Jack found Mel sitting on the porch swing with the baby, giving her a bottle. He sat beside her and played idly with Chloe's dark curls. "She seems to be doing well here," he said.

"She should," Mel said. "She's home." And it gave her deep satisfaction to know that this was true in all ways.

"I'd like to spin you around the barn a little bit," he said, leaning over the baby's head to give her a kiss.

"Another surprise. You dance?"

"I think that might be overly optimistic," he said. "I do something. I'll try not to hurt you."

Lilly came out of the house, wiping her hands on her apron. "Here, Mel, let me take her off your hands. I'll put her to bed."

Mel stood with the baby in her arms and walked into

the house, Lilly right behind her. She turned and placed the baby in Lilly's arms. Then she leaned toward Lilly and gave her a kiss on the cheek. "You have a wonderful family," Mel said. "I think you'll find just the right time to tell them."

Mel made an appointment at the Grace Valley clinic. She was surprised to learn that both doctors were available, so she requested the OB. Prenatal consult, she said. "We'll go ahead and put your patient with Dr. Stone," the receptionist said, and Mel did not correct her. After all, she'd been there before with a couple of pregnant women for ultrasounds and they knew her as the midwife upriver. After seeing a few patients, Mel headed for Grace Valley in the afternoon.

It had only been a short time since the gathering at the Stones' house and she could no longer deny the truth. She was pregnant. She already knew it. They had plenty of pregnancy tests on hand at Doc's and she'd used one. Then another one. And another. Half of her hoped it was wrong, the other half was afraid it was.

When she got to the clinic, June was hanging around the reception desk. "Hey, there." She leaned as if looking around Mel. "I thought you were bringing in a prenatal consult?"

"Yeah," Mel said. "Me."

June's eyes grew momentarily round, surprised.

"It must be the water," Mel said with a shrug.

"Come on back. You're with John, and as you know, our nurse is on maternity leave. Want me to stand in or keep out of your business?"

Mel felt a shudder of nervous emotion. "Please, come with me. I think I need to explain a few things," she said.

"Oh, boy," June said, draping an arm around her shoulders. "Sounds like it might be a little complicated."

"Not a little," Mel answered.

John came out of the back and said, "Hey, Melinda. You bring me a prenatal consult?" Before she could answer, June inclined her head toward Mel. "Oh," John said. "Well, first things first—June, set her up in there. Let's get the facts."

"Okay," Mel said, suddenly meek and nervous. "But I already know."

"Don't try to make my job so easy," he said with a laugh. "There's no challenge in that."

Mel went into the exam room where she found a gown and sheet. She undressed and sat up on the table, waiting. How was she supposed to feel about this? She'd been desperate for a baby, and now she was having one. Why did it feel so damn confusing? As though something had gone wrong, when in reality it had finally gone right.

But this wasn't what she had planned. And she knew it wasn't what Jack had planned—he'd offered to take care of their birth control needs. Oh, brother, was he going to be surprised.

John came in, June on his heels. "How are you feeling, Mel?"

"Besides terribly confused? A little nauseous in the morning."

"Damnest thing, isn't it? But you're keeping food down?"

"Yep."

June set up the instruments and pap slide while John got her blood pressure. "Want to talk first or second?" he asked her.

"Second."

"Okay. June—can you fire up the ultrasound? Thanks. Mel, lie back and slide down for me, okay?" He guided her feet into the stirrups and kept hands on her legs in case she slid too far and accidentally fell. When her position was solid, he took his place on his stool and snapped on the rubber gloves. He inserted the speculum. "You know how far along?"

"Three months," she said, her voice quieter than usual. "Approximately."

"Congratulations," he said. Beside her the ultrasound bleeped as it warmed up. He pulled out the speculum after the pap slide was complete and gently palpated the uterus, measuring for size. "You're almost as good at this as I am, Mel," he said. "You have reached the right approximate diagnosis. Good. Everything's good." He pulled the wand from the ultrasound; because this was an early pregnancy he would do an internal probe for a better reading as opposed to running the probe over her still flat belly. "Turn your head, Mel," he said. "Beautiful," he added.

She looked at the monitor. Tears slid out of her eyes and into the hair at her temples. There it was, a small mass, limbs just visible to the practiced eye, moving around inside of her. They watched the new life for a little while and she gave a hiccup of emotion, moving a trembling hand to cover her mouth.

"Just about twelve weeks," John said. "Out of the miscarriage woods. We'll print you out a picture, though the view is going to be lots better in another few weeks."

He removed the probe and helped her to sit up. June leaned a hip on the counter and John returned to his stool.

"You're in perfect health," her doctor said.

June handed Mel a tissue. "I've been there, Mel," June said. "Believe me."

Finally John said, "What's the matter, Mel? How can we help?"

She blotted her eyes. "I'm sorry to do this to you, but it's just so complicated."

John reached out to her and gave her knee a squeeze. "It probably isn't as complicated as you think."

"Oh, wait," she said with a weak, embarrassed laugh. "How about I start by telling you I'm hopelessly infertile."

He gave a little laugh. "Let's see—you have a uterus, ovaries, fallopian tubes… And I've heard this business of not being able to get pregnant from pregnant women before."

"And I went through three years of infertility treatment, including surgery, without success. We even had one very expensive, very failed attempt at in vitro."

"Well, that puts an interesting spin on things. Maybe you should back up a little. You don't have to talk to us, Mel. It's up to you."

"No, I want to. I need advice. I'm a mess. See— before moving up here from L.A., I was married. My husband was a doctor—we often worked together. We tried desperately to have a baby. He was killed when he happened into a robbery in progress. That was a year and three months ago. Almost exactly. I came up here looking for a simpler life, a safer life. I just wanted to start over."

John shrugged. "Kind of looks like you found what you were looking for."

She laughed. "Virgin River isn't all that simple. But yes, in some important ways, I found what I was looking for," she agreed. "Of course, this wasn't planned. I didn't think it was possible for me to get pregnant."

"Is the problem Jack?" June asked.

"Yes, but he doesn't know it. He's so wonderful, but he knew from the beginning that I wasn't quite over my husband. I adore Jack—you can't imagine—but I still haven't gotten to that point where I feel free to move on to—" She took a breath. "To another man." They gave her a moment and another tissue. "This is supposed to be my baby with my husband. The one we tried so hard to have." She blew her nose.

June stepped forward and took her hand. "It seems apparent that Jack loves you. And that he's a good man."

"Good with children," John put in.

"Whether you planned to or not," June said with a shrug, "it appears you have moved on. At least in some ways."

"The last time I gave my heart and soul to a man, he died," she said with a sniffle. Then she lowered her head and a couple of tears fell on the hands folded in her lap. "I don't think I could survive something like that again."

June stepped forward and took her into her arms and John was quick to join her. They comforted her for a minute. Then John gave her shoulders a squeeze and said, "Mel, I like Jack's chances. Five wars couldn't kill him."

"Five *wars?*" June asked.

John shrugged. "You didn't know that?"

"I knew he was in the marines!"

"Men actually do talk," John said.

"That husband of mine," she groused. "He's so badly trained!"

"I'm so confused," Mel said. "I don't really know what to do!"

"Naw, that's not true. It's a done deal, Mel," John said. "Now you just have to be a little kind to yourself and work through it. You wanted a baby real bad, and you're having one. Jack—he doesn't know?"

"No. He knows I'm widowed—he's the only one who knows in Virgin River. But he doesn't know how hard I tried for a baby. He's been so supportive of me in my grieving moments—he hasn't said a word to anyone, because I asked him not to. It's easier, you know—when people don't look at you that way. Like you might be in constant pain. But," she said, "he also offered to take care of our birth control concerns, and of course I told him I had it covered. I was absolutely sure I couldn't get pregnant. God, I'd never do this to a man!"

"He's a good man, Jack. He's going to understand."

"He's going to think I tricked him, isn't he? I mean, he's forty!"

"Yeah, lot of that going around, too," June said. "I remember dealing with some of these same issues when I found out I was pregnant. Jim was over forty when I broke it to him that he was going to be a father. I was afraid he'd bolt."

"I had surgery to remove endometriosis, had my tubes blown out, took hormones, took my temperature every day for two years…" She hiccupped. "We tried everything. Mark wanted a baby as badly as I did. I'm telling you—I'm completely sterile!"

"Welll…." they both said.

"It's the funniest thing," John said. "Nature suffers to fill a void. I can't believe how many miraculous pregnancies I've seen…"

"What if Jack is furious? Who would blame him?

I mean, he hasn't even been in a serious relationship, and here I come. Bouncing into town, telling him I have the birth control issue covered. What if he just says, no, thank you?"

"Something tells me he's not going to say that," John said. "But there's only one way to find out. And—at three months—I'd recommend you not wait much longer."

"I'm afraid," she said quietly.

"Of Jack?" June asked, shocked.

"Jesus, of everything! I'm not even sure I should be here! From the beginning, I thought it was a mistake, making such a big change. I'm a city girl."

"You'd never know it," June said. "You seem to fit in just fine."

"Some days I think this place was just what I needed. Other days I ask myself what I'm doing here. Not only that, do you know how scary it is to think of being committed again and opening myself up to the pain that follows when something goes terribly, terribly wrong? I'm afraid to move on—even though you're right—I already have. I still cry sometimes—over my dead husband. How can I ask another man to put up with that?" She drew in a jagged breath. "At the very least, we should have been able to plan for a possible baby before…"

June held her hand. "Hardly any of us manages to work things out that neatly," she said. June lifted Mel's chin with a finger and looked into her eyes. "I think you should try to remember two things—you have a baby inside you now, a baby you longed for. And a good man back in Virgin River. Go with it, Mel. You'll know what to do."

Mel knew John and June were right. It was important to face this head-on and tell Jack as soon as possible. Let him have time to react. Respond. When she got back to Virgin River, she intended to go straight to the bar. But there, in front of Doc's, was a car she recognized. Anne and Jeremy Givens. It was her time.

When she got inside she found the Givenses with Doc, waiting in the kitchen with a cup of tea. "So this is it?" Mel asked.

"I think so," Anne said. "I've been in labor all day, and now I'm having contractions less than five minutes apart and some spotting. That's when you said to call, right?"

"That's what we decided. Would you like to come upstairs, settle in and let me check you?"

"I'm scared," Anne said. "I didn't think I would be."

"Darling, there is nothing in the world to be afraid of. You're going to sail through this. Jeremy, why don't you let me get Anne comfortable and then you can come upstairs."

"But I want to be there for everything!" he said.

Mel laughed in amusement. "She's just going to get undressed, Jeremy. I bet you've been there for that about a million times." She took Anne's suitcase and her arm. "Come on, sweetheart. Let's go have a baby."

Once settled in, Anne proved to be only four centimeters dilated. Back at the hospital in L.A. they would call that the price of admission—anything less than four centimeters and you were sent home to labor a little longer. Mel observed a couple of contractions and they were coming strong and long. That business about sailing through was perhaps overly optimistic.

Jeremy was at his wife's side as soon as he was invited and, unlike Darryl, he was completely prepared for the rigors of labor. This couple actually had had some birthing training. Mel told Jeremy to walk his wife up and down the upstairs hallway and left Anne in his able hands to go downstairs to use the phone to call Jack.

"Hi," she said. "I have a delivery, so I'm not coming to the bar."

"You think it'll be long?" he asked.

"There's no telling. She hasn't progressed very far yet."

"Can I bring you anything? Something to eat?"

"No, Jack, not for me. Doc can walk across the street if he wants to. But listen—my instinct tells me maybe he shouldn't have a whiskey tonight."

"Don't worry about Doc—his instincts are pretty good, too. Mel? My door will be unlocked."

"Thank you," she said. "If we finish up before morning, I'll sneak into your room. Would that be all right?"

He laughed his low, sexy laugh. "It's always all right, Melinda. I might not be able to sleep for hoping."

"I'll hope, too—but for Anne's sake, not yours or mine."

Anne's blood pressure was stable and her labor was difficult. Three hours later, in spite of walking, squatting and laboring, she was still only at four centimeters. At midnight she was at a possible five. Doc suggested a Pitocin drip and breaking her water, which Mel had just been considering. Her contractions were coming every two minutes. Near midnight Mel checked her and with great relief, found that she had progressed to eight centimeters. But then, just thirty minutes later, she was back at five. Mel had been down this road before—the cervix had swollen and appeared as though it was shrinking. That indicated they might not be able to have a vaginal birth. She examined Anne during a contraction when her cervix widened and literally tried to hold her cervix open to the great discomfort of the patient, but it just wasn't working. Anne was wet with sweat and growing more exhausted by the minute.

It was three-thirty in the morning when Mel made the call to John Stone. "God, I'm sorry to do this to you," she said. "I have a delivery that might be going south. I've got a patient who's been laboring for hours, stuck at five. Her cervix advanced to eight and swelled back to five. She's not progressing. We could ride this out, but mother is wilting and I have no indication that… I think it's very possible the baby's not going to fit. I suspect I'm going to need a cesarean."

"Did you pit her?"

"Yeah. Pitocin running and I broke her water."

"Okay, stop the pit, turn her on her left side. How long has she been laboring, stuck at four or five?"

"Ten hours with me. She labored at home for about eight."

"Have you tried stretching the cervix?"

"Unsuccessfully," she said. "Our ultrasound at your clinic showed a competent pelvis and average-size baby."

"Things change," he said. "Any fetal distress?"

"Not yet. The doptone shows a strong, regular, even heart rate, but mother's pressure is up a bit."

"You could ride this out awhile, but if she's exhausted, I vote for not waiting. I'll meet you at Valley. Can you make the drive or do you need helicopter transport?"

"We've got some real good shocks on that Hummer," she said. "Either way, she's an hour or more from the hospital. I'll wake Jack. Get his help."

Mel checked Anne once more; she had finally made six centimeters, but she was weakening. Anne's heart rate was increasing and the baby's had dropped just slightly. Jeremy was growing nervous and pale despite the number of times Mel reassured him that this wasn't unusual. It was starting to look like even if the baby was going to fit, Anne might not have the energy to push him out.

It was 4:00 a.m. when Mel called Jack. He didn't sound as though he'd been asleep. "Jack, I'm going to have to transport my patient to Valley Hospital for a cesarean. John's going to meet us there. I could use some help."

"Be right there," he said.

"I'll try to get her downstairs and then if you'll—"

"No, Mel," Jack said. "Leave her where she is. I'll get her downstairs. I wouldn't want both of you to fall."

"Okay, sure. Thanks."

Then she went back to her patient. Although Doc was standing by, this was Mel's case and a decision like this was entirely hers. "Anne," she said, gently brushing the hair away from her soaking brow. "We're going to transport you to Valley Hospital for a C-section...."

"Nooo," she cried. "I want to have the baby normally."

"Nothing abnormal about a C-section," she said. "It's a good operation, and it keeps you and the baby out of distress. Fortunately, we have the time so you're not at major risk. But with the distance to the hospital, we shouldn't wait until you are. It's going to be fine, Anne."

"Oh, God," she cried.

Then she was gripped by another hard contraction and fear gave way to pain. Her husband tried the breathing with her, but after all these hours of hard labor, it was futile. She had very little space between contractions and some residual pain that made it feel, to her, as if her contractions were continual, back to back.

Mel had had tough deliveries before, but it was different in the hospital, when you could just wheel your patient down the hall to surgery and let the surgeons and anesthesiologist take over; in a hospital she would give the mother every chance to make it through, if she wanted to try. It was different for her here, when the hospital was so far away, staffed and equipped for only routine procedures and surgeries. She couldn't help but feel very disappointed for Anne, who had so looked forward to a natural childbirth with her husband.

"Anne, it's just one of those things. Sometimes a C-section is the best answer," Mel said. "You're not going to have this baby here, but we want you to have as many healthy births as you desire."

"Of course you're right," she answered breathlessly.

Mel heard the front door open, Jack's feet on the stairs and then his voice outside the door. "Mel?"

She pushed the door open.

"Let me take her down for you. I'll drive you to the hospital in the Hummer."

"Thanks. Come in. Just let her get through this next contraction."

Jack stepped into the room and nodded at Jeremy. "How you doing, man?" he asked. "I'm going to carry your wife downstairs for you—you look pretty exhausted. You and Mel can ride in back with her and I'll drive." As soon as Anne seemed to relax a bit, Jack bent over the bed and lifted her easily into his arms. "Hang on, kiddo," he said. "I'll get you down before the next one hits, how's that?"

Mel grabbed her bag and said, "Jeremy, please get Anne's suitcase." She followed Jack downstairs, grabbed her coat and while Jack held Anne, she opened up the back of the Hummer and slid out the gurney. "Anne, I want you on your left side, please." Once she was situated, Mel and Jeremy climbed in on either side of her, kneeling, while Jack got behind the wheel and took off in the direction of Valley Hospital.

Mel kept the fetoscope handy and blood pressure cuff on Anne's upper arm. She checked her pressure and the fetal heartbeat every few minutes. They were nearly halfway when she reached forward and put a thankful hand on Jack's shoulder. His hand automatically came up to cover hers. "You were still awake," she said softly.

"In case you needed anything," he answered.

She gently squeezed his shoulder, but what she really wanted to do was throw her arms around him. She so appreciated the way he instinctively supported her in her work.

When they got to the hospital they entered the emergency room and, once inside, Mel handed Jack her coat and said, "You should move the SUV. Jeremy and I will take her up to labor and delivery. John's meeting us. I hate to ask you, but…"

"Of course I'll wait. I'll be right here. Don't worry about me."

"Am I going to be allowed in?" Jeremy asked while they were in the elevator.

"That's going to be up to Dr. Stone," she said. "If it were up to me, I wouldn't have a problem with it."

Mel pushed the gurney through the swinging doors and was very happy to see John standing at the sink, finishing his scrub. Hands held up, he turned toward her and gave a nod and a smile. "Number two is set up, Mel. The anesthesiologist is here."

Beside him at the adjoining sink, pumping the faucet pedal with her foot, was a nurse in scrubs, her mask tied around her neck. She looked over at Mel and with a sarcastic twist of her lips, said, "Another botched home birth?"

Mel's mouth dropped open and her eyes widened as if slapped. John whirled on the nurse, glaring at her. Then John turned back to Mel and said, "Can you scrub in with me, Mel?"

"I'm prepared to assist, Dr. Stone," the nurse said from behind him.

"Thank you, Juliette, but I'm leaning toward someone more professional. You and I will talk later." And to Mel, "You have less than fifteen minutes."

"Certainly. Jeremy wants to be there," she said.

"Of course. Juliette, find the father some scrubs. Mel, you'll find some in the locker room. Shake a leg."

Mel pushed the gurney to operating room number two and let the circulating nurse pull Anne into the room. She donned green scrubs in the locker room and joined Jeremy at the sink, saying, "If you scrub in, the doctor might be inclined to let you hold your son when he's born. Just like this," she said, demonstrating the scrubbing technique. "No guarantees on that, so no pouting. And you'll have to stay at Anne's head."

"Have you done this before?" he asked her. "Assisted in a C-section?"

"Many times," she said.

"Mel?" he asked. "It wasn't botched, was it?"

"Of course not. What Anne experienced wasn't all that unusual. You were there, Jeremy. You see anything happen that bothered you? I trust you would've said something or at least asked a question or two." She smiled at him. "You have one stubborn little boy to raise. Fortunately, we have a very good surgeon at our disposal."

By the time they entered the operating room, Anne had received her spinal from the anesthesiologist and was much more comfortable. John was ready to begin and Mel took her place next to him, her instruments lying out on the mayo stand.

"Scalpel," he said.

She slapped it into his hand. "Thank you," she said. "For what you did out there."

"She's a good nurse, but I never figured her for jealous. I apologize for her. We're ready to retract," he said. He chuckled. "You do a damn fine job, Mel. I'd let you deliver my wife in a second."

The ride back to Virgin River wasn't exactly quiet—Jeremy was a literal motormouth. Jack heard the details of the surgery several times. While Jeremy's wife was in recovery and his son in the nursery, he needed a lift home to fetch his own vehicle so he could go back. He chattered while Jack drove, and Mel's head lolled on the seat beside him.

"Exhausted, baby?" he asked her.

"I'll be fine after a nap," she said.

"Mel assisted Dr. Stone," Jeremy sounded from the back. "He asked her to. It was incredible. The things she knows how to do."

Jack glanced over at her and smiled. "You know what's incredible, Jeremy?" Jack said. He reached over and squeezed her thigh. "She never surprises me."

It was 9:00 a.m. before they got back to Virgin River. Mel checked in with Doc. "Mother and baby came through very well. John Stone is a wonderful, fast surgeon."

"Good call," he said. "For a city girl." And then he treated her to a rare smile.

She found there were only three people scheduled for morning appointments and Doc was more than capable. She had asked Jack to give her a call in five or six hours—she didn't want to sleep all day or she wouldn't sleep that night. But the labor and delivery had been taxing and she was spent.

Jack helped Preacher serve lunch, then he went to the river to fish for a couple of hours. He had a lot on his mind. It hadn't escaped him that Mel had been moody lately. He'd seen suspicious evidence of tears. And she wasn't drinking that end-of-the-day beer—she played with it for a little while before pushing it aside and asking for ice water.

At about three in the afternoon, while Preacher worked on preparing the evening meal, he went out to the cabin. He took off his boots on the front porch and tiptoed into the house. He stripped down to his boxers and slipped into the bed beside her, gently kissing her neck. She stirred slightly, turned her head and smiled at him.

"Now this is a good way to wake up," she murmured, closing her eyes again and snuggling closer to him.

He held her for a long while, then his hands began to move. Softly and sweetly. Before even seconds passed, her hands began to move, as well, and she pressed herself against him. When she began to strain against him, he got rid of the T-shirt she slept in and the boxers he still wore. He made gentle love to her, careful to keep her comfortable and safe, even as she picked up that eager pace, that frenetic yearning that drove him wild.

He knew her body as well as she did herself by now, and he knew exactly what gave her the most pleasure.

She settled back to earth slowly. "I thought you were going to call," she said.

"Isn't this better?"

"You always know what to do," she said.

"Not always," he said, holding her close. "Right now, for example. I'm not sure what to do."

"Why?" she asked, her eyes still closed, her face buried in his chest.

"When are you going to tell me?"

She lifted her head. "Tell you?"

"About the baby."

"But Jack, you know the baby and mother are—"

"The baby inside of you," he said, placing a large hand over her flat tummy.

A startled look crossed her features. She pushed him away a little bit. "Did someone say something to you?" she asked.

"No one had to say anything. Please tell me I'm not the last to know."

"I just saw John yesterday—and how in the world would you know?"

"Mel," he said, running the back of one knuckle along her cheek, "your body's changing. You haven't had a period. For a while, I thought maybe you'd had a hysterectomy or something because I haven't noticed a period since the first time we made love, but there's a blue box under the bathroom sink. You don't drink your beer, and you get nauseous from time to time. Not to mention being more tired than usual."

"Lord," she said. "You never think a man will notice. Not things like that."

"Well?"

She sighed. "I went to see John yesterday to confirm what I already suspected. I'm pregnant. Three months."

"You're a midwife. How could you not know at three weeks?"

"Because I assumed I was sterile. Infertile. Mark and I did everything to try to get a baby—even in vitro fertilization. To no avail. This was the last thing I ever expected."

"Ah," he said, finally clear on why she might keep it from him. "So, here we are," he said.

"I'm sorry, Jack. You must think I'm an idiot."

He kissed her. "Of course not. Mel, I'm in love with you."

She was frozen for a second. "Oh, God," she finally said, plummeted into tears. "Oh, God, Jack!" She buried her face in his chest and wept.

"Hey, no reason to cry, baby. You a little surprised? No more than me," he laughed. "I never thought this could happen to me. It hit me so hard, I damn near fell down. But I love you." She continued to softly cry. "It's okay, honey. It'll be okay." He stroked her hair. "You want to have a baby, obviously."

She lifted her head. "I wanted a baby so badly, I ached. But do you?" she asked. "I mean, you're forty."

"I want everything with you. Everything. Besides, I like babies. And I'm wild about pregnant women."

"When did you decide you knew for sure?" she asked him.

"At least a month ago." He put a hand over her breast. "Sore? Haven't you noticed the changes? Your nipples have darkened."

"I was in denial," she said, wiping at her tears. "I was so desperate for a baby—but I had accepted that it couldn't happen. I wouldn't have done it this way."

"And how would you have done it, exactly?"

"If I thought it even remotely possible I could get pregnant, I would have at least been sure you wanted a family, so that we could make a decision like this together. Fully informed. So if it happened, it would be okay. I hate that you've had this thrust on you. With no warning."

"That wasn't going to happen, not under the circumstances. It never would have occurred to you to try for a baby—convinced it was impossible. So—maybe it's a good thing it just happened like this."

"And what if it had gone the other way? What if I told you the thing I wanted most in the world was a baby, asked you to try for one with me?"

He pulled her a little closer. "I'd have been happy to help out." Then he smiled into her eyes.

"I don't know what to say. You just accept everything. You're amazing. I thought you might be very pissed."

"Nah. The only thing that disappoints me is that it took me this long to find you."

"Even with all my baggage?" she asked.

"I don't consider this baggage." He leaned over and kissed her belly. "I consider this the grand prize."

"You want it?" she asked.

"I told you," he said. "I want it. It makes me happy."

"God," she said in a breath. "I was afraid."

"Of?"

"Of you saying, 'Holy shit—I'm forty! What do I want with a baby?'"

He laughed at her. "I didn't say that, did I? Nah, I'm ready. A family sounds good."

"Jack," she said, "I'm still afraid."

"Of?"

"Of believing in us. My last stab at something like this ended so, so badly. I thought I'd never get over it. I'm not sure I am yet."

"Well, you're just going to have to take a leap of faith," he said.

"I think I can do that," she said. "If you're there to catch me."

"I'm here," he said. "I haven't let you down yet, have I?"

She put her hand against his face. "No, Jack. You sure haven't."

Jack had seen his brothers-in-law, all puffed up with testosterone pride when they'd gotten their wives pregnant, when the babies came. He never pretended to really understand it. He was too busy with his career, with his troops, when it seemed to him a woman getting pregnant was probably the worst career suicide a man could suffer. He didn't get their male egos; he thought his sisters were just getting fat and mean.

He got it now. He felt as though his chest might explode. There was a fire in his belly and it was all he could do to keep from running up a flag. He couldn't wait until he and Mel could make some plans, get married, tell the world they were lifetime partners and bringing a baby on board.

She shooed him out of the cabin, told him to go take care of the dinner crowd while she showered off that long night with a patient. She promised to drive into town to have a diet cola at the bar and tell those present that Anne and Jeremy and their baby boy were doing fine. Then later, they'd go back home together.

He was almost to town when he turned around to go back. Preacher might get testy, being stuck with the bar and cooking, too, but he just had to hold her for a minute more. He tiptoed up the porch steps, took off his boots and silently opened the door. He expected to hear the shower running, but instead he heard her weeping.

"I'm sorry," she was saying through her tears. "I'm so, so sorry." Then she sobbed briefly. "I never planned this. Oh, Mark, please understand…"

He stole a peek into the bedroom and saw Mel sitting on the edge of her bed, talking to the picture of her dead husband. It cut through him like a knife; damn near ripped his heart out.

"Please understand—this was the last thing I expected," she cried. "It's just the way it happened, and it took me by surprise. Total surprise. I promise I'll never forget you!"

He cleared his throat and she jumped. She looked at him, tears running down her cheeks. "Jack!" she gasped.

He held up a hand. "I'll go," he said. "You can work this out with Mark. I'll see you later."

He turned to leave and she ran after him, tugging on his shirt. "Jack, please…"

"It's okay, Mel," he said, profound sadness showing in his eyes. He forced a smile. "It's not as if I didn't know what I was up against."

"No! You don't understand!"

"Sure I do," he said, tenderly touching her cheek. "Take your time. I'm not going anywhere. Except back to the bar. I think I need a drink."

Jack walked out of the cabin, collected his boots on her porch and got back into his truck. *So,* he thought, *probably the best day of my life, turned to total shit. She's still back there, with him. She can love you like she's yours, but she's not. Not yet.*

Hadn't he always known this was the risk he was taking, as long as he loved her? That she might not be able to let go of him? Ever?

What the hell, he told himself. *She might never really belong to me; good thing he can't come back from the grave and snatch her away. But that baby is* mine. *And I want it. I want her. Whatever she has to spare...*

Fifteen

Mel showered, put on clean clothes and prepared to go to the bar to take her medicine. She felt terrible; her heart ached when she thought of the look in Jack's eyes. He never should have witnessed that performance. It must have shattered him. She could only hope he would forgive her.

She brought a change of clothes and her makeup for work the next day. If Jack didn't want to come back to her cabin with her, she would force her company on him. They had to get beyond this. This was her fault. It wasn't just the two of them anymore. He wanted this baby. He wanted her *and* the baby. She was going to find a way to make this right.

There were only about a dozen customers in the bar when she got there—the Bristols and Carpenters sitting at a table for four, Hope and Doc at the bar, a couple of men playing cribbage with a pitcher of beer, and a young family. Jack stood behind the bar and lifted his chin slightly in greeting as she entered. It was a very subdued gesture; there was going to be penance to pay.

She stopped and chatted briefly with the Bristols and Carpenters, filling them in on the Givens baby, before going to the bar. She got onto the stool next to Doc. "Did you get any rest today?" she asked him.

"I don't sleep in daylight," he grumbled. He popped an antacid and Jack put a whiskey in front of him.

"Long night?" Hope asked her.

"Long night for the Givenses," she said. "But they're going to be fine."

"Good work, Mel," she said. "I knew I was smart to get you up here." She stubbed out her cigarette and left, chatting her way out the door.

Without being asked, Jack put a cola in front of her. She mouthed the words, *I'm sorry.* His lips curved just slightly, hurt in his eyes, but he leaned toward her and placed a gentle kiss on her brow. *Ow,* she thought. *This is bad.*

And it just got worse. They had only the most superficial conversation while Mel picked at her dinner, but determined, she waited out the emptying of the bar. It was eight o'clock by the time Preacher was sweeping the floor and Jack was putting up clean glasses. "Are we going to talk about it?" she quietly asked Jack.

"How about we let it go and move forward," he said.

"Jack," she whispered so that Preacher wouldn't hear. "I love you."

"You don't have to say that."

"But it's true. Please believe me."

He lifted her chin and put a light kiss on her lips. "Okay," he said. "I believe you."

"Oh, God," she said, tears gathering in her eyes.

"Don't, Mel," he said. "Don't start crying again. I'm afraid I won't understand why—and it'll make things worse."

She sucked it back, forced herself to still the nerves that were tightening inside her. Her fleeting thought was, *God, what will I do if he's through with me on account of that?* "I'm going to your room," she told him. "I'm going to stay there until you come to me and I'm going to convince you, somehow, that we belong to each other. Especially now."

He gave a nod that was so slight, it was almost imperceptible, so she got off her stool and walked through the back of the bar to his quarters. Once alone, she couldn't suppress the tears. They flowed freely down her cheeks. *He thinks I'm going to spend the rest of my life explaining myself to my dead husband, apologizing for how I feel about Jack. Well, that's what I was doing—what's he to think? He won't believe me if I tell him that's not true, not how it's going to be. It was just a one-time thing—the shock, the exhaustion, the high emotional state I'm in.*

Mel sat in the big chair in his room, revisiting in her mind that night she sat in this spot, drenched from the rain, and he gently undressed her, dried her and put her to bed. That was when she knew, without a doubt, there was a partner here for her, even if she couldn't admit it to herself for quite a while. Since the ultrasound, she was pretty convinced she had conceived that night. Jack opened her up, showed her passion she didn't know existed and put his baby in her. It was nothing short of a miracle—the love, the passion, the baby. She just didn't know how difficult it would be to make that transition into a new life. A second life. A completely different life.

She sat in that chair for an hour. Waiting.

Jack put up all his clean glasses and dishes, wiped down the bar and poured himself a drink. There was a particular, old single malt, an aged Glenlivet, that he saved for special occasions. Or emergencies.

Preacher put away his broom and went to the bar. "Everything okay, man?" he asked.

Jack pulled down a glass and poured a shot for his friend. He lifted his toward Preacher in something of a toast and said solemnly, "Mel's pregnant." Then Jack took the shot in one swallow.

"Aw, man," Preacher said. "What are you gonna do?"

"I'm going to be a father," he said. "I'm going to marry her."

Preacher picked up his glass and lifted it tentatively, taking a drink. "You sure about that?"

"Yeah, I'm sure."

"That what you want, man?"

"Absolutely."

Preacher grinned. "Sarge. A family man. Who'd think?"

Jack tipped the bottle once more, over both glasses. "Yeah," Jack said.

"Seems like, maybe, things aren't so hot right now," Preacher said.

"Nah," he lied. "Just found out," he further lied. "It's gonna work out great. It's gonna be perfect." Then he smiled. "You know I never do anything I don't want to do. Uncle Preacher." He threw back the second shot and put his glass on the bar. "Good night."

Jack felt bad about leaving Mel in his room for so long, but they both needed some time to compose themselves. If there were going to be more tears, this one time he wanted her to get that out of the way on her own. There's only so much one man could do, so he didn't rush to her. She was going to be feeling a little desperate—pregnant, just caught apologizing for it to the picture of Mark, afraid Jack wouldn't be able to deal with that. There was nothing either of them could do about it—Jack had known from the beginning that Mark was still there, in her life, in her heart. He would never have all of her. Well, then, he'd make the most of what he did have. He wasn't going to make her grovel; he was just going to love the heck out of her. He could manage this, even if it wasn't the most ideal situation. In time, maybe she'd come around. Mark's memory could fade enough so that even if Jack wasn't the only man in her life, he would come to feel like the most important one. Maybe when she held their child, she would realize life was for the living.

He walked in, looked across the room at her and leaned down to pull off his boots. He yanked his shirt out of his pants and took it off, hanging it on the peg in his closet. He removed his belt and tossed it aside. Then he approached her and put out a hand to her.

She put her hand in his and let him draw her to her feet. She leaned her head against his chest and said again, "I'm sorry. I love you. I want to be with you."

His arms went around her and he answered, "That's good enough for me."

Jack kissed her tenderly.

"You've had a couple of drinks," she said. "Scotch."

"It seemed like the thing to do," he said. He slowly began to undress her, leaving her clothes in a pile on the floor, because when words failed him he had never failed to be able to speak to her body. There was no confusion about this—when he touched her, she was all his. When she responded to him, she held nothing back. There might be a glitch in her heart, some of it stuck in the past. But her body came alive under his lips, his hands.

He carried her to his bed, laid her sweetly on the sheets and went to work on her. He touched her, kissed and caressed her in the ways he knew filled her up, pleased her, gave her joy, released her. She rose to him, hot and ready, wrapping herself around him, giving. Taking. Crying out.

God, he didn't know he could want this much. Love this much.

Okay, he thought—*here's the reality. He would always have this.* He would make her body sing just as she sent him reeling into the most incredible madness a man can feel. He would hold her every night and wake up with her every morning and there would be many times, like this, when they would come together in this incomparable passion and no matter what else was going on, this mutual joy belonged only to them. Just the two of them. There were no ghosts present in these moments.

Sufficient compensation. Sweet consolation.

"Jack," she said, snuggled up against him. "I hate that I hurt you."

He buried his face in her hair and inhaled the sweet scent. "Let's not talk about that anymore. It's behind us. We have a lot in front of us."

"Would it be a good idea for me to go to Joey for a little while? Give you some space? Try to get my head together?"

He rose over her and looked into her eyes. "Don't, Mel. Don't run just because we hit a rough patch. We'll work through this."

"You sure?"

"Mel," he said hoarsely, his voice a mere whisper, "you have my baby inside you. I have to be a part of that. Come on…"

She fought the tears that threatened. "I know it must be hard to deal with an emotional basket case like me."

He smiled at her and said, "I've heard that pregnant women get like that."

"I think I'm just like that, period."

"Marry me," he said.

She touched his beautiful face. "You don't have to."

"Melinda, six months ago we were two people without attachments. Two people who had accepted we would never have any—and that we'd never have families. Now we have it all. We have each other and a baby. A baby we both want. Let's not screw this up."

"Are you sure?"

"I've never been more sure about anything. I want this. If you can't stay here, I'll go anywhere you want to go."

"But Jack, you love it here!"

"Don't you realize I love you more? I need you in my life. You and our baby. God, Mel—I don't care where that happens. As long as it happens."

"Jack," she said in a whisper. "What if you change your mind? What if something happens? You have to remember, I never thought anything terrible would happen to—"

He put a finger on her lips, stopping her. He didn't want to hear his name. Not now. "Shh," he said. "I want you to trust me. You know you're safe with me."

Mel awoke humming. The song this morning was "Mamma Mia" by ABBA, of all things. It made her smile. She got out of bed and showered. When she came out of the shower and put on one of Jack's shirts, she found a steaming cup of coffee on the bathroom counter. There was a note under it. *Half-caf. Daddy.* Jack was already up and in the bar, taking care of breakfast. Taking care of her. Robbing her of caffeine.

She dressed for the day; she had been so out of focus lately, she had no idea what kind of schedule lay ahead. She couldn't remember making any appointments for the morning. Still, she wasn't rushing to Doc's. It was early and she had a very important phone call to make.

"I wish I could see the look on your face when I tell you this, Joey," Mel said. "I hope you're sitting down. I'm pregnant."

There was a gasp, then silence.

"Pregnant," she said again. "Totally knocked up."

"Are you *sure?*"

"Three months," she said.

"Oh, my God! Mel!"

"I know. Kind of blew my mind, too."

"Three months? Let's see…"

"Don't bother trying to do the math. I haven't had a period since he touched me for the first time. I guess he's potent enough for both of us. At first, I thought it so impossible, an absurd fantasy. I figured I was late because of stress, change, how weird my life is. But it's real. I had an ultrasound."

"Mel! How is this possible?"

"Don't ask me—stranger things have happened. But not around here, apparently. I'm surrounded by women who were pretty sure they couldn't get pregnant and voilà! There's a rumor about the water… I'm thinking of calling my L.A. infertility specialist to tell him about this place."

"What are you going to do?"

"I'm going to marry Jack."

"Mel—do you love him?" Joey asked, her voice subdued. Cautious.

Mel drew in a breath, trying to calm her voice, which she knew would be tremulous and emotional. "I do," she said. "Joey, I love him so much, I almost ache with it. I never thought I could love this much. I was in denial about that for a while, too."

"Mel," Joey said, then began to cry. "Oh, my sweet baby."

"It made me feel guilty, like I was doing something wrong—I was so committed to the idea that I'd lost my one true love and would never feel anything even close to that again in my life. I never considered the possibility that I might find something even more powerful. It seemed, briefly, like a betrayal. Jack even caught me crying to Mark's picture that I was sorry, that I didn't expect it to happen, and promising never to forget him. God. It was an awful moment."

"Baby girl, you haven't done anything wrong. You've been through such a lot."

"Well, in my sane state, I know that. Jack knew about my problems, and he just hung in there, just kept loving me and loving me, putting all my needs ahead of his own, promising me I'd be safe with him, that I could trust him. Oh, God," she said, tears coming in spite of the fact that she was so, so happy. "God, he's wonderful. Joey," she said in a near whisper, "he wants the baby as much as I do."

"This is just unbelievable. When are you getting married? Because we're going to be there."

"We haven't had a chance to even talk about it—I just broke it to him yesterday and he asked me last night. I'll let you know when I know."

"But does this mean you're staying there?"

Mel laughed. "You were right, you know—coming here was completely crazy. It was irrational. To think

I'd choose to go to a town where there's no mall, much less a day spa, and one restaurant that doesn't have a menu? Please. No medical technology, ambulance service or local police—how is it I thought that would be easier, less stressful? I almost slid off the mountain on my way into town!"

"Ah… Mel…"

"We don't even have cable, no cell phone signal most of the time. And there's not a single person here who can admire my Cole Haan boots which, by the way, are starting to look like crap from traipsing around forests and farms. Did you know that any critical illness or injury has to be airlifted out of here? A person would be crazy to find this relaxing. Renewing." She laughed. "The state I was in, when I was leaving L.A., I thought I absolutely had to escape all the challenges. It never occurred to me that challenge would be good for me. A completely new challenge."

"Mel…"

"When I told Jack I was pregnant, after promising him I had the birth control taken care of, he should have said, 'I'm outta here, babe.' But you know what he said? He said, 'I have to have you and the baby in my life, and if you can't stay here, I'll go anywhere.'" She sniffed a little and a tear rolled down her cheek. "When I wake up in the morning, the first thing I do is check to see if there are deer in the yard. Then I wonder what Preacher's in the mood to fix for dinner. Jack's usually already gone back to town—he likes splitting logs in the early morning—half the town wakes up to the sound of his ax striking wood. I see him five or ten times through the day and he always looks at me like we've been apart for a year. If I have a patient in labor, he stays up all night, just in case I need something. And when there are no patients at night, when he holds me before I fall asleep, bad TV reception is the last thing on my mind.

"Am I staying here? I came here because I believed I'd lost everything that mattered, and ended up finding everything I've ever wanted in the world. Yeah, Joey. I'm staying. Jack's here. Besides, I belong here now. I belong to them. They belong to me."

Right after a light breakfast, she headed for Doc's. She supposed it was in order to tell him right away, but when she walked into the house, she was greeted by quiet. Good, she thought. No patients yet. She went to Doc's office and tapped lightly on the door, then pushed it open. He was sitting in the chair at his desk, leaning back, his eyes closed. *Hmm. Doesn't sleep in daylight, huh?* She stood over him. It was good to see Doc docile for once.

Mel was about to leave and wait for a better time, but something made her take a closer look at Doc. His eyes were pinched closed, his face in a grimace and his coloring wasn't right. He was gray. She reached down and squeezed his wrist with the forefingers of one hand. His pulse was racing. Mel felt Doc's brow and found his skin clammy. His eyes opened into slits. "What is it?" she asked him.

"Nothing," he said. "Heartburn."

Heartburn does not make your pulse race and your skin clammy, she thought. She ran for the stethoscope and blood pressure cuff in the exam room, returning to him. "You going to tell me what it is—or make me guess?"

"I told you… Nothing. I'll be fine in a few minutes."

She took his blood pressure, though she had to struggle with him for cooperation. "Did you have breakfast?" she asked him.

"A while ago."

"What did you have? Bacon and eggs? Sausage?"

"It wasn't that great. Preacher's a little off on the cooking…"

His blood pressure was elevated. "Any chest pains?" she asked.

"No."

She palpated his abdomen, although excess lipid tissue on his pot belly made it impossible to feel his internal organs while he was sitting upright. And he slapped at her hand, trying to push her away. But as she palpated, he grunted in pain. "How many of them have you had?" she asked him.

"How many what?"

"Attacks. Like this."

"One or two," he said.

"Don't lie to the nice little nurse," she chastised. "How long has this been going on?" She pulled the lids back on his eyes and they had begun to yellow. He was jaundicing. "You waiting for your liver to blow?"

"It'll pass."

He was having a major league gallbladder attack, and she wasn't sure that was all. She didn't even think about it—she picked up the phone and called the bar. "Jack," she said, "come over, please. I have to get Doc to the hospital." And she hung up.

"No," Doc said.

"Yes," she said. "If you argue with me now, I'll get Jack and Preacher to put you in a fireman's carry and dump you in the Hummer. That should make your belly feel good." She looked at his face. "How's your back?"

"Terrible. This one is kind of bad."

"You're getting jaundiced, Doc," she said. "We can't wait. I suspect you're in a biliary crisis. I'm going to start an IV and I don't want any lip."

Before she could get the needle in, both Jack and Preacher arrived. "We'll get him in the car and I'll drive you," Jack said. "What's the matter with him?"

"I think it's a gallbladder attack, but he's not talking. It's serious. His blood pressure is up and he's in terrible pain."

"Waste of time," Doc said. "It'll pass."

"Please be still," she implored. "I don't want to have to ask these big boys to hold you down."

Once the IV was in, she made a mad dash to the drug cabinet while Jack and Preacher each got on either side of him, walking him slowly out the door, Jack holding the Ringer's over his head. When they got to the Hummer she joined them. Doc said, "I'm not lying down."

"I think you should—"

"I can't," he said. "Bad enough sitting up."

"All right then, we'll take out the gurney and put up the backseat. I'll pull the IV bag hook forward and sit beside you. Have you taken anything for the pain yet?"

"I was just starting to have very kind thoughts toward morphine," he said. Jack adjusted the backseat, leaving the gurney on Doc's porch. Doc climbed clumsily into the backseat. "We just don't have good enough drugs," he muttered.

"Can you make it to the hospital without drugs? Give the doctor a clean slate?"

"Arrrggghhh," he grumbled.

"If you insist, I'll give you something—but it would be better to let the E.R. decide what's best." She took a breath. "I grabbed some morphine."

He peered at her through slits. "Hit me," he said. "It's just god-awful."

She sighed and drew up a syringe from the vial in her bag, putting it right into the IV. It took only moments for him to say, "Ahhh..."

"Have you seen anyone about this?" she asked him.

"I'm a doctor, young woman. I can take care of myself."

"Oh, brother," she said.

"There's a clinic in Garberville," Jack said as he started the car. "It's closer than Valley Hospital."

"We're going to need a surgeon," Mel informed him.

"I'm not going to need surgery," the old boy argued.

"You a betting man?" was all she said.

Doc Mullins rested a bit easier with the narcotic in him, which was good since it was over an hour, even with Jack's fast and skillful driving. It wasn't the distance so much as the roads—just getting to the county road that connected with the highway twisted and turned and was slow going. Mel watched out the window, remembering that first night she came here, terrified of these sharp twists and turns, the sheer drops, steep climbs. Now, with Jack managing the Hummer, she was comfortable. Before long they were out of the hills and speeding through the valley. With her attention focused on Doc, she couldn't fully appreciate the landscape. It did occur to her, however, that every time she traveled anywhere around this county, she was amazed by the beauty as if seeing it for the first time.

She had a fleeting thought that if anything bad happened to Doc, it would be down to only her. How was she going to have a baby and take care of a town?

She thought about Joey's question—are you staying

there? It made her smile. It would hardly seem a punishment to live out her life in this glorious place.

This was only Mel's second visit to the emergency room—the first was with Connie. She had taken Jeremy and Anne to labor and delivery the night the baby came, so she didn't really know the staff in E.R. They all knew Doc, however. He'd been putting in regular appearances there for upwards of forty years. And they greeted Mel very enthusiastically, as if she were an old friend.

Doc was not one to allow fussing; he made it plain he didn't think he needed to be there. Mel and Jack were seated outside the exam room while the emergency room doctor checked him over. Then another doctor went into the exam room and Doc was heard to bellow, "Aw, for Christ's sake! Can't I get a better surgeon than you? I don't want to die on the goddamn table!"

Mel blanched, but she saw that some of the staff was chuckling. After a bit the surgeon came out to them. He had a smile on his face. He held out his hand. "Dr. Simon, Miss...?"

She stood and took his hand. "Monroe," she said. "Mel Monroe. I work with Doc. Is he going to be all right?"

"Oh, I think so. Doctors. Great patients, aren't we? I'm going to admit him and that gallbladder has to come out, but we can't take him into surgery until we get him out of this biliary crisis. That could take a day or week. Good call, Miss Monroe. I assume he didn't assist you a bit."

"He tried not to. May I see him?"

"Of course."

She found Doc in a raised position in the bed while the nurse was fiddling with the IV. The E.R. doctor was writing in the chart and when he saw her, gave a nod of

hello. And on Doc's face was the unhappy expression
she had come to view with fondness.

Mel looked around the E.R.—far smaller and less
crowded than the one she was used to in L.A. Still,
memories flooded back to her—the days and nights
she had spent working in that environment. The adrenaline rush of emergencies; the edgy environment that
had excited and stimulated her. At the nurses' station
a young doctor was bent over a nurse, reading over
her shoulder, making her laugh at some whispered re-
mark. That could have been Mel and Mark a few years
ago. She let her eyes slowly close as she realized that
she had moved completely beyond that. That familiar
pang of longing did not plague her anymore. Now the
only man she longed for waited for her just outside this
room, prepared to go through anything with her. Her
hand crept absently to her tummy, resting there. *It was
all right,* she realized. *What I suffered was very bad;
what I have is very good.*

"Young woman," Doc snapped. "You gonna be sick?"

"Hmm?" she said, coming out of the haze. "No. Of
course not."

"For a minute there you looked like you were going
to cry. Or puke."

She just smiled at him. "Sorry. I was on another
planet there for a second. Are you feeling better?"

"I'll live. You'd better go. There might be patients
back at the house."

"I'll come back for your surgery," she said.

"No! I'm probably going to die in surgery anyway
with that young pup cutting me up—you're needed back
in Virgin River. Someone has to look after things. I
guess you're in charge. God help us all."

"I'll call to see how you're doing, and I will come

back when you have surgery. And Doc? Try to behave yourself. Try not to get thrown out of here."

"Ach," he scoffed.

She put her small cool hand on his wizened brow. "Feel better. I'll watch your practice."

In an uncharacteristically soft voice, she heard him say, "Thank you."

On the drive back to Virgin River Mel said, "He's going to need time to recover before he can start seeing patients again. I suppose I'll be staying at his house for a while after he gets home."

Doc's age, weight and blood pressure put him at a disadvantage in both surgery and recovery. It was a week before the surgeon could operate, and while the normal hospital stay for a cholesystectomy was brief—couple of days at most—they kept Doc for another week.

For those two weeks, Mel drove back and forth to Valley Hospital to check on him, plus managed the meager amount of patient care in Virgin River. June and John offered assistance, should she need it, but she was holding up fine. She stayed at the clinic during the days, spent her nights with Jack across the street, and the only huge inconvenience was planning and executing a wedding.

Jack told his dad and sisters that he and Mel were marrying, news which was met with much approval and excitement. He saved the news about the baby; he wanted to see the looks on their faces when they found out. Since there were no inns or motels in Virgin River, the couple decided they'd have a small, family-only wedding in Sacramento as soon as possible—at the Sheridan house. Jack told his sisters to plan something simple, quiet and quick for three weeks from the date Doc had gone into the hospital. He and Mel would drive down, tie the knot and hurry home. "What about a honeymoon?" Sam asked.

"Don't worry about that," Jack said. And what he thought was, *I'm going to be on a honeymoon for the rest of my life.*

Rick took the news of the pregnancy and fast approaching marriage with a bit of shock. "You okay with this?" he asked Jack.

"Oh, yeah. Big time. I'm ready for a family, Rick." He put his hand around the back of the boy's neck and pulled him against his shoulder. "In addition to you and Preach, that is. You okay with it?"

"Hey, man. You're not too young, that's for sure." Then he grinned. "I really thought she was out of your league."

"She is, buddy. But what the heck."

The evening before Mel was due to pick up Doc at Valley Hospital and bring him home, Jack asked, "Do you have to spend the nights at Doc's?"

"Probably just for a few days—long enough to make sure he's getting around all right. He's ambulatory at the hospital, but he's miserable. His grimace isn't just from being ornery at the moment. He'll need pain medication—and I don't want him administering his own. He could get confused and overdose."

Jack sat in the big chair in his room and said, "Come here," to Mel. She went to him and he pulled her down onto his lap. "I have something for you." He pulled a small box out of his pocket, shocking her into silence. It was definitely a ring box. "I don't know how practical this is in a place like Virgin River. It might be a little fussy. But I couldn't help myself. I want to give you everything—but this will have to do."

She opened the box to find a diamond ring so beautiful it brought tears to her eyes. It was a wide gold band with three large diamonds set in; classy and understated, yet very rich and unique. "Jack, what were you thinking? This is beautiful! The diamonds are huge!"

"I understand if you can't wear it often, given your work. And if you don't like the design—"

"Are you kidding? It's gorgeous!"

"I went ahead and got a band like it, no diamonds. Is that okay?"

"Only perfect. Where in the world did you find this thing?"

"Not the Virgin River jewelry store, that's for sure. I had to drive over to the coast. Are you sure you like it?"

She threw her arms around his neck. "You gave me a baby," she said. "I wasn't expecting this, too!"

"I didn't know I was giving you a baby," he said, grinning. "This, I did on purpose."

She laughed at him and said, "People will think we're uppity."

"Mel—I got it a while ago. When I first thought you might be pregnant. Probably before you did. Even if it had turned out you weren't, I was set on this. This idea to marry you, to have my life with you… It's not something I feel like I have to do. It's what I want."

"God, how did this happen?"

"I don't care how," he said.

He went with her the next day to pick up Doc and bring him home. Mel got him settled in his bed at home where he proved to be a very annoying patient; however, it seemed he would make a full recovery and be back to his old schedule in no time. He might not be seeing patients by the time Mel and Jack slipped down to Sacramento for a couple of days, but he'd be able to look after himself.

Meanwhile, with all Mel had to do, running the clinic and looking after Doc, Jack, Preacher or Ricky were bringing his meals, and Mel was able to escape to the bar for an hour here and there, just for a change of scenery. Nights she spent in the hospital bed down the hall from Doc. Alone.

After just a few such nights, she was startled awake by noise downstairs. She sat up sleepily and listened. It was unusual, but not unheard-of, for someone to come pounding at the doctor's door after hours, so when Mel heard the knocking, she rolled over and looked at the clock. It was 1:00 a.m., which implied an emergency and as she was shrugging into her robe, she began to form contingency plans if she had to go out on a call. Jack could come to the house to look after Doc—or maybe go with her, leaving Doc to sleep through till morning without her.

She remembered hearing about that near-fatal truck accident some years ago and thought, *What if I'm not enough help? Who could I call?*

When she opened the front door, no one was there. Then the pounding came again and she realized that whoever it was had come to the back, to the kitchen door. She looked through the glass to see the face of that man from the compound. Calvin. If he was coming to fetch her out to that camp, she wouldn't go. She'd have to send him away. If he'd come to ask her for drugs, she thought she might have to call Jack.

She opened the door with an excuse on her lips when he rushed her, the back of his forearm against her neck. He shoved her backward with enough force that she knocked over a chair, crashed into the countertop and sent coffee cups that were drying in the dish rack hurtling to the floor. He had a snarl on his lips, a glazed look in his eyes and a big hunting knife in his hand. She screamed, a noise that was quickly cut off as he grabbed her by the hair and put the knife to her throat.

"Drugs," he said simply. "Just gimme what you got, then I'm getting the hell out of these mountains."

"They're in there… I have to get the key," she said, indicating the drug cabinet.

"Forget it," he said. As he held her, he tried kicking the wooden door. The whole cabinet shook and wobbled; she could hear the contents bouncing around.

"Don't!" she cried. "You'll break the vials! You want the drugs or not?"

He stopped. "Where's the key?" he said.

"In the office."

He pulled her backward, flipped the lock on the back door and said, "Come on. Let's move it." With one arm around her waist and the knife at her throat, he walked her out of the kitchen. She had no option but to lead him to the office.

He held her in front of him, hostage style, as they slowly shuffled down the hall to the office. As she opened the drawer to reach for the key, he started to laugh. He grabbed her hand. "I'll take this," he said, pulling at her ring.

"Oh, God," she cried, retreating. But he easily pulled her back by the hair and threatened her with the knife right in front of her face. She froze and let him pull off the ring.

He shoved it in his pocket and said, "Hurry up. I ain't got all night."

"Don't hurt me," she said. "You can have anything you want."

He laughed. "And what if I want you, too?"

She thought she might vomit on the spot. She willed herself to be brave, to be strong, to let this ordeal end.

But he was going to kill her. She knew who he was, what he'd done, and suddenly she knew—he was going to kill her. As soon as he had what he wanted, that knife would slice across her throat.

Lying on top of the desk were the Hummer keys, obvious by the trademark and remote. He scooped them up, put them in his pocket with the ring and steered her out of the office back toward the kitchen. And he muttered, "Asshole doesn't pay me enough to sit in the woods with Maxine and a bunch of old bums. But this should catch me up." And then he laughed.

Jack rolled out of bed to answer the ringing phone. "Mel's in trouble," came Doc's gravelly voice. "Someone's trying to get in the back of the house. Downstairs. She's down there. Glass broke."

Jack dropped the phone and grabbed his jeans off the chair. No time for a shirt or shoes, he took his 9 mm handgun out of the holster that hung on a hook in the closet, checked to be sure it was loaded and that he had one in the chamber and bolted out the door. He crossed the street at a dead run. He didn't think—he was on automatic. His jaw ground, his temples pulsed and his blood was roaring in his ears.

There was an old truck at the clinic beside Doc's truck and Mel's Hummer. He knew exactly who was in there.

He looked into the front door window in time to see Calvin pushing Mel into the office, and they had come from the direction of the kitchen where the drug cabinet sat. He ran around to the back of the house and looked into the kitchen door window; they were still out of sight. Then they came back into view from down the hall and Jack ducked—but not before he saw that Calvin had a big, serrated knife against her neck. He waited; he wasn't going to give him the time or opportunity to flee or to do any damage to Mel before fleeing. It was a long few seconds as he waited for them to get back into the kitchen. He could hear their movements, the man's hostile voice as he held Mel.

They were almost to the drug cabinet when Jack kicked the door. It crashed open and bounced off the opposite wall, but he was already inside. Legs braced apart, arms raised, pistol pointed at the man who held his woman, he said, "Put down the knife. Carefully."

"You're gonna let me out of here, and she'll come with me to be sure," Calvin said.

Knife against her throat, Mel looked at Jack and saw a man she had never seen before. The expression on his face should be enough to terrify the man who held her. Bare chested, barefoot, his jeans zipped but not buttoned, his shoulders and arms frighteningly huge, big tattoos on his swollen biceps, he looked like a wild man. He looked over the barrel of the gun, his eyes narrow, and a set to his jaw told her he was going to act. There was no question. He did not look at Mel, but at Calvin. And for a woman terrified of guns, she was unafraid. She believed in him. She knew, in that instant, that he would risk his life for her, but he would never put her at risk. Never. If he was going to make a move, she wouldn't be in danger. Her expression went from frightened to trusting.

Jack had less than a four-inch target—the left side

of the man's head. Right next to that was Mel's head, Mel's beautiful face. At her throat, the blade. He didn't even have to think about it—he wasn't going to lose her like this.

"You have one second."

Out of the corner of his eye, Jack saw her cast a look his way, a look that in that split second told him she loved him, believed in him. Then her eyes dropped closed and her head dipped ever so slightly to the right.

"Back off, man—"

Jack took his shot, blowing the man backward, the knife flying out of his hand.

Mel ran to Jack. The arm that held the gun was dangling at Jack's side and his other arm went around her. Jack held her close as she let out a long slow breath against his bare chest, clinging to him. He never took his eyes off the offender. A nice, neat hole was bored right into his head, a growing pool of blood spreading under him as he lay motionless.

They stood like that for a while, Mel trying to catch her breath and Jack watching. Ready. She pulled away enough to look up at him and was nearly startled anew by an expression so fierce, so angry. "He was going to kill me," she said in a whisper.

His eyes remained on the man as he said, "I will never let anything happen to you."

The sound of running footfalls came up behind them, but Jack didn't turn.

Preacher stopped suddenly in the doorway, a hand braced on each side as he leaned in, panting. He looked into the kitchen, saw the man on the floor, Mel in Jack's protective embrace, the gun dangling at Jack's side. And Preacher's expression went dark, his brows drawn close, his mouth turned down in a scowl. He walked into the kitchen, kicked the knife across the floor and bent to the man. He felt the man's neck for a carotid pulse. He looked over his shoulder at Jack and shook his head. "It's okay, Jack. It's done."

Jack put the gun on the table and, with Mel still protected against him, turned to the wall phone. He lifted the receiver, punched a few numbers and said, "This is Jack Sheridan in Virgin River. I'm at Doc Mullins's—I just killed a man."

Sixteen

It took the sheriff's deputy, Henry Depardeau, longer to arrive in Virgin River than it took him to determine that Jack had acted in defense of Mel, whose life was in danger. Just the same, Jack's second call that night had been to Jim Post, June Hudson's husband. That background in law enforcement could come in handy. Jim was there faster than Henry. And, Jack learned that night, Jim was a former DEA agent who had actually worked in the area prior to retirement.

"We better have a little look at Calvin's camp," Jim said. "If it's just a little compound of vagrants, I don't see that as a problem. But I suspect it might be more than that. If so—we'll want to tell the sheriff."

Jack was invited to spend what was left of the night with Mel at Doc's. She saw a side of him she didn't know existed. This gentle, tender giant was gripped with fury, and it was a silent and impressive fury. He held her through the night, both of them in one small hospital bed. Sleep was difficult for her and she was fitful, but every time she opened her eyes and looked at him, she found him awake, watching over her. She would look up at his face, his tense jaw and eyes narrowed in anger, but when she put her hand against his cheek, he would relax his features and turn soft eyes on her. "It's all right, baby," he said. "Try to get some sleep. Don't be afraid."

"I'm not afraid while I'm with you," she whispered, and this was the truth.

The next morning, early, June and Jim arrived in town. June came over to the clinic while Jim went to Jack's. "I just wanted to make sure you aren't having any stress-related problems with your pregnancy," June said. "Any cramping, spotting?"

"Everything seems to be fine. Except for those frequent shudders I feel when I think about what might have happened."

"I'm just going to spend a couple of hours in town," June said. "If you have patients, I'll help. Do you need to rest?"

"Jack was here last night. I don't think he slept, but I got a little rest. Where's the baby?" Mel asked.

"Susan has Jamie, and John and my dad have the clinic." She smiled. "We country folk have to be flexible."

"What's Jim doing?" Mel asked.

"He's with Jack and Preacher. They won't be long. They're going to have to take a look at that place the man came from, Mel. Be sure there's no one else out there that will come into town and threaten a life."

"Oh, God," she said.

"I think they can handle it," June said. "I guess it has to be done."

"That's not it, June. I've been out to that camp a dozen times. I didn't see Calvin Thompson there except the very first time, when I went with Doc to help him treat some injuries. But I went, though I'd been told not to. And I was a little nervous and scared, but it never once occurred to me that someone from there might hold a knife to my throat and—" She stopped, unable to go on.

"Good Lord," June said. "What were you doing?"

Mel shrugged. Her voice was small when she answered. "They looked hungry."

A slow smile grew on June Hudson's face. "And you thought you weren't one of us. What hooey."

Jack, Preacher and Jim piled into Jack's truck and drove back into the woods. The compound was less than twenty miles away, but traversed by so many old logging roads and concealed roads, it took almost an hour to get there. They were so buried, one would never be inclined to worry that these people would pose a dangerous threat.

The young man with the knife, Calvin Thompson, hadn't been with them long. He wasn't just a vagrant, but a violent felon. It hadn't taken Henry Depardeau long to learn he had a long drug-related criminal record from other California cities and had been hiding in the forest to dodge felony warrants for his arrest. It was likely that Maxine had brought him to her father's hideaway in the forest.

When they got to the camp, Jim Post said, "Yeah, that's what I figured." He pointed to the camouflaged semitrailer, a generator beside it. The three men from Virgin River got out of the truck, brandishing rifles of the caliber that would kill a black bear with one shot. Rifles that would cut a man in half. Of course there was no one in evidence. "Paulis!" Jack called.

A skinny, wasted-looking, bearded man came out of a hut. A shack. Behind him was a stringy-haired, skinny young woman. Slowly a few more men came around from the back of dilapidated trailers. This small crowd didn't display arms, but they stayed back, having knowledge of the firearms Jack, Jim and Preacher carried.

Jack approached Paulis. "Are you growing?" Jack asked.

The man shook his head.

"Did Thompson bring that operation in here?"

The girl made a sound and covered her mouth with her hand. Paulis gave a nod.

"He tried to kill a woman last night. For drugs and property. He's dead. Who brought in the trailer?"

Paulis shook his head. "We don't exchange names around here."

"What'd he look like?" Jim asked.

Paulis just shrugged.

"Come on, man. You want to go to jail for him? What'd he drive?"

Paulis shrugged again, but Maxine stepped around her father, tears on her pale cheeks. "A big black Range Rover. Lights up top. You know the kind. He paid Calvin to watch the grow."

"I know who he is," Jack said quietly to Jim. "Don't know where he is, but I have a good idea this isn't his only grow. And I happen to know the license number on that big SUV."

"Well, that could come in handy."

Then to Clifford Paulis, Jack said, "You have twenty-four hours to clear this camp and move out. The sheriff's deputy will be out here to close down this spot real quick, and if you're here, you'll be arrested—that shit's in your possession now. You have to move on now. I don't want you around. You hear me?"

Paulis just nodded.

"That woman was my woman," Jack said more quietly. "I'm going to look for you, and if I can find you, you haven't moved far enough, you understand me?"

Paulis dipped his chin once more.

The differences in the men—those from the camp and Jack, Jim and Preacher, left no doubt as to who would be the winners in any kind of conflict. Just to drive the point home, Jack raised his 30-06 caliber, bolt action rifle, aimed it at the generator beside the half-buried trailer in the compound and fired, decimating it. The report was loud enough to shake the trees. The men in view flinched, raised their hands to cover their faces or cowered back.

"I'm coming back tomorrow," Jack said. "Early."

When they were back in the truck, Jack asked Jim, "What do you make of them?"

"Vagrants. Just living in the forest. They didn't have the means to put that trailer in there—that was arranged by whoever Calvin was working for. They'll go, most likely. Deeper in the forest, where they can set up camp again and be left alone. We'll let Henry know where to find it. But you should make good on your advice just the same. They can't be here anymore. If they're not dangerous, they're willing to be taken advantage of by dangerous people."

"I didn't see any guns. They have to be armed."

"Oh, sure—but they're not armed with much. They saw what we're carrying—none of these old boys are going to be shooting at us. The ones to worry about are guys like Calvin's boss, and his boss's boss. DEA cleared out a whole town in the Trinity Alps several years ago while I was an agent—and now those boys had 'em some guns." Jim gave Jack a shot in the arm. "I'm for staying out of their business. If Forestry runs across them, they'll report them to the sheriff's department or maybe to the DEA."

The spirit of the town was tense and worried. Jack had become their favorite son, and his chosen woman—the woman who had come here to help people—had had a brush with death.

Throughout the day, neighbors came to Doc's bearing food and offering conversation. There were no patients, only friends. Doc got out of bed and dressed, coming downstairs to visit. With the exception of a short nap in the afternoon, he stayed up the entire day.

Jim and June only stayed a couple of hours, but Jack was a presence on and off throughout the day, which worked well because people who came by the house to check on Mel were anxious to talk to him. "Shot him while he held her at knifepoint, they're saying." Jack merely nodded and reached for her hand. "How'd you dare? How'd you know you wouldn't be off by a half inch?"

"I didn't have that much to spare," he said. "I wouldn't have pulled the trigger if I thought there was any chance I'd be off my mark."

Another matter of great interest was the shining ring that graced Mel's finger. The engagement was met with happiness and affection, though not surprise. There were many questions about the wedding, and a serious protest when it was learned that there would be a small ceremony in a few days for family only in Sacramento.

Jack, Doc and Mel ate a dinner made up of the food brought by well-wishers and when it was done and the dishes cleaned up, Doc said, "I'm going to bed, Melinda. You should go back to your man's bed. Those hospital beds are no place for the two of you." And up the stairs he slowly trudged.

"Yes, you should," Jack confirmed, taking her with him across the street.

Having slept so little the night before, once she was in Jack's bed, curled up against his warmth, she nearly passed out from exhaustion.

Before the sun was even up the next morning, she was awakened by the sound of amassing vehicles. She looked at the clock and saw that it was barely 5:00 a.m. She rummaged around for clothes and went through the bar onto the porch to see what all the commotion was about. There in the street were trucks, campers, AWD vehicles, SUVs, cars. Men were standing around in the street, checking their rifles, even putting on flak jackets and bulletproof vests. Some wore jeans and work shirts, some wore fatigues. She recognized faces among them—Mike Valenzuela from L.A., Zeke from Fresno, Paul Haggerty and Joe Benson from Grants Pass, Oregon. There were also neighbors and ranchers and farmers from Virgin River. She saw that Ricky was with them, looking for all the world like a grown man.

She watched them for a while before Jack noticed her standing there, her hair all mussed from sleep, her feet bare. He handed his rifle off to Paul and went to her. "You look like a girl," he said. "A little pregnant girl, but I know better." He grinned. "I thought maybe you could sleep awhile longer."

"Through this? What's going on?"

"Scavenger hunt," he said. "Nothing for you to worry about."

"Come on, Jack."

"We're going to check, see if the woods need to be cleaned out," he said.

"With weapons? Vests? My God, Jack."

He pulled her against him briefly and said, "I doubt we'll have any trouble, Mel. But we should be prepared for whatever we run into. We're just going to cut a wide circle around the town—be certain there are no drug farmers or criminals close by. No camps like the one Thompson came from. No camps for people like Thompson to hide out in."

"How will you know whether there are dangerous people in ordinary camps? I'm told there are plenty of those kind of camps scattered around. Squatters, vagrants, mountain people."

He shrugged. "Then we should know who's out there. Look for what's in their camps, check their weapons so we know what they have. Pot's pretty easy to spot—it has a real distinctive green color and it almost always comes with camouflage and a generator."

She put a hand on the vest he wore. "And you need this because—"

"Because I'm going to be a father soon, and I don't take foolish chances. One of these idiots could misfire."

"You're taking Ricky with you?"

"I look out for Ricky. We'll all be looking out for him, but believe me—he's up to this. I taught him to shoot myself. He wouldn't be left out, because it's about you."

"Is this absolutely necessary?"

"Yes," he said, and looked down at her with the expression she had learned meant he was all about business.

Jim Post was beside Jack, grinning. "Morning," he said.

"Does June know you're doing this?" she asked.

"Yes, ma'am."

"And what did she say?"

"Something like, 'You better be careful.' The hard part was convincing old Doc Hudson he couldn't come."

"Isn't this better left to the police? The sheriff?"

Jim put a foot up on the porch step. He shrugged. "We've already told Henry about Paulis's camp and gave him the description of the vehicle being driven by the man who probably had it set up. Hopefully, the Paulis camp is deserted and their plants left behind. We saw 'em, Mel—and there's no question—those old squatters didn't bring a semi in, bury it, camouflage it and set up a grow. But someone did—and there could be more of those. There's real trouble way back in there—on federal land. We're not going that far back. We'll stay out of their business. We'll leave that up to the professionals."

"It just seems so vigilante-like," she said.

"Naw, we're not going to do anything illegal, Mel. We're just going to send a little message. You don't want to give our women, our towns, any reason to feel they have to fight back. Understand?" She didn't answer. "If there's anything like that near enough to threaten Virgin River, we'll give them a chance to run for their lives before we disclose their location to authorities. It'll be fine. We'll be home by dark."

She said to Jack, "I'm going to be scared to death all day."

"Do I have to stay here with you, so you won't be scared?" he asked her. "Or can you believe in me one more time?"

She bit her lip, but nodded. He slipped an arm around her waist and lifted her up to his mouth, kissing her deeply. "You taste so good in the morning," he said, smiling down at her. "Is that normal?" he teased.

"You'd better be careful," she said. "Remember that I love you."

"I don't need any more than that," he said, putting her back on her feet.

Preacher came to the porch. He nodded at her, bushy brows drawn together in a frown that made her almost shudder. "Just send him in," Mel said. "That'll scare them all away." And to her surprise, Preacher smiled so big, for a moment she didn't recognize him.

When they had finally left in a grand parade, Mel called June. "Do you know what your husband is doing?" she asked.

"Yes," June said, sounding annoyed. "Not babysitting."

"Are you worried?"

"Only that one of them will shoot off a toe. Why? Are you?"

"Well… Yes! You should have seen them—in their vests and with those big guns. I mean, big guns!"

"Well, there are bear out there, you know. You don't want a peashooter," June said. "You don't have to worry about Jack, honey. I think it's been established he's a good shot, if he needs to be."

"What about Jim?"

"Jim?" She laughed. "Mel, Jim used to do this for a living. He won't admit he misses it just a little bit. But I swear I heard him giggle."

All day long she had visions of gun battles in the forest. The unfortunate lack of work couldn't keep her from pacing. With the bar closed and so many of the men out on the scavenger hunt, the town was impossibly quiet.

Mel spent most of the day on Doc's porch, sitting on the steps. It was about noon when the black Range

Rover pulled slowly into town. He drove up alongside the clinic and lowered his tinted window. "I heard what happened to you," he said.

"You did? I didn't know we had any mutual friends."

"I wanted to tell you a couple of things, because you did me a favor. Number one—I know about Thompson and he's a loose cannon. I know a lot of what goes on back there and there aren't any others like him, that I know of. People like Vickie—that's the woman who had the baby—she's been in some trouble, but she's not dangerous to anybody. She just flies under the radar, has had some tough breaks, doesn't know a lot of ways to make money. By the way—she's gone. Took that baby and went to a sister's in Arizona. I got her on a bus."

"You said Nevada before," Mel said.

"Did I now?" he asked, a small smile. "Well, I could be mistaken."

"I just hope you know where to send the check, since it's yours."

"I said, they'll have what they need. Didn't I say that?"

She was silent a moment, thinking. The check he was going to send would come from the sale of marijuana. There were people who thought it was no worse than a few beers, and she was about to pledge her life and love to a man who owned a bar, thought nothing of serving up a few beers. Then there were others who recognized its medical benefits. And a third faction saw it as a dangerous drug—one that, in the wrong hands, perhaps young hands, could lead to more dangerous addictions. Mel only knew two things: it was still illegal without a prescription and, because it was illegal, crime was often associated with it.

"You said you wanted to tell me a couple of things," she said.

"I'm leaving the area. There's been a death. Doesn't really matter that Thompson won't be any great loss to society," he said with a shrug. "He's associated with a couple of the operations here, so there's going to be an investigation, warrants, arrests. I'll be moving on." He smiled at her. "You get your wish. You won't be doing business with me anymore."

She leaned forward on the porch steps. "Have you done violence?"

"Not really," he said with a shrug. "Not so far. We've had our little misunderstandings. But I'm just a businessman."

"You couldn't find a more legal business?"

"Oh, sure," he answered, smiling. "I just couldn't find a more profitable one."

The window went up and he moved down the street and out of sight. She memorized the license plate, knowing that if he was any good at his profession, it wouldn't matter.

At dusk, she sat out on Doc's porch and waited. As darkness began to descend, she heard the vehicles return. As they drove slowly into town and pulled up to the bar, she tried to assess the mood of the group. Everyone seemed solemn and tired as they got out of trucks and Jeeps, stretching their backs and arms. Vests were gone, guns stowed in their racks and sleeves rolled up. But shortly they were clapping each other on the back, laughing and gathering around Jack's porch. She was so relieved to see Ricky, laughing with the men, one of the brothers, completely safe. The last truck to pull up was Preacher's, in which Jack rode, as well, and they had something large in the bed, something hanging out. When he parked, all the men gathered around, and the tempo of the group seemed to pick up. There was laughter and loud voices.

Almost afraid to know what was going on, she walked across the street. Jack was coming for her and met her halfway.

"Well? You find anything?"

"Not bad guys," he said. "Paulis's camp was busted up and what junk they left behind, we destroyed. Henry and a couple of deputies showed up to confiscate their plants. I just don't want them back in the neighborhood if they're going to let a drug operation in. Truthfully, they don't have the strength to keep them out, so we will."

"Haven't you ever thought—it's only a little pot?"

"I don't have an opinion about that," he said with a shrug. "But if it's legalized and pharmaceutical companies grow it, we won't have to be afraid for our women and children."

"What have you got in the truck? What's that awful smell?"

"A bear. Wanna see?" he asked, smiling.

"A bear? Why on earth…?"

"He was really pissed," Jack said. "Come and see—he's huge."

"Who shot him?" she asked.

"Who's taking credit or who actually shot him? Because I think everyone is taking credit." He slipped an arm around her waist and walked her the rest of the way.

She began to pick up the voices. "I swear, I heard Preacher scream," someone said.

"I didn't scream, jag-off. That was a battle cry."

"Sounded like a little girl."

"More holes in that bear than in my head."

"He didn't like that repellant so much, did he?"

"I never saw one go through that stuff before. They usually just rub their little punkin eyes and run back in the woods."

"I'm telling you, Preacher screamed. Thought he was gonna cry like a baby."

"You wanna eat, jag-off?"

There was laughter all around. A carnival-like atmosphere ensued. The serious group that had left town in the morning had come back like soldiers from war, elated, victorious. Except this war turned out to be with a bear.

Mel glanced in the back of the truck and jumped back. The bear not only filled the bed, he hung out the end. The claws on his paws were terrifying. He was tied in, tied down, even though he was dead. His eyes were open but sightless and his tongue hung out of his mouth. And he stunk to high heaven.

"Who's calling Fish and Game?"

"Aw, do we have to call them? You know they're gonna take the frickin' bear. That's my bear!"

"It ain't your bear, jag-off. I shot the bear," Preacher insisted loudly.

"You screamed like a girl and the rest of us shot the bear."

"Who really shot the bear?" Mel asked Jack.

"I think Preacher shot the bear when he came at him. Then so did everybody else. And yeah, I think he screamed. I would have. That bear got so damn close." But as he said this, he grinned like a boy who had just made a touchdown.

Preacher stomped over to Jack and Mel. He bent down and whispered to Mel, "I did *not* scream." He turned and stomped off.

"Honey," Jack said softly, "we found one other thing today." She looked up at him expectantly. "We found the black Range Rover. Ran off the road and went down a couple hundred feet…"

"Is he dead?" she asked fearfully, surprised that she even cared.

"There wasn't any body."

She gave a short, startled laugh. "God," she said. "He came by here today at about noon. All he did was roll down the window and said that because I did him a favor he wanted me to know there was no one else out there in the cannabis trade like Thompson that he knew of, and he was leaving the area. Jack, he must have ditched the truck."

"Probably," he said. "Which means he might be getting a new vehicle, new look and be back. Never go with him again, Mel. Promise me."

She was thinking, insanely, that he was one person who treated her okay and seemed to have something of a conscience. If he came to her and said someone needed medical help, it would be hard to refuse him. "Just how many children do you think he can father?" she asked with a laugh.

"Men have lapses in judgment."

"Do they? Hopefully you haven't had too many," she said.

"I haven't had any," he said with a smile.

"So. That's all you got? A wrecked SUV and a bear? Must be a little anticlimactic for you," she said.

"You calling that bear anticlimactic? Baby, that is a huge frickin' bear!"

There must have been about twenty-five men, they all smelled bad, and they were filing into the bar. Mel sniffed Jack's shirt. "Whew," she said. "You smell almost as bad as the bear."

"It's going to get worse before it gets better," he said. "Now we'll have beer, food and cigars. I have to get in there and start serving beer while Preacher and Ricky fire up the barbecue pit."

"I'll help," she said, taking his hand. "It was a waste of time, wasn't it?"

"Not in my mind. Our forest is nice and tidy, we're turning a trailer full of plants over to the sheriff and we got a mean old bear."

"You had fun," she accused.

"Not on purpose," he said. But his smile was very large.

"Is it over, Jack?" she asked him.

"I hope so, baby. God, I hope so."

For once Mel was behind the bar. She helped serve beer and drinks, tossed a great big salad while Preacher turned steaks on the grill. Plates and utensils were put out for a buffet-style service. The men poked fun at each other, their laughter getting louder and wilder as the night wore on. Although Ricky was officially working, when he'd pass one of the men, he'd be pulled into a strong-armed embrace and praised as though he was a comrade. Doc wandered across the street for a whiskey, visited with the men for a while before going back to his house. Most of the locals left before the meal was served, home to claim to their wives that they shot the bear.

It was about nine when the cards and cigars came out. Jack grabbed Mel's hand and said, "Let's get out of here. You must be exhausted."

"Hmm," she said, leaning against him. "My feelings won't be hurt if you want to hang out with your boys."

"They'll probably be around a day or two. Since they came all this way, they'll want to fish and stink up my bar. Fishing's starting to get good." He put an arm around Mel and walked her through the back of the bar. "We need to give the baby a nap."

"We need to give the baby's father a shower," she said, wrinkling her nose.

While Jack showered, Mel put on one of his shirts, her favorite soft chambray. She curled up on the sofa with one of Jack's magazines in her lap, flipping through the pages. She would have to find something better than *Field and Stream,* she decided.

She could hear the raucous laughter from the bar; she could almost smell the cigar smoke, but it made her smile. These were good people—people who came running when they thought there was a possible danger. Jack's friends, the people in town—they knew the meaning of being neighbors.

She had only known the neighbors on each side of her in L.A. With Mark's long hours, they didn't socialize as much as she'd have liked. And big cities can be less friendly. Everyone was so focused on work, on making money, on buying things. Mel used to concentrate on that, as well. Besides that Hummer, which she'd needed for work and was as much for the town as herself, she'd hardly bought a thing in six months. She patted her tummy—she would have to buy clothes soon—she couldn't get her jeans closed. As she thought about it, she didn't crave any particular label. It made her smile. Lately, she didn't recognize herself. She was not the same woman who nearly slid off the mountain six months ago.

Jack came out of the shower, a towel around his waist, rubbing dry his short hair with another one. He tossed the second towel and went to his bed, lifting the covers and inclining his head toward her. She put aside the magazine and went to him. As she slipped in, she said, "You're sure you don't want to play poker and make yourself smell disgusting? They're going to keep us up all night anyway."

He dropped his towel and got in beside her. "You're kidding, right?" He scooped her up next to him and she snuggled close.

"Have I told you how much I like sleeping with you?" she asked him. "You sleep very well. And you don't snore. But I think maybe you wake up too early."

"I like the mornings."

"I can't fit in my pants already," she said. She lifted herself up and with her elbows resting on his chest said, "You call them and they just come."

"I only called one of them—Mike in L.A.—he called the others. They're just like that. And if any of them called—I'd go." He smiled at her. "I never expected a posse like that to turn out. Says something about the way people feel about you."

"But you didn't actually find anyone scary out there."

"I liked what I found. I wasn't willing to take any chances, and neither was anyone else. The same thing would happen for any other crisis—like a bear mauling or a forest fire or someone lost in the woods. People band up, go out and take care of the problem if they can. What else are you going to do?"

She played idly with his damp chest hair. "That look you get when you're facing off with someone or something, do you have any idea how dark it is? You might want to keep that look in the closet—it's disturbing."

"I want to tell you something," he said. "I asked your sister all about your husband. Mark."

"You did?"

"Yep. I understand he was a great man. A brilliant man—and kind. He did a lot of good in the world, and he was good to you. I have a lot of respect for him."

"She didn't tell me this."

"I've been trying to figure out how to say this to you. I might muck it up, but you have to listen. A couple of weeks ago I let you cry alone, because I was pissed. I caught you talking to his picture and I got threatened. Threatened by a dead man, which makes me a true candy-ass." He touched her hair. "I won't ever do that again, Mel. I understand why you love him, why you'll always—"

"Jack—"

"No, I'm going to do this, and you're going to listen. I know you didn't want your life to change the way it did, and you couldn't control it. Just like you can't control what you feel. You don't have to pretend you don't think about him, or miss him. And if you have those moments when you're sad, when you wish you could have him back in your life, you can be honest with me. You don't have to pretend it's PMS." He smiled. "We both know you don't have PMS anymore."

"Jack, what are you talking about?"

"I just want one thing. If I can be a sport about the fact that he'll always be an important part of your life, can you try to not be sorry that we're together, having this baby? Because I have to tell you, I've never been more ready for anything. I'll do my best not to be jealous. I realize I'm not your first choice, but your next choice. That's good enough for me, and I'm sorry someone died. I'm sorry for your loss, Mel."

"Why are you saying this? It's such nonsense."

"It's what I heard," he said. "I heard you saying you were sorry you were pregnant, that it just happened, and you promised not to forget him."

Mel gave him a look of disbelief. "I thought you were hurt by what you heard me say—but you were hurt because of what you *didn't* hear!"

"Huh?"

"Jack, I'm not sorry I'm pregnant. I'm thrilled! I got myself all worked up because I realized that I was more in love with you than I thought possible. Maybe more in love than I've ever been in my life. I had a short insane moment of feeling that I'd betrayed his memory somehow. As though I'd been unfaithful or something. It's true—I didn't mean for it to happen, but it did. I know I resisted, but you just got to me. I promised Mark I wouldn't forget him. And I won't because you're right, he was a good man. And I respect him, too."

"Huh?" he said again.

"Look," she said, playing with his thick, damp hair. "I was upset and a little confused. I loved Mark very much. I didn't think I'd get to feel that again, much less for someone new. Imagine how it threw me when I realized I felt something even stronger. Something even more powerful. Jack, I was telling Mark I had moved on. I was saying goodbye—it was difficult. I'm not going to be a widow anymore, darling. I'm going to be a wife. This thing I have with you—it's amazing."

"Seriously?"

"I was in this high, emotional state," she said with a shrug. "I was tired and pregnant. Jack, I love you so much. Can't you tell?"

"Well…yeah," he said, sitting up in the bed a little. "But I thought it was mostly physical. I mean—damn,

Mel. We're really good together. The way we come together, it almost makes me weak to think about it."

"I don't mind the physical part one bit," she said with a mischievous grin. "But I love more about you than that. Your character, for one thing. Your generosity and how about your courage. Oh, there are about a million things, but I'm done talking now." She kissed him. "Now I want you to say something wonderful to me right before you tear this shirt off my body."

He rolled her over onto her back and, looking into her eyes, said, "Mel, you're the best thing that's ever happened to me. I'm going to make you so happy, you won't be able to stand it. You're going to wake up singing every morning."

"I already do, Jack."

* * * * *

Letter from Robyn Carr

Virgin River is alive! Really!

When my readers write to me to say my characters have become real to them, that they have become like friends or family, I always smile and think, *You have no idea how much so*. Sometimes they're almost *too* real for me. When I am writing a novel, my characters occupy so much space in my mind. I join them for meals, take them on walks, lie beside them in bed, wake up to them in the morning. Sometimes I feel like covering up in the shower!

They talk to me inside my head; I can imagine the sound of their voices, and there are times I've created writing exercises to help bring them to life. A few times I've interviewed characters to get a better fix on who they are. To a novelist, especially this novelist, the most authentic writing doesn't look like writing at all. It looks more like scribbling or daydreaming or, in the best of times, rocking in a hammock. I took this approach when I started writing Virgin River. Me to Mel: *What are you running away from?* Mel to me: *I lost my husband, and it was a brutal loss.*

From the very beginning of my Virgin River novels, I imagined a televised series. Over the years there has been interest from a variety of production companies, but I always knew it wasn't a story that could be told quickly. It's an ongoing story with the potential for growth and an infinite opportunity for expansion.

The Netflix production of the series is a dream come true. And I was very pleased to be invited to visit the set and watch my characters come to life.

Of course, once the announcement was made, before a single cast member was selected, I began to get letters. "They better get Jack's character right!" And the less threatening version: "I hope you have input in selecting the cast!"

However redundant these thoughts may be, we all have our own image in our heads as to what characters might look like. That's the true beauty of fiction—while our eyes scan the page, our mind is busy turning it into a movie in our minds. Will that vision be the same for everyone? Of course not.

But I knew my characters were in good hands, and I could hardly contain my excitement when visiting the set. Inside a giant warehouse was Jack's bar and several other structures, including Doc's house and clinic. There were enormous painted backdrops of the great outdoors—the monument-size trees, mountains, rivers. As I walked around the set, I was in awe. It was a town, incredible down to the smallest detail. I wandered in and out of the structures, touching the stacks of papers on Doc's desk, checking out the exam table in one of the exam rooms, looking at the small kitchen where so much action happened in the book.

I mounted the steps to Jack's bar with some trepidation —so much of the series takes place there—would it look anything like I'd imagined? I stopped just inside the door. It took my breath away. Every detail was precise. I sat on a stool at the bar and about a hundred scenarios ran through my mind. A little later in the day I watched the filming of a scene in which Mel was talking to Jack about her life as an urban nurse practitioner, tossing back a couple of shots, wobbling off the stool and needing a little assistance from Jack! Yes, the place was Jack's, down to the animal trophies on the walls. It was exactly as I'd pictured it when I first wrote about it.

And there were so many people everywhere. A large gathering of people at picnic tables outside of Doc's house turned out to be extras. They'd be called on to walk up and down the street, sit in the bar, maybe be waiting for a doctor's appointment, whatever the need.

Also within the crowd there were tradesmen: carpenters, painters, builders, cameramen, grips. A good many of them approached me, introduced themselves and asked me, usually a bit shyly, if the set met my expectations. I had to be honest—it far exceeded my wildest desires. When I said so, their faces would light up with pride. They, too, want the show to meet the expectations of the fans of the books.

Also gathered were production people: the director, sound techs and others. I found a chair with my name on the back and we gathered to watch them shoot a scene, then reshoot from several different angles. I must say, I've always had this image of actors as having a glamorous job, but what I saw was very unglamorous. They worked hard, over and over again, standing, sitting, walking, moving. And the days were long—they kept the set open, working, twelve hours a day. There were trailers in the parking lot for the stars to relax between scenes, study their lines, rest, rehearse or catch up on emails or phone calls when they weren't required on set.

And the food! This was my biggest surprise of the day. The unions are strict, and those hardworking folks need regular breaks. Every few hours tables full of catered food were put out. Between breaks, great bowls of fruit appeared.

I sat through a table reading of the ninth episode. Every actor read their lines from the script. They did this every day for several days. It was an opportunity for questions and so they could discuss their lines or delivery with the director.

The scenes that I saw or read were not what I wrote in the original book. The script can't follow the book exactly. It would be confusing, too long and the meaning could be lost in translation. The screen is a completely different format. There's no way to film a character's thoughts or internal dialogue, so adjustments are made to make the spirit of the story fit the new format. There were things I didn't recognize but so many new twists I wished I had thought of. It was true to the spirit of my work and it was excellent!

It was a brand-new adventure with some of my most beloved characters. And those people who see the televised series first will have the same experience when they read the books—fresh adventures with favorite characters.

I was on the set for two days and it was magical. I fell in love with everything I saw, but there were a couple of things that stood out. First of all, the extreme gratitude of the cast and crew, to the last. There were hundreds of people working on this series. We provided jobs—hundreds of them. This wasn't something I had done alone, even if I had created the setting and characters. This was something that evolved out of the millions of readers' love for the series. And the second thing was nestled in the heart. One of the tradesmen asked if I'd seen the sign in the bar. He took me over to show me what he meant. A closer look revealed a slice of tree trunk with some words burned into it. "Virgin River—Built By Men Of Honor For The Women They Love." It was perfect.

That is the spirit and essence of Virgin River—the town we all want to call home. I hope you enjoy the books and the Netflix series as much as I do. Please visit my website, robyncarr.com, for more behind-the-scenes information about the show.

Robyn Carr

Virgin River: Out now on Netflix

One

Maggie Sullivan sought refuge in the stairwell between the sixth and seventh floors at the far west end of the hospital, the steps least traveled by interns and residents racing from floor to floor, from emergency to emergency. She sat on the landing between two flights, feet on the stairs, arms crossed on her knees, her face buried in her arms. She didn't understand how her heart could feel as if it was breaking every day. She thought of herself as much stronger.

"Well, now, some things never change," a familiar voice said.

She looked up at her closest friend, Jaycee Kent. They had gone to med school together, though residency had separated them. Jaycee was an OB and Maggie, a neurosurgeon. And…they had hidden in stairwells to cry all those years ago when med-school life was kicking their asses. Most of their fellow students and instructors were men. They refused to let the men see them cry.

Maggie gave a wet, burbly huff of laughter. "How'd you find me?" Maggie asked.

"How do you know you're not in my spot?"

"Because you're happily married and have a beautiful daughter?"

"And my hours suck, I'm sleep-deprived, have as many bad days as good and…" Jaycee sat down beside Maggie. "And at least my hormones are cooperating at the moment. Maggie, you're just taking call for someone, right? Just to stay ahead of the bills?"

"Since the practice shut down," Maggie said. "And since the lawsuit was filed."

"You need a break. You're recovering from a miscarriage and your hormones are wonky. You need to get away, especially away from the emergency room. Take some time off. Lick your wounds. Heal."

"He dumped me," Maggie said.

Jaycee was clearly shocked. *"What?"*

"He broke up with me. He said he couldn't take it anymore. My emotional behavior, my many troubles. He suggested professional help."

Jaycee was quiet. "I'm speechless," she finally said. "What a huge ass."

"Well, I was crying all the time," she said, sniffing some more. "If I wasn't with him, I cried when I talked to him on the phone. I thought I was okay with the idea of no children. I'm almost thirty-seven, I work long hours, I was with a good man who was just off a bad marriage and already had a child…"

"I'll give you everything but the good man," Jaycee said. "He's a doctor, for God's sake. Doesn't he know that all you've been through can take a toll? Remove all the stress and you still had the miscarriage! People tend to treat a miscarriage like a heavy period but it's a death. You lost your baby. You have to take time to grieve."

"Gospel," Maggie said, rummaging for a tissue and giving her nose a hearty blow. "I really felt it on that level. When I found out I was pregnant, it took me about fifteen minutes to start seeing the baby, loving her. Or him."

"Not to beat a dead horse, but you have some hormone issues playing havoc on your emotions. Listen, shoot out some emails tonight. Tell the ones on the need-to-know list you're taking a week or two off."

"No one knows about the pregnancy but you and Andrew."

"You don't have to explain—everyone knows about your practice, your ex-partners, the lawsuit. Frankly, your colleagues are amazed you're still standing. Get out of town or something. Get some rest."

"You might be right," Maggie said. "These cement stairwells are killing me."

Jaycee put an arm around her. "Just like old times, huh?"

The last seven or eight miles to Sullivan's Crossing was nothing but mud and Maggie's cream-colored Toyota SUV was coated up to the windows. This was not exactly a surprise. It had rained all week in Denver, now that she thought about it. March was typically the most unpredictable and sloppiest month of the year, especially in the mountains. If it wasn't rain it could be snow. But Maggie had had such a lousy year the weather barely crossed her mind.

Last year had produced so many medical, legal and personal complications that her practice had shut down a few months ago. She'd been picking up work from other practices, covering for doctors on call here and there and working ER Level 1 Trauma while she tried to figure out how to untangle the mess her life had become. This, on her best friend and doctor's advice, was a much needed break. After sending a few emails and making a few phone calls she was driving to her dad's house.

She knew she was probably suffering from depression. Exhaustion and general misery. It would stand to reason. Her schedule could be horrific and the tension had been terrible lately. It was about a year ago that two doctors in her practice had been accused of fraud and malpractice and suspended from seeing patients pending an investigation that would very likely lead to a trial. Even though she had no knowledge of the incidents, there was a scandal and it stank on her. There'd been wild media attention and she was left alone trying to hold a wilting practice together. Then the parents of a boy who died from injuries sustained in a terrible car accident while on her watch filed a wrongful death suit. Against her.

It seemed impossible fate could find one more thing to stack on her already teetering pile of troubles. *Hah. Never challenge fate.* She found out she was pregnant.

It was an accident, of course. She'd been seeing Andrew for a couple of years. She lived in Denver and he in Aurora, since they both had demanding careers, and they saw each other when they could—a night here, a night there. When they could manage a long weekend, it was heaven. She wanted more but Andrew was an ER doctor and also the divorced father of an eight-year-old daughter. But they had constant phone contact. Multiple texts and emails every day. She counted on him; he was her main support.

Maggie wasn't sure she'd ever marry and have a family but she was happy with her surprise. It was the one good thing in a bad year. Andrew, however, was *not* happy. He was still in divorce recovery, though it had been three years. He and his ex still fought about support and custody and visits. Maggie didn't understand why. Andrew didn't seem to know what to do with his daughter when he had her. He immediately suggested terminating the pregnancy. He said they could revisit the issue in a couple of years if it turned out to be that important to her and if their relationship was thriving.

She couldn't imagine terminating. Just because Andrew was hesitant? She was thirty-six! How much time did she have to *revisit the issue*?

Although she hadn't told Andrew, she decided she was going to keep the baby no matter what that meant for their relationship. Then she had a miscarriage.

Grief-stricken and brokenhearted, she sank lower. Exactly two people knew about the pregnancy and miscarriage—Andrew and Jaycee. Maggie cried gut-wrenching tears every night. Sometimes she couldn't even wait to get home from work and started crying the second she pulled the car door closed. And there were those stairwell visits. She cried on the phone to Andrew; cried in his arms as he tried to comfort her, all the while knowing he was *relieved*.

And then he'd said, "You know what, Maggie? I just can't do it anymore. We need a time-out. I can't prop you up, can't bolster you. You have to get some help, get your emotional life back on track or something. You're sucking the life out of me and I'm not equipped to help you."

"Are you kidding me?" she had demanded. "You're dropping me when I'm down? When I'm only three weeks beyond a miscarriage?"

And in typical Andrew fashion he had said, "That's all I got, baby."

It was really and truly the first moment she had realized it was all about him. And that was pretty much the last straw.

She packed a bunch of suitcases. Once she got packing, she couldn't seem to stop. She drove southwest from Denver to her father's house, south of Leadville and Fairplay, and she hadn't called ahead. She did call her mother, Phoebe, just to say she was going to Sully's and she wasn't sure how long she'd stay. At the moment she had no plan except to escape from that life of persistent strain, anxiety and heartache.

It was early afternoon when she drove up to the country store that had been her great-grandfather's, then her grandfather's, now her father's. Her father, Harry Sullivan, known by one and all as Sully, was a fit and hardy seventy and showed no sign of slowing down and no interest in retiring. She just sat in her car for a while, trying to figure out what she was going to say to him. How could she phrase it so it didn't sound like she'd just lost a baby and had her heart broken?

Beau, her father's four-year-old yellow Lab, came trotting around the store, saw her car, started running in circles barking, then put his front paws up on her door, looking at her imploringly. Frank Masterson, a local who'd been a fixture at the store for as long as Maggie could remember, was sitting on the porch, nursing a cup of coffee with a newspaper on his lap. One glance told her the campground was barely occupied—only a couple of pop-up trailers and tents on campsites down the road toward the lake. She saw a man sitting outside his tent in a canvas camp chair, reading. She had expected the sparse population—it was the middle of the week, middle of the day and the beginning of March, the least busy month of the year.

Frank glanced at her twice but didn't even wave.

Beau trotted off, disappointed, when Maggie didn't get out of the car. She still hadn't come up with a good entry line. Five minutes passed before her father walked out of the store, across the porch and down the steps, Beau following. She lowered the window.

"Hi, Maggie," he said, leaning on the car's roof. "Wasn't expecting you."

"It was spur-of-the-moment."

He glanced into her backseat at all the luggage. "How long you planning to stay?"

She shrugged. "Didn't you say I was always welcome? Anytime?"

He smiled at her. "Sometimes I run off at the mouth."

"I need a break from work. From all that crap. From everything."

"Understandable. What can I get you?"

"Is it too much trouble to get two beers and a bed?" she asked, maybe a little sarcastically.

"Coors okay by you?"

"Sure."

"Go on and park by the house. There's beer in the fridge and I haven't sold your bed yet."

"That's gracious of you," she said.

"You want some help to unload your entire wardrobe?" he asked.

"Nope. I don't need much for now. I'll take care of it."

"Then I'll get back to work and we'll meet up later."

"Sounds like a plan," she said.

Maggie dragged only one bag into the house, the one with her toothbrush, pajamas and clean jeans. When she was a little girl and both her parents and her grandfather lived on this property, she had been happy most of the time. The general store, the locals and campers, the mountains, lake and valley, wildlife and sunshine kept her constantly cheerful. But the part of her that had a miserable mother, a father who tended to drink a little too much and bickering parents had been forlorn. Then, when she was six, her mother had had enough of hardship, rural living, driving Maggie a long distance to a school that Phoebe found inadequate. Throw in an unsatisfactory husband and that was all she could take. Phoebe took Maggie away to Chicago. Maggie didn't see Sully for several years and her mother married Walter Lancaster, a prominent neurosurgeon with lots of money.

Maggie had hated it all. Chicago, Walter, the big house, the private school, the blistering cold and concrete landscape. She hated the sound of traffic and emergency vehicles. One thing she could recall in retrospect, it brought her mother to life. Phoebe was almost entirely happy, the only smudge on her brightness being her ornery daughter. They had switched roles.

By the time Maggie was eleven she was visiting her dad regularly—first a few weekends, then whole months and some holidays. She lived for it and Phoebe constantly held it over her. *Behave yourself and get good grades and you'll get to spend the summer at that godawful camp, eating worms, getting filthy and risking your life among bears.*

"Why didn't you fight for me?" she had continually asked her father.

"Aw, honey, Phoebe was right, I wasn't worth a damn as a father and I just wanted what was best for you. It wasn't always easy, neither," he'd explained.

Sometime in junior high Maggie had made her peace with Walter, but she chose to go to college in Denver, near Sully. Phoebe's desire was that she go to a fancy

Ivy League college. Med school and residency were a different story—it was tough getting accepted at all and you went to the best career school and residency program that would have you. She ended up in Los Angeles. Then she did a fellowship with Walter, even though she hated going back to Chicago. But Walter was simply one of the best. After that she joined a practice in Denver, close to her dad and the environment she loved. A year later, with Walter finally retired from his practice and enjoying more golf, Phoebe and Walter moved to Golden, Colorado, closer to Maggie. Walter was also seventy, like Sully. Phoebe was a vibrant, social fifty-nine.

Maggie thought she was possibly closer to Walter than to Phoebe, especially as they were both neurosurgeons. She was grateful. After all, he'd sent her to good private schools even when she did every terrible thing she could to show him how unappreciated his efforts were. She had been a completely ungrateful brat about it. But Walter turned out to be a kind, classy guy. He had helped a great many people who proved to be eternally grateful and Maggie had been impressed by his achievements. Plus, he mentored her in medicine. Loving medicine surprised her as much as anyone. Sully had said, "I think it's a great idea. If I was as smart as you and some old coot like Walter was willing to pick up the tab, I'd do it in a New York minute."

Maggie found she loved science but med school was the hardest thing she'd ever taken on, and most days she wasn't sure she could make it through another week. She could've just quit, done a course correction or flunked out, but no—she got perfect grades along with anxiety attacks. But the second they put a scalpel in her hand, she'd found her calling.

She sat on Sully's couch, drank two beers, then lay down and pulled the throw over her. Beau pushed in through his doggy door and lay down beside the couch. The window was open, letting in the crisp, clean March air, and she dropped off to sleep immediately to the rhythmic sound of Sully raking out a trench behind the house. She started fantasizing about summer at the lake but before she woke she was dreaming of trying to operate in a crowded emergency room where everyone was yelling, bloody rags littered the floor, people hated each other, threw instruments at one another and patients were dying one after another. She woke up panting, her heart hammering. The sun had set and a kitchen light had been turned on, which meant Sully had been to the house to check on her.

There was a sandwich covered in plastic wrap on a plate. A note sat beside it. It was written by Enid, Frank's wife. Enid worked mornings in the store, baking and preparing packaged meals from salads to sandwiches for campers and tourists. *Welcome Home*, the note said.

Maggie ate the sandwich, drank a third beer and went to bed in the room that was hers at her father's house.

She woke to the sound of Sully moving around and saw that it was not quite 5:00 a.m. so she decided to go back to sleep until she didn't have anxiety dreams anymore. She got up at noon, grazed through the refrigerator's bleak contents and went back to sleep. At about two in the afternoon the door to her room opened noisily and Sully said, "All right. Enough is enough."

Sully's store had been built in 1906 by Maggie's great-grandfather Nathaniel Greely Sullivan. Nathaniel had a son and a daughter, married off the daughter and gave the son, Horace, the store. Horace had one son, Harry, who really had better things to do than run a country store. He wanted to see the world and have adventures so he joined the Army and went to Vietnam, among other places, but by the age of thirty-three, he finally married and brought his pretty young wife, Phoebe, home to Sullivan's Crossing. They immediately had one child, Maggie, and settled in for the long haul. All of the store owners had been called Sully but Maggie was always called Maggie.

The store had once been the only place to get bread, milk, thread or nails within twenty miles, but things had changed mightily by the time Maggie's father had taken it on. It had become a recreational facility—four one-room cabins, dry campsites, a few RV hookups, a dock on the lake, a boat launch, public bathrooms with showers, coin-operated laundry facilities, picnic tables and grills. Sully had installed a few extra electrical outlets on the porch so people in tents could charge their electronics and now Sully himself had satellite TV and Wi-Fi. Sullivan's Crossing sat in a valley south of Leadville at the base of some stunning mountains and just off the Continental Divide Trail. The camping was cheap and well managed, the grounds were clean, the store large and well stocked. They had a post office; Sully was the postmaster. And now it was the closest place to get supplies, beer and ice for locals and tourists alike.

The people who ventured there ranged from hikers to bikers to cross-country skiers, boating enthusiasts, rock climbers, fishermen, nature lovers and weekend campers. Plenty of hikers went out on the trails for a day, a few days, a week or even longer. Hikers who were taking on the CDT or the Colorado Trail often planned on Sully's as a stopping point to resupply, rest and get cleaned up. Those hearties were called the thru-hikers, as the Continental Divide Trail was 3,100 miles long while the Colorado Trail was almost 500, but the two trails converged for about 200 miles just west of Sully's. Thus Sully's was often referred to as *the crossing*.

People who knew the place referred to it as Sully's. Some of their campers were one-timers, never seen again, many were regulars within an easy drive looking for a weekend or holiday escape. They were all interesting to Maggie—men, women, young, old, athletes, wannabe athletes, scout troops, nature clubs, weirdos, the occasional creep—but the ones who intrigued her the most were the long-distance hikers, the thru-hikers. She couldn't imagine the kind of commitment needed to take on the CDT, not to mention the courage and strength. She loved to hear their stories about everything from wildlife on the trail to how many toenails they'd lost on their journey.

There were tables and chairs on the store's wide front porch and people tended to hang out there whether the store was open or closed. When the weather was warm and fair there were spontaneous gatherings and campfires at the edge of the lake. Long-distance hikers often mailed themselves packages that held dry socks, extra food supplies, a little cash, maybe even a book, first-aid items, a new lighter for their campfires, a fresh shirt or two. Maggie loved to watch them retrieve and open boxes they'd packed themselves—it was like Christmas.

Sully had a great big map of the CDT, Colorado Trail and other trails on the bulletin board in the front of the store; it was surrounded by pictures either left or sent back to him. He'd put out a journal book where hikers could leave news or messages. The journals, when filled, were kept by Sully, and had become very well-known. People could spend hours reading through them.

Sully's was an escape, a refuge, a gathering place or recreational outpost. Maggie and Andrew liked to come for the occasional weekend to ski—the cross-country trails were safe and well marked. Occupancy was lower during the winter months so they'd take a cabin, and Sully would never comment on the fact that they were sharing not just a room but a bed.

Before the pregnancy and miscarriage, their routine had been rejuvenating—they'd knock themselves out for a week or even a few weeks in their separate cities, then get together for a weekend or few days, eat wonderful food, screw their brains out, get a little exercise in the outdoors, have long and deep conversations, meet up with friends, then go back to their separate worlds. Andrew was shy of marriage, having failed at one and being left a single father. Maggie, too, had had a brief, unsuccessful marriage, but she wasn't afraid of trying again and had always thought Andrew would eventually get over it. She accepted the fact that she might not have children, coupled with a man who, right up front, declared he didn't want more.

"But then there was one on the way and does he step up?" she muttered to herself as she walked into the store through the back door. "He complains that I'm too sad for him to deal with. The *bastard*."

"Who's the bastard, darling?" Enid asked from the kitchen. She stuck her head out just as Maggie was climbing onto a stool at the counter, and smiled. "It's so good to see you. It's been a while."

"I know, I'm sorry about that. It's been harrowing in Denver. I'm sure Dad told you about all that mess with my practice."

"He did. Those awful doctors, tricking people into thinking they needed surgery on their backs and everything! Is one of them the bastard?"

"Without a doubt," she answered, though they hadn't been on her mind at all.

"And that lawsuit against you," Enid reminded her, *tsking.*

"That'll probably go away," Maggie said hopefully, though there was absolutely no indication it would. At least it was civil. The DA had found no cause to indict her. *But really, how much is one girl supposed to take?* The event leading to the lawsuit was one of the most horrific nights she'd ever been through in the ER—five teenage boys in a catastrophic car wreck, all critical. She'd spent a lot of time in the stairwell after that one. "I'm not worried," she lied. Then she had to concentrate to keep from shuddering.

"Good for you. I have soup. I made some for your dad and Frank. Mushroom. With cheese toast. There's plenty if you're interested."

"Yes, please," she said.

"I'll get it." Enid went around the corner to dish it up.

The store didn't have a big kitchen, just a little turning around room. It was in the southwest corner of the store; there was a bar and four stools right beside the cash register. On the northwest corner there was a small bar where they served adult beverages, and again, a bar and four stools. No one had ever wanted to attempt a restaurant but it was a good idea to provide food and drink—campers and hikers tended to run out of supplies. Sully sold beer, wine, soft drinks and bottled water in the cooler section of the store, but he didn't sell bottled liquor. For that matter, he wasn't a grocery store but a general store. Along with foodstuffs there

were T-shirts, socks and a few other recreational supplies—rope, clamps, batteries, hats, sunscreen, first-aid
supplies. For the mother lode you had to go to Timberlake, Leadville or maybe Colorado Springs.

In addition to tables and chairs on the porch, there
were a few comfortable chairs just inside the front
door where the potbellied stove sat. Maggie remembered when she was a little girl, men sat on beer barrels
around the stove. There was a giant ice machine on the
back porch. The ice was free.

Enid stuck her head out of the little kitchen. She
bleached her hair blond but had always, for as long
as Maggie could remember, had black roots. She was
plump and nurturing while her husband, Frank, was one
of those grizzled, skinny old ranchers. "Is that nice Dr.
Mathews coming down on the weekend?" Enid asked.

"I broke up with him. Don't ever call him nice
again," Maggie said. "He's a turd."

"Oh, honey! You broke up?"

"He said I was depressing," she said with a pout. "He
can kiss my ass."

"Well, I should say so! I never liked him very much,
did I mention that?"

"No, you didn't. You said you loved him and thought
we'd make handsome children together." She winced
as she said it.

"Obviously I wasn't thinking," Enid said, withdraw-
ing back into the kitchen. In a moment she brought out
a bowl of soup and a thick slice of cheese toast. Her
soup was cream of mushroom and it was made with
real cream.

Maggie dipped her spoon into the soup, blew on it,
tasted. It was heaven. "Why aren't you my mother?"
she asked.

"I just didn't have the chance, that's all. But we'll pretend."

Maggie and Enid had that little exchange all the time, exactly like that. Maggie had always wanted one of those soft, nurturing, homespun types for a mother instead of Phoebe, who was thin, chic, active in society, snobby and prissy. Phoebe was cool while Enid was warm and cuddly. Phoebe could read the hell out of a menu while Enid could cure anything with her chicken soup, her grandmother's recipe. Phoebe rarely cooked and when she did it didn't go well. But lest Maggie completely throw her mother under the bus, she reminded herself that Phoebe had a quick wit, and though she was sarcastic and ironic, she could make Maggie laugh. She was devoted to Maggie and craved her loyalty, especially that Maggie liked her more than she liked Sully. She gave Maggie everything she had to give. It wasn't Phoebe's fault they were not the things Maggie wanted. For example, Phoebe sent Maggie to an extremely good college-prep boarding school that had worked out on many levels, except that Maggie would have traded it all to live with her father. Foolishly, perhaps, but still… And while Phoebe would not visit Sully's campground under pain of death, she had thrown Maggie a fifty-thousand-dollar wedding that Maggie hadn't wanted. And Walter had given her and Sergei a trip to Europe for their honeymoon.

Maggie had appreciated the trip to Europe quite a lot. But she should never have married Sergei. She'd been very busy and distracted and he was handsome, sexy—especially that accent! They'd looked so good together. She took him at face value and failed to look deeper into the man. He was superficial and not trustworthy. Fortunately, or would that be unfortunately, it had been blessedly short. Nine months.

"This is so good," Maggie said. "Your soup always puts me right."

"How long are you staying, honey?"

"I'm not sure. Till I get a better idea. Couple of weeks, maybe?"

Enid shook her head. "You shouldn't come in March. You should know better than to come in March."

"He's going to work me like a pack of mules, isn't he?"

"No question about it. Only person who isn't afraid to come around in March is Frank. Sully won't put Frank to work."

Frank Masterson was one of Sully's cronies. He was about the same age while Enid was just fifty-five. Frank said he had had the foresight to marry a younger woman, thereby assuring himself a good caretaker for his old age. Frank owned a nearby cattle ranch that these days was just about taken over by his two sons, which freed up Frank to hang out around Sully's. Sometimes Sully would ask, "Why don't you just come to work with Enid in the morning and save the gas since all you do is drink my coffee for free and butt into everyone's business?"

When the weather was cold he'd sit inside, near the stove. When the weather was decent he favored the porch. He wandered around, chatted it up with campers or folks who stopped by, occasionally lifted a heavy box for Enid, read the paper a lot. He was a fixture.

Enid had a sweet, heart-shaped face to go with her plump body. It attested to her love of baking. Besides making and wrapping sandwiches to keep in the cooler along with a few other lunchable items, she baked every morning—sweet rolls, buns, cookies, brownies, that sort of thing. Frank ate a lot of that and apparently never gained an ounce.

Maggie could hear Sully scraping out the gutters around the store. Seventy and up on a ladder, still working like a farmhand, cleaning the winter detritus away. That was the problem with March—a lot to clean up for the spring and summer. She escaped out to the porch to visit with Frank before Sully saw her sitting around and put her to work.

"What are you doing here?" Frank asked.

"I'm on vacation," she said.

"Hmm. Damn fool time of year to take a vacation. Ain't nothing to do now. Dr. Mathews comin'?"

"No. We're not seeing each other anymore."

"Hmm. That why you're here during mud season? Lickin' your wounds?"

"Not at all. I'm happy about it."

"Yup. You look happy, all right."

I might be better off cleaning gutters, she thought. So she turned the conversation to politics because she knew Frank had some very strong opinions and she could listen rather than answer questions. She spotted that guy again, the camper, sitting in his canvas camp chair outside his pop-up tent/trailer under a pull-out awning. His legs were stretched out and he was reading again. She noticed he had long legs.

She was just about to ask Frank how long that guy had been camping there when she noticed someone heading up the trail toward the camp. He had a big backpack and walking stick and something strange on his head. Maggie squinted. A bombardier's leather helmet with earflaps? "Frank, look at that," she said, leaning forward to stare.

The man was old, but old wasn't exactly rare. There were a lot of senior citizens out on the trails, hiking, biking, skiing. In fact, if they were fit at retirement, they had the time and means. As the man got closer, age was only part of the issue.

"I best find Sully," Frank said, getting up and going into the store.

As the man drew near it was apparent he wore rolled-up dress slacks, black socks and black shoes that looked like they'd be shiny church or office wear once the mud was cleaned off. And on his head a weird WWII aviator's hat. He wore a ski jacket that looked to be drenched and he was flushed and limping.

Sully appeared on the porch, Beau wagging at his side, Frank following. "What the hell?"

"Yeah, that's just wrong," Maggie said.

"Ya think?" Sully asked. He went down the steps to approach the man, Maggie close on his heels, Frank bringing up the rear and Enid on the porch waiting to see what was up.

"Well, there, buddy," Sully said, his hands in his pockets. "Where you headed?"

"Is this Camp Lejeune?"

Everyone exchanged glances. "Uh, that would be in North Carolina, son," Sully said, though the man was clearly older than Sully. "You're a little off track. Come up on the porch and have a cup of coffee, take off that pack and wet jacket. And that silly hat, for God's sake. We need to make a phone call for you. What are you doing out here, soaking wet in your Sunday shoes?"

"Maybe I should wait a while, see if they come," the man said, though he let himself be escorted to the porch.

"Who?" Maggie asked.

"My parents and older brother," he said. "I'm to meet them here."

"Bet they have 'em some real funny hats, too," Frank muttered.

"Seems like you got a little confused," Sully said. "What's your name, young man?"

"That's a problem, isn't it? I'll have to think on that for a while."

Maggie noticed the camper had wandered over, curious. Up close he was distracting. He was tall and handsome, though there was a small bump on the bridge of his nose. But his hips were narrow, his shoulders wide and his jeans were torn and frayed exactly right. They met glances. She tore her eyes away.

"Do you know how you got all wet? Did you walk through last night's rain? Sleep in the rain?" Sully asked.

"I fell in a creek," he said. He smiled though he also shivered.

"On account a those shoes," Frank pointed out. "He slipped cause he ain't got no tread."

"Well, there you go," Maggie said. "Professor Frank has it all figured out. Let's get that wet jacket off and get a blanket. Sully, you better call Stan the Man."

"Will do."

"Anyone need a hand here?" Maggie heard the camper ask.

"Can you grab the phone, Cal?" Sully asked. Sully put the man in what had been Maggie's chair and started peeling off his jacket and outer clothes. He leaned the backpack against the porch rail and within just seconds Enid was there with a blanket, cup of coffee and one of her bran muffins. Cal brought the cordless phone to the porch. The gentleman immediately began to devour that muffin as Maggie looked him over.

"Least he'll be reg'lar," Frank said, reclaiming his chair.

Maggie crouched in front of the man and while speaking very softly, she asked if she could remove the hat. Before quite getting permission she pulled it gently off his head to reveal wispy white hair surrounding a bald dome. She gently ran her fingers around his scalp in search of a bump or contusion. Then she pulled him to his feet and ran her hands around his torso and waist. "You must've rolled around in the dirt, sir," she said. "I bet you're ready for a shower." He didn't respond. "Sir? Anything hurt?" she asked him. He just shook his head. "Can you smile for me? Big, wide, smile?" she asked, checking for the kind of paralysis caused by a stroke.

"Where'd you escape from, young man?" Sully asked him. "Where's your home?"

"Wakefield, Illinois," he said. "You know it?"

"Can't say I do," Sully said. "But I bet it's beautiful. More beautiful than Lejeune, for sure."

"Can I have cream?" he asked, holding out his cup.

Enid took it. "Of course you can, sweetheart," she said. "I'll bring it right back."

In a moment the gentleman sat with his coffee with cream, shivering under a blanket while Sully called Stan Bronoski. There were a number of people Sully could have reached out to—a local ranger, state police aka highway patrol, even fire and rescue. But Stan was the son of a local rancher and was the police chief in Timberlake, just twenty miles south and near the inter-change. It was a small department with a clever deputy who worked the internet like a pro, Officer Paul Castor.

Beau gave the old man a good sniffing, then moved

down the stairs to Cal who automatically began petting him.

Sully handed the phone to Maggie. "Stan wants to talk to you."

"He sounds like someone who wandered off," Stan said to Maggie. "But I don't have any missing persons from nearby. I'll get Castor looking into it. I'm on my way. Does he have any ID on him?"

"We haven't really checked yet," Maggie said into the phone. "Why don't I do that while you drive. Here's Sully."

Maggie handed the phone back to her dad and said, "Pass the time with Stan while I chat with this gentleman."

Maggie asked the man to stand again and deftly slid a thin wallet out of his back pocket. She urged him to sit, and opened it up. "Well, now," she said. "Mr. Gunderson? Roy Gunderson?"

"Hmm?" he said, his eyes lighting up a bit.

Sully repeated the name into the phone to Stan.

"And so, Roy, did you hurt anything when you fell?" Maggie asked.

He shook his head and sipped his coffee. "I fell?" he finally asked.

Maggie looked at Sully, lifting a questioning brow. "A Mr. Gunderson from Park City, Utah," Sully said. "Wandered off from his home a few days ago. On foot."

"He must've gotten a ride or something," Cal said.

"His driver's license, which was supposed to be renewed ten years ago, says his address is in Illinois."

"Stan says he'll probably have more information by the time he gets here, but this must be him. Dementia, he says."

"You can say that again," Maggie observed. "I can't

imagine what the last few days have been like for him. He must have been terrified."

"He look terrified to you?" Frank asked. "He might as well be on a cruise ship."

"Tell Stan we'll take care of him till he gets here."

Maggie went about the business of caring for Mr. Gunderson, getting water and a little soup into him while the camper, Cal, chatted with Sully and Frank, apparently well-known to them. When this situation was resolved she meant to find out more about him, like how long he'd been here.

She took off Roy's shoes and socks and looked at his feet—no injuries or frostbite but some serious swelling and bruised toenails. She wondered where he had been and how he'd gotten the backpack. He certainly hadn't brought it from home or packed it himself. That would be too complicated for a man in his condition. It was a miracle he could carry it!

Two hours later, the sun lowering in the sky, an ambulance had arrived for Roy Gunderson. He didn't appear to be seriously injured or ill but he was definitely unstable and Stan wasn't inclined to transport him alone. He could bolt, try to get out of a moving car or interfere with the driver, although Stan had a divider cage in his police car.

What Maggie and Sully had learned, no thanks to Roy himself, was that he'd been cared for at home by his wife, wandered off without his GPS bracelet, walked around a while before coming upon a rather old Chevy sedan with the keys in the ignition, so he must have helped himself. The car was reported stolen from near his house, but had no tracking device installed. And since Mr. Gunderson hadn't driven in years, no one put him with the borrowed motor vehicle for a couple of days. The car was found abandoned near Salt Lake City with Roy's jacket in it. From there the old man had probably hitched a ride. His condition was too good to have walked for days. Roy was likely left near a rest stop or campgrounds where he helped himself to a backpack. Where he'd been, what he'd done, how he'd survived was unknown.

The EMTs were just about to load Mr. Gunderson into the back of the ambulance when Sully sat down on the porch steps with a loud huff.

"Dad?" Maggie asked.

Sully was grabbing the front of his chest. Over his heart. He was pale as snow, sweaty, his eyes glassy, his breathing shallow and ragged.

"Dad!" Maggie shouted.

What We Find
by Robyn Carr
Available now from Mills & Boon.

More from Robyn Carr

#1 *New York Times*
bestselling author

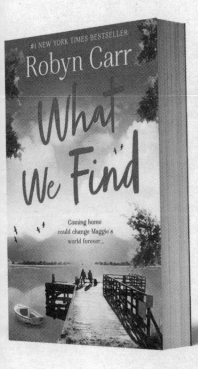

OUT NOW